Remaking Metropolis

Remaking Metropolis examines examples of both urban decay and destruction as well as urban rebirth. It shows why particular approaches were successful, or did not achieve their objectives. By bringing together innovative approaches to urban living from across the world, and by demonstrating how local initiatives can contribute to global solutions, the book establishes a framework in which to evaluate current and future developments for urban change, and to stimulate a reassessment of urban redevelopment and policies.

"Think globally, act locally" is an oft used phrase to encourage citizens to take steps close to home as part of addressing overarching environmental issues. Critics of this view point to the potential for parochial or even myopic approaches, while supporters argue that it creates both a more sustainable and a more culturally grounded environment. *Remaking Metropolis* brings together real world experiences that combine local action with a global world view, to demonstrate the continuum between the local and the remote.

At the same time the compartmentalization of contemporary perspectives toward human life in the fields of science, design, ecology, medicine, and politics is leading to increased fragmentation of the mind, body, city, and globe. By bridging these artificial divides between disciplines, this collection of individual case studies demonstrates the holistic approach necessary for a genuinely sustainable urban condition.

Edward A. Cook, Associate Professor, The Design School, Arizona State University.

Jesus J. Lara, Assistant Professor, Knowlton School of Architecture, The Ohio State University.

Remaking Metropolis

Global challenges of the urban landscape

Edited by
Edward A. Cook and
Jesus J. Lara

Routledge
Taylor & Francis Group

LONDON AND NEW YORK

First published 2013
by Routledge
2 Park Square, Milton Park, Abingdon, Oxon, OX14 4RN

Simultaneously published in the USA and Canada
by Routledge
711 Third Avenue, New York, NY 10017

Routledge is an imprint of the Taylor & Francis Group, an informa business

British Library Cataloguing in Publication Data
A catalogue record for this book is available from the British Library

Library of Congress Cataloging-in-Publication Data
Remaking metropolis: global challenges of the urban landscape / edited
    by Edward A. Cook and Jesus J. Lara.
    p. cm.
Includes bibliographical references and index.
1. Urban renewal. 2. City planning. 3. Urbanization. I. Cook, Edward,
    1955– II. Lara, Jesus J.
HT170.R456 2012
307.3'416—dc23   2012011248

ISBN13: 978-0-415-67081-4 (hbk)
ISBN13: 978-0-415-67082-1 (pbk)
ISBN13: 978-0-203-09548-5 (ebk)

Typeset in Minion by
Florence Production Ltd, Stoodleigh, Devon

Contents

PART F
Conclusions

Tables

Figures

Preface

This book explores theories, processes, and practices involved in remaking cities. It also examines the global context that both influences the way cities evolve and demonstrates how globalization can facilitate progress toward creating more sustainable cities. Recognition of the city as an essential contributor to many global environmental problems is central to the discussion, but the contributions herein also offer paths forward. The range of contributions includes theoretical or conceptual discussions of more general philosophies or approaches as well as specific projects that demonstrate how local actions can make significant contributions toward achieving more sustainable cities and in the broader sense a more sustainable planet. The urban landscape has become one of the realms in which the tension between global and local has become most prevalent. The oft used aphorism of thinking globally and acting locally has particular relevance in this context and is shown throughout this volume in the many examples of innovative and visionary work. Compartmentalization of contemporary perspectives toward human life in cities from the fields of science, design, ecology, medicine, or politics has become increasingly fragmented in recent decades. Planning and design disciplines have the potential to contribute solutions to some urban problems, but there is recognition that there must be a broader and more coordinated multidisciplinary approach taken to create more sustainable, ecologically healthy, and culturally grounded cities and regions. More voices and actions are needed that have a world view and see the continuum between local and global and are not fractured and obscured by disciplinary lenses.

The discussion included in this volume grew out of a symposium held at Arizona State University that brought together influential environmental scientists, urban planners and designers, landscape architects, architects, and others for three days to study problems and ideas and to share solutions that are being implemented in locations around the world. Subsequent contributions were invited from others who are engaged in work that provided additional geographic representation, but more importantly extended the array of possible responses to the many challenges facing contemporary cities. Through their built and written works, those who have contributed to urban landscape discourse and action provided the foundation for discussion about the future of the urban landscape in a global context. The intent is to expand the dialogue through the publication of this book. While much of the content is drawn from and applicable to North American cities, the global topic and the international perspective and origin of contributors makes this volume relevant throughout the world with similar groups in industrialized and developing nations. Additionally, the diversity of content and disciplinary interests represented extends the relevance beyond designers and planners to include social scientists, environmental health professionals, and political groups. With the emerging focus on sustainability, and in particular urban sustainability, this book should provide an interesting perspective on challenges and responses to many local and global urban problems.

Acknowledgments

We are grateful for all the assistance and support provided by numerous individuals to make publication of this book possible. Thanks to Fritz Steiner for initiating the process that led to the Remaking Metropolis: Global Challenges of the Urban Landscape symposium held in Tempe, Arizona, USA. Landscape architecture faculty, Rebecca Fish Ewan and Joe Ewan were involved in the organization of the symposium that was the impetus for the book. The Landscape Architecture Foundation and The National Endowment for the Arts provided funding to bring scholars from around the world to Arizona to discuss the ideas found in this volume. Funding was also provided by The Design School (formerly the School of Architecture and Landscape Architecture) at Arizona State University (ASU). Finally, there were a number of reviewers of various drafts of chapters that provided suggestions that helped improve the final outcome.

Edward A. Cook
Jesus J. Lara

Contributors

Penny Allan has been Program Director of Landscape Architecture at VUW since 2007, where she teaches and researches in the areas of urban resilience and adaptive design. She has a background in practice in both the public and private sector: as a principal of HASSELL and as director of Landscape Architecture at the Government Architect's Office in Sydney, Australia.

John Ball, BFA, M.Arch, is an Architect, Educator, and Student in the Arizona State University Environmental Design and Art PhD program. His 25-year professional background includes the design of numerous award winning hospitality, municipal, and corporate buildings. His public service contribution includes economic development and cultural and international sports organizations.

Martin Bryant is a Senior Lecturer at the School of Architecture and Design, Victoria University, Wellington, New Zealand. Martin shares his time between practice and university. He teaches and researches in landscape architecture and urban design and is also a director of Wraight + Associates, where he is responsible for concept planning and design of large urban projects. He has completed many award winning projects throughout Australia and Aotearoa New Zealand.

James P. Burke is the Acting Parks and Recreation Director responsible for leading 1,600 employees, managing 200+ parks and preserves, and a budget of $103 million for the City of Phoenix. He has been involved in diverse projects including: the Burton Barr Central Library, Encanto and Steele Indian School Parks, Sonoran Preserve and Papago Park Master Plans, and the Edge Treatment Guidelines.

Kimberly Collins teaches public administration at California State University-San Bernardino. Previously, she was the founding director of the California Center for Border and Regional Economic Studies, located on the Imperial Valley Campus of San Diego State University, and taught SDSU-Imperial Valley in the public administration department.

Edward A. Cook is a Landscape Architecture faculty member in The Design School at Arizona State University, where he teaches courses on urban ecological design, landscapes and sustainability, and landscape ecological planning. He has published books and articles focused on his research in urban ecology, green/ecological networks, and sustainable urbanism. He has worked on projects in landscape ecological planning throughout the world and was one of the pioneers in developing planning and design strategies for ecological networks in urban landscapes.

Hayriye Esbah is an Associate Professor in the Department of Landscape Architecture at Istanbul Technical University, Turkey. She received a Ph.D. in Environmental Design and Planning from Arizona State University and a Master of Landscape Architecture from the University of Arizona. She is currently engaged in teaching and research in sustainable urbanism.

Joseph M. Ewan, ASLA, Associate Professor of Landscape Architecture and Assistant Director in The Design School at Arizona State University co-authored the Sonoran Preserve Master Plan, and received the National ASLA President's Award of Excellence. Professor Ewan has authored and co-authored numerous articles for *Landscape Architecture* magazine on landscape architecture within the Desert Southwest.

Wolf-Peter Geitz started his professional career in landscape architecture in 1986 in the office Knoll-Ökoplan in Sindelfingen. After the successful completion of a high-profile pilot project restoring the river Enz in Pforzheim he founded and headed the river restoration department of the firm, carrying out numerous stream restoration projects. In 1999 he founded his own office in Stuttgart together with two partners. Combining their extensive expertise in landscape architecture, soil bioengineering, and hydrology the interdisciplinary team focuses on river restoration in urban areas. Through his work in professional organizations he constantly strives to further develop and promote the use of sustainable soil bioengineering techniques in restoring urban river environments and landscapes.

Lars Gemzoe is an Architect and Urban Designer with Gehl Architects based in Copenhagen, Denmark. He has authored several books on giving life to public space and has been involved in urban open space projects in cities throughout the world. He has over 30 years' experience teaching and practicing architecture and place making. He is widely considered an international authority on quality of public space and public life, having lectured at numerous universities and seminars throughout the world.

Subhro Guhathakurta is the Director of the Center for Geographic Information Systems and Professor in the School of City and Regional Planning at Georgia Institute of Technology. Prior to July 2011, he was Associate Director of the School of Geographical Sciences and Urban Planning at Arizona State

University (ASU) and among the founding faculty members of ASU's School of Sustainability. Professor Guhathakurta was instrumental in developing the Urban Modeling and Simulation Lab in ASU's College of Design. He is the author of five books and monographs and over 70 scientific papers.

Michael Hough's distinguished career in landscape architecture started at the University of Pennsylvania under the tutelage of Ian McHarg. Influenced by McHarg's ecological thinking, he turned the same philosophies to the city. Through his career as an academic and practitioner he has won many awards and has been instrumental in transforming many ordinary or forgotten landscapes into meaningful places. His two award winning books, *Cities and Natural Process* and *Out of Place*, have influenced practitioners and scholars alike. He taught at the University of Toronto and York University and has lectured throughout the world.

Khanin Hutanuwatr is a Lecturer at King Mongkut's Institute of Technology Ladkrabang. He has a background in industrial design and interior architectural research with a focus on sustainability. The tragedy of the 2004 tsunami urged him to broaden his interest to natural hazards in his Ph.D. He currently embraces a political ecology point of view, and extends his research interests to social vulnerability and resilience.

Jesus J. Lara is Assistant Professor of Landscape Architecture in the Knowlton School of Architecture at Ohio State University. His research and pedagogy are centered on sustainable urban design, community development, and socio-cultural factors in community design, from urban environments and poverty stricken areas to empty suburban malls and commercial areas at the intersection of upscale developments and highway commerce. His work emphasizes the creation of responsive and adaptive urban environments that focus on people and place, using university–community partnerships to explore the potentials for change, redevelopment, and improvement.

Desiree Martinez Uriarte is a Landscape Architect who graduated from the Technical University of Munich. She became president of the International Federation of Landscape Architects (IFLA), based in Brussels, in May 2010. Previously she served as the regional Secretary of the Americas and as Mexican delegate to the IFLA. Her professional work is focused on the restoration of public space and the promotion of sustainability, through her firm TYMSA, landscape architecture projects, urban design, and environmental management, as well as through various publications related to landscape architecture, urban ecology, and urban planning.

Devon McAslan has a Master's degree in Urban and Environmental Planning from Arizona State University. His thesis, entitled Urban Indicators: A Study and Evaluation of Urban Indicator Programs for Creating Sustainable Communities, explored how indicators are used at the urban scale and how they become effective tools for policy making.

Han Meyer has been Professor in Theory and Methods of Urban Design at the Delft University of Technology in the Netherlands since 2001. He has published a number of books concerning the fundamentals of the discipline of urbanism, the present state-of-the-art of Dutch urbanism and the transformations of port-cities. His present research focuses on 'Delta-urbanism', considering the possibility of an integrated approach of urban planning and design, hydraulic engineering, and port development in delta-areas.

Sohyun Park's background includes biology (B.S.), landscape architecture (MLA), and environmental design and planning (Ph.D.). Her research focus lies in the intersection of landscape ecology and planning for urban sustainability. Park has worked for national research organizations in Korea for six years, with a wide range of environmental and urban studies.

David Pijawka is Professor in the School of Geographical Sciences and Urban Planning and Senior Sustainability Scholar at Arizona State University. He is recognized for his publications in the areas of urban sustainability, hazards research, and environmental perceptions.

Mihir Prakash is a Researcher in the School of Geographical Sciences and Urban Planning. He is a graduate from the School, receiving his Master's degree in Urban and Environmental Planning in 2011. His work is on the application of GIS and Remote Sensing to development and policy questions as well as sustainable development. He has completed studies related to American Indian resources management, economic impacts of transportation planning, and sustainable indicators.

Edward Sadalla is Professor Emeritus in the Psychology Department at ASU. In addition to scholarly work on the topics of urbanization, spatial cognition, self-presentation, and evolutionary psychology, he has conducted applied research on issues related to urbanization, housing, transportation, energy, air quality, water quality, and quality of life.

Joseph Salukvadze is a full Professor of Human Geography at Tbilisi State University, Georgia, and a visiting professor at the Technical University of Munich, Germany. He holds the position of a vice-president of the Geographical Society of Georgia. Dr. Joseph Salukvadze was a Fulbright scholar at Massachusetts Institute of Technology (MIT), USA, and the Swedish Institute research fellow at Stockholm and Lund Universities, Sweden.

Frederick Steiner is Dean of the School of Architecture, University of Texas at Austin. He received his Ph.D. and M.A. degrees in city and regional planning and a Master of Regional Planning from the University of Pennsylvania. Dean Steiner earned a Master of Community Planning and a B.S. in Design from the University of Cincinnati. His most recent book is *Design for a Vulnerable Planet*.

Robert L. Thayer Jr. is Emeritus Professor of Landscape Architecture at the University of California, Davis. Thayer's 1994 book, *Gray World, Green Heart: Technology, Nature, and the Sustainable Landscape*, received the American Society of Landscape Architects Presidential Award of Excellence. His second book, *LifePlace: Bioregional Thought and Practice*, was published in 2003.

Michael Underhill is an Architect and Urban Designer working in Phoenix, and Executive Dean of the Herberger Institute for Design and the Arts at Arizona State University. As a professor in The Design School, he served as the coordinator of the urban design program and taught in the Master of Real Estate Development program in the business school. As a practicing architect he has received design awards for projects in Texas, Iowa, and Arizona; and his most recent work has been sustainable urban housing.

Kristof Van Assche is currently Associate Professor at the Planning and Community Development program at MN State Universities-St Cloud State. He is interested in the political, cultural, and institutional embeddings of spatial planning and design, on which he has published widely. Geographically, his work spans the US, Europe, and the areas of the former Soviet Union. He has edited several books, contributed numerous book chapters, and published in, among others, *Planning Theory, Public Administration, Memory Studies, Journal of Urban Design, Journal of Environmental Policy and Planning,* and *Planning Perspectives.*

Foreword
Designing our futures

Frederick Steiner

For landscape architects, the process of looking comprehensively at a site or a region is both an article of faith and a daily practice. This ritual involves a complex series of actions, including compiling information on its component parts, analyzing the information, developing various concepts that project ideas into the future, and engaging citizens in the process, that must be aligned into a holistic vision. The value of planning and design is accepted and assumed. Yet, in 1999, when the American Society of Landscape Architects (ASLA) commemorated its centenary and in 2000, when Harvard University, home to the first landscape architecture degree program, observed its centennial, there was little vision for the profession and no forum for dialogue that would look at the profession from a comprehensive perspective.

The Landscape Architecture Foundation (LAF) sought to address this significant need through its Landscape Futures Initiative. The purpose of this initiative was to ensure that environmental and societal goals can be achieved through credible and innovative planning and design. In order to accomplish this, the LAF explored the opportunities and challenges facing landscape architecture and provided vision for the landscape architecture profession in the twenty-first century.

Since its founding well over 100 years ago, only one major study and evaluation of the profession of landscape architecture has been undertaken—the Fein Report commissioned by the LAF in 1969 and published in 1972. Since 1972, the rate of societal, professional, and technological change has been rapid, with the result that the challenges facing the profession are more complex, the development of solutions increasingly difficult, and the need for landscape architects greater.

The Landscape Futures Initiative sought to redefine and redirect both the profession and the discipline of landscape architecture by working with key constituency groups within the profession and interested parties outside the profession to take a critical look at the present and to develop a blueprint for the future. The purpose of the Landscape Futures Initiative was to appreciably improve the significance and relevance of the profession to the issues of the future by identifying the drivers of global landscape change and by preparing the profession to assume leadership in addressing landscape change. To accomplish this goal, a series of six symposia on the drives of global landscape change were held:

1. Worldwide Urbanization—University of Pennsylvania, 2002
2. Culture and Technology—University of Virginia, 2003
3. Connectivity and Landscape Change—The University of Texas at Austin, 2004
4. Politics and Economy—University of Illinois at Champaign-Urbana, 2004
5. Global Environmental Challenges—Arizona State University, 2005
6. Population and Social Dynamics—University of California at Davis, 2005.

These symposia were organized to address the fundamental drivers of landscape change in the twenty-first century. A seventh symposium was organized in 2008 by Clemson University to pull the results of the other symposia together and to address leadership and landscape change.

Drivers of landscape change

Change does not just happen, nor is it inevitable. A variety of economic, social, and technological forces drive change. What drivers of change influence landscapes around the world? Some possibilities, identified by the LAF and others, include the following:

Population dynamics and consumption
Urbanization
Connectivity and networks
Technology, economics, and politics
Culture and the arts
Education and human services
Global and regional environmental processes.

Population growth and migration will change the demographic structure of the planet. In 2011, the number of people inhabiting Earth topped seven billion. The United Nations projects the world's population will reach around 9.4 billion by the year 2050. Population growth drives change because everyone requires water, food, shelter, clothing, and energy. However, levels of consumption vary. Our consumption patterns affect the level of resources necessary to fulfill those demands. In turn, resource use influences the character of living landscapes that provide the sources and the sinks for those resources.

We live in the first urban century. For the first time in human history, over half of the world's population lives in metropolitan regions. In the future, even more people will move to cities. By 2050, two-thirds will be living in urban regions. Various estimates exist about trends in birth and life structure as well as the distribution of income and property, but all data suggest more people living in ever-expanding urban metropolitan regions. The United Nations notes that:

The "urban footprint" stretches far beyond city boundaries. Cities influence, and are affected by, broader environmental considerations. Proactive policies for sustainability will also be important in view of climate change and the considerable proportion of urban concentrations at or near sea level.

(United Nations Population Fund 2007)

Population changes—such as growth and migration and consumption—are related to urbanization. The movement of people to cities and metropolitan regions involves the transformation of spaces from rural and natural to urban and suburban, the urbanization of the wild, the abandonment of the rural, and the recovery of the core city and older suburban neighborhoods.

Connectivity involves the ways in which new networks and information systems will alter landscapes and communities and the transfer of knowledge, time, social relationships, and education. Connecting technologies—the automobile and the Internet—may also divide people and, thus, further fragment landscapes and communities. We constantly attempt to connect through information and transportation technologies.

Global environmental processes also drive landscape changes and adaptations. Climate-change trends are well known. Increased carbon dioxide in the atmosphere leads to changes in rainfall, cloudiness, wind strength, and temperature. These changes already influence the life cycles of polar bears in the Arctic; small islands disappearing in the South Pacific as the calamities of nature increase; and the rain forest island habitats around mountaintops in Costa Rica that are dwindling with less and less cloud cover to support moisture-dependent species.

Additional environmental drivers of change influencing the global commons and specific regions include natural disasters, the nitrogen cycle, and energy use. As we learn more about these drivers, we can connect them to change occurring in urban, rural, and wilderness landscapes.

The consequences of landscape change

The consequences of landscape change are all around us. Some changes evident in our daily lives include suburban sprawl, the conversion of prime farmlands to other uses, the decline of biodiversity, social inequity, urban heat-island effects, our health, visual blight, the inappropriate location of housing and other land uses, and threats to water quality and quantity. Each consequence calls out for a landscape perspective because landscapes represent combinations of social and natural processes. Furthermore, the scale of what constitutes a landscape is fluid, but certainly larger than a specific parcel and smaller than a metropolitan or physiographic region.

Suburban sprawl

Suburban sprawl is dispersed, automobile-dependent development outside compact urban and town centers along highways and in the rural countryside. Meadows and forests are converted to strip malls and subdivisions that serve cars better than people. Such development consumes more land, water, and energy than more traditional settlement patterns. Sprawl fragments open space and tend to be homogenous in appearance. Our dependence on automobiles resulting from suburban sprawl is also associated with air pollution, motor vehicle crashes, and pedestrian injuries and fatalities (Frumkin 2002, Burchell et al. 2002).

While suburban sprawl is a well-known issue in the United States, the United Nations has now identified it as a global problem. In its *State of the World Cities 2010/2011: Bridging the Urban Divide*, UN-HABITAT observes:

> In many developing countries, urban sprawl comprises two main, contrasting types of development in the same city: one is characterized by large peri-urban areas with informal and illegal patterns of land use. This is combined with a lack of infrastructure, public facilities and basic services, and often is accompanied by little or no public transport and by inadequate access roads.
>
> The other is a form of "suburban sprawl" in which residential zones for high- and middle-income groups and highly-valued commercial and retail complexes are well-connected by individual rather than public transport.
>
> (UN-HABITAT 2010)

Landscapes provide a different lens than the individual site or the metropolitan region for understanding the impacts of sprawl. The cumulative consequences of individual parcel conversions are not obvious at the site scale and can be overlooked regionally. However, by looking at landscapes, one can start to see how places change as a result of sprawl.

The loss of prime farmland

Suburban sprawl consumes significant amounts of prime farmland. From the 1970s to the present, farmland conversions have been reported by various agencies in the United States. For example, based on U.S. Department of Agriculture data, the American Farmland Trust reports that: "In America, we've been losing more than an acre [0.404 ha] of farmland per minute. Between 2002 and 2007, 4,080,300 acres [1,651,239 ha] of agricultural land were converted to developed uses—an area nearly the size of Massachusetts" (http://www.farmland.org/resources, accessed 2, 16 2011). Furthermore, according to the American Farmland Trust:

> Our food is increasingly in the path of development. An astounding 91 percent of our fruit and 78 percent of our vegetables are produced in urban-influenced areas. Wasteful land use is the problem, not development itself. From 1982 to 2007, the U.S. population grew by 30 percent. During the same time period, developed land increased 57 percent.
>
> (http://www.farmland.org/resources, accessed 2, 16 2011)

We depend on that land for much of our food and clothing, and the conversion of prime farmland to other uses is not only a U.S. problem. As noted by the United Nations, "Since many cities are situated at the heart of rich agricultural areas or other lands rich in biodiversity, the extension of the urban perimeter evidently cuts further into available productive land and encroaches upon important ecosystems" (United Nations Population Fund 2007:45).

Agricultural land uses create a diversity of landscapes, which can be aesthetically pleasing to urban and rural neighbors. They add to the culture and traditions of places that provide character for metropolitan regions. Agriculture is related to the very meaning of landscape because both involve a mix of nature and culture.

The decline of biodiversity

Our current growth patterns also impact other species. Biodiversity refers to the variety of life and its processes, which includes the abundance of living organisms, their genetic diversity, and the communities and ecosystems in which they occur. Ill-planned development, poor land-use decisions, and bad land-management policies are often incompatible with existing natural habitats. Farm and forest lands—threatened by suburban sprawl—can contribute to biodiversity by providing habitats for a variety of wildlife, including rare and endangered species. Large, unfragmented tracts of farm and forest lands and forest corridors allow interaction and crossbreeding among population groups of the same species, which increases population health and genetic viability.

According to the Environmental Law Institute, the "primary cause of bio-diversity loss in the United States is habitat destruction and degradation, followed by competition with or predation by non-native invasive species" (2003:3). Furthermore, the Environmental Law Institute identifies the main causes of habitat destruction and fragmentation as "land conversion for development, road building, water development, outdoor recreation, agriculture, and resource extraction or harvest (e.g., mining and logging)" (2003:3). Intervention in natural processes, such as forest fires and flooding, can negatively influence biodiversity too.

In addition to habitat loss and fragmentation due to land-use changes, other global threats to biodiversity include climate change, over-hunting, invasion of non-native species, and pollution. The potential impact of global climate change on biodiversity is especially dramatic. For instance, an interdisciplinary team of scientists employed future climate scenarios to assess extinction risk "for sample regions that cover some 20 percent of the Earth's terrestrial surface" (Thomas et al. 2004:145). The team predicted based on "mid-range climate-warming scenarios for 2050, that 15–37 percent of species in our sample or regions and taxa will be 'committed to extinction'" (Thomas et al. 2004:145).

Landscapes help us understand diversity because they comprise corridors, nodes, and matrices of life. For example, corridors can be used for a species to travel across a landscape. The fragmentation of that corridor can impact the species, which, in turn, influences the biodiversity present.

Social inequity

The spatial segregation induced by prejudice and income disparities among various ethnic groups contributes to sprawl in the United States. Conversely, current patterns of suburban sprawl exacerbate social inequities. As growth and prosperity occur at the fringes of metropolitan regions, central cities, and inner, older suburbs experience a declining tax base and increasingly concentrated poverty. For example, residents of inner-city neighborhoods are more than twice as likely to live in poverty as their suburban counterparts in the United States (Policy Link 2002). Poverty is especially pronounced in minority communities, since African-Americans and Latinos have poverty rates nearly three times as high as white Americans (Institute on Race and Poverty 2002).

Global urban population growth in the twenty-first century will be largely composed of lower-income people. As the United Nations notes, "Cities are highly vulnerable to natural crises and disasters" (United Nations Population Fund 2007:59). Poor people are likely to live in the urban regions most vulnerable to natural disasters. For example, in January 2011 (as I write this), flooding has resulted in at least 842 deaths in the state of Rio de Janeiro, with another 8,777 people losing their homes. Earlier in the month, floods resulted in yet another 24 deaths in neighboring São Paulo state. Impoverished communities were particularly hard-hit.

Crime is also an especially important equity concern because crime rates are not distributed across the urban landscape. Poor neighborhoods are often cut off from protection from criminal activities. The fear of crime can prompt people to abandon communities and colonize new areas. The design of urban landscapes can exacerbate or ameliorate the potential for crime. Some places look dangerous and, in fact, are unsafe. Even if a place is not unsafe, the rapid rate of landscape change can make people feel vulnerable. People expect their surroundings to be predictable. Familiarity helps reinforce a sense of security. Change undermines that comfort. By exploring crime through a landscape perspective, we can begin to understand how safety in one place is connected to other urban places. We can also design safer public spaces. The design and use of these spaces may have a more significant effect on crime than income levels.

Urban heat-island effects

As metropolitan regions grow, the local climate changes as a result of the urban heat-island, or heat-archipelago, effect. This effect involves the additional heating of the air over urban settlements as a result of the replacement of naturally vegetated surfaces with those composed of asphalt, concrete, rooftops, and other human-made materials. For example, between 1970 and 1990, summer nighttime average temperatures in the Phoenix metropolitan region increased by 2.2°C and by 6°C between rural desert and inner urban locations (Brazel et al. 2000). Brazel and others (Brazel et al. 2007, Grossman-Clarke et al. 2010) have confirmed that this trend has continued with urban nighttime temperatures warmer than in rural areas. And, central Arizona urban and suburban temperatures continue to rise, as the region continued to grow in the early twenty-first century (Baker et al. 2002). Other desert cities around the globe are experiencing similar heating trends.

Black asphalt is an especially important urban heat-island culprit. We employ albedo, the ratio of light reflectivity to incoming light, to assess the absorption and subsequent heating of different surfaces. Thermal admittance is another surface characteristic that determines net heat storage and resultant energy flow over a surface. Surfaces with lower albedos and higher thermal admittances, like black asphalt, are warmer than those with higher albedos, unless mitigated by other microclimate factors, such as evaporation.

We can measure and study the urban heat-islands of various landscapes. A landscape of trees and bodies of water, such as parks or golf courses, will be cooler than one of large buildings and parking lots, such as central cities or shopping malls. Furthermore, landscapes help us understand the relationships between cultural activities, such as playing golf or purchasing a shirt, and natural phenomena, such as climate and vegetation.

Our health

As cities and suburbs get hotter, obesity increases, especially in the United States. According to the Centers for Disease Control and Prevention (CDC), some 60 percent of Americans are overweight and at least 18 percent are obese. A 2009 American Academy of Pediatrics policy statement estimates that "32 percent of American children are overweight and physical inactivity contributes to this high prevalence of overweight" (Committee on Environmental Health 2009:1591). The American Academy of Pediatrics links this alarming statistic to how the design of the built environment affects children's opportunities, or lack thereof, for physical activity. The lack of walking opportunities and easy access to fast food are two contributing factors. Thus, the design and planning of our surroundings, our landscapes, is an important public health issue. In most American cities, there is a lack of safe and accessible sidewalks, crosswalks, and bike paths. Transportation alternatives are limited, with little pedestrian access to buses and transit systems. Parks and recreation facilities are unsafe, ugly, and not accessible. Shopping and services cannot be accessed without automobiles. In addition to obesity, other public health issues, like heart disease, have been linked to suburban sprawl and community design (Frumkin 2002, Jackson 2003, Frank et al. 2003).

The connection between obesity and our health in general and the design of our built environment should be apparent. As Richard Joseph Jackson, formerly with the CDC and now with the University of California at Los Angeles, observed:

Medicine will not be adequate to deal with the health challenges of the 21st century, not even with the help of the sequenced genome and advances in robotic surgery. Even though the United States spends one of every seven dollars on medical care, we will not significantly improve health and the quality of life unless we pay more attention to how we design our living environments. Healthy living environments include not just a clean and heated kitchen, bath, or bedroom, but also the landscape around us. Health for all, especially for the young, aging, poor and disabled, requires that we design healthfulness into our environments as well.

(2001:1)

From France to China, we spend more time in cars. The dependency on automobile and truck transportation leads to increased respiratory problems. In addition to people, animals and plants are affected by air pollution. Many cities around the world experience ozone warning days because of traffic. Clogged highways delay travel times, which can increase our tension and anxiety.

Landscapes can enable us to understand the relationship between community design and our health. Landscapes with green corridors for walking and biking provide greater opportunities for their inhabitants to improve their health than ones dominated by highways. Landscapes may be more useful than individual sites—where the cumulative impacts are obscured—or metropolitan regions—where the consequences may not be immediately obvious.

Additional consequences

As we look around, other impacts of global change are apparent in our landscapes, including visual blight, the siting of land uses in unsafe locations, and a decline in water quality. Our contemporary surroundings are dominated by ugliness and sameness. We actually know very little about the impact of visual blight on our mental and physical well-being. Our instincts tell us that we prefer a beautiful beach or mountaintop to a highway with strip commercial development, but why? Several meanings of the word "landscape" are related to what we see. By better understanding landscapes, we might make more sense of our sight.

We often locate our homes and businesses in harm's way. Flood plain, earthquake, landslide, and avalanche zones are well known. We know that building homes in flood zones can put the lives of people at risk. Sometimes, after a flood or a hurricane, we rebuild homes and businesses in the same location where they have been destroyed, setting in motion another round of destruction. We have the ability to map with some accuracy the landscapes where earthquakes, landslides, avalanches, and wildfires will occur.

Landscape change affects the quality and amount of water available for human use and for other species. As we pave over the natural landscape, impervious surfaces increase. More hard surfaces interrupt the hydrologic cycle, increasing the water in rivers and streams and decreasing the amount of water recharging aquifers. More roads and parking lots also degrade water quality. Oil residues are picked up during rainstorms and carried into water courses. More lawns and golf courses have similar impacts on water quality, as chemical fertilizers find their way into both surface water and groundwater.

To summarize, we are losing our best farmland, while other species' habitats are disappearing. Meanwhile, the gaps between rich and poor are widening and crime—or the fear of crime—is growing. Urban and suburban places are heating up and our waistlines are expanding. Our surroundings have become ugly and traffic more congested. Water quality and quantity issues abound. These are challenges at the global scale.

Global challenges of the urban landscape

This is the second book resulting from the LAF Landscape Futures Initiative symposia. (The first was by Wescoat and Johnston, 2008, based on the Illinois symposium.) Edward Cook and Jesus J. Lara have coalesced leading thinkers about global landscape challenges to suggest strategies for remaking the metropolis in this first urban century. Clearly, the challenges indicate that we must undertake city design and planning differently than in the previous century because past patterns simply are not sustainable.

Sustainability provides a good starting point for the twenty-first century. We need to balance economic, equity, and environmental concerns to leave the planet a better place for future generations. However, we should go beyond sustainability and create regenerative cities and landscapes.

The pages that follow help provide the global perspective that is necessary to make the twenty-first-century metropolis more equitable, safe, healthy, and beautiful. The authors address environmental challenges, urban sustainability, possible futures, and action strategies. In doing so, they help define new goals for landscape architecture practice and research. In the tradition of Frederick Law Olmsted and Ian McHarg, these goals transcend the discipline of landscape architecture with profound implications for city planning, environmental management, and urban design.

References

Baker, L.A., Brazel, A.J., Selover, N., Martin, C., McIntyre, N., Steiner, F.R., Nelson, A., and Musacchio, M. (2002) Urbanization and Warming of Phoenix (Arizona, USA). *Urban Ecosystems* 6(3):188–203.

Brazel, A., Selover, N., Vose, R., and Heisler, G. (2000) The Tale of Two Climates— Baltimore and Phoenix LTER Sites. *Climate Research* 15:123–135.

Brazel, A., Gober, P., Lee, S., Grossman-Clarke, S., Zehnder, J., Hedquist, B., and Comparri, E. (2007) Determinants of Changes in the Regional Urban Heat Island in Metropolitan Phoenix (Arizona, USA) between 1990 and 2004. *Climate Research* 33:171–182.

Burchell, R.W., Lowenstein, G., Dolphin, W.R., Galley, C.C., Downs, A., Serskin, S., Still, K.G., and Moore. T. (2002) *Cost of Sprawl-2000.* Transit Cooperative Research Program Report 74. Washington, DC: National Academy Press.

Committee on Environmental Health (2009) The Built Environment: Designing Communities to Promote Physical Activity in Children. *Pediatrics* 123(6):1591–1598.

Environmental Law Institute (2003) *Planning with Nature: Biodiversity Information in Action*. Washington, DC: Environmental Law Institute.

Fein, A. (1972) *A Study of the Profession of Landscape Architecture: Technical Report*. McLean, VA: American Society of Landscape Architects Foundation.

Frank, L.D., Engelke, P.G., and Schmid, T.L. (2003) *Health and Community Design*. Washington, DC: Island Press.

Frumkin, H. (2002) Urban Sprawl and Public Health. *Public Health Reports* 117 (May–June):201–217.

Grossman-Clarke, S., Zehnder, J.A., Loridan, T., and Grimmond, C.S.B. (2010) Contribution of Land Use Changes to Near-Surface Air Temperatures During Recent Summer Extreme Heat Events in the Phoenix Metropolitan Area. *Journal of Applied Meteorology and Climatology* 49(August):1649–1664.

Institute on Race and Poverty (2002) *Racism and Metropolitan Dynamics: The Civil Rights Challenge of the 21st Century* (A briefing paper prepared for the Ford Foundation). Minneapolis, MN: Institute of Race & Poverty.

Jackson, L.E. (2003) The Relationship of Urban Design to Human Health and Condition. *Landscape and Urban Planning* 64(4):191–200.

Jackson, R.J. (2001) What Olmsted Knew. *Western City* (March):1–3.

Policy Link (2002) *Promoting Regional Equity*. Miami, FL: Funders' Network for Smart Growth and Livable Communities.

Thomas, C.D., Cameron, A., Green, R.E., Bakkenes, M., Beaumont, L.J., Collingham, Y.C., Erasmus, B.N.F., Ferreira de Siqueira, M., Grainger, A., Hannah, L., Hughes, L., Huntley, B., van Jaarsveld, A.S., Midgley, G.F., Miles, L., Ortega-Huerta, M.A., Peterson, A.T., Phillips, O.L., and Williams, S.E. (2004) Extinction Risk from Climate Change. *Nature* 427(January):145–148.

UN-HABITAT (2010) *State of the World Cities 2010/2011: Bridging the Urban Divide*. Nairobi, Kenya: United Nations Human Settlement Programme.

United Nations Population Fund (2007) *State of the World Population 2007: Unleashing the Potential of Urban Growth*. New York, NY: United National Population Fund.

Wescoat Jr., J.L. and Johnston, D.M. (eds.) (2008) *Political Economies of Landscape Change*. Dordrecht, the Netherlands: Springer.

Part

A

Introduction

Chapter 1: Edward A. Cook and Jesus J. Lara
Global dynamics of urban landscapes

Chapter 1

Global dynamics of urban landscapes

Edward A. Cook and Jesus J. Lara

Introduction

The role and importance of cities in a global context is changing. Cities are assuming prominence in our social and economic systems and are having a growing impact on the environmental condition of the planet. As cities grow in population, area and relevance, the need for resources to support them creates new stresses that are being manifested at a global scale. The complexities of urban systems are also creating challenges for urban residents that are affecting health, safety and quality of life. The tension that exists between local and global and the prospect for changing the current dynamic is emerging as an important arena for global discourse.

There is an increasing need for influential voices and actors that have a world view yet see the continuum between local and global. As the urban landscape emerges as a realm where local and global challenges meet, landscape architects, urban planners and designers, architects and others must expand their dialogue to include health professionals, sociologists, economists and others to explore problems and experiment with solutions that can lead to the creation of more sustainable, ecologically healthy and culturally grounded human environments.

This book provides an interdisciplinary view of challenges that face urbanized areas, both local and global. It also provides useful information about potential responses that could be employed by designers and decision-makers alike. Contributing authors, who through their built and written works have contributed to urban landscape discourse and action, provide the foundation for discussion about the future of the urban landscape in a global context. Various aspects of remaking cities provide an array of perspectives and responses to the urban condition from geographically diverse locations. The book expands the dialogue, extends challenges and disseminates information about emerging approaches to managing the condition of urban environments within a dynamic global context.

The book addresses topics of health challenges in cities, global environmental problems and urban sustainability, the relationship between human systems and urban form, and renewing social and natural systems of cities. Four sub-themes are introduced that frame the contributions represented in the book. Addressed first as a foundation for further development of a range of contributions from a diverse set of authors working on a variety of relevant topics are the challenges of global urbanization that currently affect cities. These include pandemics, political dynamics, global climate change, natural disaster, human/technology relationships and changes in urban territory. The second sub-theme focuses on global sustainability and shifting urban systems, addressing trends and factors affecting urban sustainability in a global context. The third sub-theme deals with possibilities for the future of the metropolis and looks at examples of plans, strategies and proposals for urban areas in developed and developing world cities that are influential in moving toward an increased level of sustainability. The fourth sub-theme is about specific undertakings that have been or are being employed in remaking the urban landscape that range from strategies for infusing public life into city spaces to reconstruction of critical ecological systems. In conclusion, the prospects for the metropolis are discussed in which the various lessons provided in this volume are reviewed as a step toward remaking a more sustainable metropolis in a global context.

The challenges of global urbanism

When it comes to dealing with issues of growth, development and the diminishing quality of life in urban areas, cities seem to be a problem rather than a solution. This is true because cities and the environmental pressures associated with them continue to spread beyond their boundaries and affect a range of issues including economic growth, migration, public health and the transformation of rural areas into urban settlements. In addition, the number of people living in deplorable conditions in many urban areas in developing regions continues to increase because of the draw of perceived, but often elusive, economic opportunities cities represent for many.

Moreno and the United Nations Global Urban Observatory (2003) estimate that most of the world's population growth in coming generations will take place in urban areas of less developed nations. By 2030, the urban population will reach 3.9 billion, 79 percent of which will be in less developed nations. Under these circumstances, cities and urban areas represent an opportunity and challenge to provide creative urban environments that are in tune with nature's rhythms and provide healthy, supportive living conditions. The current issues facing urban regions and the deteriorating links between urbanism and nature at both local and regional scales, can best be addressed with proactive and holistic approaches to planning, design and public policy focused on the unique conditions of the urban landscape.

In the quest to find ways to improve the urban condition, getting design and the resulting quality of the urban fabric right are crucial for creating more sustainable communities. This means the creation of well-designed places that put people first, make efficient use of the available space and most effectively manage environmental resources is fundamental. Well-designed places require multifaceted analysis, policy, planning and design that take into account the land, history, contemporary societal needs and economics. In addition, successfully designed interventions have to be able to respond to dynamic forces that make it difficult to achieve high-quality design that include population migration, growth and rapid urbanization. These complex issues require new ideas that can restore and improve degraded communities, rather than utilizing old or obsolete formulas to design urban areas.

The concept of remaking metropolis can be regarded, to some extent, as the reconnection of the different systems, flows or layers that make up the content of the urban landscape to create a more sustainable complex of systems. These systems are in constant need of healing and self reconstruction, but also require interventions to renovate derelict urban landscapes. This approach will provide the prospect of the persistence of sustainable urban landscapes on a global scale.

Global sustainability and shifting urban systems

The ongoing process of urbanization throughout the globe is influenced by numerous systems, at various times having greater or lesser impact on the form, quality of life and the prospect of sustainability for cities. The second sub-theme of this book, global sustainability and shifting urban systems, includes contributions from authors that demonstrate how various types of systems may affect the realization of more sustainable futures for cities. Robert Thayer, in his chapter "The World Shrinks, the World Expands: Information, Energy and Re-localization," explains how shifts in availability of information, and availability and allocation of energy resources will have a dramatic impact on achieving sustainability in the future. Hayriye Esbah, in her chapter "Urbanization Challenges in Turkey: The Implications for Aydin, Turkey," discusses how, in the context of a rapidly growing economy in a developing country, cities struggle to cope with changing conditions that often create challenging political and regulatory environments in which to promote greater attention to long-term sustainability. Kristof Van Assche and Joseph Salukvadze, in their chapter "Tbilisi: Urban Transformation and Role Transformation in Post-Soviet Metropolis," focus on changing political dynamics and ideologies that have impacted resulting urban form and content. David Pijawka, Subhrajit Guhathatkurta, Edward Sadalla, Kimberly Collins, Mihir Prakash and Devon McAslan present research in their chapter "Urban Indicators for Border Areas: Measuring and Tracking Community Conditions in the US–Mexico Border Region," about well-being and quality of life in cities that are affected by changes in international commerce, border policy and population dynamics. Each of the contributors demonstrates how shifting urban systems influence the resulting urban conditions and affect the potential for achieving a more sustainable situation.

Thayer presents the concept of remaking metropolis from a perspective that emphasizes physical, technological and economic variables in a globalizing world, and how they might influence local economies and local landscapes. Thayer and other experts expect a "big rollover" in demand versus supply of oil in the near future, and he expects the scale of the landscape will change in response to a permanent rise in the cost of transportation and shipping fuels. He foresees that air travel will become less accessible, as will shipping of high mass, low value-added materials and goods. This will require the re-establishment of more local supplies and shorter transport distances for people and goods, and for the first time in human history, the perceived size of the world will expand. In response, the "grain" of the landscape will become finer.

Thayer supports the idea that under these circumstances more people will inhabit the rural landscape, while cities and towns will become more compact. Consequently, the landscape will be influenced by the three major operative technological systems (matter, energy and information). The big question here is how cities and regions will respond to the big energy rollover. Some of the possible answers include acceleration of energy efficiency, utilization and localization of product consumption and renewable energy production. The scale of city regions becomes important and city regions will look toward replacing imported goods and services. Overall, a new relationship between supply, demand, consumption and impact may become a visible hallmark of the regional landscape. Although oil will have come and gone, information technology irreversibly changes constructions of reality and the way economies, cultures, governments and regions do business. Thayer's chapter concludes by suggesting that the bioregion, or natural "life place," is the appropriate location for the protection of biodiversity, sustained use of resources, identity and life satisfaction of local inhabitants.

Esbah makes the point that the outcomes of urbanization vary according to geographic and geopolitical situations and as Turkey responds to rapid urbanization with limited resources many challenges to forging a path toward sustainable cities emerge. As with many developing countries, in the context of a strong national economy and a changing political, regulatory and social dynamic, migration from rural areas to cities causes changes in economic, political and social structures. Esbah focuses on the challenges of land conversion and how, with inadequate regulatory frameworks, environmental and social problems become widespread.

The case of Aydin provides a clear example of how a mid-sized provincial city is being transformed as a result of a growing economy and migration from rural areas in Eastern Turkey. Esbah discusses four phases of urban evolution in Turkey. During the first phase, pre-concentration, mechanization of agriculture and investment in transportation facilitate growth in small urban centers (12,500–250,000 population). The second phase, urbanization, is currently having a significant impact on Turkey. Population growth is increasing rapidly in large cities, contributing to the growth and development of mega-cities and large metropolitan areas of the future. Polarization reversal, the third phase, is emerging in Turkey and is characterized by increased export of manufactured goods, international trade and an improved financial sector. Mid-sized cities also experience growth, and increasing suburbanization and ex-urbanization are evident.

Counter-urbanization, the fourth phase, sees increased population growth in small cities. Growth in cities is linked to the level of industrialization. In Turkey, all of these various states are occurring simultaneously in different locations.

Esbah notes that the institutional environment is critical in shaping development patterns and, historically, is more stable and a major determinant of long-term growth. Countries with historically more stable and productive political and economic institutions are generally wealthier today than those without. Economic development is closely linked with the development of the resources on which urbanization takes its course. Thus, the design of durable cooperative institutions is one key to the maximization of resources. It has been well established that successful resource management on any scale requires a system of legitimate institutions. Even though major differences exist among the institutions of developed and developing world countries, some common problems associated with rapid land use change caused by urbanization prevail around the world. For example, economic development in rural areas in most countries has declined in recent decades because government decision-makers encourage urbanization to trigger economic development. Rural landscapes possess ecological, economic and cultural qualities for humans; however, the problem of rural land conversion has become critical in many countries, including Turkey. As urbanization spreads, remnant urban open spaces are affected by rapid land development. Subsequently, these ecologically important areas are becoming smaller and more isolated and ecological values are diminishing while exotic plants and impervious surfaces increase.

Van Assche and Salukvadze contrast the planning strategies of Tbilisi, Georgia of the past few decades, from late communism to present day. Drawing on extensive fieldwork, interviews, analysis of documents and plans, their chapter reconstructs the change of course through a general shift in ideology, from Soviet planning to fragmentation of plans and policies, but also in terms of shifts in institutional networks. With the collapse of the Soviet Union, Moscow actors and Moscow knowledge disappeared, and new actors and new knowledge were introduced in the planning and design system. Architects-turned-developers introduced western architectural forms and foreign non-profit organizations introduced ecological concepts. Foreign policy advisors and western-educated Georgians gave weight to western economic visions of transition and shock therapy. With the new Georgian leadership, attitudes toward planning became more ambiguous, questioning the relevance of government intervention in spatial development, while at the same time cherishing certain results of Soviet centralized planning. This chapter attempts to answer the questions about what planning in this context can mean and what is the role of urban design. The results show institution building and clear separation of powers is needed to make the adoption of any planning model realistic. Urban design solves some of the issues confronting Tbilisi, but to be effective it has to be embedded in a fair and balanced planning system. That in turn can only emerge in a political framework where checks and balances are already functioning. Resolving this dilemma involves taking risk. It requires a combination of short-term strategies and slow institution building. The authors argue that urban design projects, if more responsive to citizens needs, can be part of the short-term strategies, creating momentum and changing the tone of long-term debates and leading to a better framework that can result in a more cohesive and sustainable city.

Pijawka and colleagues expose some of the many challenges of life in the border region between the United States and Mexico. Their chapter is viewed from the perspective of a newly forming regional urbanism that reflects many of the issues stemming from globalization. These issues include cross-border migration, regional markets with in and out daily flows, border security, drug and crime traffic, and significant flow of goods. The post-NAFTA era has led to freer movements of goods and better environmental regulations. All of these issues are impacting the quality of life in border communities. The Border Observatory Project develops data from eight border communities (four sister cities on each side of the boundary) comprising the US–Mexico border urban region. The data are in the form of Quality of Life indicators such as economic well-being, social indicators, public and health services, environmental threats and emotional well-being. On the Quality of Life Index, which represents the cumulative rating for each city, significant differences were observed. Three of the cities in Mexico had the lowest scores in overall quality of life as reported by resident perceptions, with Ciudad-Juárez, Chihuahua the lowest. The two lowest ratings correspond with the highest levels of concern over crime rates, air quality and perceived lack of local governmental responses to meet residents' needs. This suggests that preventive and mitigation measures need to be taken to avoid greater deterioration, especially in large Mexican communities, and that changes are needed to reach high quality of life ratings in any of the border communities, both in the United States and Mexico. A major finding is that in all cities, the public is concerned with the apparent lack of capacity by local governments to respond to public needs. An interesting finding is the lack of significant differences between US and Mexican communities on emotional well-being (a "happiness" scale). Despite large differences in concerns over air quality, public service delivery and trust in law enforcement, responses on the "happiness" dimension showed little variation among the eight communities. The chapter also provides explanatory factors for the findings and the potential for these perceptions to contribute to more sustainable practices in these urban conditions.

The future of the metropolis

Much of the dialogue on the topic of remaking metropolis is appropriately focused on compelling emerging themes and strategies that lead to more adaptable and conducive urban landscapes. The third sub-theme, the future of the metropolis, incorporates a series of provocative place-based planning and design approaches with scenarios that address current urban issues, with both local and regional perspectives providing directions in which the process of urbanization could evolve. Desiree Martinez Uriarte, in her chapter "Small Steps to Achieving the

Urban Sustainability of the Metropolitan Area of Mexico City," unveils the historical development of the Mexico City region and proposes a more ecologically sound proposal for coping with growing environmental problems associated with uncontrolled urban development. Han Meyer discusses the potential impacts of climate change and sea-level rise on the delta landscape of the Netherlands in his chapter "Transformations of the Urbanizing Delta Landscape." Building on the centuries of experience working with water management strategies, Meyer presents new concepts that incorporate ecology into a more flexible response. Jesus J. Lara focuses on emerging planning and design strategies employed in the Dutch Randstad region in his chapter "Sustainable Urban Design: Lessons from Dutch Cities." These are working to create a more sustainable urban region in this densely populated urban conglomeration. These three contributions provide useful models that employ a broad vision for the sustainable metropolis.

Martinez Uriarte describes the current processes and efforts for remaking the urban landscape in the Basin of Mexico, undoubtedly one of the greatest ecological disasters in human history. What was once a basin occupied by five bodies of water, surrounded by forested mountains, is now home to one of the world's largest and most densely populated metropolitan areas with consumption of resources and absorption of waste produced by a population of more than 22 million. Centuries of unsustainable resource management and the impacts of a large population have impacted the overall quality of life. The result is a deterioration of public health, environmental degradation, public and individual costs caused by inefficient city planning, and an uncertain quality of life for its inhabitants. Martinez Uriarte outlines a proposed plan to organize land use under 12 metropolitan sectors, offering their inhabitants similar opportunities for employment, commerce, recreation, relaxation, culture and health. This reorganization will play an import-ant role in sustainability by cutting distances traveled, reducing emissions of pollutants. In this way, it will be reviving pedestrian culture and encouraging the use of alternative vehicles. Once the megalopolis is reorganized into metropolitan sub-centers, the plan focuses on strategic catalyst ecological projects along with the required restoration and maintenance. These catalytic projects vary in size and scope in order to encourage the creation of public, semi-private and private green areas in new developments, as part of the green infrastructure for the metropolitan area.

The vision for the region as a group of beautiful, modern cities that also preserve their historical and urban heritage for their residents is described. Green areas are an essential part of the population's quality of life, providing valuable eco-system services and areas of relaxation and recreation, encouraging culture and social communication in the interests of creating a democratic awareness. Although the cost of cleaning up the environment of the megalopolis immediately is unaffordable, Martinez Uriarte proposes taking small steps toward a model of sustainability.

Meyer addresses the impacts of global warming in combination with an increasing process of urbanization on the Dutch landscape and presents some adaptive approaches to dealing with these issues. The history and essence of the Dutch culture is based on its relationship with the water and the landscape. For centuries the Dutch have mastered the creation of a national hydraulic system that is concerned with three aspects: the development of drainage-systems of ditches and canals to remove the superfluous water; the construction of large systems of dikes alongside the rivers and the channelizing of rivers to make them more suitable for shipping; and the construction of dikes and dams into a large coastal defense system. These aspects require complex planning and manipulation of the landscape. Under current conditions and with the effects of global warming, increasing sea levels and changes in climatic conditions have impacted the vulnerable Dutch landscape. In response, Meyer describes a new approach that tends toward a stronger emphasis on "dynamic" and "elastic" types of water management, which gives more space to the water in the rivers, more space for temporary water storage in the polders, and the replacement of the narrow coastal defense system by a wider zone of artificial and natural dunes, beaches, inlets, islands and breakwaters. Along with this new strategy, some of the existing strategies and approaches in planning and design include a transformation from a static (hard) system toward a dynamic (soft) system of water management. This also offers new opportunities for economic development, especially port development and recreation. The transformation of the urbanized delta-landscape in the Netherlands is now interwoven with the character of the territory as a coastal zone and a delta of rivers. The specific character of this watery territory transforms possibilities for numerous port-cities. The development of the landscape and the rise of cities were on the one hand defined by the ambition for maximum exploitation of the landscape for international trade activities. On the other hand, the continuous vulnerability to flooding had to be taken into account. The development of the urban landscape of the Netherlands can be understood as a fine example of the process of modernization, which has been defined by two great themes, globalization and the relationship between urbanization and natural conditions of the territory. The present-day transformation of this urbanized delta landscape can be understood as a new phase of modernization, needing a new definition of the relationship between local contexts and new global networks, and a new relationship between urban development and the natural water-oriented landscape.

Lara describes strategies or practices that improve the quality of life in the Randstad region of the Netherlands while providing the right conditions for economic prosperity. Some basic principles have been part of the planning process in the region since the Middle Ages and can be better understood through the examination of the factors that have contributed to make the Randstad the economic powerhouse of the Netherlands. The Dutch National Spatial Strategy played a crucial role in the development of the urban and rural landscape and specific planning and design strategies that have been implemented to achieve a more sustainable society. The physical and socio-cultural qualities of the region have enabled the Randstad to maintain its strong position in the Dutch economy, remaining the cultural and political center of the Netherlands. Lara notes that what sets the Dutch approach apart is an integrated means of city planning that most countries have not yet put in place. Proactive responses to pressing issues of urbanization are an integral part of the Dutch National Spatial Strategy Reports. Specific concepts and ideas are introduced to deal with issues of nature, urban entities and decentralization. Intensification approaches and strategies during the past years have shifted their focus from decentralized development and housing to improving the quality of urban life, the environment and the economy. In addition, the implementation of critical and strategic design policies and planning strategies have been crucial to the sustainability process in the Netherlands. Sustainable planning and design was elevated to a national planning strategy in 1988. This process enabled cities to provide tailor-made solutions through the implementation of piecemeal projects and a strategic planning policy that responds to each targeted location rather than master plans. Scholars and critics agree that the Dutch have embraced and intensively incorporated sustainability into their planning, design and other policies.

Remaking the urban landscape

While it is important to establish a long-term vision for the future of cities, in order to create quality living environments and build on a sustainable foundation, most cities will need to approach their various challenges on an incremental basis. Specific plans to transform, retrofit or restore urban and natural systems are usually only possible to realize when leveraging opportunities as they arise. The fourth sub-theme, remaking the urban landscape, presents a series of compelling current cases of urban landscape restoration from diverse settings around the world. The cases presented in this theme explore the various approaches with some thought of new directions that have emerged from diverse setting and contexts. Lars Gemzoe and Sohyun Park, in their chapter "Turning Cities Around," build on past work by Gehl (1987), Gehl and Gemzoe (2000) and Gehl et al. (2008) that focuses on how to bring social life back into public spaces in cities that have long been dominated by automobile-oriented and industrialized urban systems. Khanin Hutanuwatr, in his chapter "Re-urbanization in Thailand: Reconsidering Urban Development Following the Tsunami," documents the many challenges experi-enced in the re-urbanization process of Phi Phi Island following the devastating tsunami of 2004. Michael Hough presents an ecological view of city design and redevelopment in his chapter "Urban/Suburban Landscapes: An Ecological View." He builds on his previous work (Hough 2004) and the inspiration for his ecological approach to city planning and design attributed to McHarg (1969) using the Toronto Docklands to illustrate how an ecological approach can be employed to revitalize an important urban post-industrial site. Martin Bryant and Penny Allan use two cases to show how urban ecology can inform planning and design in their chapter "Tapestries and Traditions: Urban Ecology and City Making." Two distinctly different sites, an inner-city brownfield and an ex-urban greenfield site in the environs of Sydney, demonstrate how similar ecological principles can be applied in varied contexts. Edward Cook explores how urban ecosystems can provide a framework for assessing the existing conditions and the potential for sustainable design strategies in his chapter "Urban Ecosystems and the Sustainable Metropolis." He outlines a range of urban ecosystem typologies that focus on maximizing ecosystem services and ecological functions. Peter Geitz's chapter "Bringing Urban Streams Back to Life!: The Use of Modern Waterway Construction Technologies in Restoring Degraded Streams," documents work in southwest German cities to restore ecological values to degraded urban waterways. As critical contributors to ecosystem services, urban waterways are one of the key pieces to maintain healthy functioning environments in cities. Joseph Ewan, John Ball, Michael Underhill and James Burke explore the tension that exists at the edge of urbanized areas that interface with preserved natural open space in their chapter "Managing the Urban/Nature Border: Sonoran Islands in the Urbanized Desert."

Gemzoe and Park argue that in a society in which increasingly more daily life takes place in the private sphere (in private homes, at private computers, in private cars, at private workplaces and in strictly controlled and privatized shopping centers), there are clear signs that the city and city spaces have been given a new and influential role as public space and forum. Consequently, achieving exciting, meaningful, and yet safe public realms requires a balanced investment in both policy and design. Traditionally, public space has always served as meeting place, market place and traffic space, although the pattern of usage has varied in the course of history. However, since the twentieth century and even in contemporary society, the notion of public space has still been changed. Environmental issues and social problems emerge because of the shift in the use of public spaces. For example, while many urban meeting places are being eroded and violated by the ever increasing intrusion and unseemly domination of the automobile, public areas have become dangerous and polluted rather than lively and invigorating. Gemzoe and Park present the idea that contemporary experience shows that when quality city space exists, it is accompanied by extensive and multifaceted city life with many new features that reflect changes in society. They also provide cases of very successful and visionary cities around the world that are making investment in the quality of life a priority. With an emphasis on "real" streets and squares, integrated functions of city bring a rich diversity of city life to serve the daily needs of the community.

Although the case of rebuilding after a devastating event such as the 2004 tsunami is very specific, the more general process of re-urbanization following a significant devastating natural or human-induced disaster is more common and can provide useful lessons for responding to many different forms of extensive disruption in urbanized regions. Hutanuwatr describes the many challenges faced in communities where this occurs. Urbanization and redevelopment after disaster can result in great changes in urban environments. These changes may provide great opportunity for improvements in various dimensions. On the other hand, in practice they may amplify the vulnerability of local communities. Tourism-based urbanization and top-down redevelopment projects in Thailand exemplify the increase of vulnerability after disaster. Hutanuwatr's discussion is based on case study research and fieldwork in Thailand's recovery from the tsunami in 2004. The research paradigm draws heavily from the naturalistic inquiries approach. As a result, the data collection methods include in-depth interview, field examination and other secondary documents. The chapter explains the adverse impact of pressure from tourism-based urbanization in Southern Thailand. It addresses the growing demands of coastal land plots and the relationship to the difficulties in resettlement of low-income and minority communities after the tsunami. A detailed case study of Phi Phi Island is provided to exemplify the impact of redevelopment proposals after the tsunami using a centralized and expertise-based approach, aiming at converting the island into a high-end tourist destination. Sustained state–local conflicts in the planning process, resulting in delays in redevelopment and other adverse consequences, illustrate the difficulties of moving forward with reconstruction when diverse planning approaches and critical roles of participation cannot be reconciled.

Hough issues a call for a greater understanding of the essential relationships between natural systems and cities. The significance of landscape as an organizing framework for urban form that begins locally and continues at a broader scale of the larger landscape is provided in his chapter. He notes the issues facing urban and rural regions and that urbanism and nature are interconnected at local and regional scales, arguing that the issues can only be resolved with an integrated approach that pays close attention to three major issues. The first is the impact urbanization has on the various natural systems upon which cities rely, such as energy, water, plant communities and climate. The second is the role of environmental design in creating a rational basis for reshaping city form. And the third is the regional and local urban landscapes that can provide an ecological framework for structuring urban growth. He also highlights the importance of green infrastructure in the process of city making. Green infrastructure is about establishing the landscape on a site in the same way that engineers establish sewers, water, electricity, telephone and other essential services prior to planning development. A key characteristic of green infrastructure is that it is relevant at any scale. Green infrastructure also provides an appropriate way of dealing with unpredictability, since city development and change requires infrastructure as the organizing framework within which social functions evolve. Complex and stable cities and neighborhoods are not the product of grand designs or fast-track developer master plans. They are created by the people who live there, through a multitude of small decisions and choices made by untold numbers of individuals going about their daily business.

The traditional design values that have shaped the physical landscapes of our cities have contributed little to their success as civilizing, enriching places to live. Today, however, the essential relationships between natural systems and cities are beginning to be understood. Hough's chapter examines some aspects of aquatic systems and watersheds, the relationship between plants and human health and the significance of landscape as an organizing framework for urban form that begins locally and continues at a broader scale of the larger landscape. The task of remaking urban landscapes involves a fundamental principle of natural systems – that of evolution and change.

Bryant and Allan look at two projects in New South Wales, Australia. Victoria Park is 5 km from the center of Sydney and an unbuilt project at North Hawks Nest sits on the periphery, 200 km north of Sydney. Both are mixed-use developments, intended for housing and commercial uses. Both are on damaged landscapes. Both are driven by traditional urbanist principles but both have been enriched by a design process that has made urban ecology fundamental to the design of the place. Their layouts may not be much different from traditional towns, but they both have been influenced by ecological planning that weaves its way into urban form. The two projects adopt differing approaches to urban ecology as a driver of town making. Victoria Park offers a systemic, machinistic tapestry of urban ecology, revealed within the tight demands of inner city urban design. The North Hawks Nest project has a more fluid tapestry-like approach, weaving the diverse natural landscapes into a low-density urban fabric in a way that protects and enhances biodiversity.

Cook focuses on a conceptual framework by which urban ecosystems can be addressed, attributes understood and potential management strategies developed, in an attempt to preserve or re-establish lost or deteriorating environmental benefits. As a consequence of the dynamic process of urbanization, many historic-ally viable functioning natural ecosystems are being transformed in ways that are often difficult to understand and manage. Awareness of the lost services previously provided by these ecosystems is just now increasing, and there is greater interest in developing strategies to preserve, restore or reinterpret ecosystems in an urban context. Five types of urban ecosystems (preserved, restored, hybrid, synthetic and regenerated) are explored in relation to their viability within particular urban situations and to understand the potential ecosystem services and/or benefits that may be embodied within them. Preserved urban ecosystems are those that are essentially remnant natural ecosystems, but may be starting a process of decline as a result of proximate urban transformations. Principles and strategies including buffers, connectivity and preserving indigenous species are explored. Restored urban ecosystems are established through direct intervention to re-establish the structure and functions of a previously existing system. The objective is to attempt to replicate an appropriate and sustainable condition of the ecosystem and to establish the supporting structure and context. Hybrid urban ecosystems accept that urban transformation has created conditions in which preservation and restoration are not possible, but build on the deep structure of ecosystems and use some of the previously existing attributes blended with introduced elements that acknowledge the changes in the supporting structure and function of the surrounding landscape. Synthetic urban ecosystems use ecological design principles to create viable systems that provide environmental services and benefits, but are not based on previously existing ecosystems locations, structure or functions. Regenerated urban ecosystems allow for nature to take its course and naturally regenerate an ecosystem that may be different from that which previously existed. Examples are provided throughout to illustrate how these concepts can be applied in an urban context and to demonstrate the value as typologies that can be incorporated into management plans and design strategies.

Geitz's work focuses on water, especially on revitalizing streams and rivers in southwest Germany, which has suffered from immense alterations, mainly during the last two centuries. Most of the environmental dangers of today have resulted from human actions. These include global warming, forest dieback, soil erosion and flood events in urban watersheds where a high degree of impermeable surfaces prohibit natural processes, such as infiltration and retention capacity of the soil. Subsequently, large quantities of water are being flushed into streams with increasing speed and frequency, whose natural profile is not able to handle the unnatural pressure. This situation is prevalent in some of the most important rivers in the regions such as the Rhine and the Neckar, which as of today have lost 87 percent of the flood water retaining riparian zones due to the construction of flood protection dams along the rivers. For the last 14 years, Geitz has been involved in the design and implementation of river restoration projects on the Neckar River. His projects focus on restoring the aquatic habitat qualities in the river itself and in the creation of additional recreational open space in the region. The economically strong and densely populated Neckar region is also lacking parks and greenways in close proximity to the river. After centuries of focusing solely on economic growth, it has been realized that economically strong regions can only be competitive if they also possess ecological value. Landscapes which are designed taking into consideration natural processes and recreational purposes are therefore mandatory in achieving a satisfying standard of living in densely developed urban areas. The rehabilitation of these waterways requires modern natural construction methods. New ideas ask for new tools. In addition to changing the political and social view of the way residents treat their rivers and streams, they also need new goals and construction techniques to develop such interdisciplinary projects. Geitz's chapter highlights that today, landscape architects have infiltrated hard structure engineering reconstruction methods and once again made the old but newly rediscovered bioengineering bank stabilization methods acceptable (Scheichtl and Stern 1997).

Ewan and colleagues explore a cross-disciplinary design strategy focused on the interface between the edge of urbanization and open space preserves. A project based in Phoenix, Arizona is explored predicated on the idea that design should guide policy, rather than the other way around. The overall aim of the project was to endeavor to inform new policy for urban form at the edge of a new 21,500 acre natural open space preserve that has significant ecological value and is part of a larger system of preserves in the metropolitan area. Their chapter includes a review of the underlying conditions and discussion of the primary issues relevant to this edge condition within the city of Phoenix. Also included is a discussion of proposals and policy recommendations developed through the process. Political activists, pushing for more public access to and public use of open space, recently convinced the city to adopt a 60/40 rule in a rapidly developing area adjacent to the Sonoran Preserve. This ordinance requires the private side of the edge to be more than half-public. The ordinance proposes four options to meet this requirement of 60 percent access: (1) single loaded streets adjacent to the preserve, (2) cul-de-sacs opening to the preserve, (3) private open space adjacent to the preserve, and the final vague catchall (4) creative options. In practice the last option is unlikely to be used because the development community is reluctant to invest resources in an effort to discover which creative option the city would support. Of the remaining three options, it is too soon to know how the development community will respond, but the few projects required to respond to the ordinance illustrate that true public access is anathema to developers who market private and often guard-gated communities. The preferred result is a negotiated arrangement that allows access while preserving the ecological values of the open space preserve as a critical dimension of the overall sustainability of cities.

Conclusion

The selected projects and topic areas in this book reflect the desire to identify the edge of innovation in sustainability, urban planning and landscape architecture-oriented projects. Based on the selected theme areas, *Remaking Metropolis* presents a model of performance for existing urban conditions in diverse urban areas around the world, and documents the strategies and recommendations for future developments that result in concepts for new projects. Successful sustainable urban landscape initiatives are place-specific and need to be developed from local resources and in response to local conditions. This is precisely the approach that proved critical to bring about the innovative edge perceptible in the cases presented here.

Remaking Metropolis presents examples of both urban/rural destruction and urban rebirth. This examination is important to show the lessons of the past, to establish a framework in which to evaluate current and future developments for urban change, and to stimulate a region-wide reassessment of urban redevelopment and policies for the urban area being presented. In order to address the current and constantly increasing challenges of urbanization it is important to examine and critique innovative projects to determine how and why certain approaches and schemes have been successfully implemented, as well as why some of their more problematic aspects occurred. Through this learning process, a transfer of knowledge is possible in the adaptation of design principles and planning policies, because the process of adaptation provides information that is vital to the goals of creating sustainable communities. The process of remaking metropolis is still evolving and it is hoped that the contents of this book help to guide future development.

References

Gehl, J. (1987) *Life Between Buildings: Using Public Space*, New York: Van Nostrand Reinhold.

Gehl, J. and L. Gemzoe (2000) *New City Spaces*, Copenhagen: Danish Architectural Press.

Gehl, J., L. Gemzoe, S. Kirknaes and B. Sondergaard (2008) *New City Life*, Copenhagen: Danish Architectural Press.

Hough, M. (2004) *Cities and Natural Process: A Basis for Sustainability* – Second Edition, London: Routledge.

Jacobs, J. (1961) *The Death and Life of Great American Cities*, New York: Random House.

McHarg, I. (1969) *Design with Nature*. Garden City, NY: Doubleday.

Meyer, H. (1999) *City and Port: Transformation of Port Cities*, Utrecht: International Books.

Moreno, E. and UN Global Urban Observatory (2003) *Slums of the World: The Face of Urban Poverty in the New Millenium*, Nairobi: UN-Habitat.

Schiechtl, H. and R. Stern (1997) *Water Bioengineering Techniques for Watercourse Bank and Shoreline Protection*, London: Wiley-Blackwell.

Thayer, R. (2003) *Life Place: Bioregional Thought and Practice*, Berkeley: University of California Press.

Part

B

Challenges of global urbanism

Chapter 2: Jesus J. Lara and Edward A. Cook
The state of the global metropolis

Chapter 2

The state of the global metropolis

Jesus J. Lara and Edward A. Cook

Challenges of global urbanization

The challenges cities around the world face vary depending on their history, access to resources, and level of economic activity. Cities in developed, developing, and least developed regions of the world all have unique issues and challenges that require place-specific solutions. For instance, the poorest cities and their slums typically tend to have the worst local hazards, such as spread of disease due to poor access to clean water, and lack of sanitation facilities and basic public health services. In more industrial cities in the developed and developing regions, the most common challenges tend to be at a metropolitan scale, related to pollution from industry and traffic and degradation of the environment in general. Urbanization has been the focus for developing sustainable futures. With more than half of the world's population living in cities now and with more than 90 percent of future population growth expected to occur in cities, in the next 35 years it will be necessary to double the urban infrastructure that took 5,000 years to build.

Urban population dynamics and resource allocation

A review of current trends of urbanization around the world highlights the inter-connectedness between urbanization, sustainability, and the impacts population growth has on the environment. Although there is no single definition of an urban population, according to the United Nations Population Division (see Oyebanji and Mutizwa-Mangiza, 2011) an "urban population" can be defined using at least three different ideas: (1) the number of people living within the jurisdictional boundaries of a city; (2) those living in areas with high density—urban agglomeration; (3) those linked by direct ties to a city center or metropolitan area.

Historically most of the world's population grew very slowly. Prior to the seventeenth century, the world's population was small compared to the contemporary situation. It was not until the seventeenth and eighteenth centuries that mortality rates started to decline due to advances in medicine and public health. Longevity increased through the twentieth century and reached a peak at 2 percent per year in 1965–1970 (Worldwatch Institute, 2007).

In 1900, only 160 million people, or the equivalent of one-tenth of the world's population, resided in urban areas. Today the urban population continues to grow faster than the total population of the world. According to the Population Institute (2007), about three billion people or 48 percent of the total world population were then living in urban areas. In 2007, the total percentage of the population living in urban areas surpassed the 50 percent mark. For the first time, the world has more urban dwellers than rural. The proportion of the world's population living in urban areas is expected to rise to 61 percent by 2030 (Worldwatch Institute, 2006). The process of urbanization is already well advanced in the more developed regions of the world. In 2003, 75 percent of the populations in the more developed areas were living in urban areas and this is expected to increase to 82 percent by 2030.

The majority of urban dwellers are living in smaller urban settlements, while less than 5 percent of the world population lives in mega-cities (ten million inhabitants or more). The number of cities with five million or more inhabitants is projected to rise to 61 by 2015, increasing by about 25 percent in 15 years. Among these, the number of mega-cities will reach 22 by 2015. About three-quarters of the cities of five million population or greater are currently located in developing countries, where the demand for food and water already outstrips supply (see Figure 2.1).

Over the last 50 years, the world has also experienced tremendous growth in total population, increasing from 2.5 billion in 1950 to seven billion in 2011. Projections for the total world population indicate that it will likely increase by 2.2 billion over the next 40 years, reaching 9.2 billion by 2050. This increase is roughly equivalent to the overall number of people in the world in 1950 and will be absorbed primarily in less developed regions (Worldwatch Institute, 2007).

As these statistics of urban and global population growth indicate, the future poses significant challenges for cities, the environment, national governments and the world community. In addition to managing migration to cities from rural areas and the natural increase of the population from current urban residents, officials will need to create more sustainable urban environments through a range of social, economic, and environmental strategies that are coupled with proactive planning and design.

In his keynote address at the Remaking Metropolis symposium held in Phoenix, Arizona, world-renowned pathologist George Poste (2005) described a range of potential global health hazards associated with increasing urbanization. He noted that it is estimated that over the past 50 years, human activities have distorted the balance of ecosystems more rapidly and extensively than in any comparable period of time in human history. The sole purpose has been to meet fast-growing demands for basic elements such as food, fresh water, timber, energy, and fuel. In addition to the overall human population, the accelerated pace of the world's urban population growth has resulted in some alarming transformations that require serious attention. Some of these effects or byproducts of urbanization include: (1) accelerated deterioration of physical and social well-being, (2) worsening morbidity and mortality resulting from communicable and non-communicable diseases,

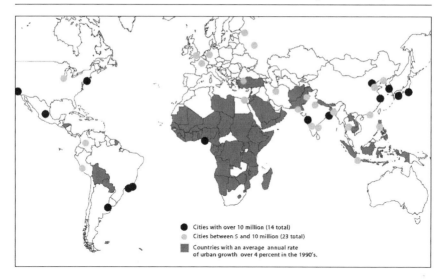

Figure 2.1 The world's largest cities, more than half located in Asia, are home to 14 percent of the world's urban population. In Africa more people live in smaller cities and towns. Courtesy of Jesus J. Lara.

and (3) increasing polar demographics that are characterized by an aging urban population and massive migration to specific areas around the globe.

Deterioration of physical and social well-being

Most critics and scholars agree that the increasing deterioration of physical and social well-being in urban areas has been as a result of three major factors: (1) population growth, (2) patterns of consumption, and (3) land use and urbanization. As populations grow and urbanize, there is an increasing need for more cars, housing, factories, amenities, roads, and other infrastructure. Ultimately, these pressures also result in the transformation of undeveloped rural areas and productive farmlands into urban development.

Urban areas have a unique impact on their surrounding environments. Often they create their own microclimate, which in turn affects the regional and global climate. They are also among the most rapidly changing environments on earth. Fast-growing, large metropolitan areas in arid climates result in some of the most extreme urban-warming rates in the world, in part because heat is being reflected, trapped, and absorbed in concrete, rooftops, and buildings that are also blocking cooling winds. At the same time, there is less vegetation to absorb the heat and cool the air through evapotranspiration. According to Brazel et al. (2007), the urban heat island (UHI) phenomenon typically occurs after sundown as heat absorbed by concrete, asphalt, and other materials during the day is slowly released back into the atmosphere at night. This results in high evening temperatures accounting for most of the differences in the urban/rural warming rates. Such is the case of Phoenix, Arizona, one of the fastest-growing cities in the Sonoran Desert in the southwest of the United States. There, UHI makes Phoenix night-time low temperatures 10–15 degrees Fahrenheit warmer than temperatures in rural areas. The main reason for an increasing UHI is the expansion of buildings farther into the desert valley. In addition, during the warmest seasons, Phoenix residents use mechanical air conditioning that releases hot air back into the environment. According to experts, it is not only the sun and the pavement, but daily urban living that is generating more heat in desert environments.

Environmental degradation is also taking place in the least developed countries where there is little or no manufacturing. In this case, it is in the form of deforestation, a common practice to provide much needed farmland and fuel for the increasing populations in these regions. According to the Population Institute (2007), in the twentieth century alone, the world lost close to half of its original forest cover, carbon dioxide emissions are up, and there is significantly less forested land to absorb carbon emissions.

Most environmental degradation and consumption on the planet can be attributed to rich, developed countries. Increasingly, however, degradation is also increasing in poorer countries with growing populations who are struggling to survive and improve their basic situation; consumption of natural resources is increasing. Population pressures have increased the consumption of basic elements such as wood used for fuel, growth of fast-growing cash-crops that exhaust the land and deplete its natural resources, and increased pressures on marine and coastal ecosystems. Those areas where population growth is highest are often least able to afford and implement environmental changes that will control current development patterns. Currently, it is estimated that more than one billion people live in ecological hotspots, areas that are both the planet's richest in biological diversity and highly threatened by increasing human activity. These hotspots comprise 12 percent of the earth's land surface, yet they contain nearly 20 percent of global population. In fact, biological hotspots are experiencing population growth that is nearly 40 percent faster than the rest of the world (Worldwatch Institute, 2007).

As populations grow, economic activity also increases, impacting ecosystems worldwide. Between 1950 and 2000 economic activity increased nearly sevenfold (Oyebanji and Mutizwa-Mangiza, 2011). Industrialized nations are responsible for the greatest amount of greenhouse gas emissions during the twentieth and early twenty-first centuries. The United States alone has less than 5 percent of the world's population, but it produces about 25 percent of the world's carbon dioxide emissions (Wackernagel and Rees, 1996). Due to current population growth and increasing demands for use of fossil fuels, China is expected to overtake the USA in carbon dioxide emissions by 2020, having potentially devastating effects on fossil fuel reserves (Population Institute, 2007). It is estimated that if the Chinese consumed as much oil as the typical American they would require 90 million barrels a day, far surpassing current daily world oil production (Worldwatch Institute, 2007). According to studies by the Population Institute

(2007), by mid-century developing countries will contribute more than half of total emissions worldwide.

An example of this trend is the increasing demand for and production of passenger cars globally. According to preliminary figures from London-based Global Insight, global passenger car production grew to 48.6 million units in 2006, a 6 percent increase from 2005 (Worldwatch Institute, 2007). During the same period China increased its production by 29 percent to 6.7 million vehicles and overtook Germany (5.7 million) to become the third largest producer. China's rise represents the most dramatic change in the world of auto industry. During the past decade, Chinese production has more than quintupled, driven by joint ventures with multinationals and the rapid growth of home-grown carmakers (Worldwatch Institute, 2007).

Land use changes and urbanization patterns have also had an impact on the environment. Land use changes that incorporate different surface types can affect the atmospheric distribution of the sun's radiation, so changes such as deforestation, irrigation, and urbanization have a severe impact on climate change. As noted earlier, for the first time in human history, more than 50 percent of the world's population lives in urban areas. As this number grows and the population urbanizes, there will be more cars, power plants, factories, and chemical production. Urban areas' unique impacts on environmental surroundings often create their own microclimate, which in turn affects regional and global climate systems. Even in countries with little to no manufacturing, environmental degradation due to unsustainable population growth is accelerating global climate change. Deforestation is ravaging the developing world to make way for much needed farmland and provide fuel for rising populations. Carbon dioxide emissions are up, and there are dramatically fewer trees to process it. Energy use for homes, cooking, and other daily activities will increase. More people means a continuing and increasing rise in greenhouse gas concentrations, guaranteeing further and more dangerous warming in the century ahead.

Recent research demonstrates that the interconnectedness between the built environment and its effects on physical well-being is much stronger than previously thought (Jackson, 2012; Donnenberg et al., 2011; Jackson and Kochtitzky, 2001). This was made obvious when infectious diseases were a primary public health threat during the industrial revolution. During the last part of the nineteenth century and the beginning of the twentieth century, as a result of industrialization, many cities and urban areas became magnets to many new residents in search of a better life and opportunities. Many of these cities were unable to cope with the influx of people as hundreds of thousands of workers crowded into unsanitary conditions, resulting in an increase in disease and epidemics and a decrease in life expectancy in many industrial cities (Rosen, 1993).

Since then, dramatic improvements in public health in industrialized nations have been made possible by changes in the built environment. Some of these measures included the installation of comprehensive sewer systems, implementation of land use and zoning ordinances that ensured that residents had access to fresh air and light, as well as the movement of residential areas away from noxious industrial facilities. The focus was on the design and creation of sound places for people: planning and public health professionals were intrinsically linked.

Over time, the priority became separation of land uses based on functions and services through zoning ordinances as an effective solution to this problem. After years of zoning to segregate land uses, a new wave of increasing disconnectedness between public health and planning/design has occurred. Segregated land use has led to increased automobile use and more sedentary lifestyles. At the start of the twenty-first century, planners, designers, and public policy makers are again realizing that planning and design can better promote healthy living (Kushner, 2007).

Thanks to advances in medical technology, many infectious diseases that plagued us in the past have now been controlled or eradicated. The diseases of developed and developing countries in the twenty-first century will likely now be characterized as "chronic" diseases, those that steal vitality and productivity, and consume time and money (Jackson and Kochtitzky, 2001). Some of the most prominent include heart disease, diabetes, obesity, asthma, depression, and unintentional injures (National Center for Health Statistics, 2002). It is now becoming clear that we can help reduce the occurrence and severity of some of these chronic diseases by how we design and build human environments. Urban planning and related professions play an important role in shaping those conditions. Nowadays, there is an increasing demand for those concerned with the built environment to integrate health considerations fully into their work, both in policy and practical terms to make long-lasting results.

The shift from infectious diseases to chronic conditions can be seen most clearly in the United States, where half the population lives in the suburbs rather than urban or rural areas. Some of the measures taken 100 years ago to improve the quality of life in cities, such as increasing de-concentration of populations and the separation of land uses through zoning ordinances, are the same measures that contribute to the increasing chronic health problems in the developed world. The expansive design of suburbs increases dependence on the automobile, leading to a more sedentary lifestyle and potential for obesity. The increased use of the automobile, in turn, contributes to air pollution with its detrimental effects, including chronic respiratory ailments.

The arrangement of buildings, green areas, public transportation, street layout and design has an impact on cities' livability. Providing sufficient parks and green areas within easy reach of residents often determines how frequently they will be used. It has become common practice for designers and developers to create urban and suburban environments that do not specifically contribute to healthy behaviors, nor provide the conditions that will support healthy lifestyles. It does not matter how much health officials can provide information about healthy living, but if people live in poorly designed physical environments, the chances that their health will suffer are more certain.

The principal contributor to a number of the chronic diseases is the high level of obesity now found in the American population (Collins, 2003). The main contributing factors to obesity are a sedentary lifestyle and poor nutrition. It has been estimated that more stroke deaths in the United States are caused by obesity and hypertension than any other behavioral risks. Obesity affects both adults and children and the percentage of obesity in the population is increasing. According to the Trust for America's Health (healthyamericans.org), 119 million, or 64.5 percent, of adult Americans are either overweight or obese. Estimates of the number of obese American adults rose from 23.7 percent in 2003 to 24.5 percent in 2004.

The way we use our land and the choices we make about where we build new homes, schools, and businesses has an impact on our collective health. Perdue et al. (2003) examined the relationship between health and the environment in which we live. The results indicate that urban sprawl can create conditions that threaten human health in different ways. Many new developments tend to be located away from city centers, existing services, and infrastructure, resulting in significant distances between work and home. This means more space taken up by roads, and residents must rely increasingly on automobiles. Currently the average American now drives 73 minutes per day and uses the automobile for almost 90 percent of trips regardless of distance (Kushner, 2007). This has several health impacts resulting from a decrease in quality of time, reduction in air quality, and increased traffic accidents and unintentional injuries.

Studies by the American Public Health Association (2005) have found that the more time commuters spent in traffic, the less time they have for quality activities that will promote health and well-being, such as exercise and leisure. The same study also found that people in high-sprawl areas are more likely to suffer from chronic diseases such as high blood pressure. Also, as the daily traveled miles increase, the pollutants from automobiles increase too. Pollution increases deaths from respiratory and cardiopulmonary illnesses. For instance, asthma among the child population in the United States has been increasing as a result of automobile pollution. Children with asthma are believed to be particularly sensitive to air pollution. According to the US Environmental Protection Agency (EPA), 25 percent of children in America live in areas that regularly exceed the ozone limits. Asthma rates among children in the United States more than doubled from 1980 through 1995, from 2.3 million to 5.5 million (Jackson, 2012).

Air pollution from automobiles is not just a problem of the developed world. This is a serious issue in large cities in developing countries, particularly in Asia and Latin America. Vehicles contribute an estimated 60–70 percent of key urban air pollutants in Latin America and 50–60 percent in India (Worldwatch Institute, 2007). Also, the increasing number of hours on the road increases the opportunity for traffic accidents and unintentional injuries. Roads designed to make it easier for vehicles to travel at higher speeds are often dangerous to people. Worldwide, traffic accidents kill some 885,000 people each year and injure many times this number (Worldwatch Institute, 2007).

Environmental, social, and economic conditions in cities can have both positive and negative effects on human health and well-being. In many cases, urban design can encourage sedentary living habits. Ubiquitous parking lots are built as close as possible to final destination points in order to increase convenience, discouraging walking even relatively short distances. Also, some of the daily basic destinations such as work, home, school, and shopping tend to be dispersed, also discouraging walking between them. To improve this condition it is crucial that all sectors in cities work together to plan and design to improve health, well-being, and quality of life.

Morbidity, mortality, and pandemics

Another critical area that has been linked to uncontrolled development and urbanization, especially in less developed regions, has been the increasing rate of morbidity and mortality resulting from infectious diseases such as SARS or AIDS. The current rate of urban population growth around the world has created conditions under which these risks spread. Also, within poor and unsanitary urban conditions and the constant encroaching of urban areas into rural areas, human–animal contact occurs in conditions that may facilitate transfer of zoonotic diseases. In most of the less developed regions where rapid urbanization is taking place, investment in public health exists but is inadequate. This often results in a false sense of security in the absence of infectious disease outbreaks, leading to reduced vigilance to effective prevention programs. It is in these areas where most of the infectious disease occurrences take place.

Historically, diseases have come as byproducts of exploration, trade, or warfare, when the movement of people, animals, or goods brought geographically isolated infections to new locations. Today, with extensive global transport, trucks, trains, massive cargo ships, and airplanes have largely replaced the slower-moving caravans and steamships of the past, increasing the possibility for disease to move from one place to another. Favorable economic conditions also provide incentives for mass movement of workers to urban centers, often across international boundaries. Thus, infections that may once have remained in obscure rural areas are now more likely to reach large populations. There are numerous circumstances in industrialized countries where high-density population centers such as schools have facilitated rapid spread of disease, once introduced.

There are a number of major factors that contribute to the emergence of these infectious diseases. Generally this is a two-step process: the introduction of an infection into the human population, followed by its dissemination. The first step is the introduction of an infection for the first time into the human population. Once a pathogen has been introduced into a population, its success will depend on establishing itself and disseminating. According to Stephen S. Morse (2007), Director of the Center for Public Health Preparedness at Columbia University, in most cases infectious diseases already exist in nature and they simply gain access to new host populations through the process of "viral traffic" (microbial traffic).

This occurs when major demographic changes, such as population migration, precipitates the emergence. Due to ecological changes, often triggered by humans, different populations come in contact with new pathogens or hosts that carry them. A recent example occurred in China. Land in China that is being converted to rice planting, necessary to support an expanding population, is also a habitat for a small field mouse which carries the Hantaan virus, a prototype hantavirus. This virus is the cause of a disease which used to be called Korean hemorrhagic fever (and is now called hemorrhagic fever with renal syndrome) (Morens et al., 2004).

The second step in the process of emerging infections is transmission. With the increasing mass migration from rural to urban areas, diseases that may once have been only local occurrences have been introduced to urban populations. Such is the case of Ebola, whose ecology is still a mystery. It is a natural infection undoubtedly of some species in parts of central Africa, probably living in the forest (Morens et al., 2004). It is speculated that as people entered the forest to collect wood or do some agriculture on the forest's edge, they would become exposed to this virus they had not encountered before. In the past the consequence may have been an unknown isolated infection. The current conditions are now different. With migration to cities, the chances of transmitting the disease are much greater.

It has also been speculated that HIV-1, the virus causing AIDS, was probably a zoonosis. It is estimated that there were probably many progenitors of HIV-1 in rural settings, possibly non-human primates in Africa. Though people may have occasionally become infected, the disease would remain localized because people did not have the means or need to move to large populated areas where it could spread.

Of significant concern to health professionals is that some of the infectious diseases can become pandemic. Due to population density and in some cases because humans create pathways to allow transmission of infections that may otherwise be poorly transmissible, the risk increases. Principle methods for spreading HIV have been through needle sharing, blood supply, and initially through the commercial sex trade (Heymann et al., 2007). HIV/AIDS is now a pandemic in spite of its relatively inefficient transmission. Mortality in the developed world is low and in most cases continues to decline, but it has been constant and in some circumstances is increasing in a number of countries with economies in transition (Worldwatch Institute, 2006).

Polar demographics – fertility and migration

Another effect of global urbanization is increasing polarization in demographics around the world. In recent years, the world population has been characterized by an aging urban population in more developed countries and a record cohort younger than 25 years in less developed countries. The former is the result of the combination of slow population growth and reduction in fertility rates in developing countries, which leads to population aging, as well as a reduction in mortality rates and increased aging due to improved health care where the proportion of older persons increases while that of younger persons decreases. It is estimated that in the more developed regions, 20 percent of the population is already aged 60 years or over and that proportion is projected to reach 33 percent by 2050 (Worldwatch Institute, 2007). According to the United Nations World Population Prospect Report (United Nations Population Division, 2003), in developed countries, the number of older persons (60 or over) has already surpassed the number of children (under age 15) and by 2050 the number of older persons in developed countries is expected to be more than double the number of children. Meanwhile, the aging population in developing countries is less advanced. In these regions, just 8 percent of the population is today aged 60 years or over but by 2050, 20 percent of their population is expected to reach that age.

The story is quite different in least developed countries: life expectancy remains low, at just 55 years, although it is projected to reach 67 years by 2045–50. In addition to fertility rates in some parts of the world, migration has been a factor for increasing populations. The more developed regions have been the net gainers of immigrants from the less developed regions. This has been a trend since the 1960s. According to studies by the Worldwatch Institute (2007) during 1990–2000, the more developed regions of the world were gaining 2.5 million emigrants annually, and about half of them (1.3 million) were directed to North America. These numbers have not changed during 2000–2010, and numbers are expected to slightly increase, bringing the emigrant population to North America to 1.5 million annually.

The major source of migrant populations is Asia, which had the most emigrants during 2000–2010, with 1.3 million annually, followed by Latin America and the Caribbean with 1.1 million annually, and Africa with 0.4 million annually. Some of the traditional countries where the migrant populations tend to go include: the United States (1.1 million annually), Canada (200,000), Germany (150,000), Italy (139,000), the United Kingdom (130,000), Spain (123,000), Australia (100,000) (Worldwatch Institute, 2007). In addition to the traditional migration of less developed regions to developed countries there are migration patterns within the developing countries that have become magnets for large numbers of migrants. Some of these regions include Hong Kong, Israel, Kuwait, Malaysia, Singapore, South Africa, Thailand, and the United Arab Emirates. During the period 2000–2010 the countries with the highest levels of net emigration included China (−329,000), Mexico (−306,000), India (−241,000), the Philippines (−180,000), Pakistan (−167,000), and Indonesia (−164,000) (Worldwatch Institute, 2007).

Climate change and natural disaster

Climate has always shaped the environment and human decisions about inhabiting places. While there has always been some unpredictability about how climate affects humans, general patterns and norms have influenced where and how cities have been established. Many of the world's largest cities are coastal and many others are located along rivers or in areas that can be seriously impacted by changes in climate. Although scientists differ about the pace of climate change and economists argue about precise figures relating to temperature rise and potential costs associated with change, there is generally agreement that climate change is happening and humans are contributing to it. Studies have shown that a number of major cities, from locations in Africa, Asia, Latin America, and the United States, will experience average temperature increases from 1 to 4 degrees Centigrade, along with increasing intensity of weather events (Rosenzweig et al., 2011). It is difficult to track climate change and therefore make accurate projections about the overall impact, but it is clear that it is an immense, multidimensional problem. Climate change is also a cumulative process and the longer it takes to undertake significant action, the more rapidly the problem accelerates and the harder it becomes to reverse.

Climate change threatens all countries to some degree and of course specific locations within countries more severely than others. There is a variety of potential impacts that will be experienced differently due to geography, economic condition, or ability to respond. The risks of climate change come in the form of a range of hazards, vulnerabilities of populations, and ability to adapt to changing conditions. Coastal cities will experience more damaging flooding related to sea-level rise and the intensity and frequency of storm events. Sea-level rise and vulnerability to storm surges have been predicted by some researchers to increase by up to 10 meters, covering 2 percent of the earth's land area while affecting 10 percent of the world's population and 13 percent of the urban population (McGranahan et al., 2007). Urban systems, such as water, energy, and transport systems, may also become vulnerable. Sudden supply changes can lead to system collapse that result in heavy environmental burdens and risk to human health. Heat waves, increased precipitation, inland flooding, landslides, drought, and other natural phenomena can also be anticipated in various locations (Dhainut et al., 2004; World Bank, 2009). Natural disasters have become more severe over the last two decades, affecting many larger cities (de Sherbenin et al., 2007). The United Nations Development Programme (UNDP) reports that between 1980 and 2000, 75 percent of the world's total population lived in areas affected by natural disaster. In 1999, there were over 700 major natural disasters, causing more than US$100 billion in economic losses and thousands of victims (Murphy and Ross-Larson, 2004). Over 90 percent of the losses of human life occurred in poor countries. At the human level, the outcome will include increased health risks and deteriorating quality of life. The ramifications on cities will vary depending on their resilience, vulnerability of the people, the quality of the urban systems, and the nature of the landscape in which they are situated. Cities will also find themselves in a downward cycle. The increase in temperature will increase the demand for air conditioning and water use, leading to greater levels of energy and resource consumption which will in turn lead to further increase in temperatures.

The disparity in cause and impact between developed and developing countries is also a significant issue and one of the current challenges to formulating global consensus for action. Cities contribute to, as well as feel, the impact. Urban areas contribute more than half of the world's carbon emissions and greenhouse gases through transportation, energy generation, industry, and biomass use (Oyebanji and Mutizwa-Mangiza, 2011). A city's contribution is also somewhat proportional to its output and energy consumption. Less dense, richer cities usually emit more greenhouse gases (World Bank, 2010). Populations in developing countries are most vulnerable and are likely to bear 75 percent of the cost of damages produced by climate change (Satterthwaite et al., 2007). The risk to the urban poor is also more severe. In developing countries, slum dwellers occupy marginal land often by railways, along slopes prone to landslides, on polluted ground, in flood plains, and in shaky structures vulnerable to earthquake or other disturbances. Because whatever urban services are available are usually makeshift, they are particularly vulnerable to any change or disturbance. Interruption of supplies and distribution can easily result in increased risk of water-borne disease, social unrest, and other serious hazards.

There are signs that efforts are being made in cities around the world to reverse this process, but the greatest challenge is to continue to develop risk assessments so that priorities are established to ensure effective use of resources. It is important to have an understanding of what disasters will cost in comparison to what could be spent to prevent future catastrophes. Objective and rational information will help move the politics along once this information is available and accepted. The larger challenge remains, however, who pays for what, considering the global variability in wealth, development, and resources.

Conclusions

It is clear that there are many challenges facing cities everywhere and although conditions vary in different parts of the world, much can be learned from how others deal with the specific problems faced where they reside. It is also clear that cities around the world are connected in important ways and problems do not remain isolated. People and disease migrate. Climate is universal, and as global communication has improved we are all becoming more aware of human tragedy as it occurs in what were previously remote places. The possibility for aid increases in these challenging times if the will is there to provide it. Finance, culture, and politics are also becoming increasingly connected and have significant influence on the way we create cities. The first step toward creating greater prospects for more sustainable cities in the future comes through understanding the challenges that exist and then sharing ideas for improving transport, land use policy, urban design, and natural systems in cities. Cities are exciting laboratories in which we are able to explore ways toward a better future.

References

American Public Health Association (2005) *The Hidden Health Costs of Transportation.* American Public Health Association: Washington, DC.

Brazel, A., P. Gober, S. Lee, S. Grossman-Clarke, J. Zehnder, B. Hedquist, and E. Comparri (2007) Determinants of changes in the regional urban heat island in metropolitan Phoenix (Arizona, USA) between 1990 and 2004. *Climate Research* 33:171–182.

Collins, C. (2003) Dietetic Management of Overweight and Obesity: A Comparison with Best Practice Criteria. *Nutrition & Dietetic – The Journal of the Dietetic Association of Australia* 60:177–184.

De Sherbinin, A., A. Schiller, and A. Pulsipher (2007) The vulnerability of global cities to climate hazards. *Environment and Urbanization* 19(1):39–64.

Dhainut, J., C. Classens, C. Ginsburg, and B. Riou (2004) Unprecedented heat-related deaths during 2003 heat wave in Paris: Consequences on emergency departments. *Critical Care* 8(1):1–2.

Donnenberg, A., H. Frumkin, and R. Jackson (2011) *Making Healthy Places: Designing and Building for Health, Well Being and Sustainability*. Island Press: Washington, DC.

Global Insight. http://www.ihs.com/products/global-insight/index.aspx.

Hahn, R.A., S.M. Teutsch, R.B. Rothenberg, and J.S. Marks (1990) Excess deaths from nine chronic diseases in the United States. *JAMA* 264:2654–2659.

Heymann, D.L., T. Prentice, and L.T. Reinders (2007). *The World Health Report 2007: A Safer Future: Global Public Health Security in the 21st Century*. World Health Organization: Geneva.

Jackson, R. (2012) *Designing Healthy Communities*. John Wiley: San Francisco.

Jackson, R.J. and C. Kochtitzky (2001) *Creating Healthy Environments: The Impact of the Built Environment on Public Health*. Sprawl Watch Clearing House Monograph Series: Washington, DC.

Kushner, J.A. (2007) *Healthy Cities: The Intersection of Urban Planning, Law and Health*. Carolina Academic Press: Durham, NC.

McGranahan, G., D. Balk, and B. Anderson (2007) The rising tide: assessing the risks of climate change and human settlements in low-elevation coastal zones. *Environment and Urbanization* 19(1):17–37.

Morens, D.M., et al. (2004). The challenge of emerging and re-emerging infectious diseases. *Nature* 430(6996): 242–249.

Morse, S. (2007) Global infectious disease surveillance and health intelligence. *Health Affairs* 26:1069–1077.

Murphy, C. and B. Ross-Larson (2004) *Human Development Report 2004: Cultural Liberty in Today's Diverse World*. Published for the United Nations Development Programme (UNDP), New York, New York, USA. Retrieved from: http://hdr.undp.org/en/media/hdr04_complete.pdf

National Center for Health Statistics (2002) http://www.cdc.gov/nchs/

Oyebanji O. and D. Mutizwa-Mangiza (2011) *Cities and Climate Changes: Policy Directions, Global Report on Human Settlements 2011*. United Nations Human Settlements Programme (UN-Habitat). Earthscan: Washington, DC.

Perdue, W.C., Lesley A. Stone, and Lawrence O. Gostin (2003) The built environment and its relationship to the public's health: the legal framework. *American Journal of Public Health* 93(9):1390–1394.

Population Institute (2007) World population is now 50% urban. *Popline* July–August.

Poste, G. (2005) Global urbanization: environment, epidemics and emerging infectious diseases. *Keynote address at the Remaking Metropolis symposium held in Phoenix, Arizona*. April 2005.

Rosen, G. (1993) *A History of Public Health*. Johns Hopkins University Press: Baltimore, MD.

Rosenzweig, C., W. Solecki, S. Hammer, and S. Mehrota (2011) *Climate Change and Cities*. Cambridge University Press: Cambridge.

Satterthwaite, D., S. Huq, M. Pelling, H. Reid, and P. Lankao (2007) *Adapting to Climate Change in Urban Areas: The Possibilities and Constraints in Low- and Middle-Income Nations*. IIED Working Paper. International Institute for Environment and Development: London.

United Nations, Department of Economic and Social Affairs, Population Division (2009). *World Population Prospects: The 2008 Revision, Highlights*, Working Paper No. ESA/P/WP.210. Retrieved from: http://csem.org.br/2009/wpp2008_highlights.pdf

United Nations Population Division (2003) *World Population Prospects: The 2002 Revision*, vol. I, Comprehensive Tables United Nations publication. Retrieved from: http://www.un.org/esa/population/publications/wpp2002/WPP2002-HIGHLIGHTSrev1.PDF

Wackernagel, M. and W.E. Rees (1996) *Our Ecological Footprint: Reducing Human Impact on the Earth*. New Society Publishers: Philadelphia, PA.

World Bank (2009) *World Development Report 2010: Development and Climate Change*. The World Bank: Washington, DC.

World Bank (2010) *Cities and Climate Change: An Urgent Agenda*. The World Bank: Washington, DC.

Worldwatch Institute (2006) *State of the World 2006: A Worldwatch Institute Report on Progress Toward a Sustainable Society*. W.W. Norton: New York.

Worldwatch Institute (2007) *Vital Signs 2007–2008: The Trends that are Shaping our Future*. W.W. Norton: New York.

Part

C

Global sustainability and shifting urban systems

Chapter 3

The world shrinks, the world expands

Information, energy, and relocalization

Robert L. Thayer, Jr.

Introduction

This chapter considers the scientific and technological backgrounds of two quite different fields: petrochemical geophysics and information technology, and their respective and opposite roles in "shrinking" or "expanding" the perceived and actual size, scale, and grain of the developed landscape. The post-"oil peak" future will necessitate a contraction, or relocalization in the source-to-end-use distances of physical goods and resources as transportation fuels become scarce and extremely expensive: for the first time in history, the world perceptually expands, as travel and freight shipping become more difficult and time-consuming. On the other hand, the continued increase in global electronic communication and consolidation of corporate ownership will continue to virtually "shrink" the world and globalize many aspects of culture. Thus, we enter a new perceptual relationship between time, scale, and sense of place unlike that ever previously experienced. As a result, we may anticipate future land patterns that respond to the relocalizing effects of scarce, expensive, and renewable transportation and shipping fuels on the one hand, and the continued globalization of culture and corporate ownership on the other.

When one contemplates a scientific basis for landscape architecture, one usually thinks of Aldo Leopold. Considered the father of land conservation, Leopold represents the quintessential conscience of land managers throughout the world, and his influence as an ecologist is irrefutable (Meine, 2004). Scientists who unknowingly contribute to the foundational principles of landscape architecture are apt to be those who concern themselves with the non-human life of the earth's surface: foresters, wildlife biologists, ecologists, horticulturists, botanists, hydrologists, or physical geographers. These disciplines, however, are not the only scientific influences on the shape and culture of the developed landscape. Today we must look beyond the most familiar boundaries of science in order to understand forces now beginning to shape the contemporary landscape, and the scientific underpinnings that give rise and explanation to those forces.

Two eccentric geniuses

This particular story begins in the 1950s, when two very different individuals, both working at the very fringes of their respective fields of science, made bold breakthroughs in the theory of their very different disciplines. In both instances, they were at first considered pariahs or eccentrics whose ideas seemed preposterous. Only later was each to become posthumously heralded as a genius whose scientific contributions now form the cornerstones of their respective disciplines.

Today, when the established work of these two contributors is considered simultaneously, a picture of the future physical world emerges which is unlike anything society has ever seen, or even imagined before. Who are these mysterious progenitors of tomorrow's unique situation?—Professors M. King Hubbert and Norbert Wiener.

M. King Hubbert (1903–89) was a petroleum geophysicist for Shell Oil Company, and later, a senior research geophysicist for the United States Geological Survey, and a professor at both Stanford and Berkeley. In 1956, he was the first to offer a scientific theory that predicted that the peak of production in American oil would come in the early 1970s, after which US production of oil would steeply decline (Hubbert, 1956). His predictions were rudely dismissed both in and outside the oil industry until 1970, when US production began to slow, then peaked in 1975. Today, nearly all petroleum experts acknowledge the validity of Hubbert's method of predicting oil supply curves and production peaks, especially as the theory applies to world oil production, even if they argue about timing (Deffeyes, 2001).

Norbert Wiener (pronounced "vee-ner") (1894–1964) was a boy-genius who graduated from preparatory school at the young age of 11 and received his Ph.D. in mathematics from Harvard at age 18. Wiener, whose broad interests included command and control systems theory in machines and animals, wrote the seminal volume *Cybernetics* in 1948, which defined the foundation of information science utilized today (Wiener, 1961). A panel of American scientists and science writers has included *Cybernetics* in its list of the 100 most important scientific publications of the last century (*American Scientist*, 1999). A broadly competent scientist and thinker, Wiener reflected upon the work of the philosopher Leibniz to build a theory, along with contemporaries Claude Shannon, Alan Turing, and Warren Weaver, explaining information as it applied both to the brains of sentient organisms as well as early computing machines (Conway and Siegelman, 2005).

Matter, energy, and information

Of pivotal concern to those of us involved in planning, designing, and managing the physical world is an earth-shatteringly simple declaration by Norbert Wiener on page 132 of *Cybernetics*: "Information is information, not matter or energy. No materialism which does not admit this can survive at the present day."

Physicists once told us there were two basic fundamentals of the universe, matter and energy, and both were conserved according to well-known laws of physics.

After the arrival of the information scientists, there suddenly were three: matter, energy, and information. Although the startling addition of this third essential characteristic can still be argued, increasingly physicists are beginning to accept that information, in its most elemental sense, is a part and parcel of the universe. Indeed, physics professor Hans Christian von Bayer, in his book *Information: The New Language of Science* (2004), states that information is "woven into the very fabric of the universe" (9).

In order to be transmitted, information must involve energy and matter, and is, therefore, supposedly governed by Einstein's universal speed limit. However, as a purely mathematical concept, information can exist somewhat independently of the other two. Norbert Wiener (1961: 11) juxtaposed information with entropy:

> The amount of information attaches itself very naturally to a classical notion in statistical mechanics: that of *entropy* [orig. emph.]. Just as the amount of information in a system is a measure of its organization, so the entropy of a system is a measure of its degree of disorganization; and the one is simply the negative of the other.

This opposition of information and entropy is the precise focus of my topic. Wiener's construction of the concept of information was reflected in the choice of his term for the new field he founded, which was called cybernetics, taken from the Greek word meaning "steersman." This referred to one of the earliest control mechanisms, the automatic devices that controlled ships' rudders to keep vessels on course. Wiener went on to describe in elaborate and brilliant terms the role of information in feedback for both living systems and automatic machines. Extrapolated to more general conditions, cybernetics, or information theory, was that universal principle which allowed living beings and latter-day computer-based systems to retard entropic processes sufficiently to allow complex ecosystems and human societies to exist. Although some biologists have since posited that life itself is an argument against the second law of thermodynamics, Wiener knew that information didn't really contradict entropy, but only slowed it down enough to form complex feedback systems in humans and animals.

Still, one can examine the past and see where the evolution of information transmission over time has involved less and less matter and energy. A phenomenon known as Moore's Law states that the information processing and storage capacity of a particularly evolving computing device doubles every year.[1] Information processing has become vastly more efficient to the point that information machines aiming at nanotechnology, utilizing organic rather than inorganic molecules as computing devices, may approach the computing energy efficiencies of the human brain (Markoff, 2007). True to Wiener's prescient opposition of information and entropy, the increasing energy efficiency of the transmission of information is opposed by the entropy inherent in the eventual exhaustion of fossil fuels.

The matter of energy: the oil peak

Geophysicist Hubbert, on the other hand, was firmly grounded in the physics of fluid flows and the strengths and behavior of various rock bodies in the context of oil fields and petrochemical geology. His breakthrough can be explained simply enough for most of us to comprehend: when approximately half of the cumulative known reserves of oil have been consumed, the production of oil "peaks," or reaches a point when demand cannot be met by supply, resulting in a bell-shaped consumption curve with roughly the same mirrored shape on the "far," or future consumption side, as was exhibited in the former, rising pattern of consumption.

This theory has been fully grasped by most oil forecasters. A particular but rapidly growing group of them, who have in the past few years organized themselves into a Society for the Study of Peak Oil, now predict that world oil production will peak (some say it already has peaked) sometime between now and the year 2015. This group includes some notables: Emeritus professor of geophysics Richard Deffeyes of Princeton (Deffeyes, 2001); Oxford Ph.D. and former Texaco and Amoco exploration geologist Colin Campbell; and perhaps most notably, long-time Houston-based Republican oil investment banker and Harvard MBA, Matthew Simmons (Simmons, 2005).[2]

As near as can be determined, the acceptance of the veracity of the coming oil peak is now about where scientific acceptance of global warming was about five years ago. Events involving the 2005 hurricanes Katrina and Rita, spiking oil and gasoline prices, bankruptcies of airlines over aviation fuel costs, political instability of oil-producing states, fears of war with Iran, and a host of other indicators are further evidence of truth in the predictions of a rapidly approaching oil peak (Heinberg, 2003).

The oil peak itself, that moment when world oil production can no longer satisfy world demand, is not the same as "running out of oil." However, it does mean the end of cheap oil. After the peak, prices can be expected to climb rapidly and never permanently return to former levels, as each additional barrel of oil takes more and more effort, money, and energy to extract in relation to that which it provides. The peak essentially marks the passing of the age of oil dependency. While some say the next energy savior is natural gas, the supply–demand conditions of natural gas, a finite resource, show a similar trend to that of oil, only perhaps with a five-year lag time or so.

The conclusions one may reach from the peaking of both oil and natural gas are stark, and some are frightening: possible economic recession or depression; potential oil wars among elite consuming nations fighting over the last oil reserves (US vs. China?); accelerated energy conservation and efficiency programs; rapid development of alternative, renewable power sources; return of national speed limits; growth and resurgence in rail and bus travel; reduction in the size of the automobile; the demise of air travel. Simmons (2005: 347–8), the most persuasive of the "peakists," as they (or I should say, "we") are being called, offers this analysis:

Once oil supply peaks, the world will be forced to create ways to *substantially* [orig. emph.] conserve our oil and other energy sources. This shift should force a rapid rethinking of the notion that transporting people and products anywhere in the world is an almost incidental cost of doing business. "Transportation" turns out to be the biggest single user of oil, and we need to begin finding ways to minimize everyone's transportation needs and make use of transportation fuel as efficiently as possible. If we do not alter our transportation systems as a matter of policy and public planning, the inexorable operation of the pricing mechanisms will do it for us.

Meager alternatives

Exhaustive study of alternative transportation fuels leads to few realistic hopes. Coal gasification (as was done by the Nazis during the end of WWII) provides a means to turn coal into liquid fuel, but at great environmental and monetary costs, and significant energy inefficiency. The energy returned on energy invested (EROEI) for turning coal into modern liquid fuel would necessitate a manifold increase in price per British thermal unit (BTU), to say nothing of the impact such processes would have on CO_2 emissions and potential climate damage (Heinberg, 2003). Such procedures would require technically complex and environmentally risky sequestration of carbon dioxide in deep wells beneath the surface of the earth.

Canadian tar sands require natural gas (itself subject to an only slightly delayed price peak than that of oil) to extract useful petroleum, with low efficiencies, high consumption of fresh water, and vastly increased CO_2 emissions (Roberts, 2005; Hawkins et al., 2006).

Hydrogen is for many the currently envisioned panacea. However, hydrogen expert Joan Ogden reminds us that hydrogen is not really an energy source but a means of transporting energy (Ogden, 2006). Hydrogen requires an alternative source of energy to split it from the oxygen in water. Such sources of hydrogen are either "brown" (i.e., fossil fuels like natural gas or coal), or "green" (i.e., solar or wind-generated electricity). Neither wind nor solar energy has sufficient energy density or energy flux (kiloJoules per acre per year) to provide the massive quantities of hydrogen that would be needed to replace oil and gas at their current rates of consumption. Some experts suggest that any future excess capacity in renewable energy should be more efficiently used to displace fossil fuel electrical plants, not create hydrogen for transportation (Romm, 2005). Although one encounters the occasional industry-based optimist who banks on some new technology (pond scum which can photosynthesize hydrogen directly, for example), or proposed alternative fuels like ethanol or biodiesel, the conclusion one must reach after exploring alternatives is quite simple: the world will be very different after the oil and gas peaks have exerted their market influences on our existing transportation and land use patterns. In short, the post oil-peak world will psychologically and perceptually re-expand as the new difficulties of travel and shipping become evident. Travel and shipping that are more difficult than they have been in the past, rather than less, constitute a completely new perceptual phenomenon in the world; one that has never been experienced before. This will translate directly into altered land use patterns, as we shall soon see.

The impact on transportation and shipping

To understand the landscape/geographic impacts of oil supply peaks and declining fuel supply for transportation, one must consider the relative intensity, or energy efficiency of the major modes of passenger and freight transport. Table 3.1 compares general values of transportation energy efficiency for different modes for the year 2000. Note that the figures in Table 3.1 are offered in units independent of fuel type: thousands of kBTU/passenger-mile or ton-mile. This fact is critical: to a great extent, regardless of which future fuel type is utilized, differing modes of transportation have basically different efficiencies. As transit fuels become scarcer and much more expensive, we might conclude that the more efficient modes will begin to be emphasized while less efficient modes may decline, regardless of type of fuel used.

When one considers that petroleum products now provide for nearly all the utility in the transit means identified in Table 3.1 (except walking and bicycling), one may get an inkling of the scope of impact that the oil peak will have on future transportation and shipping.

Table 3.1 Relative energy intensities of transportation and shipping modes

Passenger transport	kBTU/passenger-mile
Air	4.0
Auto, US	3.5
Auto, European	2.8
Bus, US (transit)	3.7
Bus, European	1.4
Rail, Amtrak	2.1
Rail, European	1.4
Walking	0.3
Bicycling	0.1
Freight transport	kBTU/ton-mile
Air	31.0
Trucks	4.9
Ship	0.41
Rail	0.35

Note: Figures are based on actual, not theoretical, passenger and freight load factors vs. actual fuel consumption.

Source: Oak Ridge National Laboratory, 2004; Bureau of Transportation Statistics, 2005.

Figure 3.1 Bicycle and Amtrak. The combination of bicycling and heavy passenger rail combines the most energy efficient non-powered and powered land transit modes, respectively. Image courtesy of R. Thayer.

Therefore, it is possible to draw some conclusions about the implications of the oil peak and fuel supplies on the future scale of the landscape and, in turn, the source-to-end-use distances involved in modern material welfare:

- Passenger travel by car will decrease significantly.
- Passenger travel by rail will increase significantly.
- Passenger travel by bus will increase.
- Passenger travel by air will decrease significantly.
- Passenger travel by ship will increase.
- Travel by bicycle and walking will increase.
- Freight by rail will increase.
- Freight by truck will decrease.
- Freight by air will decrease significantly.
- Freight by marine shipping may decrease slightly.

Although freight by marine shipping is highly fuel efficient compared to trucking and air, the long distances and total fuel consumption implicit in marine shipping may curtail it somewhat, forcing a trend toward more local sources of goods and resources. High-mass, low-value commodities and goods such as coal, aggregates, water, wood, bulk foods, and so on, will be produced and consumed more locally. Low-mass, high-value commodities and goods such as electronic components, luxuries, and so on, will continue to be made and shipped globally, although slow-downs in delivery can be expected in proportion to mass of goods shipped. Even when measured by current economic value added and not by bulk or weight, 40 percent of shipped goods are items delivered by air—escalating airplane fuel costs may significantly decrease this percentage in the near future.

Of course, increased fuel efficiency will be sought in all transit modes (air, rail, truck, bus, auto, and marine).[3] In sum, the implications of the coming oil supply peak and steeply increasing transport fuel prices are considerable for the "grain" of the landscape, for the economy, for food, energy, and water supply chains, for travel and tourism. Part of the "re-expanding" physical world we will encounter will feature a significant relocalization of provision of physical necessities.

Tourism: the substitutability theory

During the oil embargoes and subsequent "energy crises" of the 1970s, leisure theorists posited a "substitutability" hypothesis, in which it was presumed that constraints on gasoline would lead recreation visitors to substitute nearby leisure destinations for far ones. The post-oil-peak reality is apt to test this hypothesis at an order of magnitude much more severely than its originators dreamed. "Nearby nature" will become even more critical than it is today, and the entire landscape of tourism will most certainly be transformed. Tourist destinations that are capable of replacing remote international visitors with local and regional visitors will thrive.[4]

Post-oil-peak patterns of tourist change have the potential to occupy many Ph.D. dissertations and books. Just from the standpoint of pure physics, tourism must change when fossil fuels become very scarce and very expensive. This inevitability will have enormous impact on the landscape.

Opposite influences from information technology

Information, on the other hand, presents us with a completely different landscape manifestation. Much has been said and written about the implications of electronic communication technologies on globalization, centralized economics, cultural imperialism, and the emergence of near-virtual realities. What is critical to emphasize at this juncture, however, is that while the effect of scarce, expensive oil on the physical environment will be significant, the effect of constrained fossil fuel supplies on the electronic, largely "virtual" environment will be nearly negligible. The reason is simply a matter of scale.

While, as Wiener noted early on, useful information requires a certain degree of physicality and energetics to be encoded, transmitted, and decoded, the amounts of mass and energy (particularly in comparison to the economic value added) required to send and receive information pale in comparison to sending and receiving physical goods or traveling for business or pleasure, and those mass and energy expenditures per information "bit" are declining rapidly. Technical advances continually increase the amount of information that can be carried per unit of matter or energy, until, as Wiener implies, the true, mathematical nature of information may be approached: "Information is information, not matter or energy."

Consider the concept of money. The invention of currency was perhaps the first singular step in the dematerialization of economics. Whereas the early Etruscans once traded pigs for various goods, coins began to represent pigs, and the physical notion of "money," while possessing some mass in its metal likenesses, displaced the physical need to exchange actual pigs. The same process can be considered in the postmodern electronic era, as electromagnetic waves sent via satellite replace money, and codes of information define ownership in globally dispersed, invisible networks. Ownership is information, and information is power and control. However, as Wiener's aforementioned rule goes, information is information, not matter or energy. Therefore, ownership—in its pure sense—is ubiquitous, electronic, cybernetic, and hardly constrained at all by the second law of thermodynamics. It is important to stress that nothing inherent in the post-oil-peak transition shows any indication of impeding the consolidation of ownership due to global dissemination of information. In short, ownership will continue to consolidate. For many of us, the inevitability of continued global consolidation of ownership is very frightening.

Push-pull: possible economic futures

So we reach the very crux of the argument: that the world after the oil-peak will be pushed—or pulled—in two very different cultural directions at once. Information will continue to be relatively accessible, ubiquitous, and valuable, while the physical environment will relocalize and reorganize into much more efficient, fine-grained landscape-shaping networks of supply and demand, provision and consumption, origin and destination. This is the strange new world that the very different work of both Wiener and Hubbert have laid before us, yet perhaps neither anticipated the influences of the other. We, who will occupy and manage the evolution of this strange new world, are solely responsible for its outcome.

Consider the possible geographical and ownership relationships between the sources, distribution networks, end uses, and waste or recycling locations of the things we need for modern life. There are basically three different possible future scenarios as to how these conditions might relate:

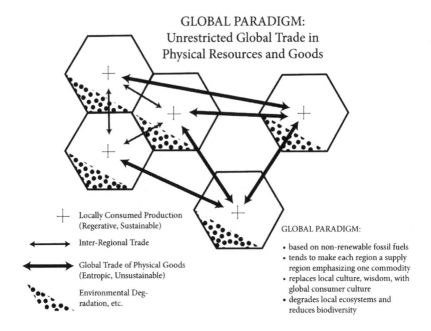

GLOBAL PARADIGM:
Unrestricted Global Trade in
Physical Resources and Goods

─┼─ Locally Consumed Production
     (Regerative, Sustainable)

◄───► Inter-Regional Trade

◄═══► Global Trade of Physical Goods
       (Entropic, Unsustainable)

••• Environmental Deg-
     radation, etc.

GLOBAL PARADIGM:

• based on non-renewable fossil fuels
• tends to make each region a supply
  region emphasizing one commodity
• replaces local culture, wisdom, with
  global consumer culture
• degrades local ecosystems and
  reduces biodiversity

Figure 3.2 Global Paradigm. Regions provide one major resource or commodity to world markets in exchange for all other necessities. Image courtesy of R. Thayer.

Figure 3.3 Wal-Mart. The global paradigm at work. Image courtesy of R. Thayer.

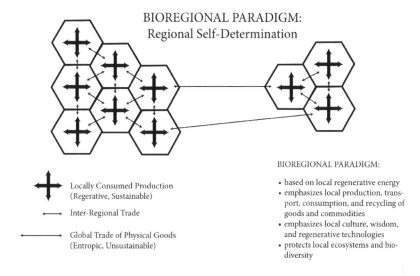

BIOREGIONAL PARADIGM:
Regional Self-Determination

Locally Consumed Production
(Regerative, Sustainable)

Inter-Regional Trade

Global Trade of Physical Goods
(Entropic, Unsustainable)

BIOREGIONAL PARADIGM:

- based on local regenerative energy
- emphasizes local production, transport, consumption, and recycling of goods and commodities
- emphasizes local culture, wisdom, and regenerative technologies
- protects local ecosystems and biodiversity

Figure 3.4 Bioregional Paradigm. Regions provide for their own local needs to the maximum extent possible, trading only surpluses to macro-regional and world markets. Image courtesy of R. Thayer.

Figure 3.5 Davis Farmers' Market. The bioregional paradigm at work. Image courtesy of R. Thayer.

Scenario One: Resources are harvested, products are produced, and both are shipped across vast distances, consumed, and wastes disposed of globally, where ownership of means of production is shared by a globalized network of investors (Figure 3.2–3.3).

Scenario Two: Resources are harvested, products produced, consumed, and recycled locally, where capital ownership of means of production is also localized within naturally definable regions concurrent and coincident with local cultures and economies (Figure 3.4–3.5).

Scenario Three: Resources are harvested, products are produced, consumed, and recycled locally, but capital ownership of means of production is shared globally and consolidated within a few giant corporations in each sector.

I am convinced (and Hubbert's work certainly predicts) that Scenario One is actually a physical impossibility. Trends toward this future direction will inevitably end, and sooner than we think. However, as much as I might wish for Scenario Two with its local control of local resource supply chains, it is Scenario Three— relocalized production and distribution with globalized ownership—that I believe is the most likely evolutionary scenario.

The world expands ... AND shrinks

Notwithstanding a continued barrage of optimism from corporate energy sectors like the coal, hydrogen, and nuclear industries, it now seems obvious that the post-oil-peak reality will reverse a formerly one-way trend that has existed since time immemorial: the notion that travel always gets easier, and that the world, in perceptual terms, therefore, continues to "shrink," or seem increasingly smaller and more accessible (see Table 3.2). For the first time in human history, we will reach a "Y," or fork, in the perceived size and physical accessibility of the world: energy and entropy constraints will tend to make it "re-expand" or seem larger, just as electronic communication continues to make it "shrink," and seem smaller.

The very wealthy, of course, will continue to travel long distances, but the point bears repeating for emphasis: for most of the middle and lower economic classes, the door to world travel will partially close for the first time in human history. They will travel less frequently, for shorter distances, using modes that take more, rather than less, time as I discuss below. The peculiar combination of the effects of scarce and expensive transportation fuels on the physical and perceptual world, coupled with continued globalization of culture and economic ownership driven by electronic information, make for some startling potential realities:

• Electronic information will continue to erode sense of place, as individuals adopt increasingly smaller, less expensive, and more powerful communication devices that are able to trump both space and time.

Table 3.2 Energy, information, and relocalization

	Time	Place	Ownership	Supply chain	"World size"
Information energy (post-Peak)	Speeds up	Erodes	Consoli-dates	____	Shrinks
	Slows down	Re-inforces	____	Shortens	Expands

Note: The new relationship between the effects of a post-carbon, post-oil-peak physical reality and the continuing globalization of information presents a duo of forces acting on the American landscape that have never before been experienced.

- Continuing globalization of ownership will also erode the sense of place and any sense of responsibility of globalized shareholders to the relocalized effects of physical resources and supply chains.
- Relocalized sources, physical transport means, end uses, and fate of physical goods in the landscape will tend to focus sense of place on smaller, and more naturally defined and constrained regions.

What is perhaps even more interesting is the combined effect of accelerating information flow and constrained physical movement of people and goods on the perception of time. Because energy efficiencies are maximized at slower speeds, traffic and shipping will slow down. Speed limits may return, freight will shift from faster, more energy consuming modes to slower, more energy efficient modes. In response to horrendous costs for aviation fuels, airlines may be forced to trade time for fuel efficiency. Furthermore, individual travelers who choose more immediate rather than distant destinations to save energy expenditures will gain additional time at destinations and lose less time en route.

Another rather subtle but potent factor affecting time perception after the Hubbert Peak is that renewable resources have inherent speed limits. With the gradual switch to renewable energy sources, the time needed for renewable energy sources to regenerate will directly influence the pace of human life. If energy is dependent on wind to blow, sun to shine, hydroelectric dams to fill, batteries to recharge, crop residues to be converted to biofuels, and so on, one may not speed up these processes beyond their natural rates of regeneration. This fact is diametrically opposed to the influence of several centuries of fossil fuel use on human perception of time. In fact, the entire fossil fuel era has been robbing matter (accumulated over many eons) to save time. By the laws of thermodynamics and entropy, this must change, and the changes are apt to be dramatically perceived.

On the other hand, as information continues to be processed by more and more efficient means, and as the size and power requirements of computing and communicating devices drop exponentially (as has been the case), it appears that there will be no comparable slowdown in transmission of information, nor any real drop in the volume of information transferred. As a result, information saturation and the exploding ubiquity of communication devices and means will continue to tend to accelerate our sense of time, and give us the perception of the informational world "speeding up."

We tend now to think in terms of "either-or"—either the world will seem to speed up, or it will seem to slow down, and it will either "shrink" or "expand," but not both. Since it has been speeding up for generations now, we can hardly be expected to think otherwise. But we will enter a new stage of landscape perception and sense of reality characterized by "virtual acceleration and world shrinkage" combined with "physical deceleration and world re-expansion." Let us now attempt to bring this scenario "back to the ground," and talk about landscape.

Landscape effects

It is extremely difficult to predict the effects of these combined, yet opposing influences on the future human perceptions of space, region, and landscape. One such constraint on prediction is whether the limits to transportation and energy expenditures will be manifested first by global warming or by the oil peak. Earth just experienced the Northern Hemisphere's warmest winter in history. According to the National Climatic Data Center (2007), the global temperature for December 2006 through February 2007 averaged 1.3 degrees Fahrenheit above normal. Will carbon fuels be voluntarily restricted following the massing of undeniable evidence of the acceleration of global warming? Or will the oil peak arrive to put an automatic damper on the release of extra carbon into the atmosphere? To a certain extent, this point is moot—a fact recognized in the title and content of a recent special issue of *Scientific American* entitled "Energy's Future Beyond Carbon."[5]

In a graduate studio course in landscape architecture and environmental planning at Berkeley in the fall of 2005, students and faculty examined the entire Napa River watershed region, including the famous Napa Valley, as a post-oil-peak retrofit with a target date of 2030. Teams of graduate students explored hybrid transit systems, the relationship of energy and movement systems to housing and development patterns, a more localized agriculture, and the effect of energy on wine shipping and wine-based tourism. We envisioned more compact cities and towns predominantly with infill, rather than greenfield development, linked to the San Francisco Bay Area by ferry and to land destinations via rail and hybrid electric bus. Students planned to reintroduce local food production, sought locations for generating or co-generating renewable energy, focused on walkable neighborhoods, and balanced local housing with local jobs. Although idealized, as one might expect the creative work of young, future-oriented planners and designers to be, the students' ideas were by and large quite possible, and hopefully, will actually come about in some future form (Thayer and Harper, 2006).

The one wild card in our course prognostications that seemed to evade landscape expression, however, is the third scenario mentioned previously: relocalized provision of essential physical goods and services, accompanied by globalization

Figure 3.6 Bay Street, Emeryville, California. Image courtesy of R. Thayer.

of ownership. Imagine this future: Budweiser may own three-quarters of the microbreweries in continental North America; our "local" dairy may be owned by Carnation, Inc.; our local organic farm by Archer Daniels Midland; our local water supply by the Nestlé Group; our local timberlands by Weyerhauser International; our transportation fuel by a single consolidated energy giant called "Exxon/Mobil/Texaco/Shell/BP."

There are a few salient examples of the kinds of landscapes that are physically "relocalized" yet globally owned. One good example is Bay Street, the faux main street in Emeryville, California, where major world-brand stores masquerade as small shops among massive three-story condominiums (Figure 3.6).

The best example of this strange global/local admixture may be the commercial strip on Kalakaua Avenue just inland from the large beachfront hotels of Waikiki in Honolulu, Hawaii. Tourists who walk this street pass by many small, seemingly local shops. But if one walks a half mile or so in either direction along this strip, one finds that the small franchised shops repeat each other every third of a mile or so: three Starbucks, three Local Motion surf wear shops, three Crazy Shirt stores, and so on. Rather than build a singular, central megastore, the marketers have determined that a more physically dispersed, faux-local pattern presumably maximizes profits while appealing more to a sense of human scale. And finally, the founder of Starbucks, the best physical example of locally scaled yet globally ubiquitous business, says that the company has "lost its soul" (Harden, 2007). Most coffee aficionados, bioregionalists, and food localists have a one-word, three-letter response: "Duh!"

One could take this contemporary Starbuckesque pattern and, using some future-oriented interpretation of the ironies of electronic globalization/physical relocalization, predict that the commercial landscapes of the future will be smaller and finer grained than today's hyper-centralized big boxes, yet they will be owned by enormous consortia, centered far away—or worse, not "centered" or "located" at all. The physical patterns of supply and demand constrained by physics in an oil-scarce world will have absolutely zero spatial relationship to the globally dispersed distributions of stockholders. At this juncture, I must emphasize that I (and perhaps the majority of others) would rather see a concurrent relocalization of ownership as well as supply of physical goods, so that each finite life-place or bioregion can maximize control of its own destiny. The truth is that there is nothing whatsoever on the horizon powerful enough to withstand the continued shrinking of the financial world and the consolidation of ownership, not even the Hubbert Peak and the inevitable transition to renewable energy and resources.[6]

Convergent relocalization

In spite of this somewhat gloomy economic prediction, there are a number of converging influences that, taken together, give us some cause for optimism. During the 1990s my focus was on the growing tendency of people to identify with naturally definable regions, or "life-places." The individual's increasing identification as a citizen of a particular river watershed, coastal region, mountain range, prairie, or forest land coincided with professional and academic trends toward more comprehensive and applied science disciplines as ecosystem management, ecological restoration, conservation biology, and landscape ecology, all of which served to legitimize the bioregional focus as a means for comprehensive environmental stewardship.

Beyond this brew of new scientific and geographic efforts was added the public's burgeoning identification with naturally definable life-places, forming "Friends of" (river, mountain range, etc.) groups exponentially. For example, the 2005 Land Trust Alliance's National Rally (one of the most well-attended and uplifting conferences I have ever experienced) demonstrated that land trusts are quint-essentially local, bioregional, successful, and highly optimistic, being involved quite literally with saving the nature of local regions. Fortunately, the land trust movement is accelerating each year.

The effects of electronic communication and globalizing ownership notwith-standing, these combined forces of relocalization will assert themselves on our future landscapes, communities, and regions. The scientific legacies of M. King Hubbert and Norbert Wiener will inevitably reach some equilibrium, with a considerable dose of Aldo Leopold included in the mix. The challenge for planners and designers is to attempt to anticipate and help bring about this proper reconciliation at all possible scales, from the creation of backyards to the planning of entire bioregions.

What will this new, electronically globalized, physically relocalized world with its strange, new landscapes look like and feel like to those of us who will inherit and live within it? The patterns we might expect to emerge out of the communities and bioregions of the future could include:

- finer-grained, smaller shops and stores
- a more thorough and serious revival of "Main Street"
- dispersed, localized energy sources, such as rooftop PV solar arrays, rural and urban wind farms, cogeneration of biomass, and energy by agriculture and industry
- radically reconfigured street corridors with multiple transit modes accommodated in the same right-of-way
- housing finely mixed with commercial, office, and light industrial uses
- vegetation aimed at moderating solar shade and access, ameliorating climate, cleansing or extracting carbon from the air, or providing local food or critical habitat (instead of just "looking good")
- transparent expression of local utilities such as water, waste, and electricity (which will, for better rather than worse, be "in our back yard")
- redensification of remote, sprawled suburbs, starting with reclamation of formerly antiquated, one-story shopping centers now in seas of asphalt being reconfigured as dense, mixed-use village centers
- reinforcement of the center city as the most sustainable and high-class residential location
- evolution of much more fine-grained, flexible, and multi-use zoning allowing more land use complexity and variety in any given size parcel or zone
- more emphasis on local parks and regional wildlands
- "escape routes," which allow non-motorized circulation from dense residential neighborhoods to "nearby nature"
- smaller vehicles of all kinds (probably rechargeable hybrid-electric flex-fuel vehicles running on ethanol or biodiesel) including scooters, two-, three- and four-wheeled vehicles that are much smaller than cars of today[7]
- shrinking the grain, scale, and current ubiquity of residential streets, parking lots, and garages
- fewer, less dispersed, but larger airports
- air travel that increasingly caters only to the very wealthy, with luxury emphasized rather than mass transportation
- more ferries and ferry terminals
- railroads returned from the brink of nostalgia to operational status
- reversal of the abandonment of rail rights of way ("Rails to Rails?"), with train tracks being considered as irreplaceable assets
- high-speed electric trains
- micro light-rail systems for short-distance travel
- regional tourist getaways
- zoning for protection of existing prime agricultural soils

- reclamation of good agricultural soils long-buried by excessive asphalt or concrete
- diverse reclamation and revitalization of older, industrial era manufacturing zones for local renewable resource-based industry.

A simple glance at the above list obviates the need for well-trained, professional land planners and designers at all scales and stages, from policy generation, regional planning, through site design and detail construction.

The lure of the local

Perhaps the most shocking, yet inevitable manifestation of this "world shrinks, world expands" future is the effect it will have on high culture and academic thought. After years of fossil-fueled snobbery and academic dismissal of all things local, the humanities, sciences, and design arts will begin to seriously contemplate, examine, and recognize the local region, while electronic communications continues to shrink our economic, and to some extent, perceptual world. What I predict, therefore, is the end of dualistic thinking about global and local, and the beginning of a very serious "both-and" kind of focus on living locally in a global world. At the very least, we may soon expect to study and seriously contemplate the regional and local along with the global as co-equal influences in the halls of academe. As case in point, the University of Idaho has recently been awarded a 1.6 million dollar grant for a new university-wide initiative on "Bioregional Planning and Sustainable Community Design" that will not only establish a graduate degree program but also offer a two-way interchange between the graduate students and local planning and governmental officials. "Relocalization" has finally penetrated the halls of the academy.[8]

In accommodating this new world order, it may pay to bear in mind that the landscape of the next four or five decades will undergo considerable rapid evolutionary change as a strange admixture of global and local affairs tugs on the formative dimensions of our wild, rural, and urban landscapes. Keep your eyes peeled for these astonishing changes in the landscape as the world shrinks and expands at the same time, as we slide down the far side of the Hubbert Oil Peak, chattering away on our tiny combination cell phone/iPod/microcomputer/TVs. As this future unfolds, I am convinced that Manuel Castell's declaration will be borne out: there is, indeed, no such thing as a true "citizen of the world." Welcome to a future landscape we have never seen before.

Acknowledgment

Thayer, Robert L., Jr. "The World Shrinks, the World Expands." Originally published in *Landscape Journal* 27 (1) (2008): 9–22. © 2008 by the Board of Regents of the University of Wisconsin System. Reproduced courtesy of the University of Wisconsin Press.

Notes

1. Moore's Law, while originally intended to address the increasing complexity of transistors on computer chips, is easily extrapolated to the declining size and energy requirements versus increasing speed and power of information devices, as per Markoff (2007). For accessible information on Moore's Law, see http://en.wikipedia.org/wiki/Moore's_law.

2. Matthew Simmons, who was one of the not-so-secret energy policy advisors to the Bush–Cheney regime died in 2010. He was the most outspoken and persuasive of them all, and maintained a web site (www.simmonsco-intl.com) where lay people can review his polished presentations and impressive statistics. Simmons has also garnered the support of several Nobel laureates, and by standard measures of scientific/academic persuasion, his conclusions were taken seriously.

3. It remains to be seen whether current hidden transit subsidies and hidden penalties for various modes will be removed or rectified. For example, fuels for shipping and air travel are at present not taxed, nor regulated for air pollution impacts, while rail, truck, and auto fuels are taxed, and auto emissions are regulated.

4. For years my family and I have been going to a 100-plus year-old resort town, Calistoga, in the northern Napa Valley for getaways that feel much farther "away" than they really are. Calistoga, no doubt, will enjoy prosperity after the oil peak, while Hawaii, the most remote islands on earth and an economy almost entirely dependent upon tourism via air travel, will suffer tremendously.

5. This issue of *Scientific American* is perhaps the most comprehensive, accessible, and dispassionate examination of post-carbon fuel alternatives for the next several decades. It is a must-read for any student of the subject.

6. Since my second, rather optimistic book, *LifePlace* (2003) was published, I have unfortunately soured somewhat on the chances of genuine local economic control commensurate with physical relocalization. I hopefully await evidence that some social mechanism for asserting local control will evolve with power enough to resist information-based global conglomeration of ownership.

7. There is strong evidence that the plug-in electric flex-fuel ethanol or biodiesel hybrids coupled with rooftop-mounted solar photovoltaic electricity-producing systems are key to a more sustainable future for many Americans. Hybrids that could use battery power only for up to 60 miles in range would cut the need for any petroleum or liquid fuel at all for 90 percent of personal vehicle trips. See Andrew Frank (2007) and Sherry Boschert (2006). (I currently ride a 14 kW/19 hp, all-electric motorcycle that charges from my 4 kW rooftop photovoltaic array.) If a transition to plug-in electric/biofuel hybrid vehicles were coupled with land use and transportation policies that emphasized mass transit and dispersed essential land uses to village/city centers no greater than 30 miles apart from each other, most of the polluting carbon footprints of contemporary land use could be avoided.

8. Among the many fine contributions to the growing literature and theory of localism is Lucy Lippard's excellent volume, *The Lure of the Local* (1997).

References

American Scientist. (1999). American Scientist's 100 or so books that shaped a century of science. 87 (6) (November–December), http://home.comcast.net/~antaylor1/amscientists 100.html (accessed April 26, 2012).

Appenzeller, T. (2004). The end of cheap oil. *National Geographic Magazine* 205 (6): 80–109.

Boschert, Sherry. (2006). *Plug-in Hybrids: The Cars That Will Recharge America.* Gabriola Island, BC: New Society Publishers.

Bureau of Transportation Statistics. (2005). *National Transportation Statistics, 2004.* Washington, DC: US Department of Transportation.

Conway, F., and J. Siegelman. (2005). *Dark Hero of the Information Age: In Search of Norbert Wiener, the Father of Cybernetics.* Cambridge, MA: Basic Books.

Deffeyes, K. (2001). *Hubbert's Peak: The Impending World Oil Shortage.* Princeton, NJ: Princeton University Press.

Frank, Andrew. (2007). Plug-in hybrid vehicles for a sustainable future. *American Scientist* 95 (March–April): 158–165.

Harden, Blaine. (2007). Is malaise brewing at Starbucks? *Washington Post,* March 4, http://www.washingtonpost.com/wp-dyn/content/article/2007/03/03/AR2007030301100.html (accessed April 26, 2012).

Hawkins, D., D. Lashof, and R. Williams. (2006). What to do about coal. *Scientific American* (September): 68–75.

Heinberg, R. (2003). *The Party's Over: Oil, War and the Fate of Industrial Societies.* Gabriola Island, BC: New Society Publishers.

Hubbert, M. K. (1956). *Nuclear Energy and the Fossil Fuels.* Publication #95, Shell Development Company, June.

Leopold, Aldo. (1949). *Sand County Almanac.* New York: Oxford University Press.

Lippard, Lucy. (1997). *The Lure of the Local: Sense of Place in a Multi-centered Society.* New York: New Press.

Markoff, John. (2007). Intel says chips will run faster, using less power. *New York Times,* January 27.

Meine, C. (2004). *Correction Lines: Essays on Land, Leopold, and Conservation.* Washington, DC: Island Press.

National Climatic Data Center. (2007). State of the Climate Global Analysis 2007. http://www.ncdc.noaa.gov/oa/climate/research/2007/feb/global.html (accessed April 26, 2012).

Oak Ridge National Laboratory. (2004). *Transportation Energy Data Book.* Office of Energy Efficiency and Renewable Energy, US Department of Energy.

Ogden, J. (2006). High hopes for hydrogen. *Scientific American* 295 (3): 94–101.

Roberts, P. (2005). *The End of Oil: On the Edge of a Perilous New World.* New York: Houghton Mifflin.

Romm, J. (2005). *The Hype about Hydrogen: Fact and Fiction in the Race to Save the Climate.* Washington, DC: Island Press.

Scientific American. (2007). Energy's future beyond carbon. Special Issue. 295 (3).

Simmons, M. (2005). *Twilight in the Desert: The Coming Saudi Oil Shock and the World Economy.* New York: John Wiley & Sons.

Thayer, R. L. (1994). *Gray World, Green Heart: Technology, Nature and the Sustainable Landscape.* New York: John Wiley & Sons.

Thayer, R. L. (2003). *LifePlace: Bioregional Thought and Practice.* Berkeley: University of California Press.

Thayer, R. L., and A. Harper. (2006). Water, oil, and wine: Regional planning and design for a post-fossil fuel. Napa Valley. FrameWorks. College of Environmental Design, Berkeley.

United States Bureau of Transportation Statistics. (2004). http://www.bts.gov/publications/national_transportation_statistics/2004/index.html (accessed April 26, 2012).

Von Bayer, C. (2004). *Information: The New Language of Science.* Cambridge, MA: Harvard University Press.

Wiener, N. (1961). *Cybernetics: Control and Communication in the Animal and the Machine.* 2nd ed. Cambridge, MA: MIT Press.

Chapter 4

Urbanization challenges in Turkey

Implications for Aydin, Turkey

Hayriye Esbah

Introduction

Urbanization is a worldwide phenomenon. Estimates indicate a level of urbanization in the world of only 1.6 percent in the seventeenth century. This number grew to 47 percent by 2000, and is expected to grow to 60 percent by the year 2025. Currently, developed nations have a higher percentage of urban residents than less developed countries (Antrop, 2004), but the speed of urbanization is five times faster in less developed countries (Lopez et al., 2001). Subsequently, most new urban growth is expected to occur in less developed nations and in smaller cities and towns. Typically, these places have fewer resources to respond to the magnitude of the change. Satellite images show that all urban sites (including internal green and built up areas) constitute only 2.8 percent of the terrestrial landscape of the world (GRUMP, 2008). Although this proportion is not large, it contains half of the world's population. A recent study commissioned by the World Bank shows that modern patterns of city growth are increasingly land intensive (Angel et al., 2005), they have increased rates of expansion, and where additional land is incorporated into the urban fabric, significant social and environmental implications result for present and future populations (UNFPA, 2007).

The outcomes of urbanization vary according to the geographical and geopolitical position of the region (Timar, 1992). Extension of the market economy and trade, encouraging migration to cities, are the forces behind this diffusion process (Vink, 1982). Urbanization involves changes in the economic and political structures of a region. Urbanization also causes cultural and sociological change by transforming rural life styles into urban ones. Alteration of life style changes people's perception about their environment, and the way they use the environment (Antrop 2000a, 2000b), triggering change in land use management approaches.

The effects of urbanization extend beyond the urban boundaries, and various factors involved in the process shape the dynamics in a larger landscape (Forman, 2008). Urbanization gradually results in a changing spatial pattern and causes profound changes in the ecological functioning of the landscape. Even though major differences exist among the developed and developing countries in terms of urbanization characteristics, some common problems associated with rapid land use change prevail all around the world. For example, rural landscapes in most countries have declined significantly over the past decades, because local and state decision makers encourage urbanization to trigger local economic development. The rural landscape possesses ecological, economic, and cultural qualities for humans but also provide habitat for wildlife (Wasilewski and Krukowski, 2004). The problem of land conversion in these areas has become one of the most current and urgent in many countries.

The rapid growth of cities restrains the provision of services such as energy, education, health care, transportation, sanitation, parks, and physical security. When governments have limited understanding of sustainability and limited revenues to spend on the provision of services, cities can become areas of serious environmental problems and widespread poverty in developing countries. Good governance plays a crucial role in such situations. The term "urban governance," formerly equated with urban management, refers to the processes by which local urban governments—in partnership with other public agencies and different segments of civil society—respond effectively to local needs in a participatory, transparent, and accountable manner (UNFPA, 2007). Good governance is possible when the institutional environment is responsive to the long-term needs of the society and nature.

Thus, the institutional environment is critical in promoting sustainable land use patterns, as this environment is a major determinant of long-term growth. This environment consists of formal rules such as property rights (Hanna et al., 1996), laws, constitutions, international treaties, and informal constraints such as norms of behavior, conventions, and self-imposed codes of conduct (North, 1991) and characteristics of their enforcement. In this framework, organizations, which include political, economic, social, and educational bodies, are also important. Countries that had better political and economic institutions in the past are generally richer today than those that lacked these structures (Hall and Jones, 1999). Economic development is closely linked with the development of resources, on which urbanization will take its course. Subsequently, the design of durable cooperative institutions could be the key to the overexploitation of resources (Ostrom, 1990). It has been well established that successful resource management on any scale requires a system of legitimate institutions (Richerson et al., 2002).

This chapter elaborates the specific implications of the institutional environment on urbanization patterns. It highlights the typical characteristics of the institutional environment with respect to urbanization in Turkey. The efforts to improve the institutional environment since 2000 are also discussed. The impacts of an inefficient institutional structure on the transformation of the landscapes are illustrated through landscape- and municipal-scale examples from the urban area, a rapidly urbanizing part of western Turkey. Lessons learned in Aydin's case may aid in the development of policies that provide better management of the landscapes in Turkey, and other countries with similar spatial and institutional structure.

Urbanization in Turkey

Turkey is a developing country with an increasing population density. Turkey's first population census was taken in 1927 and counted a total population of about 13.6 million. This number had reached almost 68 million in 2000. In the same period, the population density went up from 18 persons/km^2 to 88 persons/km^2. Significant population growth occurred between 1950 and 1980; however, the rate of growth has been slowing gradually since. Turkey's annual population increase is relatively higher than that of European countries. Thus, the European Union (EU) has cited the high population growth rate as one of the justifications for delaying a decision on Turkey's long pending application to join the EU (Metz, 1995).

Migration from rural areas to cities has contributed to urban inflammation in the country. Kongar (1999) notes that the urbanization process in Turkey is formed by an immigration phenomenon where city poorness is preferred to country destitution. In Turkey, rural population exceeded urban population until 1960. The acceleration of rural populations slowed by 1985, and then started to decline. What pushed people out of the villages was the decline of the agriculture sector in GNP from almost 50 percent in 1950 to around 13 percent in 2003 (Esbah, 2007). Agriculture's share in GNP is planned to be 7.8 percent by 2013 (SPO, 2006). This signals continuing migration in the near future unless other measures are taken with regards to rural development. The relatively poor showing of the agricultural sector reflects, in part, government policies that have made rapid urbanization and industrialization a national priority (Country Studies, 2003).

The evolutionary stages of urbanization in Turkey follow four phases: pre-concentration, urbanization, polarization reversal, and counter urbanization (Gedik, 2003). Economic incidences after World War II set the stage for the pre-concentration, which is characterized by rural to urban and intra-provincial migration. At the end of the 1940s, Turkey had searched for international aid (e.g., Truman doctrine, Marshall Aid) to solve its economic problems. The result, contrary to expectations, didn't bring prosperity to the country due to improper use of the loans and the lack of long-term plans (Gur et al., 2003). Mechanization of agriculture and investments in transportation pushed excess labor in rural areas to migrate to cities. The initial phase of urbanization, pre-concentration, occurred in 1955–60. During this period, the proportion of the urban population was 25.1 percent in Turkey. The small urban centers (125,000–250,000 population) experienced the highest population growth (Gedik, 2003). The time span for the pre-concentration lasted differently in each region, roughly corresponding to its level of development.

The urbanization phase started in about 1960 and continues now. This phase is characterized by a high population growth rate in large cities that eventually became the metropolises of our time. The next stage, polarization reversal, emerged during 1975–80 (or more markedly after 1980). In this period, a liberal economy, international trade, export of manufactured industrial goods, and improvement in the finance sector were emphasized. Medium-sized cities grew more than large and small cities. None of these cities were near any of the metropolitan areas of that time, indicating inter-regional deconcentration and polarization dispersal. Also, suburbanization and ex-urbanization started in this period, and the urban to urban flows far surpassed the rural to urban flows (Gedik, 2003).

The counter urbanization phase corresponds to the period 1990–2000. At the beginning of this period, the percentage of the urban population was 59 percent. This number reached 65 percent by 2000 (SPO, 2000). Although the population growth rates of small urban areas were the highest, slight differences in the rates exist among small, medium, and large cities. Today, the population of Turkey is almost 74 million and the proportion of people living in urban areas is 76.3 percent (TUIK, 2010). Industrialization plays a major role in the development of Turkish cities. The industrialized cities most probably will grow faster regardless of their size. Turkish cities need a longer-term strategy for expected change.

Institutional structure

There is a direct relationship between urbanization and environmental policy. As in other parts of the world, environmental policy making in Turkey is initiated and enforced by the government. Development of the necessary policy and legislation has limited history, because the attention toward environmental problems is relatively new in the nation. For instance, the topic was only a part of health policy as of the 1980s, and the legal grounds for the environmental regulations were the "right to health" in the Constitution of the 1961 (Article 49). This changed with the Constitution of 1982, which contains individual articles that directly concern the environment. Article 56 says that everyone has a right to live in a healthy and balanced environment, and that it is the duty of the state and its citizens to improve the environment, to protect environmental health, and prevent environmental pollution.

With regards to urbanization, the Turkish constitution mentions planning for the use of resources to promote economic and social development. It affirms that the state orchestrates urbanization within a planning framework that respects the dynamics of the cities and environmental conditions (Article 57). Article 23, with respect to the limitation of the free choice of settlement, could be a warrant for uncontrolled urban expansion. In the article, one's freedom of where one settles would be limited in order to generate a healthy and reasonable urbanization. Based on this article, it is possible to develop particular laws to enable different approaches to development problems and to more effectively manage immigration from rural areas to cities. Nevertheless, because such laws must be enacted within a democratic society and politicians fear they will not be re-elected if they place too many limitations on the freedom of citizens, no such limitation has been enacted.

Nonetheless, the Turkish Constitution constructs a legal foundation to develop sustainable environmental policy, and based on that, a vast amount of legislation related to urbanization and environment exists (e.g., Environment Law, Municipal

Law, Forestry Law, Public Works Law). The Environment Law was enacted in 1983. The concept of sustainable development was added to the law in May 2006. The law primarily focuses on the prevention of pollution and has limited power in terms of preventing unsuitable land use development and green space loss. Likewise, the Municipal Law empowers municipalities to take every possible action to control and upgrade urban sanitation and falls short of taking action to provide an ecologically sound open space system. The Public Works Law defines the duties and responsibilities of different public offices that are authorized to generate land use plans at different scales. An article to protect agricultural lands from development was added to the law in 2005. Other than this, the law falls short on issues related to ecologically sound planning of urban environments. These main legal documents have a common denominator: economic development has priority and environmental concerns will be dealt with only if financial constraints permit. This means that the degree of national political will to further protect and to enhance environmental quality is curtailed (Yasamis, 2006).

Government agencies vary in terms of both spatial and functional scope in their urban activities, and their ability to concentrate resources can be a critical factor in urban development (Danielson and Keles, 1985). Different government agencies work in the implementation of the government policies with regards to urbanization. Among them, the ministries of Public Works and Housing, Industry and Commerce, Culture and Tourism, and Environment and Forestry are the most prominent. The local offices of the aforementioned ministries are in charge of implementing the government policies at local level in their jurisdiction, and providing related services for local citizens.

Municipalities are local institutions authorized to generate land use plans in their jurisdiction. Municipalities also provide infrastructure and services. They are legally responsible for managing solid waste, installing and operating water, gas, and urban transport services, and constructing and repairing streets. Although sewage and bus services are not specified among municipal duties, they have been assumed in practice. Since 1980, the privatization and corporatization of municipal services has improved the provision of infrastructure and services in cities. Nevertheless, local authorities have limited human resources to undertake their responsibilities and are not autonomous in their ability to set salaries for qualified personnel, create or eliminate positions as needed. Most municipalities are deficient in monitoring and enforcement tools, limiting the effectiveness of environmental regulations. Local governments tend to prioritize economic over environmental goals in local development and land use planning (Esbah, 2007).

Different agencies are involved in preparing plans related to environment and urbanization. The State Planning Organization (SPO) under the Prime Minister's Office prepares the Development Plans, which set the short- and long-term economic, social, spatial, and environmental policies of the nation. The Ministry of Environment is in charge of preparing 1:100,000 and 1:25,000 scale Environmental Plans. These plans are prepared in favor of industrialization and urbanization and have limited capacity to promote sustainable landscape planning.

The Ministry of Tourism is in charge of preparing the plans for those areas defined as the tourism development regions. Their plans are prepared to boost tourism revenues with inadequate consideration to environmental carrying capacity. Municipalities and the Office of the Governor are responsible for the development of the land use plans (1:5000 and 1:1000 scales) in the municipal boundaries and its surrounding rural areas, respectively. Various other plans are produced by other agencies under various laws. Not having a national land use planning and land protection law causes complications about who is authorized to deal with land use and planning (Coskun, 2005).

Although numerous plans are developed, their usefulness can be limited. For example, land use plans do not keep pace with rapid population growth and changes in settlement patterns and therefore may be irrelevant. The plans are also confined to physical dimensions, not integrated with projections and targets of other plans, and are frequently changed. Moreover, a conflict of authority and responsibility exists with respect to devising plans and implementing them (SPO, 2007)

The involvement of NGOs in environmental issues has increased since the early 1990s. This is putting pressure on the central and local authorities for good governance. Some of the most influential NGOs are either established or have been supported by the private sector (Kalaycioglu and Gonel, 2005). Their activities primarily concern re-forestation, especially on rural landscapes, and combating erosion and pollution, and disregard the unsustainable land use and open space transformation issues. Moreover, their role in challenging the authorities to protect and maintain ecological integrity of the urban landscapes is minor. NGOs also face constraints that affect their ability to participate. They have difficulties mobilizing membership, developing proposals, and financing activities and technical equipment. In spite of various legislative arrangements that were introduced to ensure the right to participate, transparency is also a problem (SPO, 2007).

Less than two decades ago, decentralization and delegation of powers from the central government down to the local governments started in Turkey. Following the United Nation's action plan for sustainable development—Agenda 21—Turkey has made good progress in terms of public participation. Local Agenda 21 implementation in Turkey commenced at the end of 1997, and enabled a style of government more responsive to the citizens' demands. The UNDP selected the Local Agenda 21 Program of Turkey as a model of world-wide "best practice" in 2001, and presented this program to world leaders at the UN Rio+10 Summit in Johannesburg (SPO, 2006).

Turkey's environmental policy is predominantly shaped and enhanced by a variety of international commitments on environmental issues such as the International Agreement for Biological Diversity and the Ramsar Convention. Turkey signed the European Landscape Convention in 2003 and assumed the responsibility to protect and manage all types of natural and man-made landscapes as well as possible. Subsequently, the Office of Landscape Protection was established under the Ministry of Environment and Forestry. Even though their role in protecting and managing natural and cultural landscapes in urban areas is insufficient, the ratification of the convention and the establishment of the office set the stage for the sustainable use of Turkish landscapes in the future.

Turkey has been knocking on the EU door since 1987 and was granted candidate status in 1999. EU accession negotiations were officially launched in 2005. There are 35 key chapters under negotiation with the EU. In order to harmonize the national law and regulations as well as physical and social structure with the EU, Turkey has been following some EU programs such as PHARE, ISPA, and SAPARD that provide specific support to spatial development in candidate countries (SPO, 2006). The ongoing EU accession process has required many improvements in the institutional environment of the nation and may continue to help focus on environmental, urbanization, and land use issues.

Development plans

Turkey's overall urbanization policy is presented in the periodic Development Plans prepared by the State Planning Agency since 1963. The development plan is the main instrument for coordinating government policies, including those for environmental management and urbanization. Initial plans did not favor the limitless growth of the cities, and promoted an optimum urban size concept, which basically recommended development correlated with the employment opportunities in the region.

The latter plans regarded urban development as the outcome of economic, social, and especially industrial development and suggested that urbanization become an economic stimulus. Starting around 1980, one principle in the plans was to promote livable cities and to answer the needs of urbanites instead of slowing the urbanization process in the nation. According to this plan, as a natural and inevitable result of development and industrialization, the urbanization process must be managed in the best possible way and measures had to be taken to increase its contribution to economic development. Also, in the 1980s, the concept of specialization was introduced and cities were defined based on their characteristics such as touristic, industrial, or commercial. The 1980s represented a time of accelerated institutional development with the addition of new related articles to the constitution, international agreements, and the establishment of the Ministry of Environment. For the first time in the country's history, the notions of preventing uncontrolled development on agricultural lands and socio-economic equity in the selection of new industrial sites appeared in the development plans.

The plan of the 1990–95 period acknowledged some problems associated with urbanization, mainly in the area of land resources, infrastructure, housing, education, and health. Special emphasis was put on the completion of city plans and efficient supervision of development of surrounding rural areas related to these plans. The dramatic magnitude of migration to urban areas was recognized and policies were developed to reduce the rate of migration by the late 1990s. The plans included not only the economic and physical aspects of urban development, but also social, esthetic, cultural, and educational aspects.

The Seventh Development Plan period (1996–2000) recognized the fact that environmental issues had not been adequately incorporated into economic and social decisions. In the plan, protection and improvement of the environment was one of the objectives and it proposed a set of policies that include: preventing pollution, developing regional and ecobasin strategies, ensuring integration with EU norms, enhancing the financing system for environmental protection and management, promoting environmental awareness, and harmonizing legislation to ensure compatibility between economic development and environmental protection. The instruments to implement these policies included a priority project entitled Institutional Arrangements on the Environment and the preparation of a National Environmental Action Plan (the NEAP).

The Eighth Development Plan period (2000–05) is significant in terms of improving the institutional structure. In this period, the duties, authorities, functions, and responsibilities of all public institutions and organizations were redefined. The plan raises the concept of urban culture (life style) within the main frame of national values, while it prepares the cities to meet the demands of globalization. Therefore, the establishment of international-scale commercial centers (cities) and the extension of organized industrial districts around the country were recommended along with the formation of techno-cities.

The Preliminary National Development Plan (PNDP), which covers the 2004–06 period, was prepared to determine the medium-term main priority areas to be financially supported in the field of economic and social harmonization during the EU accession. In the plan period, local development initiatives, strategic operational regional development programs with independent budgets, and cross-border cooperation programs (INTERREG) were started.

The current plan, the Ninth Development Plan, was prepared as a basic strategy document that would contribute to the EU accession process. The plan period was determined as 2007–13, considering the EU fiscal calendar. In comparison with previous plans, the ninth plan includes effective monitoring and evaluation mechanisms in order to ensure efficiency and transparency in the implementation. In the ninth plan, strategic development axes were defined in order to sustain stable economic growth and social development: increasing competitiveness and employment, strengthening human development and social solidarity, ensuring regional development, and increasing quality and effectiveness in public services. The plan proposes improvements in urban infrastructure and some solutions to environmental problems encountered in urban areas. It does, however, overlook the issue of ecological integrity in urban areas.

Environmental implications

The policies and recommendations of the aforementioned development plans seem to be comprehensive and idealistic. The implementation of the plans in the real-world situation has proven to be challenging. Instability and inconsistency in their implementation has undermined the overall impact (Yasamis, 2006). The suggested measures in the plans have not been effective. Existing laws sometimes contain conflicts of interests, and are insufficient to prevent unsuitable development. Despite the array of measures, enforcement efforts are weak. For example, illegal settlements were allowed and regularized in the 1980s through several squatter settlement amnesties (gecekondu). The Environmental Impact Assessment (EIA) process was hampered by an insufficient budget and public participation, an unreliable database, and the Ministry of Environment's unwillingness to apply EIA to major investments for public interest.

There is a need for viable economic and environmental strategies to provide sustainable resource use (Irtem et al., 2005). According to Wasilewski and Krukowski (2004) environmentally sound urban planning will only take place in the presence of mechanisms that safeguard environmental interest. Such mechanisms may include procedures that provide a role for governments and programs to raise public awareness in preserving valuable landscapes. In contrast, the case of Turkey generally shows a lack of the environmental awareness and foresight required to anticipate the negative effects of uncontrolled urbanization.

Unsustainable urban development prevails in the form of rapid, sprawling, and uncontrolled urbanization in Turkey. The type of urbanization causes social and economic erosion (Erturk, 1997). Traffic and inadequate parking, drinking water and power supplies, public transportation services, infrastructure, schools, libraries, and green spaces are the signs of such erosion. The development of informal slum settlements on the periphery is very common (Keles, 2004). Municipalities often struggle with establishing adequate infrastructure before the development takes over these areas. Especially in recent years, the dispersion of commercial and residential land uses from inner urban areas to the outer urban ring is common due to the demand for higher quality of life. Hence, compared to inner areas, the rate of population increase is higher in the outer ring (Maktav et al., 2002).

Environmental interests in the preservation of open space remain marginal. A typical urban development causes fragmentation in the natural or open space systems, diminishing ecological integrity in the urban and peri-urban matrix. Most often urban open spaces are converted to residential uses or their structure is changed from natural to man-made. A substantial amount of prime agricultural land is transformed for different land uses, however, local communities do not consider land withdrawal from agricultural production a casual factor in the loss of rural landscape (Esbah, 2004).

Although no official statistics exist regarding agricultural land conversion in Turkey, some individual scholarly work exists to display the general trend. Doygun (2005) investigated the consequences of urban development in the fourth biggest metropolitan area of Turkey, and found out that Adana and its surroundings experienced 107.58 percent urbanization between 1984 and 2000, and agricultural lands decreased 34 percent due to this development. Other research on the coastal areas of the same geographic area found that the expansion of agricultural practices over ecologically sensitive natural areas was evident, and urban settlements continued to grow mostly at the expense of prime agricultural land in their close vicinity (Alphan and Yilmaz, 2005). In the rapidly developing, heavily industrialized city of Bursa, Aksoy et al. (2004) found that 3,006.1 ha of agricultural land were converted to urban uses, corresponding to a 73.9 percent change from 1984–98. Maktav et al. (2002) investigated urban growth in Buyukcekmece, Istanbul between 1984 and 1998 using satellite images, ancillary data, and remote sensing technology. Their results indicate approximately 288.2 percent overall population increase. Due to the migration triggered by industrialization, the urban area expanded approximately 20 percent, resulting in a decline of open systems and agricultural lands. Agricultural lands decreased 26.4 percent over those 14 years.

From an ecological stand point, the outcome of these examples is increasing horizontal and vertical difference in the structure of the landscape and changing function that signals the type of development in the near future. Although the study area in the present work, the City of Aydin, Turkey, possesses somewhat different socio-cultural, economic, and spatial attributes, the initial observations indicate that the development pattern might exhibit similar outcomes.

Landscape-scale changes

The City of Aydin is located in Aydin Province of the Aegean Region of Turkey. The City is comprised of three municipal districts, Aydin, Umurlu, and Dalama. Extending to 62,700 hectares, it is the administrative center of the total of 16 cities in the province. The population of the City of Aydin has increased continuously over the years, and reached approximately 208,000 in 2000 and 252,000 in 2010. Between 1940 and 2000, the population rose by 108.7 percent, with the fastest increase occurring between 1980 and 1985. Most of the population increase occurred in the urban areas (DIE, 2000). This resulted from Development Plans created in the late 1970s and early 1980s which prioritized urbanization to stimulate economic growth. Migration from rural to urban areas and from eastern to western Turkey accelerated during this period of social and economic transition.

The City of Aydin is located in the Big Meander River Basin. During its history, the Big Meander Valley was always an important business and agriculture area due to its location on major transportation routes. The first railroad was constructed in 1853 by the British to supply cotton to the U.S. during the American Civil war. The arrival of the railroad opened a new era in the regional economy. Subsequently, cotton production, the related textile industry, and mining were important industries. After the foundation of the Turkish Republic in 1923, agriculture became more significant. Today, the Big Meander Valley is one of the most prominent agricultural areas of Turkey. It holds second place in the country's cotton production (Keskin and Bircan, 2002), and exports more dried figs and chestnuts than any other part of Turkey.

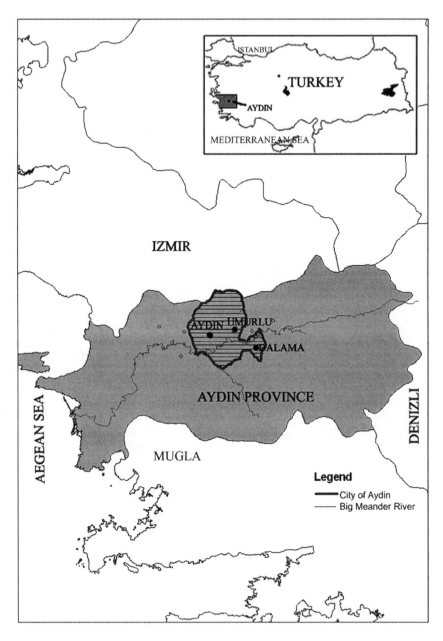

Figure 4.1 Study area, the City of Aydin, Turkey. Image courtesy of Hayriye Esbah, 2011.

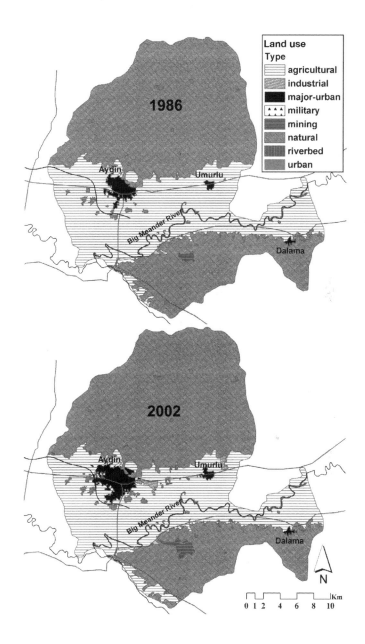

Figure 4.2 Land use change in the City of Aydin between 1986 and 2002.
Image courtesy of Hayriye Esbah, 2011.

Although the social and economic structure of the City of Aydin is shaped by agriculture (Mazlum, 2000), the latter's role in the local economy has been diminishing since the 1980s due to the national industrialization policy. Currently, two large-scale organized industrial zones exist in the city. Mainly food processing, agricultural machinery, and textile industries are operating in these zones. Moreover, individual factories are mushrooming on the fertile agricultural lands. In fact, in the City of Aydin, urbanization and industrialization are acting at the expense of the agricultural landscape as in many other urban cases in Turkey, though the magnitude of the conversion is not extraordinary.

Between 1986 and 2002, agricultural lands decreased 3.19 percent. Fifty-seven percent of this land was converted into major urban areas; 23 percent was converted to industrial use; and 16 percent was converted to peri-urban use (Esbah, 2007). Alteration in the social and economic structure of the area created new urban settlements, further fragmenting the landscape matrix.

Although agricultural lands were lost in some areas, new areas were reclaimed from natural land elsewhere. Most of the converted natural land was near existing agricultural land, in areas with gentle slopes. Overall a 1.74 percent decline occurred in the natural areas between 1986 and 2002 (Esbah, 2007). This is very low considering the rates of conversion reported for other cities in Turkey (Alphan and Yilmaz, 2005) and abroad (Kienast, 1993). Natural areas chiefly comprise the mountainous landscape on the north and south of the City where topography is not suitable for development. Unlike examples from developed countries such as the United States (Burke and Ewan, 1999), these areas were not preferred for urban development because of the high cost of construction. However, deforestation of these areas occurred as a result of government policies that give property rights to farmers if they cultivate strips of natural lands bordering on existing agricultural areas for a certain period.

Industrialized areas increased 100-fold between 1986 and 2002. Industrialization has several major ecological drawbacks: the amount of impervious surfaces is very high in such land use (Deniz, 2005), industrialization contributes to groundwater depletion and salinization (Paul and Meyer, 2001), and air and water pollution increase when the new establishments do not comply with the environmental regulations (Kalaycioglu and Gonel, 2005). If the transformation of natural and agricultural lands into industrial and urban land uses continues in the City of Aydin, it will represent a case of the tragedy of the commons (Hardin, 1968). In addition to these landscape-scale changes, municipal-scale land use transformation has also occurred, to the detriment of urban open spaces.

Municipal-scale changes

The largest urban area, the municipal district of Aydin, is located in between the transition zone from hilly natural landscape on the south part of Aydin Mountain to the flat agricultural landscape of the Big Meander River Basin (KHGM, 2001). Tabakhane stream, running north to south in the City, traverses the plain and

Figure 4.3 Changing housing silhouette in Aydin. Image courtesy of Hayriye Esbah, 2011.

reaches to the river. Aydin is the fifth fastest-growing urban area in Turkey (Mazlum, 2000), stretching in an east–west direction along the major road connecting two major industrial cities, Izmir and Denizli. Its population has grown continuously in the past five decades. The urban population had increased 5.3 times and reached 188,337 by 2010. The inevitable consequence of this rapid population growth is urban sprawl. Urban sprawl is the disorderly and unregulated expansion of housing, industrial, and commercial development in and beyond the periphery of metropolitan areas (Cho, 2005). According to Tregoing et al. (2002), sprawl consumes precious open space and spoils the landscape with unsightly development. In Turkey, sprawl usually occurs with the formation of squatter districts in peripheral areas. However, in Aydin's case, relatively upscale suburban developments were built in these areas, because the Municipality of Aydin took necessary measures and provided affordable housing for low-income families. Also, strict monitoring and law enforcement against squatter development contributed.

The tendency toward suburbanization could be a result of changing social and cultural structures due to globalization. Advances in transportation and the media are exposing more people to the sorts of life styles experienced in developed countries, and many of these people prefer to live in lush landscapes. Unlike in northern Europe, America, and other larger metropolitan areas in Turkey (e.g. Istanbul), this process didn't begin to accelerate in Aydin until the past decade (Deniz et al., 2005), and while different to other Turkish cities with squatter settlements, the urbanization did degrade the condition of the surrounding natural and agricultural landscape (Esbah and Deniz, 2007).

The isolation of small patches of formerly agricultural land by roads and housing developments is evident at the municipal scale. The construction of the highway in 1998 caused fragmentation of agricultural patches into smaller parcels, made them less efficient, and sometimes led to loss of biodiversity in the agricultural areas (Esbah and Deniz, 2007). The abandonment of agricultural land in anticipation of imminent urban development has been common. These abandoned agricultural patches have been mostly transformed into residential uses (Deniz, 2005). A variety of public policies and programs, such as zoning, use value assessment, purchasing of development rights, and purchasing conservation easements, could protect the ecological integrity of the peri-urban landscapes.

The magnitude of natural land conversion was not striking in peripheral areas, because Aydin did not expand toward the natural lands in the north due to the rugged characteristics of the natural landscape and the cost of bringing infrastructure. However, the structural incompatibility between the urban system and the natural system could increase the magnitude of any edge effects. Therefore, even though the conversion of natural land to urban land has been low, the ecological integrity of the natural system might be in danger due to its proximity to a high-impact urban system. Despite these issues facing the peri-urban open spaces, important parts of the city plans focus on existing developed areas (urban core areas), with peripheral areas receiving far less detailed attention.

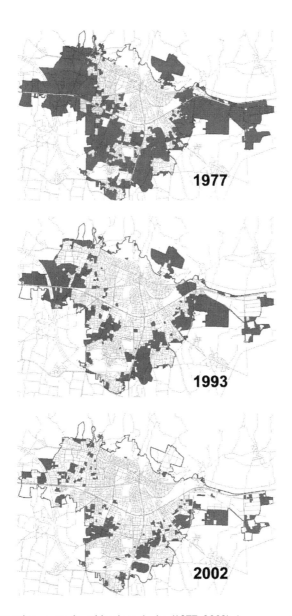

Figure 4.4 Diminishing agricultural lands in Aydin (1977–2002). Image courtesy of Hayriye Esbah, 2011.

Figure 4.5 Different sections of Tabakhane stream corridor from north to south. Top: in a natural setting; center: in the urban matrix; bottom: in the agricultural landscape. Image courtesy of Hayriye Esbah, 2011.

Urban open spaces are the direct expression of what is on the local and national agenda. Their design and perception is affected by socio-economic policies, mostly leaving no space for ecological thinking. Esbah and Deniz's (2007) research shows that ecological integrity of the highly dense urban core area in the city is questionable due to changes in the open space system. In Aydin, natural areas in the urban core area were converted to anthropogenic uses between 1977 and 2002. Significant change occurred in the natural drainage corridors such as Tabakhane stream corridor (Esbah and Deniz, 2007; Tuncay and Esbah, 2006). The parts of the corridor in the urban matrix were taken over by less ecologically compatible high density residential and commercial uses, and the stream was canalized, losing its ecological integrity. Canals are examples of artificial corridors (Cook, 2002). If they comprise substantial green areas along them, they may still contribute to the open space system of the city. However, in Aydin's case opportunities for green areas along the canal are limited to a couple of neighborhood parks.

The City of Aydin puts a great deal of effort into bringing nature to the urban landscape through parks. Thus, the number of parks has increased gradually over the years. However, contribution in the more ecologically sound open space system was, and is, very low (Esbah and Deniz, 2007; Esbah, 2006). These parks are very small in area, and are dominated by impervious surfaces and exotic plants. Sustainable and ecologically sound design of urban parks is crucial in Aydin to improve their various open space qualities. NGOs and citizens' participation in the planning and management of the parks could be beneficial. These parks are mostly on a neighborhood park scale. A large urban park and even a preserve in the northern section may be the first steps to improving ecological integrity in the city.

The man-made patches of public open spaces such as cemeteries, gardens of hospitals, and campuses of government offices, school yards, and outdoor complexes hold a great potential for the environmental and social enrichment of Aydin. The investigation of aerial photographs shows that these anthropogenic open spaces increased from 3.85 percent in 1977 to 23.08 percent in 2002 (Esbah and Deniz, 2007). In Aydin, transportation routes and industrial and archeological land uses increased, especially after 1993. The realization of the potential of these areas is necessary, as they possess vast amounts of open space within their property boundaries and rights of way (Deniz, 2005; Esbah and Deniz, 2007). The changing face of the open spaces from natural and agricultural to man-made is an indicator of the changing social, economic, and cultural face of the city. As more anthropocentric land uses dominate the urban landscape of Aydin, open spaces change to fit the anthropogenic needs of the residents. In the absence of mechanisms to safeguard the ecological integrity of these areas, promoting sustainable urban development is not viable (Esbah et al., 2009).

Revitalizing the institutional environment (2000–11)

Increasing environmental problems, poor quality of living in urban areas, high rates of migration, and the EU accession process led Turkey to revitalize its institutional environment by the end of the 1990s. The development plan of this period recognized the inadequacy in incorporating environmental issues into social and economic decisions. Subsequently, in 1999, Turkey's State Planning Organization, together with the World Bank, coordinated a project called the Turkish National Environmental Strategy and Action Plan (NEAP) for integrating environment and development. The timeline of implementation varied from five to ten years. The goals of the NEAP identified by the preparation process were better quality of life, increased environmental awareness, improved environmental management, and sustainable economic, social, and cultural development (MOE, 1999). The NEAP was organized into three components that were formed by working group meetings and stakeholder workshops: (1) a program and supporting actions to develop a more effective system of environmental management; (2) actions for enhancing information and public awareness; and (3) investments for critical problem areas. Urban areas and natural resource management were recognized as among the problem areas. Improving waste management, encouraging clean technologies and energy sources, and upgrading urban slums were proposed to deal with problems in urban environments. To improve natural resource management, a large investment to upgrade rural environmental infrastructure was proposed.

The improvement of social, economic, and physical infrastructure in rural areas was one of the major policies to keep people in their villages. Nevertheless, Turkish cities continued to be insufficient in meeting the population pressure created by intense migration movements. This situation required an integrated regional development approach. The EU accession process enabled radical changes in regional development strategies and implementation of the policies. To this end, the official Nomenclature of Territorial Units for Statistics (NUTS) system started in 2002. NUTS helped in the formulation of the regional development policies, the collection of regional statistics, and the creation of a statistical database compatible with the EU regional statistics system. In 2004, new incentives were put into practice with the aim of accelerating the increase in investments and employment, and increasing the role of the private sector in regional development. Within this framework, in 2003, discounts in income tax and social security premium payments were implemented in provinces with negative Socio Economic Development Index (SEDI) values.

In order to ensure development in the rural areas, the National Rural Development Strategy was prepared in 2006. The main purpose was to create a framework for rural development projects and to solve harmonization problems of the rural areas during the EU accession. The legal and institutional regulations to implement the rural development policies are continuing. In this period, the General Directorate of Rural Services, the agency in charge of settlement issues in rural areas, was closed. Its settlement-related duties were transferred to the Ministry of Public Works and Settlement while other duties were transferred to provincial administrations. This enabled the allocation of funds to local administrations in 2006–08, initiating a project for supporting the infrastructure of villages (KOYDES). However, the scattered and disorganized pattern of rural settlements challenged the effective and widespread provision of physical and social infrastructure services.

Important regulations related to the institutional structure were realized in the 2000–05 period. The Ministry of Culture and Ministry of Tourism were merged. Likewise, the Ministry of Environment was merged with the Ministry of Forestry. The Ministry of Agriculture was made the authority for all types of rural issues. A report, "Reviewing the General Institutional Structure in the State," was prepared in 2003. This document explains the duties, authorities, functions, and responsibilities of all public institutions and organizations. In it, the replication of authority and duties among the institutions were identified and recommendations for solving duplication were provided. In spite of the report and all the regulation to improve the institutional structure, the administrative, financial, and personnel problems still exist in the local administrations. Furthermore, the central government still needs to determine standards of its services and to supervise compliance with these standards (SPO, 2006).

In 2006, the law on the Establishment, Coordination and Duties of Development Agencies was enacted to facilitate collaboration among public and private sectors and NGOs. This law ensures efficient use of resources and provides regional development based on activating local dynamics and internal potential. Moreover, the authorities and responsibilities of local administrations were increased through the laws on special provincial administrations, municipalities, metropolitan municipalities, and local administration unions, hence increasing the capacities and resources of local administrations, especially in less developed regions. In addition to the changes in the local institutional structure, an improvement occurred in terms of the authority dissonance. Progress has been made in the establishment of connections between plans, clarification of responsibilities, and coordination of organizations at central and local levels during the plan preparation and implementation.

The ninth Development Plan and its policies, strategy documents of the UN, the European Commission, and the European Union have provided a foundation for the most recent policy instrument regarding urbanization in Turkey, the Integrated Urban Development Strategy and Action Plan (or KENTGES) (Table 4.1). Ratified in November 2010, the action plan is based on three policy axes: restructuring the spatial planning system, improving quality of life in urban settlements, and strengthening economic and social structure. In the plan, the problems of urbanization in Turkey are outlined as uncontrolled growth of cities and providing infrastructure; migration from rural areas to cities and lack of effective rural development strategies; illegal housing and squatter settlements; urban areas vulnerable to disasters; inadequate infrastructure especially in terms of sewage, solid waste, and water supply and an inadequate public transportation system; lack of organization among planning-related institutions; lack of coherence among different planning levels; failure in integrating planning and implementation powers of the local governments; inadequate numbers of stuff and finance in municipalities and special provincial administrations.

Table 4.1 Policy axes and strategies of KENTGES

Restructuring the spatial planning system

- Strengthening the spatial planning system by a comprehensive framework law and a regulatory and supervisory institution at the central level; monitoring and controlling mechanisms between the plan hierarchies; and an efficient information system. Increasing the capacities of local governments through the Municipal Law and the special provincial Administration Code. Enhancing coordination and defining ethics and code of conducts of spatial planning.
- Increasing the capacities of local governments through the Municipal Law and the Special Provincial Administration Code. Enhancing coordination among local governments. Defining ethics and code of conducts of spatial planning.

Improving quality of life in settlements

- Implementing urban macro form for limiting expansion.
- Providing housing opportunities for different income groups. Adopting new construction technologies for decreasing cost and time, and increasing construction quality. Employing new land allocation system to utilize state lands for development. Utilizing international standards for promoting environmentally friendly practices.
- Revitalizing central business districts and sub-centers by rational site selection and construction of shopping malls. Utilizing urban design projects, and maintenance/operation, financing, participation, and management approaches for improving livability in city centers.
- Establishing sustainable urban transportation system by integrating comprehensive transport plans with city plans. Improving pedestrian and bicycling paths and maintaining high standards in their design. Promoting transportation plans based on accessibility, safety, comfort, reliability, sustainability, and cost efficiency. Developing efficient and more environmentally sound public transportation systems.
- Integrating urban infrastructure plans into spatial planning by infrastructure master plans and infrastructure impact assessments. Pursuing sustainability principles when providing and improving infrastructure services. Generating legislation for the use of renewable energy resources in urban areas.
- Ensuring balanced and adequate service distribution at the city and neighborhood levels.
- Providing open and green areas. Adopting a system approach for planning urban parks. Discovering new open and green space typologies and standards.
- Ensuring protection of natural and cultural assets and values in the spatial planning process. Monitoring and control mechanisms for sustainable use of all natural resources. Harmonizing different protection efforts.
- Considering all social, cultural, and economic dimensions in urban transformation projects.
- Ensuring integrated and effective disaster management system by legislative arrangements.
- Planning and designing safe settlements with high quality of life.
- Strengthening and preserving historical, natural, and cultural patterns.
- Establishing environmentally sensitive living spaces by adopting concepts such as maintaining ecological balance, preventing pollution, environmental conscience, energy efficiency, and sustainable natural resource use in the planning process.

Strengthening the economic and social structures of settlements

---

- Improving spatial and economic structure and quality of life in small and mid-size cities and rural areas to facilitate reverse migration.
- Increasing social solidarity, integration, and tolerance in cities.
- Providing urban services for disadvantaged groups and people in need. Opening occupational training programs and skill courses to reduce urban poverty.
- Ensuring citizen participation in every phase of spatial planning.
- Promoting urban culture, sense of belonging, and awareness of urban rights.

Source: Ministry of Public Works and Settlements (2011).

Created as part of Turkey's program for alignment with the EU acquis (the body of European Union law), KENTGES assumes urban development as a fundamental element of regional development. Economic, social, spatial, and legislative matters of urban development are addressed through a participatory process. The plan was prepared in two years with the participation of 151 institutions including universities, state institutions and organizations, local authorities, occupational associations, the private sector, and NGOs. Therefore, the action plan is the most comprehensive and up-to-date policy instrument concerning sustainable urban development in Turkey. KENTGES is an urbanization vision of the country up to the year 2023, the one-hundredth anniversary of the establishment of the Republic of Turkey (MOPW, 2010).

A vision for sustainable landscapes

Turkey has experienced rapid social, economic, and environmental changes since the 1980s. The institutional environment has played a major role in this transformation. The planning objective of promoting economic growth without considering sustainability shows signs of causing serious detrimental changes in landscapes. Unfortunately, Turkish environmental policies were far from becoming efficient, systematic, and stable until the 2000s.

The EU accession process is a good opportunity to improve the policies, regulations, and institutions with regards to urbanization in Turkey. EU policies and programs have significant implications for future urban development in member and candidate countries. In this regard URBAN I and II, URBACT, and Urban Audit are some of the influential Community initiatives. The European Spatial Development Perspective (European Commission, 1999) and Guiding Principles for Sustainable Spatial Development of the European Continent (CEMAT, 2000) are two other major policy reference documents that are influential in promoting sustainable spatial development. Though they are not binding, the aforementioned policy instruments orchestrate the implementation of various treaties that are shaping spatial dynamics in the EU member and candidate states such as Community Competition Policy, Trans-European Networks, Structural Funds, Common Agriculture Policy, Environment Policy, Research Technology and Development, and the Loan activities of the European Investment Bank. Turkey has been benefiting from most of these treaties, and has taken them as a base for generating regional and rural development strategies. Subsequently, significant changes have occurred in the institutional environment of Turkey during the last decade. Time will show the efficiency of the implementation in years to come.

The case presented in this chapter offers a good example of the impacts of the institutional environment on land use dynamics at local and landscape scales. Industrialization is playing a significant role in the development of the study area by altering the social and economic structures and by changing spatial patterns. At a larger landscape scale, urban and industrial areas have both exhibited large proportional increases, largely at the expense of agricultural areas. Agricultural expansion has occurred, in turn, at the expense of natural areas. Compared to other areas of Turkey, the overall land use transformation has not been striking because of the relatively recent history of urbanization and industrialization in the region. At the municipal scale, the transformation of open space systems has resulted in an unhealthy urban environment. Semi-natural open spaces were changed to artificial open spaces with more exotic plants and impervious surfaces. The negative consequences of these landscape and municipal-scale changes may accelerate in the future if a strategy to control urban expansion and conversion of land is not developed.

The policy makers should consider, for the future, where the expansion would be accommodated, how ecological integrity at the landscape scale will be preserved, how infrastructure is to be paid for and provided, and how this can be done with minimal budget and with minimal environmental impact. At the municipal level, ecologically sound approaches to the establishment of urban open space systems are crucial during the preparation of the city plans and the evolution of open space designs. As urban open spaces are key ingredients in the city's sustainability, variability in open space types should be recognized to enhance the ecological integrity of the highly complex urban matrix.

The task of promoting sustainable urban landscapes demands a coordinated, proactive, and broader political and spatial approach and realistic, equitable, and enforceable regulatory regimes. Efforts are currently underway to revitalize institutional environments relating to urbanization, decentralization of power to local governments, promotion of regional and rural development, and industrialization to accelerate economic growth in Turkey. Well-deserved attention is being given to social and economic development to answer society's major needs of employment, social solidarity, equity, and access to infrastructure, all of which are expected to mitigate migration pressures. Considerable attention is also being given to the ecological, economic, and cultural qualities of rural landscapes. However, protecting natural and semi-natural areas as well as providing high-quality open spaces in urban and peri-urban areas seems to be overlooked. In this regard, the policy recommendations of the most recent policy instruments are implicit.

Effective urban open space planning can contribute to a framework for sustainable urban planning in developing countries. Local governments should consider how an urban open space system can help in limiting the expansion of cities in environmentally valuable areas and those with potential environmental risks; in what capacity urban open spaces can serve in diminishing the tendency toward suburbanization and raising the quality of life in inner urban areas; how open spaces should be planned and designed to mitigate social exclusion; in what way open spaces can support effective and environmentally friendly public transportation systems; how their benefits can be maximized in protecting and enhancing floodplains and narrow strips of water bodies; what their role is in conserving and promoting cultural heritage; and how open spaces can serve to maintain ecological integrity in urban environments and vice versa.

References

Aksoy, E., Ozsoy, G., and Sezgin, E. (2004) "Determining urbanization development and its adverse effect on soils of the alluvial plains at the Bursa Province using multi-date satellite data." *Proceedings of ISC on Natural Resource Management for Sustainable Development.* Erzurum, Turkey, 300–308.

Alphan, H., and Yilmaz, T. K. (2005) "Monitoring environmental changes in the Mediterranean coastal landscape: the case of Cukurova, Turkey," *Environmental Management,* 35 (5): 607–619.

Angel, S., Sheppard, S. C., and Civco, D. L. (2005) "The dynamics of global urban expansion, Washington, D.C.: Transport and Urban Development Department," the World Bank. Online. Available http://siteresources.worldbank.org/ (accessed April 20, 2011).

Antrop, M. (2000a) "Background concepts for integrated landscape analysis," *Agriculture, Ecosystems and Environment,* 77: 17–28.

Antrop, M. (2000b) "Changing patterns in the urbanized countryside of Western Europe," *Landscape Ecology,* 15: 257–270.

Antrop, M. (2004) "Landscape change and the urbanization process in Europe," *Landscape and Urban Planning,* 67: 9–26.

Burke, J., and Ewan, J. (1999) "Sonoran Preserve master plan: an open space plan for the Phoenix Sonoran Desert," City of Phoenix Parks, Recreating and Library Department.

CEMAT (2000) "Guiding principles for sustainable spatial development of the European continent," European Conference of Ministers Responsible for Regional Planning, Hannover.

Cho, J. (2005) "Urban planning and urban sprawl in Korea," *Urban Policy and Research,* 23: 203–218.

Cook, E. A. (2002) "Landscape structure indices for assessing urban ecological networks," *Landscape and Urban Planning,* 58: 269–280.

Coskun, A. A. (2005) "An evaluation of the environmental impact assessment in Turkey," *International Journal of Environment and Sustainable Development,* 4: 47–66.

Country Studies (2003) "Country studies-area Turkey," Federal Research Division of the Library of Congress, USA. Online. Available http://countrystudies.us/turkey/56.htm (accessed August 1, 2006).

Danielson, M. N., and Keles, R. (1985) *The Politics of Rapid Urbanization: Government and Growth in Modern Turkey,* New York: Holmes and Meier.

Deniz, B. (2005) "Use of landscape structure indices in assessing urban land use transformation and their contribution in urban planning practices: case of the city of Aydin" (in Turkish), Unpublished Dissertation, University of Ege, Izmir, Turkey.

Deniz, B., Esbah, H., and Kucukerbas, E. V. (2005) "Determining the change in agricultural landscape matrix resulted from urban sprawl in the case of Aydin urban area," *Proceedings of X. European Ecological Congress,* Kusadası: Turkey, 83–94.

DIE (2000) "Census of Population," Report, State Institute of Statistics, Ankara.

Doygun, H. (2005) "Urban development in Adana, Turkey, and its environmental consequences," *International Journal of Environmental Studies,* 62: 391–401.

Doygun, H., and Alphan, H. (2006) "Monitoring urbanization of Iskenderun, Turkey," *Environmental Monitoring and Assessment,* 114: 145–155.

Erturk, H. (1997) *Urban Economics,* Bursa: Ekin Press.

Esbah, H. (2004) "Agricultural land loss due to urbanization," *Proceedings of Agro-Environs,* Udine: Italy, 231–238.

Esbah, H. (2006) "Investigation of urban parks in Aydin through some ecological quality criteria," *Ekoloji,* 15(58): 42–48.

Esbah, H. (2007) "Land use trends during rapid urbanization of the City of Aydın, Turkey," *Environmental Management*, 39: 443–459.

Esbah, H., and Deniz, B. (2007) "Effects of land use development on urban open spaces," *Journal of Applied Sciences*, 7(8): 1138–1144.

Esbah, H. E., Cook, A., and Ewan, J. (2009) "Effects of increasing urbanization on the ecological integrity of open space preserves," *Environmental Management*, 43(5): 846–862.

European Commission. (1999) "European spatial development perspective," Report, European Commission, Potsdam. Online. Available http://ec.europa.eu/regional_policy/sources/docoffic/official/reports/som_en.htm (accessed March 12, 2011).

Forman, R. T. T. (2008) *Urban Regions: Ecology and Planning Beyond the city*, Cambridge: Cambridge University Press.

Gedik, A. (2003) "Differential urbanization in Turkey, 1955–97," *Tijdschrift vooe Economische en Social Geografie*, 81(1): 100–111.

GRUMP (2008) "Global rural urban mapping project," Alpha version, Center for International Earth Science Information Network (CIESIN), Columbia University. Online. Available http://sedac.ciesin.columbia.edu/gpw (accessed November 14, 2010).

Gur, M., Cagdas, V., and Demir, H. (2003) "Urban rural interrelationships and issues in Turkey," *2nd FIG Regional Conference* Marrakech: Morocco. Available http://www.fig.net/pub/morocco/proceedings/TS1/TS1_6_gur_et_al.pdf (accessed February 12, 2010).

Hall, R. E., and Jones, C. I. (1999) "Why do some countries produce so much more output per worker than others?," *Quarterly Journal of Economics*, 144: 83–116.

Hanna, S., Folke, C., and Maler, K. G. (1996) *Rights to Nature: Ecological, Economic, Cultural, and Political Principles of Institutions for the Environment*, Washington DC: Island Press.

Hardin, G. (1968) "The tragedy of the commons," *Science*, 13: 1243–1248.

Irtem, E., Kabdasli, S., and Azbar, N. (2005) "Coastal zone problems and environmental strategies to be implemented at Edremit Bay, Turkey," *Environmental Management*, 36(1): 37–47.

Kalaycioglu, S., and Gonel, F. (2005) "Business perspectives on environment in Turkey," *Proceedings of Business Strategy and the Environment Conference*, September 2004, Leeds, 1–7.

Keles, R. (2004) *Urbanization Policy*, 8th edition, Ankara: Image Press.

Keskin, S., and Bircan, M. (2002) "Aydin agricultural master plan," Report. Tarım Il Mudurlugu, Aydin.

KHGM (2001) "Aydin land inventory," Report, Ankara: KHGM press.

Kienast, F. (1993) "Analysis of historic landscape pattern with GIS – a methodological outline," *Landscape Ecology*, 8: 103–118.

Kongar, E. (1999) *Turkey in the Twenty-First Century*, Istanbul: Remzi Press.

Kurucu, Y., and Chiristina, N. K. (2007) "Monitoring the impacts of urbanization and industrialization on the agricultural land and environment of the Torbali, Izmir region, Turkey," *Environmental Monitoring and Assessment*, 136: 289–297.

Lopez, E., Bocco, G., Mendoza, M., and Duhau, E. (2001) "Predicting land cover and land use change in the urban fringe: A case in Morelia city, Mexico," *Landscape and Urban Planning*, 55: 271–285.

Maktav, D., Erbek, F. S., and Akgun, H. (2002) *Remote Sensing of Urban Areas*, Istanbul: Metgraf Press.

Mazlum, S. C. (2000) "Environmental inventory of the City of Aydin as a tool for environmental management," Unpublished Dissertation, Adnan Menderes University, Aydin, Turkey.

Metz, C. H. (1995) "Turkey: A Country Study," Washington: GPO for the Library of Congress. Online. Available http://countrystudies.us/turkey (accessed April 21, 2011).

Ministry of Public Works and Settlements (2011) *Integrated Urban Development Strategy and Action Plan, 2010–2023*, Republic of Turkey.

MOE (1999) "National environmental action plan of Turkey," Report, Ministry of Environment, Ankara.

MOPW (2010) "KENTGES: integrated urban development strategy and action plan 2010–2023," Report, Ministry of Public Works, Ankara.

NEAP (1999) "National Environmental Action Plan," State Planning Organization, Ankara. Online, Available http://www.unescap.org/stat/envstat/neap-turkey.pdf (accessed January 2, 2011).

North, D. C. (1991) *Institutions, Institutional Change and Economic Performance*, Cambridge: Cambridge University Press.

Ostrom, E. (1990) *Governing the Commons: The Evolution of Institutions for Collective Action*, Cambridge: Cambridge University Press.

Paul, M. J., and Meyer, J. L. (2001) "Streams in the urban landscape," *Annual Review of Ecology and Systematics*, 32: 333–365.

Richerson, P. J., Boyd, R., and Paciotti, B. (2002) "An evolutionary theory of commons management," in Dietz, T., Dolsak, N., Ostrom, E., and Stern, P. (eds.) *The Drama of the Commons*, Washington, DC: National Research Council, National Academy Press.

SPO (2000) *Settlements and Urbanization* (in Turkish), Report, Ankara: State Planning Organization.

SPO (2006) *Ninth Development Plan 2007–2013*, Report, Ankara: State Planning Organization. Online. Available http://www2.dpt.gov.tr/konj/DPT_Tanitim/index1.html (accessed January 12, 2011).

SPO (2007) "Settlements and urbanization" (in Turkish), Ninth Development Plan Specialty Commission Report, Ankara: State Planning Organization.

Tagil, S. (2006) "Change of habitat fragmentation and quality in the Balikesir Plain and its surroundings with landscape pattern metrics (1975–2000)," *Ekoloji*, 15: 24–36.

Timar, J. (1992) "The main features of suburbanization in the Great Hungarian Plain," *Landscape and Urban Planning*, 22: 177–187.

Tregoing, H., Agyeman, J., and Shenot, C. (2002) "Sprawl, smart growth and sustainability," *Local Environment*, 7: 341–347.

TUIK (2010) *Population Census of Turkey – 2010*, Report, Ankara: Turkish Statistics Institute.

Tuncay, A. A., and Esbah, H. (2006) "Understanding the effects of historic land use pattern on an urbanized stream corridor," *Journal of Applied Sciences*, 6(8): 1873–1881.

UNFPA (2007) *State of World population – 2007*, Report, New York: United Nations Population Fund. Online. Available http://www.unfpa.org/swp/2007/ (accessed June 12, 2009).

Vink, A. P. A. (1982) "Anthropocentric landscape ecology in rural areas," in Tjallingii, S. P. and Veer, A. A. (eds.) *Perspectives in Landscape Ecology: Contributions to Research, Planning and Management of Our Environment*, Wageningen: Center for Agricultural Publishing and Documentation.

Wasilewski, A., and Krukowski, K. (2004) "Land conversion for suburban housing: a study of urbanization around Warshaw and Olsztyn, Poland," *Environmental Management*, 34: 291–303.

Yasamis, F. (2006) "Assessing the institutional effectiveness of the state environmental agencies in Turkey," *Environmental Management*, 38: 823–836.

Chapter 5

Tbilisi

Urban transformation and role transformation in the post-Soviet metropolis

Kristof Van Assche and Joseph Salukvadze

Introduction

Tbilisi is the capital of Georgia, a country in the Caucasus that gained independence in 1991. Before that time, it was part of the Soviet Union, and as such was subjected to Soviet urbanization policies. In the USSR, urban development efforts, as well as urban design efforts, were focused on the capital cities of the republics (French and Hamilton, 1979; Hough and Fainsod, 1979). Also within the republics, the drive for urbanization was supported, in the frame of a general ideology of progress, and under the influence of Moscow incentives. An elaborate planning system enabled planning at various scales (Andrusz, 1984). After the dissolution of the union, planning in most republics moved to the background, one of the reasons being the association with socialism (Andrusz et al., 1996). Each of the new states followed its own path, in a double transition that was supposed to lead to democracy and a free market (Anderson 1999; Kornai and Rose-Ackerman, 2004).

Despite the specificity of each transitional path, some urban problems could and can be discerned in many post-Soviet countries (Boren and Gentile, 2007; Elster et al., 1998). We will map out the evolution of Tbilisi before, during, and after the Soviet era, and reflect on the specificity of that evolution. In that endeavor, the researchers undertook fieldwork (expert and resident interviews, document analysis) in 2006, 2007, and 2009, and telephone interviews (experts) in 2008 (overall $n = 147$). In 2006, a survey ($n = 200$) with residents of five neighborhoods gauged their interpretation of urban qualities, issues, and professional roles. Before reviewing results from fieldwork in Tbilisi, the researchers briefly outline some features of urban governance that can be observed in much of the post-Soviet space. The new states all had to face similar issues. Integrated within the text of this chapter are comments from Tbilisi residents.

First of all, each country and each city had to deal with the issue of privatization (Allina-Pisano, 2008; Elster et al., 1998). The choices made there further shaped the options for urban governance, including planning and urban design (Kornai and Rose-Ackerman, 2004). Second, there is the question of local governance: how autonomous should municipalities be, what are their resources, and how do they represent local interests and desires (Ruble, 1995)? Third, which form of democracy and which form of market is chosen (Wilson, 2005)? Contrary to popular (mostly American) beliefs in the 1980s and 1990s, many forms exist (Anderson, 1999; Wilson, 2005; Wheatly, 2005). A different way to say this is that markets are necessarily embedded in and shaped by other institutions, by politics, law, and culture in a broad sense. The relation between market, politics, and law will further determine which form of planning is possible (Van Assche et al., 2010; Kornai and Rose-Ackerman, 2004)

Empirically, 20 years of post-Soviet urban planning show a remarkable variety of answers and solutions (Boren and Gentile, 2007; Kornai and Rose-Ackerman, 2004; French, 1995). Still, certain phenomena are widespread. In most areas, affordable housing is becoming more and more of a problem (Vardosanidze, 2009). For people who could cling to the apartment they received after privatization, this is not a major problem, but for other groups, including younger people, it is. Because jobs are now even more concentrated in the capitals, the pressure on the housing markets is generally high there (Andrusz et al., 1996). Then there is the problem of public space, green and otherwise. In most post-Soviet capitals, the pressure on public spaces is high, and local planning rarely represents a real counter-pressure. Third, service provision, including schools, in many neighborhoods less attractive for private developers, is declining fast. Fourth, larger projects, such as large-scale infrastructure projects or new neighborhoods, are hard to coordinate in the absence of strong government planning (Allina-Pisano, 2008; Van Assche et al., 2010; Gachechiladze, 1995; Shavishvili, 2003). Finally, suburban development in many places undermines the financial base of inner cities. Heritage rarely plays a role in urban development, with the exception of heritage that is deemed instrumental in the reconstruction or reinforcement of national identity (French, 1995; Manning, 2009).

In many places, the capital is also perceived as a symbol for the nation, and, as the seat of the president or prime minister, the actual control of urban space is often shared by local and national government, in modes and relations that are opaque and shifting. Some more centralized regimes attach special importance to urban planning and design, mostly in the capitals, while in others this is left to the market, or is simply neglected. The similarity in resulting city spaces indicates that the variety in formal arrangements hides a greater similarity in driving forces and choices. One such similarity, we argue, comes from the fact that in all the different regimes that sprang from the USSR, it is very hard to find one where planning still occurs in a more or less consistent and comprehensive manner. In the post-Soviet realm, officially socialist places, neo-liberal regimes, social-democratic states, authoritarian ones, or states that exist mostly on paper, have in common that planning, as coordination of policies and practices of spatial organization, rarely works.

A second similarity is that the rule of law is rarely encountered in post-Soviet places. That implies that large-scale development has to rely on a constant cultivation of ties with top-level politics (cf. Wilson, 2005; Gallina, 2010). It makes such development a risky endeavor, and therefore more rare, and this in turn reinforces the impression that planning is not necessary, since there is no demand for development anyway. On a smaller scale, legal insecurity creates problems for buyers and owners of real estate. Property rights rarely have the implications they should formally have (Allina-Pisano, 2008; Ledeneva, 2006). Unclear and disrespected property rights can be a blessing for developers with political ties (allowing the appropriation of other properties to redevelop) but for these same developers, the volatility of politics makes long-term calculations and long-term security unlikely.

A third similarity is that in few places is the role of local government fully crystallized, and made immune to sudden interventions by higher-level politics (Ruble, 1995; Gallina, 2010; Allina-Pisano, 2008). In some places these interventions can be interpreted in a positive manner, as resulting from a modernizing drive emanating from central government. In the long run, however, the unclear authority of local government impedes a re-institutionalization of local planning, and therefore, with that, the possibility to guide development towards common goals. In many post-Soviet cities, the absence of strong and stable local government aggravates a problem that was supposed to disappear with transition: control by the top is difficult (Kornai and Rose-Ackerman, 2004). Whereas Soviet governance was much less centralized than many western observers believed, post-Soviet regimes often strive for centralization, with local institutions and Soviet checks and balances weakened. Thus, both controls from the top and local control are difficult, and the resulting situation is too unstable to stimulate either planned or private development. Major exceptions exist where, as mentioned, large corporate players, local government, and central government coexist in a more stable manner, that is, in capitals of the more politically and economically successful authoritarian successor regimes. How can Georgia and Tbilisi be located in this bigger picture?

Tbilisi was once considered one of the most attractive cities of the former Soviet Union. It is rich in history, has a splendid landscape setting, excellent food, a pleasant climate, and an easy-going atmosphere (Suny, 1994; Van Assche et al., 2009). Soviet development peaked in the 1960s and 1970s, and then slowed down with the economic decline of the Union (Gachechiladze, 1990). After independence (1991), the city went through a very turbulent period. Stabilization around the turn of the century gave way to a new wave of intense development activity since 2003. With the dramatic changes in Georgia, new issues emerged in Tbilisi, as in many other post-Soviet cities. Lack of social housing, green space and public space in general, homelessness, poor construction quality (not entirely new), and chaotic development practices led to problematic densities and environmental problems (Vardosanidze, 2000). Meanwhile, Tbilisi's renowned historic center is in need of urgent renovation (Shavishvili, 2003; Baburov, 1977).

Development patterns and planning strategies

Before communism

Tbilisi was founded in the fifth century AD, and one century later became the capital of the Eastern Georgian kingdom. In times of unification of the country, it served as the national capital. For most of the Middle Ages, it was a prosperous, multi-ethnic, multi-religious city, thriving on long-distance trade, located on one of the few routes connecting Central Asia and the Black Sea with relative ease (Lang, 1966). However, Tbilisi also experienced devastating invasions (for a historical overview see Suny, 1994). The last Persian invasion, in 1795, virtually razed the city to the ground. The Russians, with whom the Georgian king (Irakli II), seeking protection, signed a treaty in 1783 (the Georgievsk treaty), stepped in only after this tragic event. Protection, however, turned into a takeover of the Georgian kingdom (Lang, 1957). After the devastation of 1795, Tbilisi had to be rebuilt, and this took place in the nineteenth century, under Russian rule. This was the start of a new, post-medieval period in Tbilisi's development.

Russian and European architects participated in the reconstruction and expansion of the city. The Mtkvari (Kura – in Russian and European languages) river remained the city's defining structural feature, together with the surrounding

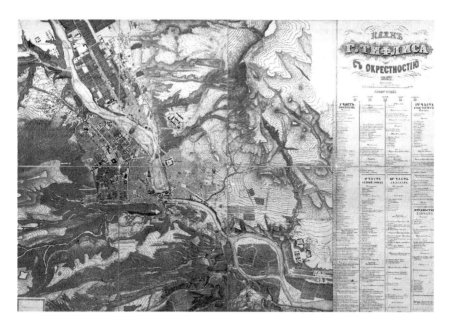

Figure 5.1 1867 Czarist Tbilisi, the Russian empire engaged in urbanist programs, adding new sections to the old town and rebuilding that old town in a hybrid style, incorporating various western and oriental architectural references. Image courtesy of Joseph Salukvadze.

Figure 5.2 Tbilisi's old town was and is a unique blend of architectural and cultural traditions. In recent years, renovation and reconstruction programs inspired by tourism and national pride have saved a considerable part of it, but other parts are still in limbo. Image courtesy of Joseph Salukvadze.

landscape of volcanic hills, ravines, streams, springs, and waterfalls (Ziegler, 2006). Armenian merchants dominated the economy until the early twentieth century, and had a strong say in city politics (Suny, 1994). Several neighborhoods (especially north of the river) had a strong Armenian flavor; others were predominantly Muslim (mostly Azeri, but also Kurdish, Persian, and others). Over the centuries, Tbilisi developed a distinct city culture that mixed elements of many ethnic origins (Gachechiladze, 1990), transcending its original ingredients: many people felt Tbilisian before Armenian, Georgian, Azeri (Manning, 2009). The Georgian language, and a unique Tbilisi culture, marked all neighborhoods in the city, Georgians differentiated themselves from their peers in the countryside, and the Tbilisi Armenians and Azeris spoke mostly Georgian.

Russian rule brought neo-classical architecture and city planning to Tbilisi. Squares were connected by boulevards, parks, a botanic garden, and theatres, museums, schools, and government buildings were established on conspicuous locations in this spatial structure (Rhinelander, 1972). Quite often, despite the generic neo-classic architecture deployed, Russian city planning efforts tried to capitalize on the surrounding landscape. The splendid botanical garden in a narrow valley (the former Royal forest), the new main boulevard (currently Rustaveli Avenue) stretched out on a terrace south of the river, punctuated by open spaces providing excellent views. The old town, surrounding the eastern sections of the new boulevard, was rebuilt from ruins, but did not attract much interest from the new administration. The density was too high, the road pattern and spatial structure too distinct and "unreasonable" for imperial town-planning. The old town was also perceived as potentially hostile to the Russian ruling elite, bureaucracy, and army. Therefore, the new administration turned its back on the old city, ignoring the river as a natural axis of growth, and started building an alternative city, in mostly neo-classical fashion (Suny, 1994; Rhinelander, 1972). The old town was mostly rebuilt in a style that referred to the older Persian-influenced architecture, maintaining street patterns, recreating the labyrinthine structure of courtyards and balconies, with shade and privacy. Western influences are visible in neo-renaissance, neo-baroque, and neo-classical ornaments and patterns, as well as a peculiar Russian orientalism that sometimes comes close to Italian Gothic (Ziegler, 2006; Baulig et al., 2004).

The Soviet period

This is, in a nutshell, the Russian imperial inheritance the communists had to work with. After a brief independence in 1918–21, the USSR established a firm grip on Georgia, and the country was an integral part of the Union until 1991. Tbilisi today is largely a Soviet city. Most people live in neighborhoods that were developed under Soviet rule, and the overall spatial structure, including the transportation network, is Soviet-made (Salukvadze, 1995; Ziegler, 2006; Van Assche et al., 2009). A period of Stalinist neo-classicism (or, more precisely, monumentalism with neo-classical elements), notably visible in extensions of Rustaveli Avenue, gave way to mass-produced architecture and neighborhood design. A neighborhood, a so-called *mikrorayon*, was supposed to have an array of amenities and local services, but in practice the level of service provision was very uneven (Andrusz, 1984; Bater, 1980; interviews). The neighborhoods started to look different when buildings grew taller than the standard five floors established under Khrushchev, the Secretary General of the Communist party of the USSR (CPSS) and author of all-Soviet programs for cheap mass housing. Under Brezhnev, the next Secretary General of the CPSS (French, 1995), building height extended to 16 floors and sometimes more. "In the beginning, people were proud of the tall buildings, and at least they had a home," explained an older political scientist. Later—as also testified by our survey—people became more critical of the late-communist neighborhoods.

Under the Soviets, three Master-plans (*Genplan*) were produced for Tbilisi, the first one in 1934 and the last one in 1969 (Van Assche et al., 2009). None of those plans was fully implemented, but local experts agree that the third plan had most impact. Planners were not the most important players in the game of economic development in the USSR (French, 1995; Boren and Gentile, 2007; Huzinec, 1978). Economic development had priority over city planning, and economic ministries, as well as some (industrial) enterprises under their umbrella, could quite easily ignore existing city plans (Huzinec, 1978). Tbilisi is not an extreme case in

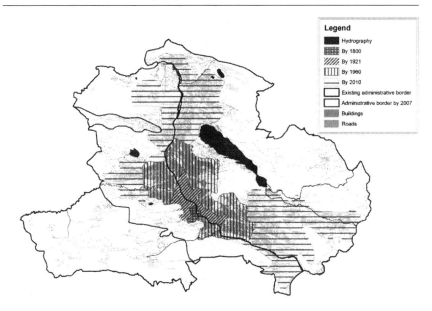

Figure 5.3 A major phase in Tbilisi's growth: before 1800, the Tbilisi of Georgian
nobility and multi-ethnic merchants were restricted to a small area circling
around fort and market. The pre-1921 phase represented Russian imperial
additions, while most of the other additions date from the communist
period. Image courtesy of Joseph Salukvadze.

this respect; nonetheless, large industrial complexes were plonked in the city fabric
in places that did not make sense for the early planners working in Tbilisi or in
Moscow.

Within the sphere of planning, physical planning (*planirovka*) was mostly
important because the physical planning agencies (*Giprogorstroi* and its branches)
were responsible for meeting production targets in housing construction (Bater,
1980; Andrusz, 1984; Frolic, 1972). Urban design was much lower on the agenda
and the same holds true for planning as the search for better spatial organization
(Frolic, 1972; Hough and Fainsod, 1979). Specialized design institutes existed, but
they often played a role close to that of an experimental research station for civil
engineering. "Good, safe jobs, not supposed to be consequential," one architect
reflected. The most influential research institute, according to all voices heard,
was the Moscow institute where building norms (the so-called SNIP, *Stroitel'nye
normy I pravila*, e.g., USSR council 1976) were established. The construction
codes (extending to street and neighborhood design) determined the appearance
of most Soviet city spaces (French and Hamilton, 1979; Shaw, 1991). So, despite
relative marginality of planners, cities still had a "planned look." In the survey
results from this study, many respondents did appreciate the "clean look of the
Soviet places," albeit finding them "boring."

With the emphasis on production targets came a very uneven quality of construction and planning (Shaw, 1991). Some neighborhoods were mere collections of apartment blocks, devoid of services, lacking even elementary landscaping and streetscape. There, city and countryside overlapped in the most literal sense; high-rise buildings were simply dumped in the countryside and "the chickens still roamed freely in the unfinished green spaces" (interviews and observation). Other neighborhoods did receive some services, like a neighborhood school or a pharmacist, but lacked easy connections with the city center. Extension of the metro system was too expensive. "You knew where to apply for, which places were better, but you couldn't always get in," several older academics declared. The quality of planning and construction were not always correlated either. Some neighborhoods were poorly planned, but had sound and safe buildings ("ugly but rock-solid," according to a group of architecture students), while others were well planned but lacked well-constructed buildings (Bater, 1980).

In terms of spatial structure, seven decades of Soviet rule stretched Tbilisi even further along the Mtkvari River (Ziegler, 2006). There is no ring road, and traffic was already a problem before independence. In the narrow valley, river, railroads, highways, and local roads have to share space. Some newer Soviet neighborhoods moved up into the highlands, still generally in an east–west corridor, and with very poor connectivity ("No way to get there," "can take hours"). In the last Masterplan there were ideas about a possible expansion around the artificial lake called "Tbilisi Sea," altering the elongated city form, but this never happened. The focus on new construction (as opposed to preservation and renovation), combined with poor access and quality of the far-flung new developments, led to a clear local preference for the late imperial and early Soviet neighborhoods, between old town and fringe (Gachechiladze, 1995; Salukvadze, 2009). The neighborhoods of Vera and Vake are the most famous examples, deemed desirable under the Soviets, and up to the present day (Gachechiladze, 1990; Van Assche et al., 2009).

The old town, meanwhile, has received some attention since the 1970s, because of local activism, good connections with Moscow, and "some Russian willingness to listen to arguments about the heritage of a small and old Christian nation to the south." Georgian architects were active and influential in Kiev Rus, contributing greatly to the style of twelfth- and thirteenth-century Russian architecture (Brumfield, 1997; Velmans and Alpago Novello, 1996). Georgian history was well known in Russia, and, last but not least, Russians enjoyed their vacations (and "work vacations" according to a geographer) in Georgia. On the part of the Georgians, heritage protection was a relatively safe way to foster the national identity. Tbilisi (with Kiev) took a lead in the heritage protection movement in the USSR, and since the late 1970s, some parts of the old town have been preserved, renovated, and rebuilt (Ziegler, 2006; Baulig et al., 2004; Baburov, 1977; French, 1995).

After independence

The collapse of the USSR had profound implications for the development of Tbilisi. Large projects were hard to envision in the absence of the resources and organizational capacity of the USSR. "The spoils of empire" (words of a diplomat) were hard to come by after the empire crumbled. Tbilisians left the country, to be replaced, largely, by new arrivals from the countryside, where agriculture completely failed for about a decade (Gachechiladze, 1995; Vardosanidze, 2000). With that segment of the urban population, much economic, social, and intellectual capital disappeared. Small projects were quicker to pick up, due to rapid privatization of apartments and the emergence of a new actor, the developer. In the 1990s, development was largely unregulated ("chaos"), small scale, and marked by low construction quality ("people didn't know how to build anymore"), shady financial deals, and hit-and-run strategies. These sentiments were expressed in many interviews, and evident from direct observation, and it is hardly surprising, since in the 1990s, Georgia was in reality a failed state. Several regions were de facto independent, and the government could not provide safety and basic services to the citizens (Steavenson, 2004). Tbilisi was a dangerous place for several years (especially 1992–94), when private militia roamed the streets, and sometimes, the president was forced to make deals with even the tiniest interest groups (Suny, 1995; Steavenson, 2004). One can imagine easily that development could hardly take off in this risky environment, let alone regulated development. Because capital was so hard to come by for developers, as well as for home buyers, a mortgage market was non-existent and development almost by definition relied on black market capital and shady connections.

The development pattern that slowly emerged in these years, which accelerated after 2000, and even more after the Rose Revolution in 2003, is sometimes called "investor urbanism" (Ziegler, 2006). What is left of government planning is located at the city level, but the few planners that are actually at work there have little influence on the larger projects ("why do you even talk to them?" an architect wondered). Investors with political connections and politicians with real estate connections in all likelihood take the big decisions, on large projects devoid of long-term strategies (Gallina, 2010; Allina-Pisano, 2008). In 2009, after many tribulations, a new Master-plan was adopted, but up to the time of writing its impact seems minimal.

The resulting development pattern is one of extreme densities in already desirable neighborhoods, like Vera and Vake. Risk was deemed low there, quality of living high. Unfortunately, because of a lack of regulations, the problems with "investor urbanism" are most pressing in these prestigious neighborhoods (Shavishvili, 2004). In the last few years, some restrictions have been placed on land use (a land use plan for the central city was implemented in 2005) but even so, subdivision regulations are not adopted. That means that even cases where the 2005 land use plan and the 2009 Master-plan are followed, the quality of urban design can be very poor. Parking space is scarce, sewer systems inadequate ("can you imagine they didn't even upgrade them?," a resident asked rhetorically), access unclear, public spaces, especially green space, too rare ("all taken out, no money in them"). The privacy screening of many new buildings is also problematic (but "at least now I can see my neighbor taking a shower"). Even when Soviet plans were usually not fully implemented, these issues were usually handled adequately, "boring, but everything worked," according to some older residents (French, 1995; Bater, 1980).

In addition, open spaces, or spaces that could be cleared relatively easily, between the historic districts and the newer Soviet areas, are the victim of "investor urbanism." Here, the possibilities for larger volumes and the prox-imity to the attractive areas, create the draw. Open spaces and spaces unused in the often wasteful Soviet land use (Gachechiladze, 1990; Salukvadze, 2009), attracted attention, but also spaces with a small number of institutional (and not too well-connected) users were targeted ("We'll see how long we last here," an NGO director wondered). In the 1990s, even parks were not safe, but the public outcry that resulted did motivate the political elite to step on the brakes in these cases. Also, construction quality seemed to have improved since that chaotic era ("although some of that [1990s construction] is waiting to collapse," several architects noted). The relative stability since 2000 reduced the hit-and-run

Green areas

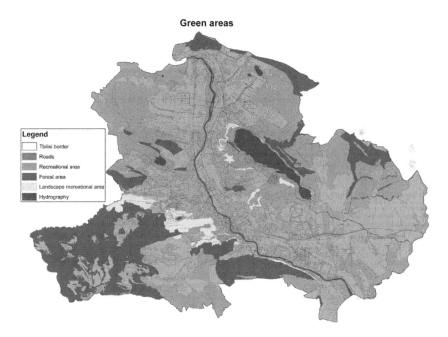

Legend
☐ Tbilisi border
▨ Roads
▨ Recreational area
▨ Forest area
☐ Landscape recreational area
▨ Hydrography

Figure 5.4 Green areas. Tbilisi is a green city, partly owing to the communist interest in green public spaces, partly due to the natural landscape that makes construction difficult in many places, a landscape that has also been appreciated and preserved since the middle ages. Image courtesy of Joseph Salukvadze.

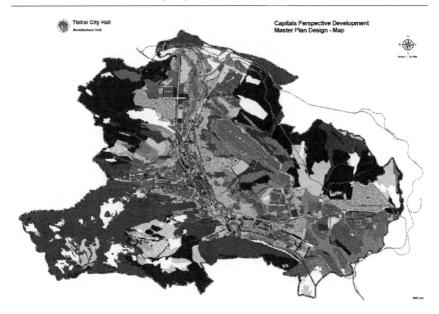

Figure 5.5 The Master-plan adopted in 2009, the fourth, represents a democratic compromise after a long struggle at various levels of government, after a long search for a new meaning of "planning" after communism. Darker areas around the edge comprise 5 per cent and are to be saved for green/public spaces. Image courtesy of Joseph Salukvadze.

strategies of developers, and forms of self-organization and self-regulation in the developers' guild contributed to the improvement ("we had to do something ourselves," said a developer).

Since 2000, historic Tbilisi, the old town, enjoys a form of protection, under the form of a special land use ordinance. According to most sources, that ordinance is more strictly enforced than the 2005 land use plan and the 2009 Master-plan. Combining old and new buildings in a harmonious manner is a consistent topic of conversation, often controversy, among architects and critical intellectuals, but also among politicians, developers, and in society at large (Van Assche and Duineveld, 2006). Old Tbilisi is an important symbolic space for Georgia, a place with a high density of historical buildings and many markers of national identity (Shatirishvili, 2009). Densities were always high and the urban fabric intricate in the maze of courtyards and balconies. The special ordinance, together with very complicated divided ownership of many buildings, protected most historic neighborhoods against ruthless redevelopment. At the same time, the very same legal complexity, in conjunction with the poor condition of most houses, makes renovation costly and reinvestment risky.

The more recent (1960–1990) Soviet developments generally lacked reinvestment and reinvention ("Nothing happens there and it won't for a long time," a developer shared). It would probably take a consistently enforced vision for the

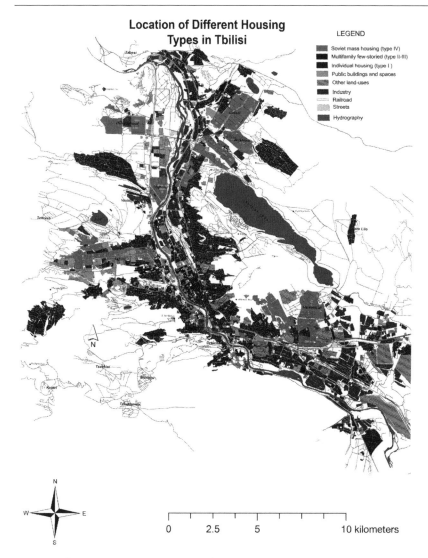

Figure 5.6 The current spatial structure of Tbilisi. Most of the city space is dominated by residential high rises, a communist legacy. Fortunately, much public space, old and more recent, has survived. Image courtesy of Joseph Salukvadze.

whole city to direct investment to the fringes, but this seems unlikely in the near future. Now defunct industrial complexes within the city limits negatively affect the quality of life in adjoining Soviet-era neighborhoods. They offer formidable challenges (and opportunities) for redevelopment, but once again, this would require a long-term vision and a scale of investment that can only come from a government interested in spatial planning. Outside the old city limits (in a few cases inside the new 2007 city limits) some suburban development can be observed. These are mostly gated communities at a modest scale (Sulukhia, 2009). Further away, in the mountains and sometimes on the coast, the more prosperous strata in society own their *dachas* or summer homes. Tbilisi can be quite empty in the hot summer months. There is some upscale development in a few recreational suburbs (like Tskhneti, Tsavkisi), but the scale is relatively small.

New players on the scene

Moscow disappeared behind the horizon for planners. In the Soviet period, there was no proper planning education in Georgia. Several Georgian architecture and engineering programs were highly regarded all over the Union, but urban/town planning was taught only in a few Russian graduate programs. With the collapse of the Union, that connection disappeared. The influence of architecture in spatial organization increased, since many new developers had an architectural background, and because large-scale planning as such was nonexistent.

With that, a new influential actor was introduced: *the developer.* With the improvement of financial markets, the size of projects grew (Shavishvili, 2003; Sulukhia, 2009). As mentioned before, the developers opted for self-organization and self-regulation before the government stepped in and imposed its rules. According to the researchers' (2006) survey, and more recent interviews, people still have great trust in developers, even if they don't like much of the development they see. Many developers, especially in recent years, were not opposed to planning. Hit-and-run strategies became less prevalent now than in the 1990s, according to most observers; "you'll have to deal with the same people again" a developer reflected. Developers hoped to be in business for a long time, and knew then that reputation counts. They were also aware of the fact that the actions of other developers impact the quality of life—and therefore real estate values—in neighborhoods they hoped to work in. It was acknowledged that coordination and regulation can protect and create value, reflecting on how early American zoning was initiated by economic elites.

Developers also employed many young architects. For them, western architecture, in all its modernist and post-modernist variations, and to a lesser extent Georgian traditional architecture, was the main source of inspiration. At architecture schools, in discussion groups, and through exchange programs or study abroad, many of them were very well informed about the latest trends and award-winning projects. The internet was also a great leveler, since architectural magazines and travel are expensive. Often through these young employees, but not exclusively, ideas on urban design are introduced. Several projects now underway show influences of Dutch, Scandinavian, and Spanish urban design. Occasionally, foreign architects participate in development projects, especially when supported by the national government.

A western orientation in design does not, however, signify a western-inspired financing structure, or western-style regulatory environment. For a Georgian developer, rules and regulations are more flexible than for European or American counterparts. Unpredictability is also higher, making investment riskier (and more stressful). Sometimes, Soviet-era rules or norms are imposed again, or suddenly and selectively, the letter of the recent law is followed ("What the f . . .?! Now that's the game?," we overheard several times). In some cases, law enforcement could be selective, depending on, among other things, the interests and mutual positioning of elite members (shifting connections and relations). For financing, developers are dependent on banks that are still not as reliable as western banks, less stable, and more expensive. An alternative is to work with private investors. In that case, there are usually political connections, few questions asked, and few rules imposed.

Citizens are rarely heard, both in the Soviet planning systems and in the new developer-driven system (Vardosanidze, 2009). New coalitions of actors take decisions, and the free market, ideally a rich source of signals about citizen's preferences (Kornai and Rose-Ackerman, 2004), is not as free as it seems. The new elite, with foreign (and pseudo-foreign) investors, determines supply and demand becomes even less relevant when a significant part of new developments is not meant to be inhabited, but acquired to launder money or for speculative purposes. Citizens are often critical about Soviet planning, but they do expect the government to guarantee a high-quality living environment. In other words, they do expect a form of planning.

Conclusion

In Tbilisi, the urban problems that have emerged since independence could be addressed by means of urban planning and urban design strategies. Urban design, however, cannot be part of a consistent strategy if it is not embedded in a planning framework, and planning cannot be consistent and legitimate outside the context of democratic institutions (Van Assche et al., 2010; Kornai and Rose-Ackerman, 2004). Separation of powers, in all its facets, is a precondition for institution-building that can allow for planning to re-emerge. Mitchell (2009) speaks of a false dichotomy created by the current regime between state building (new laws and organizations, now) and building democracy (maybe later). The authors concur, and consider revamped laws and governmental organizations only useful if they function in a framework of democratic decision-making. The intricate checks and balances that come with a clear separation of powers are integral to the success of any planning system that would be opted for, whether it be an American-style property model (currently the professed one), or a more social-democratic model of community visioning.

Coming back to the question of specificity, the authors argue that the new role of the developer has acquired a very specific character in Tbilisi. Developers are, more than in other transitional countries, influenced by the values and appreciations of the architecture profession, and the special attention of the president. In addition, the relatively small size of the developers' community makes reputation and a long-term vision important. Thus, a reinvention of planning is in the making, perhaps paradoxically, because it comes from the guild of developers rather than from the national government, operating on a mix of neo-liberal policies, pride of place, and suspicion of local government. Autonomous municipal planning or participatory planning, involving citizens more directly, could not be observed. Recent developments, especially the successful 2010 municipal elections, do inspire hope for stronger local governments, and, with that the inclusion of different voices and a gradual separation of powers.

References

Allina-Pisano, J. (2008) *Post-Soviet Potemkin villages: Politics and property rights in the Black Earth*, Cambridge: Cambridge University Press.

Anderson, L. (1999) *Transitions to democracy*, New York: Columbia University Press.

Andrusz, G. (1984) The built environment in Soviet theory and practice. *International Journal of Urban and Regional Research*, 11, 478–98.

Andrusz, G., M. Harloe, and I. Szelenyi (Eds.) (1996) *Cities after socialism: Urban and regional change and conflict in post-socialist societies*, Oxford: Blackwell.

Baburov, A. (1977) *Historic cities of Georgia: Some aspects of preservation*, Tbilisi. Academy of Sciences of Georgian SSR.

Bater, J. (1980) *The Soviet city: Ideal and reality*, London: Edward Arnold.

Baulig, J., M. Mania, H. Mildenberger, and K. Ziegler (2004) *Architekturfuhrer Tbilisi*, Kaiserslautern: Technische Universitat Kaiserslautern.

Boren, T., and M. Gentile (2007) Metropolitan processes in post-communist states: An introduction. *Geografisker Annaler B*, 89, 95–110.

Brumfield, W. C. (1997) *A history of Russian architecture*, Cambridge: Cambridge University Press.

Elster, J., C. Offe, and U. Preuss (1998) *Institutional design in post-communist societies*, Cambridge: Cambridge University Press.

French, R. (1995) *Plans, pragmatism and people: The legacy of Soviet planning for today's cities*, Pittsburgh: University of Pittsburgh Press.

French, R., and F. Hamilton (Eds.) (1979) *The socialist city: Spatial structure and urban policy*, Chichester: Wiley.

Frolic, B. (1972) Decision making in Soviet cities. *American Political Sciences Review*, 66, 38–52.

Gachechiladze, R. (1990) Social-geographical problems of a metropolitan region within a Soviet republic (A case study of the Tbilisi metropolitan region, Georgia). *Geoforum*, 21, 4, 475–82.

Gachechiladze, R. (1995) *The new Georgia: Space, society, politics*, London: UCL Press.

Gallina, N. (2010) Puzzles of state transformation: The cases of Armenia and Georgia. *Caucasian Review of International Affairs*, 4, 1, 20–34.

Higley, J., and G. Lengyel (2000) *Elites after state socialism: Theories and analysis*, Lanham, MD: Rowman & Littlefield.

Hough, J., and M. Fainsod (1979) *How the Soviet Union is governed*, Cambridge, MA: Harvard University Press.

Huzinec, G. (1978) The impact of industrial decision making upon the Soviet urban hierarchy. *Urban Studies*, 15, 2, 139–48.

Kornai, J., and S. Rose-Ackerman (Eds.) (2004) *Building a trustworthy state in post-socialist transition*, New York: Palgrave.

Lang, D. M. (1957) *The last years of the Georgian monarchy*, New York: Columbia University Press.

Lang, D. M. (1966) *The Georgians*, London: Thames & Hudson.

Ledeneva, A. (2006) *How Russia really works: The informal practices that shaped post-Soviet politics and business*, Ithaca, NY: Cornell University Press.

Manning, P. (2007) Rose colored glasses? Color revolutions and cartoon chaos in post-Socialist Georgia. *Cultural Anthropology*, 22, 2, 171–213.

Manning, P. (2009) The city of balconies: Elite politics and the changing semiotics of the post-socialist cityscape. In K. Van Assche, J. Salukadze, and N. Shavishvili (Eds.) *City culture and city planning in Tbilisi: Where Europe and Asia meet*, Lewiston, NY: Mellen Press.

Mitchell, L. A. (2009) Compromising democracy: state building in Saakashvili's Georgia. *Central Asian Survey*, 28, 2, 171–82.

Pallot, J., and D. Shaw (1981) *Planning in the Soviet Union*, London: Croom Helm.

Rhinelander, L. (1972) *The incorporation of the Caucasus into the Russian empire: The case of Georgia*, PhD dissertation, Columbia University.

Ruble, B. (1995) *Money sings: The changing politics of urban space in post-Soviet Yaroslavl*, Washington, DC: Woodrow Wilson Center Press/Cambridge University Press.

Salukvadze, J. (1995) New trends in the urban land-use management in the transition period. *Proceedings of the II British-Georgian Geographical Seminar*, London–Birmingham–Oxford, 28 June–5 July. Tbilisi.

Salukvadze, J. (2009) Market versus planning? Mechanisms of spatial change in post-Soviet Tbilisi. In K. Van Assche, J. Salukadze, and N. Shavishvili (Eds.) *City culture and city planning in Tbilisi: Where Europe and Asia meet*, Lewiston, NY: Mellen Press.

Shatirishvili, Z. (2009) National narratives, realms of memory and Tbilisi culture. In K. Van Assche, J. Salukadze, and N. Shavishvili (Eds.) *City culture and city planning in Tbilisi: Where Europe and Asia meet*, Lewiston, NY: Mellen Press.

Shavishvili, N. (2003) View from Tbilisi: Georgia's painful transition from Soviet republic to independent state is chronicled in its architecture. *The Architectural Review*, 1275 (May): 32–3.

Shavishvili, N. (2004) Vake is not a residential district. *Caucasus Matsne*, 3, 112–17.

Shaw, D. (1991) The past, present and future of the Soviet city plan. *Planning Perspectives*, 6, 2, 125–38.

Steavenson, W. (2004*) Stories I stole*, New York: Grove Press.

Sulukhia, T. (2009) Suburbanization in Tbilisi: Global trend in local context. In K. Van Assche, J. Salukadze, and N. Shavishvili (Eds.) *City culture and city planning in Tbilisi: Where Europe and Asia meet*, Lewiston, NY: Mellen Press.

Suny, R. G. (1994) *The making of the Georgian nation*, Bloomington: Indiana University Press.

Suny, R. G. (1995) Elite transformation in late-Soviet and post-Soviet Transcaucasia, or: What happens when the ruling class can't rule? In Timothy J. Colton and Robert C. Tucker (Eds.) *Patterns in Post-Soviet leadership*, Boulder, CO: Westview Press.

Taubman, W. (1973) *Governing Soviet cities: Bureaucratic politics and urban development in the USSR*, New York: Praeger.

USSR Councils of Ministers, State Committee for Civil Construction (1976) *Construction norms and regulations: Design norms*, Moscow: Stroyizdat Press.

Van Assche, K., and M. Duineveld (2006) On context, harmony and Tbilisi, Kamara. *Annual Journal of Georgian Technical University Faculty of Architecture*, 6, 2, 100–9.

Van Assche, K., J. Salukvadze, and N. Shavisvili (Eds.) (2009) *City culture and city planning in Tbilisi: Where Europe and Asia Meet*, Lewiston, NY: Mellen Press.

Van Assche, K., G. Verschraegen, and J. Salukvadze (2010) Changing frames: Citizen and expert participation in Georgian planning. *Planning Practice and Research*, 25, 3, 377–95.

Vardosanidze, V. (2000) Georgian culture and urbanization. *Urban Design Studies*, 6, 105–15.

Vardosanidze, V. (2009) Social dimensions of urban development in post-soviet Georgia: The quest for participatory planning in shattered social landscapes. In K. Van Assche, J. Salukadze, and N. Shavishvili (Eds.) *City culture and city planning in Tbilisi: Where Europe and Asia meet*, Lewiston, NY: Mellen Press.

Velmans, T., and A. Alpago Novello (1996) *Miroir de l'invisible: Peintures murales et architecture de la Georgie*, Melleray: Zodiaque.

Wheatly, J. (2005) *Georgia from national awakening to Rose Revolution: Delayed transition in the former Soviet Union*, Berlin: Ashgate.

Wilson, A. (2005) *Virtual politics: Faking democracy in the Post-Soviet world*, New Haven, CT: Yale University Press.

Ziegler, K. (2006) *Stadtebau in Georgien: vom sozialismus zur Marktwirschaft*, Kaiserslautern: Kaiserslautern University Press.

Chapter 6

Urban indicators for border areas

Measuring and tracking community conditions in the U.S.–Mexico border region

David Pijawka, Subhrajit Guhathakurta, Edward Sadalla, Kimberly Collins, Mihir Prakash, and Devon McAslan

Introduction

The border region between the United States and Mexico reflects many of the problems stemming from globalization and bi-national boundary issues. Such problems confront most border regions and often reflect asymmetrical development, but they are nearly always indicative of rapid urban growth rates coupled with cycles of economic imbalances and fluctuations (Anderson and Gerber, 2007; Collins, 2006). In most border areas, despite wide-scale regional cooperative agreements, there are serious governmental inabilities to manage cross-boundary air and water pollution and monitor the health of bioregions and watersheds that transcend national boundaries. Moreover, multi-national socio-political issues are also common in border regions across the globe that include illegal cross-border migration, regional markets with clogged transportation flows, inadequate local infrastructure, drug traffic, and the lack of capability to regulate the significant flow of goods. Migration overflow problems require substantial policy attention in most border regions (Collins, 2006).

As expected, the post-NAFTA (North American Free Trade Agreement) era in the U.S.–Mexico urban border has led to freer movements of goods, industrial investment in northern Mexico by international firms, and improved bi-national environmental regulations. However, the last two decades have seen the emergence of myriad serious urban problems that decrease the quality of life in the border communities. Few systematic studies have been conducted regarding how these changes in urban conditions along the border affect the quality of life of residents in trans-border communities. Furthermore, few models exist for measuring quality of life impacts in border communities and their longitudinal monitoring.

This chapter is based on the results of a five-year effort of the *Border Observatory Project* to develop, collect, and interpret data for eight border communities (four sister cities on each side of the boundary) comprising the U.S.–Mexico border region. Using both objective and subjective indicators, it offers a framework for

Quality of Life (QoL) assessments and policy development that can be applied to other border regions of the world. The data are in the form of QoL indicators such as economic well-being, social conditions, public and health services, environmental threats, and emotional well-being. This chapter reports on QoL indicator data collected and analyzed for the *Border Observatory Project* which includes both objective indicators (e.g., levels of air and water pollution, crime rates, availability of and access to health facilities, and other factors), and subjective data (e.g., perceived levels of satisfaction living in a particular community). The subjective data were obtained from conducting household surveys of residents in each of the eight cities. The sample of households for individual city surveys was carefully selected as a basis used to extrapolate to the entire population of each city. To date, data were also obtained from longitudinal, repeat, follow-up surveys for four cities. The subjective data reflect residents' perceptions of quality of life in their respective communities along multiple dimensions.

The QoL indicators used in this research were derived from a review of academic studies of quality of life in different parts of the world. Previous QoL studies in the border region have been funded by the U.S. Environmental Protection Agency, the United Nations, and Mexico's SODESOL, but until the present study, no program has collected or developed systematic QoL indicator data for the entire urban border and over time. Such data are crucial for informed decision-making and urban planning. The *Border Observatory* has collected longitudinal data in order to document differences among urban areas based on size, demographics, and side of the border. We assess which border cities are doing well and which indicators of quality of life are improving or declining. Importantly, this research utilized both objective and subjective QoL indicators. The ability to demonstrate through a set of comprehensive indicators how one bi-national border region is doing over time may serve as a model to evaluate border regions elsewhere – especially in cases where there are dissimilar data and variant geographical scales of governmental reporting.

Concern about the present and future quality of life for residents of the U.S.–Mexico border region has emerged as a salient policy issue in both countries. One significant impediment to policy-making in the border region has been the lack of systematic and comparable QoL data for border cities. The *Border Observatory Project* was initiated to address this gap. Beginning in 2004, the *Observatory* began to collect data in eight communities in the border region, four on the Mexican and four on the U.S. side. These communities include: Ciudad Juárez; Mexicali; Tijuana; San Luis and Somerton, Arizona; El Paso; Calexico; the San Diego urban region; and San Luis Rio Colorado. The *Observatory's* objective is to obtain QoL data for each pair of sister cities in the region and to provide these data to decision-makers in a timely manner. The attributes of quality of life for which data were collected fall into 14 indicator groups. These include: (1) economic well-being, (2) accessibility to health facilities, (3) level of social integration, (4) environmental quality, and (5) emotional well-being and happiness, among others. The *Observatory's* longitudinal data permits decision-makers in these cities to identify what QoL indicators have changed over time, the direction of these changes, and their magnitude. The indicators from the longitudinal analysis can be used as measures of progress along QoL dimensions. As such, they can be utilized as drivers of urban policy, either to reverse deteriorating conditions or enhance successful existing programs.

The border region

The U.S.–Mexico border region is a unique bi-national region of the world because of its growing social, economic, and cultural integration. It is a complex and dynamic area with one nation representing a rapidly developing country; and the other a major industrialized global power. The region consists of four U.S. and ten Mexican states, with both small communities and large, complex, rapidly changing metropolitan areas. Despite current economic difficulties, rapid population growth continues unabated in the region from internal migration from Mexico and overflow from northern Mexico to the U.S. Unpredictable fluctuations in local economies are creating significant instabilities; the border communities have consistently experienced serious deficiencies in infrastructure provision.

These economic and demographic factors in the border region have seriously weakened the abilities of local governments to respond to pressing basic needs. As economic conditions worsen and the population climbs, finding resources for long-term solutions continues to be challenging. Crime rates are exploding in the larger Mexican border cities and high levels of air and water pollution continue across the border. Both past and future trends reveal significant challenges. The emergence of the maquiladora economic sector in the border has resulted in substantial immigration to the Mexican border states, with resulting population overflow problems in the U.S. border cities. Even with the large-scale employment generation that the maquiladora provides, immigration and related social and economic imbalances are apparent. The *colonias marginales* have grown in population and area extent, resulting in serious environmental problems that affect public health. The provision and maintenance of basic infrastructure have not been able to meet the needs of the dynamically growing population. In 2005, one population estimate had the border region at over ten million persons (Peach and Williams, 2000). By 2020, the population of this region is likely to double to 20 million people (Anderson and Gerber, 2007). The largest cities in northern Mexico have experienced the most rapid growth, and yet these cities have also experienced the most severe urban pathologies coupled with minimal, or even absent, abatement strategies.

In the last few years the ten northern Mexican states have seen economic growth decline due to global competition. Thus, the significance of the maquiladora as an income and employment generator is declining relative to the rest of the economy. These major fluctuations in local economies may exacerbate already vulnerable socio-economic, housing, and infrastructure vulnerabilities. In the border region, one institutional capacity factor is that the most southern U.S. counties (except for San Diego) are also the poorest in the U.S., experiencing both population

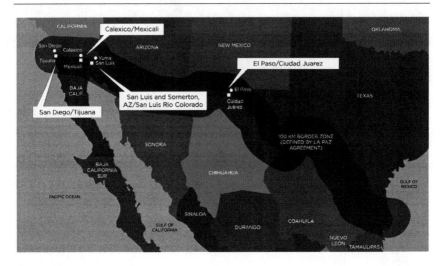

Figure 6.1 The U.S.–Mexico border region. Image courtesy of David Pijawka. 2011.

influxes from Mexico and infrastructure deficits resulting in large-scale environmental degradation.

Border indicators

During the last decade, several attempts have been made to develop indicators for the U.S.–Mexico border. The U.S. EPA established the largest set of indicators, but this program was suspended because of problems with the application of indicators. Not surprisingly, these problems have included issues of data availability, program implementation, data consistency in areas, and border data collection. These difficulties are known for most indicator programs and staying-power is a principal weakness for indicator programs in general and for the U.S.–Mexico region specifically.

Two other programs are additionally noteworthy. The first pertains to the efforts by SCERP (Southwest Consortium for Environmental Research and Policy) housed at San Diego State University to provide policy-relevant environmental data for the entire border region over the last 15-year period (Pijawka et al., 2003). Although topically important, the data are piecemeal, not systematic, and originally derived from specific unrelated research projects and programs at five U.S. and ten Mexican universities. While these data are available, they are not usable for border-wide monitoring of conditions, nor are the data suitable for longitudinal analysis. Further, there is a notable paucity of usable data on social conditions, infrastructure capacity, and community well-being. Another program source of data on QoL stems from the U.N.'s effort at comparing QoL indicators for cities around the globe (the U.N. Urban Observatory). This program is based on 45 agreed-upon indicators that have been applied to cities around the world. There are about 10–15 cities that are in this program in Mexico, but thus far are only available for two border communities – Mexicali and Tijuana. There is no evidence that these two programs provide longitudinal indicator data.

Before the *Border Observatory Project*, it was difficult to examine the U.S.–Mexico border region and evaluate whether it demonstrated improvement or deterioration (and in which areas). Available studies are few and use indicators that are not applied consistently, hence making comparative studies nearly impossible. New data collection efforts on environmental quality such as the *Border Environment 2012 Report* (2011) are piecemeal, often dependent on information that happens to be available. Furthermore, they are not based on relevant data that are needed or on systematic data that enable comparisons to be made over time and space. A systematic approach for the border region that incorporates all the urban areas, over time, and for a comprehensive set of urban conditions has not been developed except for the *Observatory*. One set of indicators showed promise – the study completed by Anderson and Gerber (2007) that used an adjusted United Nations Human Development Index for communities in the border originally established to measure progress at the national level. This use of national-based indicator metrics, however, lacked grounding in specific community-connected problems or in a regional policy context. These types of databases typically are limited to income and education metrics and cannot address the inherently more complex community-based problems that need resolution; they are best at providing crude indicators in terms of income or education and poverty levels and do not help in providing the bases for prescriptive remedies. A related issue pertains to the fact that border cities have not been compared longitudinally to determine what areas are doing well or deteriorating and why. There is some recent thinking about introducing different types of indicator frameworks at one place that can provide explanatory data for change in quality of life.

The basis for the border indicators

Although the use of statistical measurements as indicators can be traced back 200 years, their current use constitutes a hybrid of two distinct indicator movements: the community indicator movement of the 1980s and the sustainable development indicator movement of the 1990s. These two movements trace their lineage to indicator work done during the social and environmental movements of the 1960s and 1970s.

In the 1960s, an interest in social indicators developed, which stemmed from the success gained by economists in previous decades using economic indicators to guide the formulation of economic policy (Cobb and Craig, 1998). Many initially thought that social indicators should remain objective given the degree of success achieved by economic indicators. However, not all proponents of social indicators embraced this view. Some theorists argued that "social goals were more ambiguous than economic ones, social problems were less clearly understood, and the theoretical foundations of economics were much clearer than those underlying the analysis of social problems" (Cobb and Craig, 1998). The development and use of social indicators flourished in the 1970s but often had little effect on policy due to a failure to discern a link between indicators and the underlying causes of social problems.

Community indicators emerged in the 1980s to address QoL concerns, which incorporated not only social issues but also economic and environmental issues (Sawicki and Flynn, 1996). The term *community indicator* is a broad term for an indicator that measures any aspect of a community's well-being. Community indicators are "measurements of local trends that include all three dimensions of what it takes to build a healthy community – economic, environmental and social" (Redefining Progress, 1997). One of the main characteristics of community indicators is that they are created through a bottom-up approach – one that possesses high levels of stakeholder input and community participation. This approach developed in response to the deficiencies noted in previous indicators performed only at the national level and created with a top-down approach that often had minimal scalability at the local level.

In 1987, the concept of sustainable development was introduced as a new way of thinking about growth and development by integrating economic and social growth with concerns about environmental well-being and resource depletion. In 1992, the U.N. released *Agenda 21* which stated that "indicators of sustainable development need to be developed to provide solid bases for decision-making at all levels and to contribute to a self-regulating sustainability of integrated environment and development systems" (UNCED, 1992). *Agenda 21* helped to reignite national and local interest in indicator work, which was now focused on sustainable development goals. *Agenda 21* facilitated the development of a new type of indicator altogether – a *sustainability indicator.* Prior to this, indicators had been relatively simple statistical measurements that only measured a single variable. Sustainability indicators were multidimensional and recognized the linkages among the environment, society, and the economy. Innes and Booher (2000) noted that for indicators to be useful there must be not just opportunity, but there must be a concurrent requirement to report and publicly discuss the indicators in conjunction with policy decisions that must be made. To respond to this objective, we made our indicator reports and surveys publicly available, and established a web site for the purposes of public discourse. It was important that a systematic approach to QoL indicators in the border region be pragmatic and linked to urban policy.

The *Observatory's* 2010 report, *The State of U.S.–Mexico Border Cities* (Guhathakurta et al., 2010) was produced to ensure that the indicators are relevant *both* to the community and to policy (Levitt, 1998; de Vries, 2000; Innes and Booher, 2000; Miller, 2007). An indicator is relevant in that it "tells you something about the system you need to know and is meaningful to the community" (Redefining Progress, 1997). The indicator must also be appropriate for that community (Phillips, 2003). Another issue noted in the academic literature concerns the problem of measurement. Indicators must be measurable (Redefining Progress, 1997; Levitt, 1998; Leitmann, 1999; de Vries, 2001; Phillips, 2003). If the data to measure an indicator cannot be collected, then the indicator cannot be reported in the literature, on the web, and within other informational venues. The data should be already available as in the case of our objective indicators (Leitmann, 1999), or it should constitute a practical method for collecting the data (Redefining Progress, 1997). What to measure is the critical issue in indicator use; for this reason, we utilized a number of measurements for each indicator for internal validation purposes. Longitudinal indicator data are also critical, especially in the border areas as those conditions can change rapidly and require governmental responses. A number of researchers have commented that indicators need to have consistent and reliable time series data (Maclaren, 1996; Redefining Progress, 1997; Leitmann, 1999; Miller, 2007). Trends can provide indirect information about future conditions (Maclaren, 1996). Knowing whether a system is improving or worsening allows a decision-maker to improve the state of that indicator. In border studies of community conditions, indicators must be sensitive to change (Leitmann, 1999; de Vries, 2001; Miller, 2007).

QoL indicators are one of several "frameworks" falling within the conceptual or theoretical indicator types (Phillips, 2003). Quality of life is "the level of enjoyment and fulfillment derived by humans from the life they live within their local economic, cultural, social and environmental conditions" (Redefining Progress, 1997). Quality of life has been cited as the most frequently used conceptual framework for urban indicator programs (Redefining Progress, 1997). The early QoL indicator programs developed in response to the lack of success that social and environmental indicators had in local public policy making. They aimed to combine many dimensions of a community into a single, often comprehensive report. The *Border Observatory* is consistent with this goal.

An important aspect of QoL indicator programs is their employment of both objective and subjective indicators. Objective indicators are used to measure concrete aspects of systems and are based on observed statistical data (Santos and Martins, 2007). These observable and measurable phenomena include such divergent entities as air quality and crime levels. Subjective or perceptual indicators involve data collected through field surveys in which citizens are asked to estimate or evaluate various qualities (e.g., air quality, crime rates) within their living environments (Santos and Martins, 2007). Although subjective indicators offer important insight to the views of urban residents, it has been noted that they also can cause confusion among policy makers. This happens when "there are disparities between what people say they want and need and what the objective conditions indicate" (Dluhy and Swartz, 2006).

Border objective indicators

This section compares objective indicators for the eight communities in the U.S.– Mexico border region. The same measures are applied to all cities in the border.

Two sets of data were utilized for the objective indicators of quality of life for communities on both sides of the border. The first set had their basis in the United Nations' Human Development Index (HDI) that was modified for communities in the border region by Anderson and Gerber in their volume, *Fifty Years of Change on the U.S.–Mexico Border* (2007). The HDI was established by the U.N. to compare countries on human development factors, and included indices such as educational attainment, income, and health. Based on a Two-Sample T-test and data for 2000, we found significant differences between cities on each side of the border in the proportion of families below poverty given ($t = -4.03$, p 0.05) with Mexican cities having significant larger means. US cities had higher means when it came to income ($t = 4.46$, p 0.05), and education ($t = 8.46$, p 0.05) as well as in the health index. As objective indicators, these adjusted HDI measures proved to be an improvement because they could be applied systematically across most border cities to make comparisons, and they allowed for the observation of the magnitude of changes over time. However, they were prone to similar criticisms that characterized the HDI at the national level. That is, they provided a rather constrained indicator set in terms of providing a comprehensive and robust set of objective QoL indicators at the community level. With a focus on GDP it fails to assess how the revenues from economic growth are directed to real QoL factors. To address these limitations, we developed an alternative set of QoL objective indicators reflective of the wide array and key variables argued for in QoL community-based livability programs. The indicators include poverty rates, infant mortality, crime rates, number of schools per 100,000 population, high school completion rates, percentage of homes without water connections, number of physicians per 100,000 population, and several others.

Measures of Poverty. Three types of poverty measures are used in Mexico – nutritional, socio-economic, and "overall" poverty levels. The "overall' poverty measure is closest to the one employed in the U.S. for the percent living in poverty although the amount of income differs between the two countries on what defines the level of poverty. The "overall" poverty indicator in Mexico is defined as the "percent of people whose per capita household income is below the level necessary to cover consumption needs for nutrition, clothing, shelter, health, transportation, and education." The average "overall" poverty level for the four Mexican border cities in our study was around 25 percent. In contrast, the average poverty level for the four cities on the U.S. side of the border was 19.3 percent. The average for the U.S. cities in the border was lower but not by much. In fact, the poverty rate for the four U.S. cities in the border region was higher than the U.S. national average and for the states in which these cities are located. This is not a surprise as household incomes in the U.S. counties bordering Mexico are generally lower than elsewhere in the U.S.

The small community of San Luis Rio Colorado experienced the highest poverty level of the four communities studied in Mexico, with 41.1 percent of its 2005 population living in poverty. This was followed by Ciudad Juárez with a 33.4 percent poverty rate. However, the largest city in the border region, Tijuana,

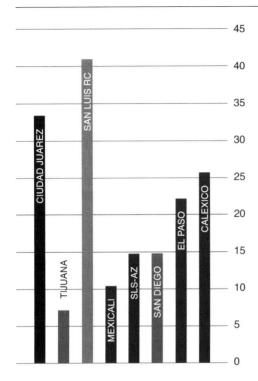

Figure 6.2 Poverty rates in the U.S.–Mexico border region. Image courtesy of David Pijawka. 2011.

had only 7.1 percent of its 2005 population living in "overall" poverty. Another low rate was the City of Mexicali, with a poverty rate of 10.3 percent. For the Mexican side of the border, poverty rates are not uniform; there are both high and low poverty rates, some lower than rates found on the U.S. side of the border. Overall, poverty levels in the border cities are relatively high even for the U.S. cities. Two of four cities in our study on the U.S. side had poverty levels at or above the study's average – El Paso and Calexico. The case of the sister cities, Calexico and Mexicali, is interesting in terms of their contrast on this measure. For a U.S. border community, Calexico experienced a relatively high level of poverty, 25.7 percent, in 2005. In contrast, Mexicali has a comparatively low level of poverty at 10.7 percent.

Infant Mortality. Infant Mortality (IM) per 1,000 live births is an important health-based indicator of quality of life. The average IM rates for the four Mexican cities in this study are around 21/1,000 live births. IM rates decrease substantially for U.S. cities: El Paso has an IM rate of 3.7/1,000 births and San Diego 5.4, respectively. Differences between U.S. and Mexican rates in the border region on this indicator are significant and certainly related to factors such as nutrition, health status, physicians' access, education of soon-to-be-mothers, among other factors.

These data corroborate the earlier IM measures from Anderson and Gerber (2007) and other sources of objective measures.

Health Care. Availability of physicians and access to health facilities is a fundamental factor in considering quality of life in any place. Here, we looked at two objective data sets: the number of physicians per 100,000 population and the number of hospitals and clinics per 100,000 population. The four cities on the Mexican side of the border averaged 100.8 physicians per 100,000 persons compared to 154 for the four cities on the U.S. side of the border. This represents a major difference in health care provision. Of the four Mexican cities, Ciudad Juárez ranks the lowest in terms of number of physicians, with 75 physicians per 100,000 persons, and Mexicali ranks at the top with 119 physicians. U.S. border cities are around 1.5 times better on this indicator than Mexican cities. Among the U.S. border cities considered, Calexico stands at the bottom of this indicator and San Diego at the top with 266 physicians for 100,000 persons. The best measure for health availability in a Mexican border community is less than the worst in our U.S. border database. The health availability indicator is much lower in the U.S. border cities compared to the U.S. national average, which is at 230 physicians per 100,000 persons.

Public Safety. The recent emergence of violent crime connected to drug trafficking, especially in Mexican border communities, has serious consequences

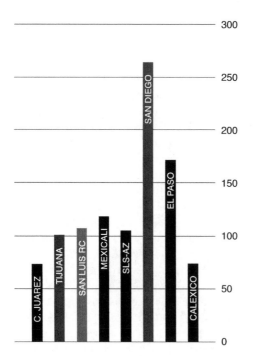

Figure 6.3 Physicians per 100,000 population. Image courtesy of David Pijawka. 2011.

for the quality of life in these communities. Violent crime rates are about five per 100,000 population on average in U.S. cities, including the U.S. border cities. Violent crime rates in Mexico as a whole are about 2.5 times those in the U.S. However, it is an entirely different matter for cities on the Mexican side of the border, with rates averaging 25 times those of U.S. border cities. In Ciudad Juárez alone, the violent crime rate reached 250 incidents per 100,000 persons in 2005. The surge of violent crime and the disappearance of women in Juárez have become international humanitarian issues.

Objective indicators of quality of life in the eight border communities show significant differences between communities on each side of the border on key indicators. On the whole, these indicators show lower QoL measures in the U.S. side of the border relative to the same measures for the U.S. as a whole and for the states in which the border communities are located. As corroborated by Anderson and Gerber (2007), QoL measures are generally better for Mexican border cities than the country as a whole. If these measurements are correct, we can expect a continuation of population movement from central to northern Mexico, including a related population overflow to the U.S. side.

Subjective indicators

Subjective indicators presented in the following pages are based on systematic household surveys of the eight border communities.

Personal Quality of Life. The overall "personal quality of life" in a place measures a person's subjective well-being as a holistic concept that subsumes many of the individual QoL components such as housing conditions, economic health, and crime, among others. This measure represents a summary judgment about the totality of life for the individual in that *place.*

The totality of people's lives in terms of QoL is quite distinct from the sum of their judgments about individual components. The subjective rating of their "overall personal quality of life" is measured on the basis of a nine-point scale, where 9 is excellent and 1 is a poor personal quality of life. Scores of 6 and 7 are indicative of fair to good ratings on this question. Only Ciudad Juárez falls below a score of 7 on overall quality of life, with a score of 6.4. The range of scores for personal quality of life is highly clustered from a low score of 6.4 to the highest score of around 7.4, a difference of only 1.0 on the 1 to 9 scale. Residents in all border cities expressed a fair to good personal quality of life in their respective cities. As a place to raise children, another summary QoL indicator, we did not observe pronounced low ratings for border cities except for Ciudad Juárez.

Education. In international surveys, the availability of adequate education is one of the most commonly used QoL indicators. As we have seen earlier, the United Nations Human Development Index uses just three indicators to rank countries collectively by level of human development – education, GDP, and life expectancy. The World Bank and other multilateral institutions now agree that investments in education are the new keys to economic development. It is well known that the

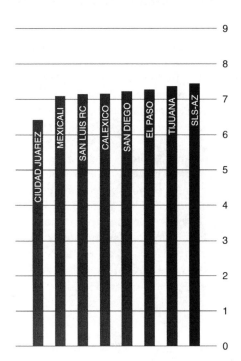

Figure 6.4 Overall quality of personal life. Image courtesy of David Pijawka. 2011.

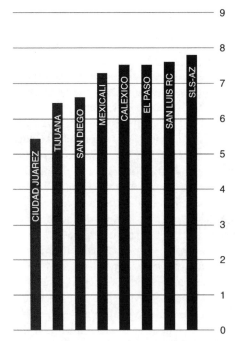

Figure 6.5 Rating places to raise children. Image courtesy of David Pijawka. 2011.

quality of education provided in public schools in the U.S. varies widely, and similar findings would be expected in Mexico. Earlier we evaluated objective indicators for educational achievement and access. The *Observatory* also explores residents' subjective satisfaction with schools and universities in the border region and the extent to which perceived education quality varies from city to city. When the question concerned the *quality of schools in their area for children*, differences among border cities were apparent. Residents of Ciudad Juárez were the least satisfied with their schools, followed closely by San Diego. Residents of San Luis Rio Colorado gave the quality of their children's schools the highest relative rankings. Largely because of the high levels of satisfaction in San Luis Rio Colorado, schools in the Mexico side of the border ranked higher on perceived quality than those on the U.S. side of the border.

Public Safety. The actual or perceived incidence of crime significantly influences an individual's sense of personal security. This sense of security is considered to be among the most vital components in the perception of quality of life. Where the daily news is dominated by drug-related violence and other serious crimes, public safety has become a serious concern both for residents and visitors. As expected from the subjective indicators on crime, five out of eight border cities rated crime as very serious and impacting their quality of life. Residents of two cities, Ciudad Juárez and El Paso, rated crime as an extremely serious problem with scores of less than 3.0 on a scale of 1 to 9, where 1 is worst and 9 the best. Residents of five out of eight cities rated the problem as under 4.0 – very poor conditions. Even the best ranked cities on crime, such as Calexico and San Diego, did not rate much above 6.0. Crime is a serious problem across the entire urban border, and for some cities, the most critical concern of the public in terms of quality of life. Of all the QoL indicators, "the problem of crime in your neighborhood" received the poorest ratings of all QoL indicators.

Public concerns over crime, especially in Mexican border communities, are also reflected in the objective indicators on crime, showing a very high incidence of *violent* crimes in several Mexican border cities. It is in the public safety domain that both the objective and subjective indicators align. The survey also specifically asked about "feeling safe walking home after dark." In this case, the higher the scores on the 1 to 9 scale, the safer people feel in their communities. *None* of the border city populations feel generally safe walking alone after dark in their neighborhoods. However, residents in Tijuana expressed the highest concern about risks of walking alone after dark with a score of just over 3.0. This ranking was followed by Ciudad Juárez and Mexicali, which showed ratings of between 4.0 to 5.0. People indicate they are somewhat less threatened in the U.S. border cities (walking alone after dark) compared to their counterparts south of the border.

Environmental Quality. Air and water quality are two serious environmental issues in the U.S.–Mexico border region because of notable disparities in environmental regulation and enforcement on the two sides of the border. Mexico and the U.S. share airsheds and watersheds and therefore necessarily also share either the adverse effects or the benefits of air and water quality. In our surveys, no one

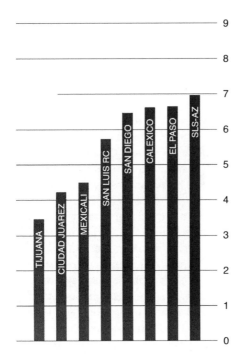

Figure 6.6 Feeling safe walking home after dark. Image courtesy of David Pijawka. 2011.

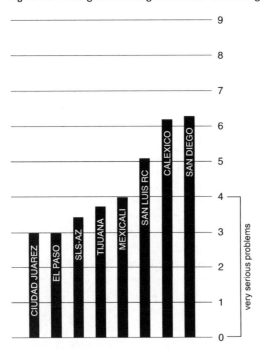

Figure 6.7 Seriousness of crime in border communities. Image courtesy of David Pijawka. 2011.

community rated air quality as very good or excellent (over 7.0). The range of responses is from 4.0 in Ciudad Juárez (poor quality) to around 7.0 (good) for both the San Diego area and San Luis and Somerton, AZ. Most of the cities in our survey – San Luis and Somerton AZ, El Paso, Tijuana, and Calexico – had scores between 5.0 and 6.0, relatively low on our barometer of public perceptions for air quality. If the ratings for air quality are generally poor, does this translate into concerns over residents' health? In this light, we asked residents in our surveys to rate their level of concern with the effect of local air pollution on their health. The community expressing the greatest concern was Ciudad Juárez. Not surprisingly, Ciudad Juárez also showed the poorest perceived level of air quality in our surveys.

Economy. The economic health of families and households has an inordinate influence on the quality of life given that the ability to enjoy many of the finer (i.e., non-survival) aspects of life is based on access to wealth and income. Economic status is usually measured in terms of availability of jobs, income potential, and economic product of a region. For this study we asked households about their satisfaction with their current economic condition, availability of jobs, and about their future expectations regarding economic security. The surveys show that residents of these communities are generally satisfied with their economic condition. Mexican citizens report on their economic well-being perceptions relative to the prevailing economy in Mexico and their life-long experiences. Most residents, regardless of their location, thought that their economic situation had

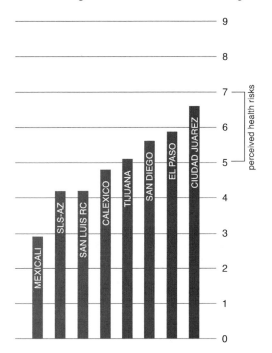

Figure 6.8 Perceived health risk from air pollution. Image courtesy of David Pijawka. 2011.

improved from the previous year and felt optimistic about even further improvement in the following year – 2008. Among the Mexican cities, the lowest level of satisfaction with the current economic situation was found in Ciudad Juárez. Residents of San Luis and Somerton, AZ, on the U.S. side, expressed low levels of satisfaction with their economic condition compared to other U.S. cities. These findings predate the economic crisis of 2008–10; hence, these results cannot be construed to reflect current conditions.

Happiness and Life Satisfaction. There has been recent interest in developing measures on "happiness" and overall "life satisfaction." The results from mostly survey-based research vary significantly, but all show substantial regional differences in happiness and life satisfaction. For example, the World Database of Happiness ranks how much people report enjoying their life on a scale from zero to ten. The findings were based on random samples of people from different countries from 2000 to 2008. In these surveys happiness ratings for Mexico were high (behind Iceland, Denmark, Colombia, and Switzerland) with an average rating of eight out of ten. Although Mexico's gross domestic product per capita pales in comparison to its northern neighbor, its residents' happiness ratings surpassed those in the U.S. (Veenhoven, 2006). The factors that make people happy typically vary from one country to the next. For example, personal success and self-expression are frequently reported as the most important contributors to happiness in the U.S., while in many Asian and Latino cultures, family cohesion and spending time with people you like tend to be valued more highly. The *Border Observatory Project* assesses happiness and life satisfaction in the U.S.–Mexico border region as important QoL indicators. We are interested in whether there are measurable differences among cities or between U.S. and Mexican cities in the border.

We collected ratings of "Life Satisfaction" on a nine-point scale where 9 indicated excellent and 1 indicated poor life satisfaction. Residents in seven of the cities reported fair to good ratings with scores near or above 7.0 and under 8.0. Ratings of Life Satisfaction in the eight border communities did not show any major differences based on the size of the communities or whether the communities were in Mexico or in the U.S. Our data on "Emotional Well-Being" indicate that border residents are generally happy with their daily lives. Generally, residents reported positive emotions, with an average rating of about 7 on a nine-point scale for the four different indicators of emotional well-being. Our surveys indicate that at an experiential level, there are few significant differences either in overall life satisfaction or in the emotional quality of life between the U.S. and Mexican border cities. However, despite high perceived ratings of "happiness," residents of border towns in Mexico indicated that they would find the quality of their lives much improved if they resided on the U.S. side of the border.

Implications for border policy

Based on longitudinal indicators data (Guhathakurta et al., 2010), we found that substantial declines in quality of life in the border region can occur rapidly, especially when no corrective action is taken. Most residents perceive weaknesses in local governmental responsiveness to problems. There certainly is room to enhance and improve QoL factors in the border cities. The five-year indicators study reveals that downturns can happen quickly with changes in local economies and without institutional capacities to build community resilience. The border is a dynamic place, and the implementation of focused, strategic actions can definitely improve conditions when they worsen. Inaction by government can very quickly lead to severe and adverse conditions concomitant with very long-term and sluggish recovery. The indicators data also reveal that some issues are well beyond local control and recovery (such as crime and environmental quality), and the redress of such problems will necessitate the involvement from extra-local governmental organizations. In terms of quality of life, the border communities both in the U.S. and Mexico are in a precarious balance. At around 6.0 on our nine-point subjective scale, quality of life is slightly on the upper half of the scale, but it is only barely so. The next step may be the entrenchment of long-term community imbalances unless institutional improvements can be made in governmental responsiveness to these problems. Yet the data demonstrate that local governments are under stress, and only partially responsive to an abundance of significant and often competing needs. Concerns over crime and the apparent lack of governmental responsiveness at the community level are principal public concerns that should drive local policy initiatives. These data indicate it is critically important that initiatives be taken to improve and expand local governments' capacity to respond to fundamental urban problems that already impact QoL in these eight communities.

The Border Observatory Project is a long-term, longitudinal study of both subjective and objective QoL indicators. It should be noted that the use of subjective QoL indicators to guide policy decisions has been controversial. Some scholars have suggested that measures of subjective well-being require additional research and refinement before they are used in the formulation of policy decisions. Others argue that the use of such measures is long overdue. The present project is based on the assumption that subjective measures are a necessary complement to objective QoL indicators. The data from this study clearly indicate that objective indicators are difficult to obtain given the absence of systematic and timely data at the same level of geographical aggregation. Some are only available with the decadal census that does not permit evaluations of changing conditions on any basis less frequent than decadal data. It should be kept in mind that subjectivity is what guides individual decision-making. For this reason, data on both objective and subjective indicators of QoL are useful as guides to policy in the border region. The *Border Observatory* has demonstrated indicator approaches for border regions that can be considered as urban areas become increasingly more complex. Given significant uncertainties and complexities in global transnational borders, longitudinal indicators are an appropriate tool for adaptive planning and management at the local and regional levels. New urban areas are forming around the globe and existing ones growing rapidly, especially in developing countries.

Bi-national regions with large urban populations and socio-political problems related to borders will have great needs to retool to be on top of emerging trends. The *Observatory* indicators described in this chapter may provide a useful model for identifying and tracking community conditions and their impacts on quality of life.

References

Anderson, J. and Gerber, J. (2007) *Fifty Years of Change on the U.S.–Mexico Border.* Austin, TX: University of Texas Press.

Cobb, C.W. and Craig, R. (1998) *Lessons Learned from the History of Social Indicators.* San Francisco CA: Redefining Progress.

Collins, K. (2006) "Local Government Capacity and Quality of Life in the U.S.–Mexican Border: The Case of Calexico and Mexicali," unpublished doctoral dissertation, El Colegio de la Frontera Norte.

De Vries, W.F.M. (2001) "Meaningful Measures: Indicators on Progress, Progress on Indicators," *International Statistical Review,* 69 (2): 313–31.

Dluhy, M. and Swartz, N. (2006) "Connecting Knowledge and Policy: The Promise of Community Indicators in the United States," *Social Indicators Research,* 79 (1): 1–23.

Gudmundsson, H. (2003) "The Policy Use of Environmental Indicators – Learning from Evaluation Research," *The Journal of Transdisciplinary Environmental Studies,* 2 (2): 1–12.

Guhathakurta, S., Pijawka, D., and Sadalla, E. (2010) *The Border Indicator Project: The State of U.S.–Mexico Border Cities.* Arizona State University and the Southwest Consortium for Environmental Research and Policy.

Innes, J.E. and Booher, D.E. (2000) "Indicators for Sustainable Communities: A Strategy Building on Complexity Theory and Distributed Intelligence," *Planning Theory and Practice,* 1 (2): 173–86.

Leitmann, J. (1999) "Can City QOL Indicators be Objective and Relevant? Towards a Participatory Tool for Sustaining Urban Development," *Local Environment* 4 (2): 169–80.

Levitt, R. (1998) "Sustainability Indicators—Integrating Quality of Life and Environmental Protection," *Journal of the Royal Statistical Society. Series A,* 161 (3): 291–302.

Maclaren, V.W. (1996) "Urban Sustainability Reporting," *Journal of the American Planning Association,* 62 (2): 184–202.

Miller, C.A. (2007) *Creating Indicators of Sustainability: A Social Approach.* Winnipeg, Manitoba, Canada: International Institute for Sustainable Development.

Peach, J. and Williams, J. (2000) *Population and Economic Dynamics on the U.S.–Mexico Border: Past, Present, and Future,* Austin, TX: CEDRA

Phillips, R. (2003) *Community Indicators.* Chicago, IL: American Planning Association.

Pijawka, D., Ganster, P., and Van Schoik, R. (2003) *Overcoming Vulnerability: An Environmental Research Agenda for the U.S.–Mexican Border Region.* San Diego, CA: San Diego State University Press.

Redefining Progress. (1997) *The Community Indicators Handbook: Measuring Progress Toward Healthy and Sustainable Communities.* Oakland, CA: Redefining Progress.

Redefining Progress. (2002) *Sustainability Starts in Your Community: A Community Indicators Guide.* Oakland, CA: Redefining Progress.

Santos, L.D. and Martins, I. (2007) "Monitoring Urban Quality of Life: The Porto Experience," *Social Indicators Research*, 80 (3): 411–25.

Sawicki, D.S. and Flynn, P. (1996) "Neighborhood Indicators," *Journal of the American Planning Association*, 62 (2): 165–83.

UN Habitat. (2001) *Global Urban Indicators Database*. Version 2. New York: United Nations.

UN Habitat. (2004) *Urban Indicators Guidelines: Monitoring the Habitat Agenda and the Millennium Development Goals*. New York: United Nations.

United Nations Conference on Environment and Development (UNCED). (1992) *Agenda 21*. New York: United Nations.

United Nations Department of Economic and Social Affairs (UNDESA). (2007) *Indicators of Sustainable Development*. New York: United Nations.

Veenhoven, R. (2006) World Database of Happiness. Erasmus University Rotterdam. Available at: http://worlddatabaseofhappiness.eur.nl

World Bank. (2006) *The Current Status of City Indicators: Part of a Study to Assist Cities in Developing an Integrated Approach for Measuring and Monitoring City Performance*. Prepared by Environmental Resources Management (ERM).

World Bank. (2007) *Global City Indicators: Definitions and Methodologies*. Prepared by Environmental Resources Management (ERM).

World Bank. (2008) *Global City Indicators Program Report: Part of a Program to Assist Cities in Developing an Integrated Approach for Measuring City Performance*. Prepared by Environmental Resources Management (ERM).

Part

D

The future of the metropolis

Chapter 7

Small steps toward achieving the urban sustainability of the metropolitan area of Mexico City

Desiree Martinez Uriarte

Introduction and background

Global concerns about the transformation of the planet and associated conse-quences such as climate change, loss of biodiversity, and social pressure concerning natural resources and inequality have triggered the need for a profound reflection on the history of these transformations. These transformations have been provoked by human activity that can be observed in the landscape and correspondingly in its many ecosystems. Understanding these processes may represent a first step in redefining our goals of achieving a more sustainable way of living. This chapter examines a number of small steps taken toward achieving urban sustainability in the metropolitan area of Mexico City.

The ecological history of the Basin of Mexico is a chronicle of one of the greatest ecological disasters in human history. What was once an endorheic basin occupied by five bodies of water, surrounded by mountains with forests of oak, pine, and oyamel fir, is now home to one of the world's largest and most densely populated examples of urban sprawl. The demand for resources and services, together with the waste produced by a population of more than 20 million people, has an impact that is felt far beyond the area itself.

Water once distinguished the area now comprising the Metropolitan Area of the Valley of Mexico (MAVM). However, inadequate water management is causing ecological and economic damage and is harming the quality of life of the inhabitants of both the MAVM and the regions from which the water is taken. Over-extraction of groundwater to supply 20 million people is destabilizing urban land, causing subsidence and many of the springs in the mountains around the basin to dry up. In other cases, sources of spring water have been enclosed. All this has altered conditions in the rain forests. The oyamel fir forests have been especially hard hit. About 40 percent of the water is lost through leakage, either at the time of extraction, in the pipelines, or in domestic plumbing.

A significant part of Mexico City's drinking water comes from outside the region from the Lerma and Cutzamala systems. The effects of pollution are also felt outside the region. The resulting scarcity of water in these regions is a source of economic hardship and social conflict. The sewage from the region is discharged into the

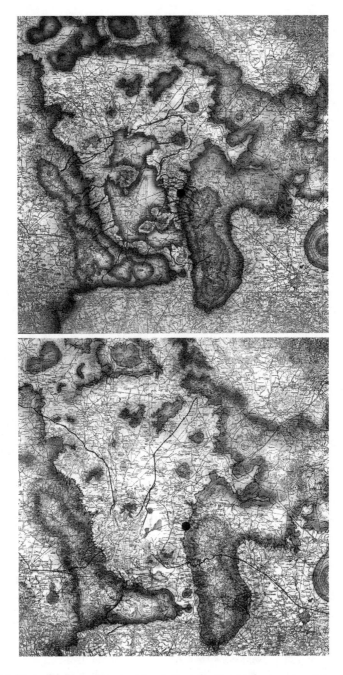

Figure 7.1 The area covered by the lakes before the Spanish conquest and the situation in the Metropolitan Area of the Valley of Mexico today. Image courtesy of Fernando Islas, 1999.

River Tula basin. The resulting pollution harms agricultural production, is a source of social conflict, and causes public health problems, all of which increases costs in the public and private sectors. The ecology of this neighboring basin has been radically transformed by the excess of polluted water as well.

At present, less than 10 percent of the water used in the MAVM is treated, and existing water treatment plants are operating at less than 60 percent of capacity. Its failure to implement a project supported by the Inter-American Development Bank to solve the sewage problem and thus comply with Official Mexican Ecology Standard NOM-ECOL-001-1996 has made the Mexico City Government liable for an annual fine of 700 million pesos (Instituto Nacional de Ecologia, n.d.). Much of the untreated sewage is discharged into ravines, rivers, streams, and canals, where it forms sources of infection with a high cost to public health. There is little justice in the way that water is used in the city. In some areas it goes to waste, in others it has to be supplied with water tankers at a far greater economic, physical, and social cost.

Added to the problems with water, air pollution also has negatively impacted public health and the quality of life in the MAVM and neighboring regions. In large measure, this is due to traffic congestion brought about by shortcomings in public transport and lack of city planning, forcing workers and shoppers to make long and frequent trips. It seems clear then that the MAVM is in a perilous situation, with high public health costs, environmental fines, public and individual costs caused by inefficient city planning, and above all, a dubious quality of life for its inhabitants. The state of the country's economy, and more specifically that of Mexico City and its surrounding conurbation, makes it highly unlikely that the massive expenditure involved in cleaning up the Basin will ever be made. In view of this, the proposals outlined in this chapter consist of small doable steps aimed at achieving an ultimate goal. Their starting point is sustainable city planning.

A sustainability proposal

The purpose of the proposal is to outline urban development measures that can lead to the gradual ecological recovery of the basin, greater sustainability, a more efficient city, and, above all, a better quality of life for all the inhabitants of the region. Specifically the plan targets the following issues:

- The creation of a Green Network based on existing and newly created green spaces and corridors
- Sustainable water management
- Waste management
- Economic energy use.

The environmental sustainability of an urban area is intrinsically linked to its efficiency. At present the MAVM is inefficient in the sense that its inhabitants are obliged to travel long distances in vehicles that are wasteful and by and large a source of pollution. This is why the plan is linked to a reorganization of land use and the introduction of comfortable, efficient, and environmentally viable public transport. The basis of the plan for land use is to organize the vast urban sprawl into 12 metropolitan sectors, each with a radius of about 8 km, which will offer the inhabitants similar opportunities of employment, commerce, recreation, relaxation, culture, health, and more. This reorganization will play an important role in sustainability by cutting distances traveled, reducing emissions of pollutants, and making the use of private cars less necessary. In this way, it will be possible to revive the pedestrian culture and encourage the use of alternative vehicles such as bicycles for journeys of up to 10 km (Islas et al., 2006). With the megalopolis reorganized into metropolitan sub-centers, the plan converts underused areas into a network of green and pedestrian areas with central preservation zones, broad pavements, parks and gardens, areas of historical interest, bodies of water, canals, and rivers.

The advantage of a network with a large number of linear spaces is that it occupies great length without taking up too much surface area and affords optimal accessibility. From an ecological point of view the green corridors provide habitat to a significant number of desirable native flora and fauna. They can also fulfill environmental functions (Hellmund and Smith, 2008).

The starting point for the plan is the present situation in the MAVM. It complies with the international collaboration agreements signed by Mexico, as well as the National Development Plan and local, state, municipal, and district plans and programs, all of which make sustainable or sustained development an essential part of policy. Among its features are sustainable development, reduction of the production of CO_2 to a minimum level, and protection of biodiversity. Mexico is one of the world's most biologically diverse countries and this strategy attempts to recognize the inherent characteristics of the landscape.

The plan also focuses on rescuing the cultural treasures of the MAVM, a region which at different times in its history was home to two of the most beautiful cities in the world, Tenochtitlan in pre-Hispanic times and the "City of Palaces" from the seventeenth to the nineteenth centuries.

A number of other important features are to be included in the implementation. First is reduction of the amount of space used for urban development (by encouraging "redensification" of currently developed urban land), urban rehabilitation, and improvement of the quality of life in areas where it is deficient. Industrial areas are to be redeveloped so that "clean" industries (technology, services, etc.) are mingled with residential areas for different income levels, as well as public, semi-public, and private green areas.

Second is cyclical water use, encouraging its collection, storage, treatment, and reuse. This involves encouraging the building of cisterns with autonomous collection and purification systems. Before being reincorporated into the cycle, sewage is to be treated at estate, block, or even building or house level. Fundamental to this is the reduction, and ideally the elimination, of the amount of sewage discharged into the drainage system, which at present carries its overflow into the

Figure 7.2 Proposed metropolitan sectors in the MAVM. Image courtesy of F. Islas, D. Martinez, and A. Alceda, 2006.

River Tula Basin. This also includes works to further the replenishment of the aquifers with rain water and to protect the rain water from pollution from sewage. Generally speaking, "closed cycles" are to be encouraged so that water can be collected and reincorporated into the aquifers at the same place.

Third is discouraging the use of private motor vehicles by encouraging efficient and comfortable public transport and also by reorganizing the city so that its inhabitants can find jobs, shops, services, education, health, and recreation within the 8 km radius of their sub-metropolis. Cutting distances to the sub-centers makes alternative means of transport feasible (e.g., bicycles along sub-metropolitan cycle paths). Walking is facilitated by creating pedestrian precincts with shopping, recreational, and cultural opportunities that improve the quality of life of the inhabitants of all the urban sub-centers.

Fourth is rescue and conservation of the varied historical and cultural facets of the MAVM by promoting artistic and cultural activities.

Fifth is improvement of the existing green areas and the creation of new areas in a spirit of ecological awareness. The green areas should be improved so that as far as possible they fulfill their environmental functions by increasing the capacity for collecting, storing, and refiltering water, for filtering dust and pollutants, and for producing oxygen, while fulfilling their functions as habitats for native flora and fauna, preferably for species native to the basin. The gradual replacement of non-native species is planned in accordance with management and maintenance programs.

Sixth is the creation of public space in green areas and corridors, centers of historical interest, shopping precincts, avenues, and linear parks with recreational, artistic and cultural, and sporting events. These encourage social development with an emphasis on integration, culture, family unity, democracy, and a social conscience.

Seventh, existing technology creates significant opportunities for environmental rehabilitation. Although this may call for substantial early investment, the technology will pay for itself within a reasonable period and the benefits for society (public health, social well-being, etc.) include the saving of other costs that may over time become unaffordable (including environmental fines).

Green networks and ecological rehabilitation

The development of a green network is an important dimension of ecological rehabilitation of the MAVM. To accomplish this, the series of actions to be taken include:

- Ecological rehabilitation and adaptation of ravines and bodies of water (reservoirs, lakes, canals, rivers) for recreational purposes.
- Restoration of the Lake of Texcoco.
- Restoration, maintenance, and creation of green areas of importance for the metropolis:
  - Chapultepec
  - Bosque de Aragón
  - Important city parks (Naucalli, Tezozomoc, Tarango, Los Álamos, Bosque de Tláhuac, Bosque de Tlalpan, etc.).
- Design and implementation of management and maintenance programs and specific actions for ecological regeneration in conservation areas, ecological areas, protected natural areas, heritage sites, and others around the MAVM.
- Optimization of existing green areas (parks, gardens, central reservations, etc).
- Utilization of unused and underused areas, such as unused road space, wide pavements, and empty lots.

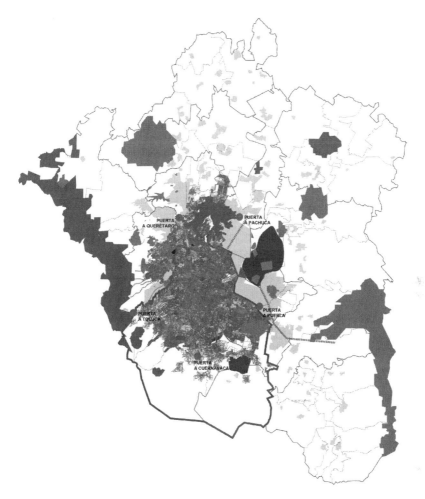

Figure 7.3 The proposed network of MAVM green areas. Image courtesy of F. Islas, D. Martinez, and A. Alceda, 2006.

- The creation of public, semi-private, and private green areas in new developments and urban restoration works.
- Restoration and pedestrianization to adapt historical sites for relaxation and cultural purposes.
- Restoration and maintenance of traditional avenues and promenades.

The network of MAVM green areas also includes the protected natural areas in the surrounding region. Inside the urban continuum it consists of neighborhood parks connected by linear parks set in the wide central reservations of the roads. The tree cover along the urban motorways can also be optimized. The ravines to the west link the forests in the mountains to the sprawling city. It is also important to restore the historical parks and avenues and to open the sites of historical interest to pedestrian use. The appearance of the access routes to the MAVM can be upgraded to make them more dignified with a complementary strategy.

The plan creates a network from the existing green areas by restoring their ecology, embellishing them, making them more comfortable in all seasons, and making them more pedestrian-friendly. Underused and waste land will be similarly improved (as specified in the objectives) and included in the network.

The system consists of the belt of protected natural areas, national and state parks, and agricultural and forest land surrounding the metropolis. It includes heritage sites such as Xochimilco and wetlands such as Tláhuac. The restoration of the basin of the former Lake of Texcoco will clearly be capable of contributing significantly to the restoration of lakes in the Basin of Mexico in the medium and long term.

Each metropolitan sector is to have an internal system of green areas, especially urban and neighborhood parks and central reservations that are connected to each other by regional corridors such as linear parks.

A fundamental part of the ecological restoration of the basin is the protection and restoration of the ravine area to the west of the MAVM. This will include the restoration of the reservoirs that receive a large amount of the runoff from the ravines and have great ecological and recreational potential.

The largest urban parks (e.g., Chapultepec, San Juan de Aragón, Bosque de Tlalpan, Parque Fuentes Brotantes, Parque Tarango, and Parque "los Álamos"), together with the medium-sized parks (Alamedas, etc.), neighborhood parks, and sports areas, are "green islands" which should be re-established to restore plant life, ecology, and social functions.

The MAVM contains a large number of historical sites and by heightening awareness of their culture, a sense of local identity among the inhabitants of the different metropolitan sectors will be created. The pedestrianization of the beautiful public areas will create places for culture and for people to meet.

The link between the "green islands" and pedestrian areas in the city will be achieved by:

- Using central reservations that are suitable for conversion into linear parks
- Restoring historical avenues and promenades and buildings of historical interest
- Restoring canals and rivers and routes that were formerly streams, canals, aqueducts, and rivers
- Creating promenades of contemporary design alongside the urban motorways and avenues with sufficiently wide pavements.

This approach creates possibilities for a great number of projects, some of which are listed and prioritized in this proposal. However, because of the size and complexity of the MAVM they can only be dealt with here in a general manner.

Both the government and civil society (specifically local residents and businesses) should play a role in the restoration, optimization, and creation of green areas. Their participation should be governed by general guidelines (laid down in the applicable regulations) and specific designs. It is essential that any businesses in the green areas make a real contribution to their optimization and maintenance.

The creation of new green areas in the MAVM is especially difficult in the central districts and towns within the urban continuum. Efforts in the outlying districts and towns should be focused on limiting urban expansion.

To increase the number of square meters per inhabitant in the central areas of the city a series of principles can be established and are described as follows:

- Development in former industrial urban areas that have been recycled (especially in underused corridors) should be linked to public and semi-public green areas and urban spaces.
- Recovery of mines as green areas.
- Areas that have not yet been developed should be consolidated as green areas with intrinsic environmental value.
- New road building should be accompanied by the creation of linear parks with paths for pedestrians and cyclists. Roads and paths must be made at the same time because experience has shown that if the landscape and paths are not done together with roads they are often postponed and are never done.
- Development and implementation of an urban reforestation program along treeless roads (e.g., urban motorways), planting Mexican species suitable for the urban climate, compacted soil and minimal water.
- Utilization of unused areas as green areas establishing neighborhood parks and green areas for local residents.
- Creation of green bridges and pedestrian links over sunken roads and underpasses.

Cultural and historical facets

The purpose of this plan is to raise the quality of life by turning the historical sites of Mexico City and the MAVM conurbation, including the broad avenues that were at one time synonymous with the city, into contemporary public spaces linked to the metropolitan network of green areas. Due respect would be paid to their historical value and residents would be provided with places for meeting, strolling, and chatting, cultural events, and recreation.

The following actions are proposed to reinforce cultural and historical aspects:

- Conversion of historical sites in the MAVM into areas of social coexistence by restoring and improving pedestrian safety. Because of the way that urban development has taken place, such sites are more or less evenly spaced throughout the MAVM.

Table 7.1 Existing green areas

Type of area / Main functions within the metropolitan green area network	Amelioration activities within the network of green areas
a) Protected Natural Areas and National and State Parks	
• Collection of rainwater to replenish groundwater • Production of oxygen • Mitigation of urban climate and provision of cool, fresh air to the urban area • Habitat for native flora and fauna (source of biodiversity) Filtering of pollutants • Weekend recreation	• Design and implementation of management programs aimed at optimizing environmental services and recreational opportunities for the population
Heritage "chinampa" areas and remaining wetlands	
• Mitigation of the urban climate at regional level thanks to the presence of vegetation and a large amount of water • Remains of pre-Hispanic Mexican culture (UNESCO World Heritage Sites) • Central tourist attraction in the Basin of Mexico • Habitat for native flora and fauna with a great number of endemic species (an important source of the basin's biodiversity)	• Updating and implementation of management programs focused on restoring the natural conditions and cultural heritage of these areas • Ecological restoration of polluted bodies of water • Treatment to improve the water quality, removal of sewage content • Restoration of drained and dried up bodies of water • Control of the capacity of the systems, especially for tourist use • Encouragement of the recreational use of cleaned up and restored bodies of water
b) Urban woodland	

• Enhancing the urban climate
• Recreation and sport (at weekends and daily for local residents)
• Filtering of pollutants and production of oxygen
• Helping to collect water to replenish the aquifers
• Habitat for native flora and fauna (source of biodiversity)
	• Creation and implementation of management programs including:
	  • Cleanup of damaged and overused areas
	  • Amelioration of recreational facilities and regulation of businesses in the areas (channeling business revenues to the maintenance and optimization of the areas)
	  • Incorporation of compost areas and oozing wells to improve rainwater collection capacity

Urban and neighborhood parks	
• Daily recreation and sport for local residents • Filtering of pollutants and production of oxygen • Helping to collect water to replenish the aquifers • Enhancing the urban climate at local level	• Restoration of trees and gardens • Improvement of pavements and street furniture and sporting and recreational facilities. Installations of safe children's play areas • Incorporation of compost areas and oozing wells to improve rainwater collection capacity
Bodies of water	
• Flood control basins in case of heavy rainfall • Potential areas for water-related recreational activities	• Excavation to increase their capacity so as to conserve their function as flood control basins

Table 7.1 Existing green areas

Type of area / Main functions within the metropolitan green area network	Amelioration activities within the network of green areas
• Habitat for native flora and fauna (at present they are extremely damaged)	• Design and construction to make the areas suitable for recreational use and as habitats for flora and fauna
c) Ravines	
• Funnels that carry fresh air from the forest areas around the metropolis • Areas where rainwater can seep into the aquifers, especially in the areas with a large number of faults • Filtering of pollutants and production of oxygen • Habitat for native flora and fauna (source of biodiversity) • Biological corridors that form linear connections between the green areas	• Delimitation of ravine areas under *Rule 21* in order to stop illegal land-grabbing and building in dangerous areas • Design and implementation of management programs aimed at optimizing environmental services and above all to conserve the areas • Utilization of ravines as linear parks within the green area system, taking safety into account when making paths and installing street furniture
d) Rivers and canals	
• Presence of water in the metropolis (its nature as an area of lakes) • Local improvement of the urban climate resulting from water and vegetation • Present or potential habitat for native flora and fauna • Biological corridors connecting green areas • Paths for walkers and cyclists • Sporting and recreational areas whose linear form gives them a large catchment area	• Water treatment in polluted canals • Cleanup of rivers, construction of drains on the banks to prevent contamination by sewage • Design and construction of paths for walkers and cyclists along their banks (linear parks) • Restoration of the vegetation and/or planting of trees alongside the rivers and canals where necessary
Central reservations	
• Links between the green areas with the potential (if wide enough) for the incorporation of cycle paths and street furniture • Potential contribution to the collection of rainwater and seepage • Large catchment area because of their linear nature	• Design and construction of linear parks with paths for walkers and cyclists and street furniture, etc. • Adjustment of levels to improve rainwater collection, construction of hollows and seepage wells • Restoration of trees and gardens.
Pavements and urban trees in neighborhoods	
• Integration and coordination of the urban image • Improvement of the immediate and local urban climate by providing shade and moisture	• Program to restore pavements according to neighborhood and metropolitan sector • Restoration and coordination of urban tree system according to neighborhood and metropolitan sector (trees should be thought of as part of an entire system, not in isolation) • Installation of underground cables in prioritized stages throughout the *entire MAVM*

- Recovery of traditional urban avenues as corridors for shopping and relaxation with restaurants, cafes, and malls. Good landscaping is essential if the city is to recover its image.
- Restoration of views of important regional features such as mountains, volcanoes, and urban landmarks.
- Restoring dignity to the city's image in rundown areas through public–private programs. Models may include partnerships where the government provides the materials and residents the labor or discounts from city taxes may be offered to residents who make improvements. Similar plans have been successful in Calle Tacuba in the historical center of Mexico City.
- Improvement and coordination of urban tree systems according to neighborhood.
- Creation of "urban gateways" to the city. This involves redesign and the creation of landmarks where the roads access the city from Querétaro, Pachuca, Texcoco, Puebla, Cuernavaca and Toluca. The Santa Fe Gateway is already in place.

Water management

Water should be managed cyclically to ensure sustainable use. Broadly, it should be managed in accordance with the following guidelines:

- Creation of a regional water management plan and the reincorporation of water as a core element in the MAVM.
- Encouragement of measures to save water at all stages, including extraction, conveyance, supply, and use.
- Creation of local water cycles by encouraging the use of local water combined with the reincorporation of water into the system through reuse and re-infiltration.
- Encouraging sewage treatment and reuse.
- Encouraging the collection of rainwater and, once treated, using it for all kinds of needs.
- Encouraging technologies for the collection, treatment, and storage of rainwater.
- Separation of domestic and industrial sewers from storm drains so that clean rainwater can be used separately from sewage water.
- Encouraging the use of rainwater infiltration systems in green areas and public spaces, and improvement of local small- and large-scale infiltration conditions so that the water can be reincorporated into the aquifers.
- Inclusion of springs, fountains, canals, ponds, and other bodies of water in the urban surroundings by restoring existing water features and creating new ones in public areas. In this way, not only will the presence of water perform an environmental function; it will also encourage a culture of respect for water.

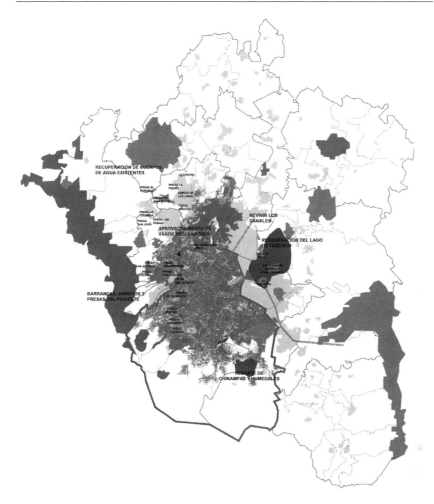

Figure 7.4 Regional water management strategies. Image courtesy of F. Islas,
    D. Martinez, and A. Alceda, 2006.

Although most of the rivers in the MAVM have now been encased in pipes and
practically all the lakes have been drained, there are still some bodies of water worth
restoring. Because of this, the regional planning strategy for water management
concentrates on existing bodies of water.

It may take more than 20 years, but the restoration of the lakes in the Basin of
Mexico should be a core part of the MAVM development goal. It is essential for
the restoration of the region's ecological balance and quality of life. The restoration
of a lake basin in the MAVM would also restore its former temperate climate,
tempering extremes of heat and cold. It can also provide residents with exceptional
opportunities for recreation and relaxation. The region would regain its ecological

importance in the Americas for migratory birds and other species of flora and fauna. Pollution from suspended particles would be reduced significantly and improved water quality would also have a positive effect on environmental values overall. This would obviously reduce the costs of public health and raise the quality of life. For this goal to be achieved, the following measures are outlined:

- New urban development or any type of building on the beds of the lakes should be prevented.
- Small bodies of water such as the Nabor Carrillo Lake should be restored with a view to incorporating them in larger bodies of water in the long term.
- Ecosystems should be restored by re-establishing habitats and reintroducing native aquatic and riparian plants, fish, amphibian species (including the *ajolote*).

Flood control basins like El Cristo and Carretas can be cleaned up by treating sewage that is discharged into them. If they are made deeper, their capacity will be maintained, allowing them to continue performing their flood control function. This will make it possible to reclaim green areas for recreation and relaxation. The cleaner bodies of water will provide other environmental benefits by improving the local climate, and reclaiming space for the habitats of native flora and fauna. They will also provide a variety of options for relaxation and sport. Their restoration as part of the urban plan will have a direct beneficial impact on the quality of life.

The ravines in the western part of the MAVM play a vital role in the ecology of the Basin. As the direct links to the mountain forests in the west and southwest (Sierra de las Cruces, Ajusco, and Chichinautzin), they provide the MAVM with essential ecosystem services. On the one hand, lines of oak trees act as funnels through which fresh air is carried from the mountains to the lower regions of the basin and on the other they carry rainwater to the lakes. The many geological faults in the area are especially important for the infiltration and reincorporation of water into the aquifers.

In general, the ravines are in poor condition. They receive large amounts of mainly domestic sewage and are used as dumps for garbage and rubble by local residents and even by the local authorities. Although the governments of Mexico City and the surrounding cities and districts allocate funds for cleaning up the ravines each year, their decay is unchecked. To clean up ravines a number of actions can be undertaken that include:

- The installation of sewers linked to treatment plants
- The treatment of domestic sewage
- Returning treated water to the ravines because it is important that the ravines remain humid
- Passing the cost of cleaning up the ravines on to the producers and end users of polluting materials (the producers of soft drinks, PET, disposable diapers,

etc.) by charging an environmental tax as part of a general program of garbage recycling.

- The ravines should be made into linear parks for recreation and sport by providing them with paths for walkers and cyclists where physical and ecological conditions permit.

In many cases, the ravines in the western part of the MAVM run down to reservoirs whose only function, at present, is to contain floods in the event of heavy rain. These bodies of water are in a state of total abandonment. With practically no ecological value, they are disease-causing pockets of pollution.

Ravine restoration must be linked to the collection, conveyance, and treatment of sewage and the separation of clean rainwater that can be allowed to run straight into the bodies of water. Reservoir capacity can be maintained by excavating them deeper and removing sediment. This would also make them less likely to be left without water during the dry season. Like the flood control basins, the reservoirs would make recreation and relaxation possible and their presence would enhance the culture of water and encourage the population to interact with it.

Although *chinampas*, canals, and wetlands still survive in the south and southeast of the MAVM, they face a variety of perils. Urban growth, illegal development, sewage pollution, solid waste pollution, lack of maintenance, and overuse of tourist areas has accelerated problems. The aquifers that used to feed the system have been diverted in pipes and lack replenishment with clean water. The *chinampas* and wetlands of Xochimilco, Tláhuac, and Chalco are the only significant remaining pre-Hispanic landscapes in the MAVM. The *chinampas*, tethered and reinforced with *ahuejote* willows (*Salix bonplandiana var. stricta*) and surrounded by canals, were a distinctive feature, first of Gran Tenochtitlan, and then of the outskirts of Mexico City, from colonial times until the first half of the twentieth century. Because of this, UNESCO protected Xochimilco by naming it a World Heritage Site. However, because of the area's unceasing decay and the lack of a functioning management program, this protection is on the verge of being lost.

The restoration of the ecology and heritage of Xochimilco, Tláhuac, and Chalco should include the creation and above all the *implementation* of management programs for all the territory in the lake system. As well as specifying what land use is permitted and what prohibited, the programs must define maximum permitted intensities of use in order to prevent further damage to the environment. Strategies to achieve this include:

- Creating zoning regulations that define different intensities of use in accordance with environmental vulnerability.
- Diversifying economic activities and uses, with a focus on biodynamic agriculture and fishing. The use of traditional methods of production can restore regional cultural values and provide local inhabitants with a source of income other than giving boat rides to tourists.
- Encouraging projects that will attract more cultural tourism.

Figure 7.5 The Canal Nacional before and after clean up and redesign. Image courtesy of D. Martinez, 2007.

For a long time, canals were traditional throughout the lake area of the MAVM. Unfortunately, today, those that have not been enclosed in pipes carry sewage and are foul-smelling sources of gastrointestinal, respiratory, and other infectious diseases. To achieve sustainable water management, the following water collection, storage, conveyance, and treatment works projects could be carried out:

- Adaptation of roofs to collect rainwater and convey it in pipes.
- Planting roof gardens so that the vegetation and substrate will help filter rainwater.
- Construction of rainwater storage cisterns.
- Separate drains for rainwater and sewage.
- Allow open canals to carry rainwater so they are both functional and attractive.
- Introduce plants employing efficient sewage treatment technology (bio-membranes, among others).
- Create treatment wetlands in green areas (parks, central reservations, waste land) for the treatment of domestic sewage and its reuse in irrigation or reinfiltration.
- Use small plants to make rainwater drinkable at domestic level or for groups of houses (biomembrane, electrolytic treatment, etc.).
- Make industrial facilities responsible for treating their water with technologies that are suitable for the type of waste produced.

The more sewage builds up and gets mixed, the more difficult it is to treat. Therefore, local sewage-treatment solutions, established by block, building, or industrial facility, should be encouraged. Reintroduction of water into the aquifers can be facilitated by leveling green areas to allow surface water to be conveyed toward them. The construction of hollows and grease traps with sedimentation and absorption tanks will allow rainwater to be reincorporated into the local cycle and replenish the aquifers in green areas, central reservations, and waste land. Bioengineering works can also improve infiltration in ravines and forests in accordance with studies and plans that take into account the ecological conditions of each area through inclusion in management programs.

Waste management

Because "garbage" is one of the greatest problems faced by urban society, waste management is an essential part of the sustainability proposal. Total municipal solid waste (MSW) produced in the Metropolitan Area of Mexico City, including the Federal District and 17 cities in the State of Mexico, is thought to exceed 18,000 tons per day (Institute Nacional de Ecologia, n.d.)

According to figures produced by the National Institute of Ecology in 2007, organic waste accounts for about 47 percent of this total. About 38 percent of all MSW produced by the country's major cities consists of used containers and

Figure 7.6 Artificial wetland for the treatment of sewage contaminated with domestic organic material. This is a series of interconnected tanks and layers of gravel to filter the water. The flora provide oxygen and their roots house the bacteria that digest the pollutants. Image courtesy of D. Martinez, 2010.

packaging. On the basis of these figures, appropriate management of organic waste and used containers and packaging could reduce the volume of garbage produced in the Metropolitan Area of Mexico City by 85 percent.

Energy use and management

Energy should also be managed in a sustainable way. The core features of sustainable energy management are saving, self-generation, and utilization of energy generated as a by-product. Many conservation strategies are known, but the key is to educate for implementation. Self-generation minimizes energy transmission losses and opens the door to the incorporation of clean generation technologies. The utilization of energy generated as a by-product is often achieved in the decomposition of organic matter or in some industrial processes.

Table 7.2 Proposed approach to waste management

No.	Feature	Strategy	Instruments
1	Encouragement of aware consumption	• Inform and educate consumers at all levels	• Programs for schools • Publicity campaigns • Economic incentives to encourage consumers to participate in collecting and sorting waste for recycling (e.g., sorted garbage would be put in special bags and be collected free of charge. Unsorted garbage would be put in other types of bag and its collection would be charged for)
2	Encourage environmentally responsible production processes and use of containers and packaging	• Provide incentives for recycling and for reducing production of waste, containers, and packaging • Discourage the use of products that are hard to recycle or to integrate in natural cycles	• Environmental taxes on non-recyclable products and on production processes without a recycling system • Tax incentives for companies which show that their processes are environmentally responsible • Tax incentives for businesses that include a recycling system in their production cycle • Environmental standards for the handling of different types of waste
3	Restructuring of the municipal and district garbage collection systems	• Collection of sorted waste in sorting trucks • Installation of containers for the collection of materials such as glass, cardboard and paper, aluminum, etc. • Transformation of garbage transfer centers into Recycling Collection Centers	• Concessions for the collection and sale of recycled materials
4	Inducements for making and using compost	• Separate collection of organic waste in special bags • Collection and use of biogas as a by-product of compost • Use of compost earth in public green areas with poor soil (in the west of the MAVM) and sale of compost earth to discourage the removal of leaf mold and top soil from natural forests	• Installation of compost centers in green areas with preference given to technologies that increase the efficiency of the process • Concession for the utilization of biogas and compost • Tax incentives for companies that set up compost centers offering service to the community

Conclusions

While the environmental situation in the MAVM is unique, the consequences of environmental degradation are phenomena that are also occurring in other cities. Pollution, floods, atmospheric inversions, and the concentration of gaseous pollutants and particulate matter are occurring in many locations. Similarly, the consequences of urban inefficiency are common problems for many large cities, particularly those in developing countries.

The proposals described in this chapter were designed for the MAVM. Nevertheless, similar measures are being applied in urban areas throughout the world. The increase and improvement of green space and greenways, water management, the promotion of public transportation as well as general urban efficiency, coupled with sound management of energy and waste are some of the urban policies which are increasingly transforming cities. At the same time, they can simultaneously foster social equity and a higher quality of life for urban residents. It is evident, given the fluctuating global economic situation that it is impractical to transform a metropolis in the short term. However, it is important to focus each new urban development project toward a carefully researched objective that is based on sustainability. In this way our cities will be gradually transformed in favor of their inhabitants. Each city's history, environment, culture, and its population is unique and accordingly each city will also have distinct challenges. For this reason, we must understand the specific processes of each city and plan accordingly. To understand a city's physical, biological, cultural, economic, and social processes is to understand its nature and we must all design with nature.

References

Hellmund, P. and D. Smith (2008). *Designing Greenways: Sustainable Landscapes for Nature and People.* Island Press: Washington, DC.

Instituto Nacional de Ecología (n.d.): Online. Available http://www.ine.gob.mx/ueajei/publicaciones/libros/22/resumen.html (accessed June 2010)

Islas, F., D. Martínez and Á. Alceda (2006). *Reestructuración Urbana Regional del Área Metropolitana de la Ciudad de México.* Fundación ICA and Metropolis 2025.

Mexico: Identifying Complementary Measures to Ensure the Maximum Realization of Benefits from the Liberalization of Trade in Environmental Goods and Services, Case Study Mexico: Online. Available. http://www.cce.org.mx/cespedes/publicaciones/otras/DesafioAgua/agua00_3.PDF (accessed June 2010)

Chapter 8

Transformations of the urbanizing delta landscape

Han Meyer

Introduction

This chapter was completed in March 2011, just after the horrible news of the tsunami in Japan. This disaster shows the risk of living in a coastal zone in an extreme way. This time it is not a developing country where the poorest slum-areas are hit by a flood. It is the third largest economy of the world, with a high living standard and advanced infrastructure. In the world of hydraulic engineering, the infrastructure of Japanese super-levees is considered as the most powerful and efficient flood defence system of the world (De Graaf and Hooimeijer, 2008). When even this country, with its developed water defence system, can be hit so seriously, it becomes clear that every risk cannot be avoided. Even the most advanced system can fail. It forces us to reconsider the balance between risk prevention and other aspects which define the quality of life.

These days more than 13 per cent of the urban population of the world lives in coastal zones with an increasing vulnerability for flooding (UN-Habitat, 2008). Delta areas, especially, function as magnets for urbanization. Thirteen of the 20 mega-cities in the world (more than ten million inhabitants) can be found in delta areas. The vulnerability of these urbanized deltas comes from two directions: from the sea and sea level rise, and from the rivers, with increasing peak discharges because of intensified rainfall and erosion in catchment areas. The 2005 Katrina disaster in New Orleans was regarded as a 'wake up call' for what can happen in urbanized coastal and delta areas. Considered from this context, many eyes are directed to the Netherlands. This country is essentially the delta of the rivers Rhine and Meuse. Seventy-six per cent of the urban population lives below sea level, which makes this country fourth on the list of countries with the highest proportions of their urban population living in low-elevation coastal zones (McGranahan et al., 2008). However, because of a century-long tradition of hydraulic engineering, living in this country is considered to be extremely safe.

Still, this tradition has become the subject of debate and of fundamental reconsideration over the past 20 years as national policy changed from focusing on *resistance* towards a policy which tries to emphasize *resilience* and building with nature. This change has a large impact on the typology of landscapes and urbanization patterns in the Netherlands. The transition from resistance to resilience might be relevant for all urbanized and urbanizing deltas worldwide. The Netherlands can be regarded as an interesting laboratory of implementing and testing this transition.

The Dutch landscape as a hydraulic system

Urban growth and urban planning in the Netherlands are interwoven with the character of the territory as a coastal zone and a delta of rivers. The specific character of this watery territory offered the conditions for the settlement of numerous port cities. The development of the landscape and the rise of cities were on the one hand defined by the ambition to exploit the landscape for international trade activities to the maximum extent, while on the other hand the vulnerable character of the territory to floods had to be continuously taken into account.

The development of the urban landscape of the Netherlands can be understood as a fine example of the process of modernization, which has been defined by two great themes. One theme concerns the process of globalization, with all kinds of contrasts and conflicts, but also fruitful combinations between globalization and local context. The second theme concerns the relationship between urbanization and the natural conditions of the territory, which should be treated carefully in order to avoid excessive exploitation of nature, soil, water and air. The present-day questions of transformation of this urbanized delta landscape can be understood as a new phase of modernization, which makes it necessary to define a new relationship between local contexts and new global networks, and a new relationship between urban development and the natural (water) landscape.

The roots of modern urbanism in the Netherlands can be traced back to the sixteenth and early seventeenth centuries. It is the period in which the Netherlands, according to the American professor Jan de Vries and his Dutch colleague Ad van der Woude (1997), became the first modern society in the world. Essential to the concept of modern is the rational action of man. The old, pre-modern society is characterized by unspoken, unquestioned acceptance of traditions and rituals. The characteristic of modern society is then the break with the unquestioned traditions and the beginning of *Homo oeconomicus*, the rational man who makes conscious choices based on concrete information. The origin of the modern condition is rational action, and the process of urbanization forms part of this rationality. Urbanization was not a spontaneous process, and it was even less so in the wet swampy territory of the United Republic of the Netherlands. The sixteenth-century map of Holland reveals a landscape covered with swamps, rivers, creeks and sea inlets with inconsistent water levels. The ingenuity and perseverance that must have played a role in the creation of a new, rationally ordered landscape is impressive.

The area of the Netherlands was – and still is – a delta of some large European rivers (Rhine, Meuse, Scheldt), and as such, is an *intermediate zone* between the

Figure 8.1 The Dutch landscape as a hydraulic system. Beemster polder. Image courtesy of Photograph Pandion – Peter Bolhuis, 2004.

mainland and the sea. It is a zone where land and sea are interwoven and influence each other; a hybrid, wet area, not really mainland but also not really open sea. This landscape of the river delta has very poor conditions for agriculture and for urbanization. The relationship between land and water is changing continuously. It is a dynamic landscape which has been transformed dramatically by floods, changing river courses and changes of the sea level over time. Human settlement is in danger in extreme conditions and is at least inconvenienced at other times. The quality of the soil is poor. The peat ground is too wet for agriculture and human settlement, and it is also too soft for other built construction. To be able to use the landscape for agriculture and human settlement, drainage of groundwater and protection against flooding from rivers and the sea were key issues for survival and economic development.

Because of human interventions, the Dutch landscape was transformed into a large hydraulic system in the course of the eleventh to seventeenth centuries. Technological innovations in drainage (for example the introduction of the windmill in the sixteenth century) and dike construction produced conditions suitable for large-scale exploitation of the landscape and for both agriculture and urbanization. From the nineteenth century onward, hydraulic engineering and water management became a primary concern of the nation-state of the Netherlands.

The creation of this hydraulic system concerns three main aspects:

1. The development of drainage systems of ditches and canals to remove super-fluous water. During the eleventh–fifteenth centuries, large systems of rational patterns of ditches, reservoirs and canals overtook the wild character of the Dutch wetlands. These patterns were based on a parcelling of land which provided agricultural plots, large enough for development of an agricultural operation, and at the same time small enough to be drained by the surrounding ditches.
2. The construction of large systems of dikes alongside the rivers to protect the land against flooding. In addition, rivers were channelized to improve their function as navigation channels for shipping.
3. From the nineteenth century, the state administration initiated construction of a large system of coastal defence systems including dikes and dams. The effect of this was that the fitful coastline became stabilized and straightened, ultimately resulting in an enormous reduction of the total length of the coastline.

The Dutch city as a hydraulic construction

Why was this enormous effort undertaken? Of course, the peat and clay areas of the landscape were very fertile and the rivers and sea were an inexhaustible reservoir of fish and shellfish. But the main motive was the extremely favorable location for trade and commerce. This coastal zone of lowlands and the position of this area as an intermediate zone between mainland and sea seemed to be the ideal situation for 'the modern condition', the place to develop these lowlands as the main 'hub' of the sixteenth- and seventeenth-century trade economy. The increase of port cities, ruling and controlling international trade and traffic, transformed these lowlands into the most densely and intensively urbanized country in the world around 1600, which was the substance of this 'first modern economy'. Urbanization had increased so that about 61 per cent of the entire population of the country lived in cities and towns of more than 5,000 inhabitants in 1675 (de Vries and van de Woude, 1997).

In the framework of the landscape as a hydraulic system, the Dutch port city was a hydraulic construction, creating the conditions for urban settlement, for urban life and activities, as well as for transhipment and other port activities. City and port were interwoven with each other. The port was located *in* or at the immediate border of the city. In this enclosed system of the port city, the harbour was a *marketplace* and *the* final destination on the transportation route. The port's infrastructure was organized within the enclosed character of the city (Meyer, 1999).

The urban port infrastructure was a transformed and manipulated part of the landscape drainage system. The systems of harbours and canals in cities like Amsterdam, Rotterdam, Dordrecht, Vlissingen, Hoorn, Harlingen and others,

Figure 8.2 The Dutch city as a hydraulic construction. Amsterdam inner-city, ca. 1990.
    Source: anonymous.

functioned as port infrastructure, drainage system and main structure of the
urban fabric. The elements of hydraulic engineering (canals, quays, dikes, dams,
sluices) were at the same time the main framework of the urban fabric. The quays
and dikes were the most important urban streets and the dam was the main square
and the core of the Dutch water city. City, port and water management infrastructure were interwoven completely (Hooimeijer et al., 2005).

From intermediate zone to sharp border

In the subsequent centuries, especially the nineteenth and twentieth, the development of the struggles of Dutch engineers against the danger and inconvenience of
water was assisted by new technical innovations like steam and electric energy. This
resulted in an ongoing enlargement of scale of the landscape as a hydraulic system.

The possibilities for drainage and coastal defence seemed to be endless and produced the idea that it is possible to totally control nature. At the end of the nineteenth century it was no longer considered necessary to interweave the water systems and the urban network because the reliance on water as traffic and transport system was diminishing. The introduction of steam, electricity and oil meant also that the role of water networks was overtaken by railroad and road networks. In addition, the urban water networks were at full capacity by the end of the nineteenth century (Hooimeijer et al., 2005).

With the experience of transforming the landscape, manipulating the water and controlling urban growth, the Netherlands was a strong breeding ground for the modernistic conception of the idea of *planning*, establishing the possibility to define and precisely control future processes (Van Vught, 1979). This idea is based on a belief in the unlimited possibilities of state institutions to regulate and control all aspects of social and economic life. Urban planning and urban design, in both Western and Eastern Europe, was strongly influenced by this idea of the making of society.

As a result, these modernistic conceptions led to the idea of the separation of different functions, institutionally and spatially. During the nineteenth century most European cities had just one public works department, which was responsible for the integral development of the public domain and the infrastructure. By the mid-twentieth century, most cities had evolved and had created separate urban planning, traffic and port authority departments and others. Most of the waterfront had been reconstructed under the responsibility of the port authority, which developed specialized quays for large-scale cargo handling. Meanwhile, much of the remaining area was under the control of the traffic department for the construction of large-scale motorways. In Holland, a third institution played a role. The water boards (water management authorities) claimed the waterfront areas to construct new barriers against the danger of high water.

The ongoing efforts to get the water-dominated landscape under control, however, produced a paradox. With the reclaimed polders, the channelized rivers and the coastal dikes and dams, the Netherlands had increasingly transformed from an intermediate zone between mainland and sea, into a part of the mainland with a sharp border along the sea and the rivers. The overwhelming focus on safety that resulted in straightened coastlines, closed inland seas and inlets, high dikes and dams, produced a sharp separation between open water and inland and between zones 'outside the dikes' and 'inside the dikes'.

This development had several effects. The first concerned the number of port cities and the relationship between cities and ports. During the period of the sixteenth to nineteenth centuries, the Netherlands was characterized by a very long coastline with a great number of smaller and larger port cities. More recently, because of a significant reduction in the area directly connected to the open water of sea and rivers (the 'outside the dikes' areas), the possibilities of port development have been reduced dramatically and are mainly concentrated in the 'Europort-zone' near Rotterdam. At the same time, a separation between port and

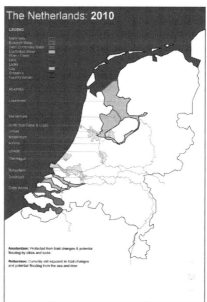

Figure 8.3 Shortening of the coastline in the twentieth century by construction of the Afsluitdijk (closing dam) in the north and the Delta-works in the southwest. Image courtesy of TU-Delft.

city occurred, where the city represents the controlled and well-planned civilized world, and the port is regarded as a 'terra incognita' outside the civilized world. Now, at the end of the twentieth century and the beginning of the twenty-first, the economic use of the urban water edges is essentially changing. The port and transport economy and the technological world are undergoing fundamental shifts. Some port activities need large-scale concentration and deep water, while other port and transport activities need more decentralization and an effective logistic organization (Meyer, 1999). These days, there is increased interest in the roles played by hierarchy and by the division of tasks among port cities, leading to the development of larger ports into main ports, or, in other words, into the most important ports serving large continental areas from which goods could continue being distributed. The modern twenty-first-century port tends to consist of various specialized distribution hubs, which together form a network.

Second, water management has become increasingly problematic through the centuries. Because of continuous drainage, the peat grounds are shrinking, resulting in subsidence of the ground level. For this reason, the western part of the Netherlands has now subsided several metres (some parts more than six metres) below sea level. This means more pumping energy is required to move groundwater to the open water. This process has become more serious because of the changing climate with the effects of a rising sea-level, a larger inflow of river water and greater amounts of rainfall alternated by periods of serious dryness. Several floods caused by heavy rainfall and subsequent extremely high water levels in the rivers led to the threat of dike failures during the 1990s and made clear that the relationship between water and territory is *not* under control. A fundamental change in attitude concerning water management is taking place, resulting in new policies which aim to develop a more dynamic relationship between water and land, methods of storage of rainwater and more dynamic coastal and river systems.

Third, the reduction of the coastal zone to a narrow strip has produced enormous pressure on this area. Economic growth, urbanization and recreation facilities have been concentrated mainly in this coastal zone. These days the 'Randstad Holland' is the most densely populated area in the Netherlands. Six million inhabitants, or 40 per cent of the total Dutch population, are concentrated in this region which only covers 14 per cent of the country. Port activities are mainly concentrated in the port of Rotterdam, with a few small ports along the coast. Recreation and tourism are increasingly concentrated in the coastal zone, which takes on the character of a long recreational park.

Towards a new relationship between hydraulics, landscape and urbanization

Since the 1980s, a new approach to the relationship between the urban environment and the characteristics of the watery delta landscape has emerged. This approach had a cultural motive. The presence of water in the landscape and the urban environment has been discovered as an important aspect of 'identity' of the post-modern city. Rotterdam is an interesting example. Through most of the twentieth century, the river functioned as a broad physical barrier between the two parts of the city. With the re-conversion of the obsolete docklands in the 1980s and 1990s, the urban river landscape was transformed into a central zone connecting the north and south of the city. A new central boulevard, with the recent introduction of the landmark Erasmus Bridge as its highlight, became the physical centre of this connection. Also, the layout of the Rotterdam city plan changed radically as a result of the implementation of this new central boulevard. The new bridge, the new quays and river-oriented squares and parks became part of a new integral civic design of the public domain.

Similar examples in other port cities try to focus on the waterfronts as central elements in city plans; new structures create new types of attractive urban environment which break with the negative image of the industrial port city (Meyer, 1999). In these examples, the civic design of the city is not limited to the borders of the urban ensemble. It engages the urbanizing landscape of the regional territory. The operational quality of this strategy is that it presents a framework of a new coherence between the several urban fragments. The process of the re-conversion of the obsolete docklands is to be regarded as the first step in this strategy. This approach of water oriented urban design has increased due to the new developments in the framework of water management itself.

Figure 8.4 Conversion of abandoned docklands: The *Kop van Zuid* area, 1975.
Conversion of abandoned docklands: The *Kop van Zuid* area, 2006.
Source: anonymous / Image courtesy of dS+V Rotterdam, 2006.

In previous times, 'modern' water management was geared to produce more safety, but it simultaneously reduced the potential economic and recreational use of the land. This approach to water management essentially established and was confronted with its own limits. The recent radical change in water management policy provides a stronger emphasis on 'dynamic' and 'elastic' approaches, giving more space to the water in the rivers, more space for temporary water storage in the polders, and replacement of the narrow coastal defence system by a wider zone of artificial as well as natural dunes, beaches, inlets, islands and breakwaters. This approach creates new possibilities for attractive urban water landscapes, which combine water management functions with public space, leisure and recreation. The change from a 'resistant' towards a 'resilient' water management, from just 'hard' towards more possibilities for 'soft' coastal defence, also offers new opportunities of economic development.

Port and transport economy and technology have been undergoing fundamental changes since the end of the twentieth century. In the nineteenth century, the Rotterdam port focused on the transhipment of bulk (oil, coal, iron). In the twentieth, a large petrochemical complex was added, which made Rotterdam the second largest petrochemical complex in the world. In the coming decades, the port is facing the need to adapt to processes of energy transition. The new energy port of the twenty-first century can only survive if established as a *smart* port, supported by new energy systems and intelligent logistic systems. These can only be developed in a climate of an innovative knowledge-based and creative economy.

For the flowering of this economy, attractive urban and natural environments are necessary (Florida, 2002). This breakthrough insight is the reason for a new relationship among port authority, city administration and environmental organizations. New extensions of the port territory into the sea, like the 'Maasvlakte 2' (under construction), have become possible after intensive negotiations with environmental organizations and as a result address the importance of the delta ecosystems (WWF, 2010).

Figure 8.5 Proposal by H+N+S Landscape Architects for Maasvlakte, Rotterdam. A new artificial dune-landscape combines flood-defence, underground storage, recreation and natural biodiversity. Image courtesy of Port Authority Rotterdam, 2007.

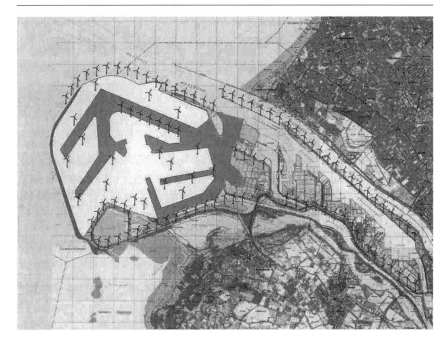

Figure 8.6 Proposed wind turbines on the Maasvlakte, port of Rotterdam. Image
courtesy of Feddes, 2010.

The port authorities have been required to forge new relationships with the
environmental movement and the city, and to collaborate with water boards to
develop new concepts and construct new attractive urban landscapes. This means
new types of water-management and new hydraulic concepts are necessary to create
an exciting new urban landscape, which can be considered fundamental for a
flourishing innovative knowledge-based and creative economy, while still
providing the functioning 'hardware' of the port.

The search for new concepts which show the result of these new collaborations
is the reason for an interesting experiment of the Rotterdam Port Authority. In
2007, the authority commissioned eight landscape architects and urban designers
to present ideas concerning improving the spatial attractiveness of the port area,
combined with an intensification of the land use (Port of Rotterdam, 2007). These
ideas delivered important components for a future strategy concerning the
combination of land use intensification, flood defence and new metropolitan
landscapes. These experiments are also linked to development of large-scale wind
turbine parks in the Rotterdam port area. This means new conditions for internal
spatial organization of the port area. On the one hand, there is the question of
what to do with the vacant land if coal and oil terminals are abolished. And, on
the other hand, the introduction of several hundreds of windmills in the port area
will result in a quite different impact on the surrounding rural and urban areas.

A realistic vision of the future might include, instead of a series of smoking oil refineries and coal hills, the skyline of a port dominated by extended ranges of windmills (Feddes, 2010).

Conclusions

Designing and planning the new urban delta landscape has become a complex matter. The Netherlands comes from a situation of a strong belief in the 'makeable' society. This is expressed by a strong top-down policy of the central government, a strong belief in mathematics and engineering and strong coherence of spatial planning and hydraulic engineering policy with a national policy of industrialization and agriculture. This whole political, economic and ideological system has disappeared and there is not yet a clear alternative system. Parts of the new situation planners and designers will confront include:

1. Complex multi-actor systems with new concepts of governance instead of a central government dominated approach.
2. Greater attention paid to the delta ecosystems instead of a one-dimensional focus on safety.
3. A focus on natural richness of the delta that will deliver a new breeding ground for new types of economic life instead of a focus on industrialization.
4. New combinations of the functions of city, port and nature delivering advantages for each of these functions, producing new types of urban landscape instead of strict separation of different functions in the delta.

Considered from this point of view, not only the context and assignments of urban and landscape design are changing, but also the role and content of design itself. In the process of attempting to create new concepts of governance, new combinations of functions in the delta, new integrations of natural ecosystems in urban environments, design plays more a role of a survey, a reconnoitering of new possibilities. The fundamental changes in the Dutch approach are relevant for many other urbanized areas, which often suffer from a high vulnerability to flooding and serious ecological problems, while residential areas lack interesting relationships with the water because of waterfront port and industrial developments. The Dutch experiments can be considered as attempts to develop a more sustainable approach to the delta, where safety policy, economy and natural environment should not compete with each other but can be combined.

References

De Graaf, R. and Hooimeijer, F. (2008) *Urban Water in Japan*, London: Taylor & Francis.
De Vries, J. and van der Woude, A. (1997) *The First Modern Economy. Success, Failure and Preservance of the Dutch Economy 1500–1815*, Cambridge, MA: Cambridge University Press.

Feddes, Y. (2010) *Een choreografie voor 1000 molens*, The Hague: College van Rijksadviseurs

Florida, R. (2002) *The Rise of the Creative Class*, New York: Basic Books.

Hooimeijer, F., Meyer, H. and Nienhuis, A. (2005) *Atlas of Dutch Water-cities*, Amsterdam: SUN.

McGranahan, G., Balk, D. and Anderson, B. (2008) A summary of the risks of climate change and urban settlement in low elevation coastal zones. In *The New Global Frontier: Cities, Poverty and Environment in the 21st Century*, G. Martine, G. McGranahan, M. Montgomery and R. Fernandez-Castilla (eds), London: Earthscan.

Meyer, H. (1999) *City and Port. Transformations of Port-cities – London, New York, Barcelona, Rotterdam*, Utrecht: International Books.

Meyer, H., Bobbink, I. and Nijhuis, S. (eds) (2010) *Delta-Urbanism: The Netherlands*, Chicago: APA.

Port of Rotterdam (2007) *Haven Zicht. Beeldkwaliteit van de haven. Een verkenning* (Port view. Image quality of the port. An exploration), Rotterdam: Port of Rotterdam.

UN-Habitat (2008) *State of the World's Cities: Harmonious Cities*, London: Earthscan.

Van Vught, F. (1979) *Sociale Planning. Oorsprong en ontwikkeling van het Amerikaanse planningsdenken* (Social Planning. Origin and development of American planning philosophy), Assen: van Gorcum.

WWF (World Wildlife Fund) (2010) *Met Open Armen. Voor het belang van natuur, veiligheid en economie* (With open arms. For the interest of nature, safety and economy), Zeist: WWF.

Chapter 9

Sustainable urban design
Lessons from Dutch cities

Jesus J. Lara

Introduction

There is an old saying that God made the world, but the Dutch made Holland. To a certain extent, this is true. From the Middle Ages to the 1980s, the Dutch have been actively involved in the process of land reclamation. Without the elaborate system of dikes, dams, and flood control gates that the country has developed over the last millennium, almost two-thirds of the Netherlands would be under water. Practically the entire west and low north of the country consists of polders: drained lands mainly surrounded by dikes within which groundwater levels can be controlled. There are some 5,000 polders in all (van de Ven, 2002). Over the centuries, reclaiming land on the sea while protecting existing land has produced some of the most outstanding features of the Netherlands' geography. Likewise, the unparalleled planning and design approaches that have sustained and advanced urbanization in the Netherlands could be used as a model for other cities. Although the Randstad's (ring of cities) long tradition of land reclamation and planning makes it a good model, it is important to understand the dynamics of this system before ideas and knowledge can be transferred or adapted to another urban region. To grasp the dynamics and complexities of the Dutch institutions, planning traditions, and design approaches and their outcomes, it is crucial to explore and analyze: (1) the factors that have contributed to making the Randstad the economic powerhouse of the Netherlands, (2) the impact of the Dutch National Spatial Strategy, and (3) approaches that have encouraged innovation in Dutch planning and design.

Randstad Netherlands

The first step in understanding Dutch planning and design traditions is to analyze some of the factors that have contributed to making the Randstad the economic driver of the Netherlands. Two characteristics define the Randstad: (1) the *physical* structure (size, location, and topography) of the region, and (2) *socio-cultural* characteristics (growth-density, economy, and political institutions) that establish the different socio-political divisions in its four major cities: Amsterdam,

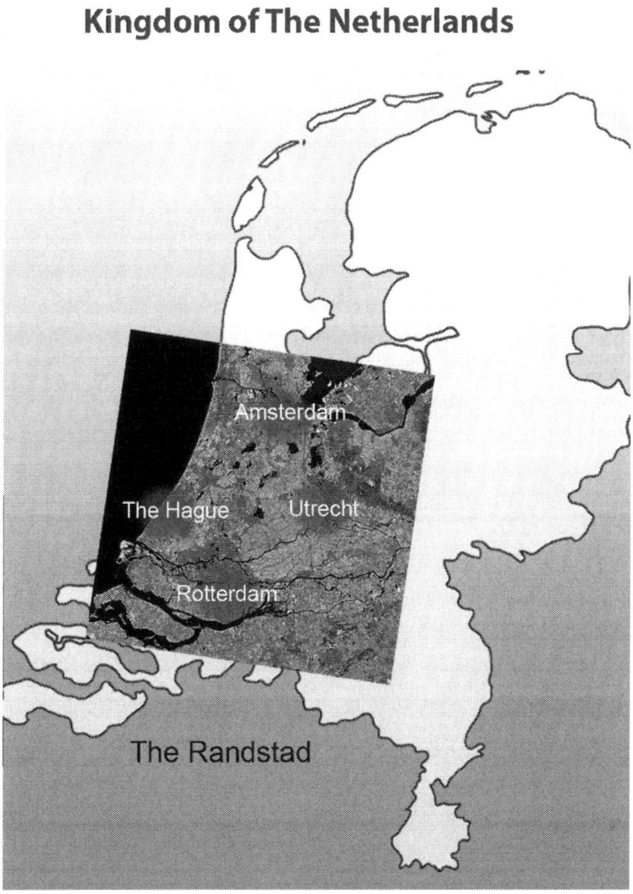

Kingdom of The Netherlands

Figure 9.1 The Randstad region with its four major cities: Amsterdam, Rotterdam, The Hague and Utrecht. Image courtesy of Jesus J. Lara, 2010.

Rotterdam, The Hague, and Utrecht. According to planning and design scholars, the physical structure of the Randstad was largely determined by geographical characteristics and historical accident (Hall, 2002).

Before discussing the physical structure of the Randstad, one must start with an understanding of the term "Randstad" itself. It is not a city; it has no official status, no mayor, and no municipal council. Its boundaries are not clearly marked and there is no organization especially responsible for land use planning in the Randstad. The term "Randstad" was first used in the 1930s to denote a group of towns and cities located relatively close together in the west of the Netherlands that are oriented in a generally horseshoe-shaped line approximately 110 miles in length. The word "Rand," which means "rim" or "ring" in Dutch, is used because the Randstad encircles an open area called the Green Heart. The Randstad extends across the four provinces of North Holland, South Holland, Utrecht, and Flevoland. The name is thus considerably younger than the towns and cities it represents. Each city is separated from its neighbors by a green buffer zone. Rural areas have increasingly felt the impact of urban sprawl, with more traffic on the roads, more people engaged in leisure pursuits, and encroaching suburbanization. As a result, the trend is now to refer to the whole area—the cities and their immediate vicinity and the Green Heart—as the Randstad.

The geography of the Randstad, and the Netherlands in general, is unique and fascinating. The Netherlands largely consists of totally flat landscapes dominated by water. Nearly one-quarter of the country's territory is below sea level and half of the country, including the most densely populated areas, would flood were it not for the dikes. The Dutch have lived with these conditions for generations and have organized spatial planning accordingly. The country's vulnerable location and small size have been the primary motivators for strategic innovations that have drawn international attention.

An important factor in making the Randstad a vibrant region has been its polycentric urban setting. "Polycentric" here refers to the existence of a number of urban centers in a certain area. A polycentric urban area derives its meaning from the patterns and dynamics of functional interrelations and cooperation (versus competition) among these centers through a series of networks of visible and invisible infrastructures, including transportation, communications, and/or public services (Bosma and Helinga, 1997). Under these polycentric conditions, none of the cities can claim to be the undisputed "capital." There is no major hierarchy, since the four largest cities—Amsterdam, Rotterdam, The Hague, and Utrecht—each fulfill a separate role and have their own specializations. Amsterdam (population 736,000) is the main financial, cultural, and air transport center; Rotterdam (population 599,000) has the largest port not only in the Netherlands but in the world; The Hague (population 454,000) is the seat of government; and Utrecht (population 261,000), as the hub of the rail system, has become an important center for services like higher education. The region includes 12 additional cities with more than 100,000 inhabitants and another ten in the range of 70,000–100,000. The co-existence of many smaller and larger cities in a relatively small area gives the Randstad its polycentric appearance (Hall and Green, 2005).

For decades, the Netherlands has had the fastest population growth in Europe. From 1950 to 1995, the population increased over 50 percent, from 10.1 million to 15.4 million (Rosemann, 2005). Randstad, with an area of 2,092 square miles, is the most highly urbanized area of the Netherlands. The urban areas of the Randstad contain approximately 6.6 million inhabitants. Some 48 percent of the population of the entire country resides in just one-quarter of its surface area. The Randstad provinces boast 50 percent of the total number of dwellings in the Netherlands, and 41 percent of the entire Dutch population lives on 16 percent of its territory. This results in an average density of more than 3,300 inhabitants per square mile (Randstad, 2005).

The Randstad is the business and economic center of the country, producing 70 percent of the Netherlands' domestic growth product (Van de Beek, 2006). It is home to some three million jobs, most of them in the service sector, and 50 percent of the nation's employment is concentrated in the Randstad. It is also the site of 70 percent of the head offices of the 100 biggest Dutch companies (Simmonds and Hack, 2000). A dense network of roads and railway corridors connects the cities of the Randstad with one another, other parts of the country, and Northwest Europe, providing optimal conditions for business and employment.

The Randstad's place as the cultural and economic powerhouse of the Netherlands came about due to a combination of geographical, historical, and, perhaps most importantly, cultural factors. Historically, the Netherlands has had to struggle to exist as a land mass. About 50 percent of the land is below sea level, and were it not for the dikes, artificial dams, and water works, the country would not exist in its current form. The Netherlands is the only nation that literally created its own living space, or at least large parts of it. In addition to the difficulty of keeping the country above water, there are obstacles to overcome such as population growth and the lack of domestic raw materials, and these have been the driving forces behind the growth and development of this small country. The polycentric characteristic of the Randstad's urban areas has resulted in highly differentiated areas that provide the economy, knowledge industry, innovation, business, financial services, and tourism in the Netherlands. With its two major ports, Rotterdam and Schiphol, the entire region forms one of Europe's major intersections in the rapidly changing global network community.

Impacts of the Dutch National Spatial Strategy

The second step in understanding Dutch planning and design successes is to acknowledge the pervasive influence of the Dutch National Spatial Strategy on many aspects of Dutch life and culture. High population densities in the Netherlands mean that issues associated with land uses have to be carefully considered. Dutch planners have often been admired for developing highly urbanized areas, with a number of separate cities grouped around a more or less open central area, while also maintaining each city's individual identity.

Traditionally, the planning process in the Randstad and in the Netherlands corresponds to the political characterization of the "Polder Model" (Betsky, 2004). This model is based on inclusive deliberation and restraint on the part of all actors (Simmonds and Hack, 2000), and it means that nobody leaves the negotiating table until a consensus has been reached. The polder model has three dimensions. The first is within the government, as there must be discussion between different ministries at the national level and also with regional and local authorities. The second dimension is between the government, nongovernmental organizations, citizens, and the private sector. Finally, the third dimension is an international base, with a special emphasis on the European Union. The polder model is the general policy framework of urban planning in the Netherlands. It is based on transparency and the unity of all, and coordination of stakeholders. The model is "centralized where necessary and rather decentralized where possible" (Faludi and van der Valk, 1994). The core of planning relies on reaching consensus through formal and informal personal networks and negotiations and exchanges of knowledge within relevant governmental institutions. All participants might not be completely happy under these conditions, but they can work together to achieve a result.

The branch of the Dutch government that is responsible for space development and national space planning is the Ministry of Spatial Planning, Housing, and the Environment (VROM). VROM collaborates with the ministries in charge of agriculture, nature preservation, the environment, water management, and transportation to set policies and to determine both guidelines and budgets for regional and local planning authorities.

Table 9.1 History of national spatial planning concerning the Randstad

Period	Major policy document	Key words/concepts
1960–1973	• First national policy document on spatial planning (1960) • Second national policy document on spatial planning (1966)	• Randstad wings: North and South • Decentralized metropolis • Radiation outwards • Concentrated deconcentration • Central open area • Agricultural central area
1973–1988	• Third national policy document on spatial planning (1976)	• Concentration in urban districts • Intensification of fringes • Refining open central area • Growth centers • Buffer zones • Compact city
1988–1998	• Fourth national policy document on spatial planning (1988) • Fourth national policy document on spatial planning Extra – VINEX (1991) • De Ruimte van Nederland (1996)	• Randstad metropolis • Randstad international • Ecological infrastructure • ABC Policy for business locations • Compact city
1998–Present	• Draft fifth national policy document on spatial planning (2000)	• Network city • Urban networks • Delta Metropolis • Green heart and green belts • Diversity

The national government sets the direction and parameters of what is to be achieved in spatial planning through periodic Spatial Planning Reports prepared by the interdepartmental National Spatial Planning Commission. The commission implemented the present planning act in 1965, and since that time the act has been regularly amended to adapt to new developments in spatial planning law. An important element of these National Spatial Planning Reports has been the priority given to the concept of nature and its relation to urban entities. Views of decentralization have varied over the years, with the focus shifting from housing to the environment to, later, the economy.

In summary, the creation of space in the Netherlands is a fundamental part of government policies, and this is reflected in their National Planning Reports. Because of the destruction caused by World War II, the main objective in the second half of the 1940s and the 1950s was to create adequate housing facilities under the centralized management of the government. In the 1960s, emphasis shifted toward aspects of land use planning. In the 1970s and the 1980s, however, urban renewal and centers of urban growth were high on the agenda. During the 1990s, physical planning was oriented toward reinforcing the metropolitan economy by improving the climate for business investments in the Randstad. The proposed planning emphasis for the period of 2000 to 2020 can be characterized as a turning point in which two main ideas are central: (1) reduce top-down planning regulation and further shift planning responsibilities to regional and local levels of government; and (2) focus on spatial and economic concepts such as the Delta Metropolis that would allow the Randstad to compete with and be part of international urban networks.

Approaches to planning and design

The third step in understanding Dutch planning and design traditions is to explore both some planning approaches that have been implemented in the Randstad and the policies that ensure the advancement of such approaches. The Dutch have an international reputation for achieving high standards for design and making the most of their natural and urban settings. The Randstad region is faced with challenges in improving the spatial quality of life due to a combination of high demand for new homes, jobs, and facilities, and the creation of a means of access to these newly urbanized areas. While this region is under constant pressure from both urban and green spaces, its current conditions represent an opportunity to develop approaches and implement strategies that support new sustainable technologies and a more sustainable urban development pattern. The Dutch have been aware of the significance of sustainable development when shaping urban policies, and they have experienced favorable outcomes. Some of the most innovative planning and design approaches currently being introduced include: (1) the practice of multiple land use, (2) the development of the concept of "Rurban," and (3) the implementation of sustainable design programs. All of these approaches have had positive outcomes and may serve as models for other urbanizing regions in the world. These approaches and others are discussed below in detail.

Multiple land use

The western part of the Netherlands used to be a collection of mid-sized cities, each with its own history and distinct identity, dialect, and architecture. Traveling through this part of the country used to reveal each town as a separate entity, clearly visible in a flat landscape of canals, black and white cows, farms, and windmills (van der Hoeven, 2004). Over the past three decades, though, these traditionally compact and dense Dutch cities have been transformed into a vast urban region that has swallowed smaller towns and villages. Many Randstad residents feel that the Randstad region is full. There is a general desire to accommodate some of the demand for urbanization elsewhere in the country while also creating extra space for nature and recreation. Most residents agree that available land or open space has become a scarce commodity that needs to be cherished and carefully managed. The Randstad has almost 7.1 million people, with six million living in or near the cities. Growing populations in the districts of major cities have resulted in several problems, such as a shortage of decent housing, too little land on which to build, and widespread commuting that has led to enormous traffic problems. There is limited space available for recreational facilities and there has been an increase in environmental pollution (water, air, soil, and noise pollution).

Urban areas in the Randstad have shown dramatic growth over the past three decades; current trends of land consumption cannot continue to be supported in this region. There is a tremendous need for land use practices that can preserve the choices that consumers have made in the past decades. Some scholars argue that the growing population is no longer the main cause of rapid urban sprawl. Socio-economic developments and the shift in consumers' needs are the main causes for the existing population's desire to consume more space for its urban functions than ever before.

According to a study by the Ministry of Housing (2001), within the past 30 years there has been a nearly 50 percent decrease in the number of occupants per household and in the number of units per hectare, while the floor area per home has increased by almost 80 percent. The average Dutch dwelling was home to four persons in 1960, but by 1995 this figure had dropped to 2.5 persons (van der Hoeven, 2004). In the pre-war areas of the major cities like Amsterdam, Rotterdam, and The Hague, the size of the average home was about 60 square meters of net floor area. In more recent residential areas, this size has increased to somewhere between 80 and 120 square meters of net floor area, depending on whether housing is subsidized by the government or is more upscale and privately owned (van der Hoeven, 2004). In the same period, the average housing density fell from gross 70 to 80 units per hectare before the war to a gross of 30 to 40 units per hectare after the war (van der Hoeven, 2004). What is called a "lack of space" is merely the result of a transition of public space into the private realm that translates into bigger

Figure 9.2 Examples of multiple land uses: City of Almere (top image) and City of Nijmegen (bottom image). Courtesy of Jesus J. Lara, 2009.

houses with gardens and garages. Consequently, Dutch cities have to explore new and innovative ways to provide room for more development in urban areas.

Traditionally, the western part of Holland has dealt with its limited space by expanding horizontally, turning water into land. Most of the potential for land reclamation was exhausted in the last century, and reclaiming land from water through the process of poldering has reached environmental limits (van der Hoeven, 2004). Remaining open water is needed for nature, recreation, and agriculture. Rather than expanding horizontally, the Dutch have shifted to multiple land use, which is characterized by two principles that result in a more compact and densely built-up environment: (1) use space left over after plan implementation or infill development; and (2) use the urban transformation and processes of abandoned and dilapidated area.

Space left over after plan implementation: Urban planning practices of the 1960s and 1970s left vast amounts of internal unbuilt space scattered all over cities (van der Hoeven, 2004). Since the 1980s, most Dutch cities have evaluated these resources in connection with the compact city policy that was mandated in the fourth National Planning Report. With current population increases in urban areas of the Randstad, cities are facing challenges of urban intensification where the leftover space provides untapped resources for existing built-up areas. These leftover spaces struggle with noise, emissions, and external risks of various kinds associated with infrastructure, facilities, and factories that will require special environmental mitigation in order to provide new uses and services. Nonetheless, they have been successfully adapted for new uses, such as the cases of Kop Van Zuid in Rotterdam, The New Ceramique in Maastricht, or the Eastern Docks in Amsterdam.

Urban transformation processes: The transformation of obsolete and abandoned facilities into new uses and services helps to mitigate the lack of space for new development in already congested urban areas. For example, dock areas in both Amsterdam and Rotterdam have been transformed into vibrant mixed-use developments with all of the amenities and services typically available in city centers. This process of reuse has been taking place throughout the Netherlands in the past 20 years, but it has been the most successful in the Randstad, where innovative and environmentally conscious projects have been unparalleled. Projects like the Koop Van Zuid in Rotterdam, the Eastern Docks in Amsterdam, and the New Ceramique in Maastricht, have been able to absorb some of the demands for urban live–work types of environments, thus bringing economic vitality to the area.

Rurban developments

For the past two decades, the Netherlands has seen an increase in mobility and economic affluence that has triggered changes in housing demands. Housing preferences have shifted from the traditional inner-city housing projects of the 1950s and 1960s socialist era to rural living with all of the amenities and services

Figure 9.3 Examples of re-adaptive use projects in urban centers. Kop Van Zuid, Rotterdam is a project that has been the result of a shift of the port activities westward (top image); The Ceramique is a large-scale infill project that occupies 57 acres of the east bank on the Maas river in Maastricht (bottom image). Images courtesy of J. Lara, 2009.

of a city environment. For many housing consumers in the Randstad, the ideal residential environment is close to services and amenities, employment, and transport, while at the same time maintaining a green and village-like character. Given the lack of space and strict compact city regulations, such residential environments are scarce or nonexistent in many parts of the Randstad. A study by van der Wouden et al. (2005) shows that this is not only disappointing for housing consumers, it is also unsatisfactory for towns and cities. Because the towns and cities are not meeting demands for green urban residential environments, their middle- and higher-income residents are leaving. This has resulted in economic losses for the area (Bukman, 2004).

Like other Western urban societies, the Netherlands has its own "rural idyll," or idealization of country life. This rural idyll has been a strong influence on the type of homes that people desire and the residential environments in which they prefer to live (van Dam, 2005). Studies have shown that many urban dwellers looking for new homes in rural environments can fulfill their housing desires by settling down on sites near or even in cities (van Dam, 2005). To meet the demand for rural residential environments around towns and cities, the Netherlands Institute for Spatial Planning has implemented what it calls "Rurban" development. This involves transposing valued characteristics attributed to the countryside, such as peace and quiet, open green spaces, convivial social structures, small-scale character, and safety, to the urban edge or even into urban areas themselves.

Studies have identified two dimensions to the demand for Rurban living. First, the morphology (the form) of the residential environment plays a role: there is a high demand for spacious homes built at low densities on large plots in a green and tranquil environment. Second, the sociology (the essence) of the residential environment is important because housing consumers display a marked preference for small-scale, orderly, and safe residential environments (van Dam, 2005). Moreover, there is a general preference among consumers not only for privacy, but also for a sense of community, a convivial atmosphere, and social engagement and solidarity. Rurban developments can fulfill all these needs. Optimally, Rurban residential environments can be developed around all of the main towns and cities or urban conurbations in the Netherlands where the need for housing is the greatest.

Sustainable design programs, practices and technologies

Sustainable design has been part of the planning and design agenda in the Netherlands for at least 35 years. While sustainable design technologies did not enjoy full support from national and local governments during the 1970s and 1980s, sustainability has since become a national priority that is highlighted throughout the fourth and fifth National Planning Reports. As a result, the Dutch Ministry of Housing, Spatial Planning and the Environment (VROM) produced white papers in 1995, 1997, and 1999 that contain programs and action plans to get sustainability on the agenda of all actors involved in the built environment (Bueren and Boonstra, 2001). One of these programs is the "City and Environment" program, outlined below.

The Fourth National Policy Document of 1990 placed a high priority on creating compact cities and minimizing environmental demands. One way to achieve this was to use space for multiple purposes, allowing green space around cities to remain open as areas for recreation and preservation. However, intensified building within urban areas in an attempt to achieve compact urban forms had negative social and environmental consequences. These consequences included, but were not limited to, noise, air, and soil pollution, and safety problems (Ministry of Housing, 2003). Avoiding these problems is especially difficult in such locations as railway stations and inner-city industrial parks given the high number of stakeholders involved in the process and the high number of issues that needed to be addressed. As a result, the Dutch government initiated the City and Environment Program to help environmentally challenged urban areas use place-based policy and strategy to come up with creative ways to make them more livable. The main features of the City and Environment Program are: (1) an area-based approach; (2) cooperation among parties (national, regional, and local authorities and companies; organizations; and local residents); (3) integration of different sectors (environment, spatial planning, health, economics); and (4) a flexible application of regulations, if necessary (Ministry of Housing, 2003).

The success of the City and Environment Program is due to its ability to create tailor-made solutions for particular locations and its emphasis on involving all parties in the decision-making process (Ministry of Housing, 2003). At the beginning of each complex urban redevelopment project, all parties concerned are encouraged to participate. In some cases, the process involves bringing together environmental experts, spatial planners, commercial parties, local residents (or their representatives), and stakeholder organizations. Environmental and health issues are included in spatial plans from the very beginning. Currently, 25 locations have been identified to participate in this program. According to the Ministry of Housing (2004), an important characteristic that has made this program successful since its inception back in the mid-1990s is a three-step approach involving tailor-made solutions that solve problems at the source and provide a little bit of flexibility with regard to environment law.

Step 1) Source policy: Major environmental issues are solved by dealing with them at their source. For example, lowering the speed limit from 100 to 80 kilometers per hour on the A13 motorway that cuts through the residential district of Overschie in Rotterdam greatly reduced the region's air and noise pollution levels (Ministry of Housing, 2003).

Step 2) Tailor-made solutions: Creative thinking is used to produce solutions within the law. An example of this is the municipality of Smallingerland in the north of the Netherlands, where polluted sludge and waste from a refuse dump has been used to build a noise barrier between an industrial estate and a new residential area. According to the municipality, this approach allows them to kill two birds with one stone, solving soil pollution and noise problems simultaneously.

Step 3) Possible deviation from environmental legislation, regulations, and procedures: This option, which currently applies to only the 25 municipalities participating in the City and Environment Program, necessitated a special Experimental City and Environment Act that has been drawn up for the possible deviation from environmental legislation (Ministry of Housing, 2003). A good example of this is the case of the municipality of The Hague, which decided to revitalize the Scheveningen Harbor area near the North Sea by constructing flats on the quay with a view out to the sea. Measures have been taken to combat noise problems at the source, but environmental permits have been limited and the central government has given the municipality permission to slightly exceed noise levels near the quay. By way of compensation, the new homes will be fitted with extra noise insulation and more green areas and playgrounds will be constructed in the residential area. Projects taking place in the 25 municipalities participating in the City and Environment Program can be divided into five categories to facilitate comparison among the various problem areas and possible solutions: (1) railway station areas, (2) harbor and riverbank areas, (3) inner-city areas facing a mix or change of functions, (4) post-war residential areas, and (5) inner-city industrial estates.

According to VROM, the experimental phase of the City and Environment Program was completed in 2004. After 2004, all local authorities in the Netherlands were given the option of relaxing environmental legislation and regulations to improve quality of life in urban areas. Under certain conditions, cities were allowed to deviate from environmental quality requirements with respect to noise levels, external safety, and soil and air quality. Under this program, the decisions taken by local authorities are intended to decrease the role of central government (Ministry of Housing, 2003).

This section has presented some of the most effective examples of urban development initiatives that have been developed in the Netherlands, including multiple land use practices, the implementation of Rurban developments as a response to shifting preferences among home owners, and approaches like the City and Environment Program that minimize environmental impacts in dense urban areas. In addition to the examples presented, there are many other initiatives that have been created in response to the complex challenges of urbanization. The planning programs and design strategies discussed in this section are among the most recent examples of how the Dutch government intends to deal with: (1) challenges related to the lack of space as a result of population increase as well as a new preference for larger homes, (2) the rehabilitation of neglected and abandoned urban areas to accommodate new uses and services, and (3) policies and programs that focus on making sustainability the driving force of every aspect of society. These urban development initiatives offer a model approach for cities and urban areas in any country with the necessary flexibility to enable a relatively easy transfer of knowledge.

Key factors that contribute to successful planning and design

Achieving sustainable development requires the attention and participation of all parties involved in the process, beginning with the initial stages of design and implementation and ending with post-occupancy project evaluation. Government support is a critical factor to the success of any sustainability initiative. Having back-up support from a government through policies and regulations can further ensure the realization of any sustainability initiative (Beatley, 2000, 2004; Bueren and Boonstra, 2001). In the Netherlands, the success of sustainable initiatives can be attributed to Dutch sustainable building and planning policies. Some of the key factors that have facilitated sustainable development in the Netherlands include but are not limited to: (1) A strong national government with embedded powers at different levels of the national planning system. The national government exerts power over important infrastructure, such as the freeway, rail systems, and airports. (2) There are stipulations in the national planning reports that support sustainable development; such is the case with the 1993 National Spatial Policy Plan. (3) A general awareness about the existing expansion conflicts among urban areas in the Randstad and the need for preservation and improving the quality of the Green Heart. (4) Lastly, the budget for sustainable development practices originates from the national tax base, not from the local tax base.

Dutch approaches: shifting emphasis

In addition to the influence of the factors mentioned above, the Netherlands has experienced a shift in the way in which urban design professionals and the general population approach environmental issues (Bueren and Boonstra, 2001; Vlassenrood, 2004). In addition to increasingly using sustainable materials, planners now look to larger-scale development. While they may have concentrated on single building blocks in the past, they now attempt to design or redesign neighborhoods, districts, and entire communities, all of which tend to have a larger impact on urban sustainability.

In the past 20 years, the increase in urban density and the lack of available space for new development, combined with the desire to promote urban living and increase vitality in cities, has led city planners to turn to recycling brownfield areas for new development rather than building new housing and offices in greenfield sites.

In addition, there has been a shift from the implementation of the physical system to the social system. The social environment in which sustainable building takes place has become important. There is no ecological sustainability without social sustainability. Issues such as social segregation, quality of life, and community involvement have acquired a prominent place on the agenda of Dutch politicians and designers.

Figure 9.4 Examples of shifting emphasis from materials and energy to other ecological themes. Delft University of Technology Library, a building of glass and grass. The climate façade, the grass roof, and the cold storage are the most important sustainability measures included in the library design (top image). Kattenbroek in Amersfoort, is a community planned and designed on ecological principles (bottom image). Images courtesy of Jesus J. Lara, 2010.

Practical innovations in the Netherlands: uncovering design and policy principles

Case studies are crucial to illustrate how planning and design approaches are carried out. The Randstad region in the Netherlands is an excellent example because it is home to some of the greatest concentrations of dynamic and innovative approaches in the world. Urban design and planning practices in the Randstad may provide lessons for other regions in the areas of urban planning and design.

The projects are documented under three main categories: (1) urban extensions, (2) compact infill, and (3) retrofitting urban areas. These case studies demonstrate urban design and planning qualities that reflect the desire to identify the "edge" of innovation in sustainable urban design-oriented projects. The diversity of project types is intentional, covering a range of activities, scales, and locations across the Randstad to ensure wide appeal to the general public and to illustrate as many principles as possible. Selected projects demonstrate the practical application of urban design principles and the benefits that come from good practice as well as areas where further improvements could be made. The methods for each case study analysis consisted of collecting background information for each site, including summary facts and project statistics. Next a description of the design process and urban design issues are explored, followed by an evaluation of the project's success and limitations, lessons learned, and the value gained.

Urban extensions/VINEX locations

In the Netherlands, the quality of urban design and the conditions for urban planning have been set out in the plans for the VINEX sites by VROM. The VINEX policy is an urban compaction policy designed to meet regional needs for housing, employment, health care, and urban facilities on a regional scale. In qualitative terms, the VINEX projects represent an opportunity to design genuinely new city areas with urban character, compact building development, varied programs, and a strong relationship with the existing city, by which I mean the built environment and existing social connections. In some cases, opportunities for relationships with the existing city are achieved through a combination of public transport and business premises or through the creation of socio-cultural facilities. The three Vinex projects explored in this research are: (1) Ypenburg (The Hague), (2) IJburg (Amsterdam), and (3) Leidsche Rijn (Utrecht).

The VINEX projects, which were introduced in the Fourth Policy Document on Spatial Planning Extra (Boeijenga and Mensink, 2008), are supported by policies that promote the implementation of compact cities. The Fourth Policy Document contained massive house-building targets, and mobility objectives played a key role in the policy. Therefore, the location, layout, and accessibility of new VINEX housing developments were designed to help reduce non-essential car use. This concentration of urban development aims to provide a critical mass for urban

Figure 9.5 IJburg, a VINEX housing project, involves the reclamation of six artificial
islands of different size and consists of 18,000 dwelling units for some
50,000+ inhabitants (top image); Ypenburg is situated in the conurbation of
the Randstad between The Hague, Delft and Rotterdam and consists of
12,000 homes, subdivided into several projects (bottom image). Images
courtesy of Jesus Lara, 2010.

services and amenities and limit further urban expansion and encroachment on rural areas while also curbing growth in mobility (Ministry of Housing, 2000; Boeijenga and Mensink, 2008).

To keep up with increasing housing demands from its growing population, the Dutch government plans to build approximately 750,000 housing units between 1995 and 2015. A common goal among these developments is to provide the quality of life found in large residential areas within the city. The locations of the VINEX projects are strategically situated close to existing city centers, to which they can easily be connected via existing public transportation and road infrastructure. An important aspect of the programmatic design of the VINEX projects is the attention given to the social structure of these urban extensions. For example, key percentages of housing units are allocated for private owners in addition to rental units (Ministry of Housing, 2000). These practices allow different income and ethnic segments of the population to live in these newly designed communities.

It is anticipated that the VINEX projects will be a major force in the way that cities and urban areas in the Netherlands will be shaped in the future, given their scale, location, and the lifestyle they promote. For instance, approximately 360,000 dwellings are planned in the seven largest urban areas—100,000 of them in the inner cities of those areas; 161,000 in the remaining urban areas; and 177,000 outside the urban areas (Ministry of Housing, 2000). To put this in perspective, the housing stock for the city of Utrecht alone is about 103,000 housing units, meaning that the entire proposed new housing would be almost eight times the size of Utrecht, the third largest city in the Netherlands, approximately 828,145 units. This results in an annual task of adding approximately 55,000 dwellings to the existing stocks (Roo, 2003). The vast majority of the urban population currently lives and works in expansion districts rather than the historic city centers. The quality of life in VINEX projects has influenced the daily living environment of the contemporary urban dweller, which has shifted from the traditional city center to its periphery; the periphery has become their center.

Compact infill

Compact infill development is an urban strategy frequently implemented in the Netherlands. It is intrinsically connected to the National Compact City Policy, which has been highly regarded by the planning authorities of the Netherlands since the 1980s. Given the Netherlands' small size and high density, cities are the most popular places to live and work. The compact city is seen as the answer to two main problems that plague the Randstad and other densely populated areas: (1) fast urbanization of open space and (2) the continued increase of mobility. As a result of these two urban issues, VROM introduced the Compact City Policy as part of the Fourth Physical Planning Report Extra in 1990. The idea was that such polices would contribute to the spatial quality of both urban and rural areas. In addition, one of the expected positive byproducts of compact city policies was a positive effect on the environment because of reduced traveling distances.

Figure 9.6 Examples of compact development: Nieuw Sloten, Amsterdam (top image), and the City of Almere downtown area (bottom image). Images courtesy of Jesus J. Lara, 2009.

The next two case studies under this category included two major projects dealing with compact infill development in highly urbanized parts of the urban fabric: (1) New Centrum in the city of The Hague, and (2) The New Ceramique in the city of Maastricht. Although the latter case study is not located within the Randstad region, I strongly believe that it represents a very interesting and successful example of a compact urban infill project.

Current urban design and planning in the Netherlands is striving to improve quality of life in general. The process of improvement is achieved by providing the physical and social conditions for a good living and a productive climate. Under the Ministry of Housing's general policy, which calls for the mixed use of space for housing, work, and recreation, first priority is given to developments that take place within existing cities and in areas bordering existing cities. In addition, it is expected that about 1.1 million new homes will be built by 2015. About one-third of these new housing programs will have to be implemented within city limits. Roughly another one-third will cause further expansion of the city due to the development of new residential areas. Another one-third will be built away from city boundaries and, consequently, will contribute to the further urbanization of the countryside (Roo, 2003). Consequently, compact infill of any form of available or underutilized space in the urban area, especially in the highly urbanized Randstad, has to be carefully planned and designed to accommodate a high density of use and activities.

Modernizing infrastructure/retrofitting urban areas

Space in the Netherlands is scarce, so any available space is highly valued. Therefore, the sustainable use of such space is a major concern of the Dutch planning authorities. The increasing concentration within urban areas has forced planning authorities to provide alternative new spaces for redevelopment within existing urban areas. As a result, there has been a shift in the way that the Dutch approach issues of scarce land for development. Some of the new developments are taking place on former brownfield areas, leftover spaces from planning, and in former industrial areas. In these situations, the activation of urban spaces with obsolete uses and functions represents a feasible solution for new uses and densities within the urban context. In this way, urban areas in the Randstad have been part of the urban transformation of inner-city industrial areas, harbors, factories, public utilities, and hospitals over the past 10–20 years. These new urban spaces play an important role in adapting the city to the changing demands of its residents.

Conclusion

Planners in the Randstad region are always in search of design and planning practices that will improve the quality of life for its citizens and thus provide the right conditions for economic prosperity. These basic principles have been part of the planning process in the region since the Middle Ages, and they can be better

Figure 9.7 Examples of modernizing infrastructure: Eastern Docks in Amsterdam (top image) and The Hague New Centrum (bottom image). Images courtesy of Jesus J. Lara, 2010.

understood through the examination of: (1) the factors that have contributed to make the Randstad the economic powerhouse of the Netherlands; (2) the crucial role of the Dutch National Spatial Strategy and its impact on the urban and rural landscape development of the entire country; and (3) the critical function of some of the specific planning and design strategies that have been implemented to achieve a more sustainable society.

The physical and socio-cultural qualities of the region have enabled the Randstad to maintain its strong position in the Dutch economy and remain the cultural and political center of the Netherlands. What sets the Dutch apart from development in other parts of the world is an integrated means of responding to city planning that most countries have not yet even discussed, let alone put in place. Proactive responses to pressing issues of urbanization are an integral part of the Dutch National Spatial Strategy Reports. In the reports, specific concepts and ideas are introduced to deal with issues of nature, urban entities, and decentralization. Intensification approaches and strategies have shifted their focus from decentralized development and housing to improving the quality of urban life, the environment, and the economy. In addition, the implementation of critical and strategic design policies and planning strategies have been crucial to the sustainability process in the Netherlands. Sustainable planning and design was elevated to a national planning strategy in 1988. This process moved away from master plans, enabling cities to provide tailor-made solutions through the implementation of piecemeal projects and a strategic planning policy that responds to each targeted location. Scholars and critics agree that the Dutch have embraced and intensively incorporated into their planning, design, and other policies explicit considerations of sustainability. The concept of sustainability is generally a higher priority in Holland and Europe than it is in the United States (Beatley, 2000).

Overall, the "Dutch Model" involves creative technologies and innovative solutions; it is a reliable testing ground for transformations that have been altering the physical and social makeup of urban areas. This model and the examples presented in this chapter may be a benchmark for other countries and urban regions. They also provide an opportunity for architects, planners, and urban designers worldwide to rethink the ways in which urban infrastructure can be revitalized and modernized.

References

Beatley, T. (2000). *Green urbanism: Learning from European cities.* Washington, DC: Island Press.

Beatley, T. (2004). *Native to Nowhere: Sustaining Home and Community in a Global Age.* Washington, DC: Island Press.

Betsky, A. E. (2004). *False flat: Why Dutch design is so good.* New York: Phaidon.

Boeijenga, J., and Mensink, J. (2008) *Vinex Atlas.* Rotterdam: Uitverij 010 Publishers.

Bosma, K., and Helinga, H. (1997). *Mastering the city: North-European city planning, 1900–2000.* Rotterdam: Nai Uitgevers Publishers.

Bukman, B. (2004). *Hybrid landscapes: Designing for sprawl in the Netherlands 1980–2004*, Stichting Lijn in Landschap.

Bueren, E. M., and Boonstra, C. (2001). Sustainable design in the Netherlands. In Edwards, B. (ed.) *Architectural Design (Special Green Architecture Issue), 71*(4), 76–81.

Faludi, A., and van der Valk, A. J. (1994). *Rule and Order: Dutch planning doctrine in the twentieth century*. Boston, MA: Kluwer Academic Publishers.

Hall, P. (2002). *Urban and regional planning*. London: Routledge.

Hall, P., and Green, N.(2005). *Commuting and the definition of functional urban areas*. Amsterdam: Institute of Community Studies/The Young Foundation & Polynet Partners.

Ministry of Housing. (2000, 2001, 2004). *Compact cities and open landscape: Spatial planning in the Netherlands*. The Hague: The Ministry.

Ministry of Housing. (2003). *Livable cities: A Dutch recipe for environmental spatial planning in the city and environment project*. The Hague: The Ministry.

Roo, G. (2003). *Environmental planning in the Netherlands: Too good to be true: From command-and-control planning to shared governance*. Burlington, VT: Ashgate.

Rosemann, J. H. (2005). The strategies of planning, urban transformation and governance: The case of the Netherlands. Exploring Urbanism lecture series (reader fall 2005), Delft, the Netherlands, Delft University of Technology.

Simmonds, R., and Hack, G. (2000). *Global city regions: Their emerging forms*. London: Spon Press.

van de Ven, G. P. (2002). *Man-made lowlands: History of water management and land reclamation in the Netherlands*. Utrecht: Uitgeverij Matrijs.

Van de Beek, H.M.C. (2006). *Statistics: Randstad Region Europe*. Randstad Region, the Province of Zuid-Holland, Utrecht, the Netherlands.

van der Hoeven, F. (2004). Multiple land-use through effective usage of subsurface dimension. Retrieved from http://www.bouwweb.nl/ob/vdhoeven/ (accessed April 27, 2012).

van der Wouden, R., Dammers, E., and van Ravesteyn, N. (2006) Knowledge and policy in the Netherlands: The role of the Netherlands Institute for Spatial Research. *NSL network city and landscape*, DISP-Online. Retrieved from http://www.nsl.ethz.ch/index.php/en/content/view/full/1198 (accessed May 15, 2012).

Part

E

Remaking the urban landscape

Chapter 10

Turning cities around

Lars Gemzoe and Sohyun Park

Introduction

Increasing urbanization is a critical issue that many cities in the world face. While developing countries go through severe environmental (e.g., air quality) and social problems (e.g., gentrification) and trade-offs for urban and economical development, many large cities in developed countries suffer from extensive urbanization or post-urbanization issues resulting in urban sprawl, suburbanization, downtown decline, and even rural sprawl. In order to cope with these challenges and create more livable and sustainable cities, trends such as neo-traditional approaches or new urbanism have emerged as alternatives to retrofit cities with more improved spaces and innovative ideas. In particular, significant efforts have been made to enhance public spaces in cities all over the world. For example, trams and bicycles that emerged in the late nineteenth century are being introduced again to the city center. New squares and parks are being created or re-established and practical strategies to improve pedestrian environments are being implemented in many city laboratories. This chapter describes the public spaces combined with the city life in changing society and explores urban regeneration strategies by introducing successful examples in urban design practice and policy.

Changes in human activity

From necessary to optional activities

The principle "form follows function" has been effectively proven in many parts of urban design. However, the function of public spaces in contemporary society appears to be determined by temporal and cultural processes as well. Indeed, public spaces have co-evolved with changing society from industrial to consumer city. While past city life relied heavily on "necessary" activities (e.g., waiting for the bus), contemporary city spaces provide more extensive and multifaceted experiences allowing "optional activities" (e.g., skating, social gathering). Such transition brings up the issue of quality of space and increasingly it becomes a crucial parameter in its use. Gehl et al. (2006) demonstrate how people have used public spaces in association with interplaying between public space design and social life. As shown in the example of Copenhagen, Demark, many cities during the twentieth century have undergone dramatic changes in the context of city life. In the early 1900s, necessary work-related activities dominated the streets where people had to use the space for their daily activities. This tendency had significantly decreased by the turn of the century. During the past several decades, necessary activities played only a limited role because indoor spaces have taken over what outdoor public spaces used to do. In contrast, both passive (e.g., people watching) and active (e.g., skateboarding) optional activities have grown exponentially. While the former has been recreational behavior for a long time, the latter is a more recent characteristic of city life. On another front, the invasion of the automobile began in the mid-1950s. The pressure of functional planning in the 1960s triggered a counter-reaction to reclaim city space. In the following 40 years this reaction was reinforced and developed nationally and internationally in an ongoing process (Gehl et al., 2006).

As city life in the public arena has changed in both character and purpose, the demands on quality in city space have grown accordingly. While necessary activities happen regardless of space quality, optional activities tend to occur only with the existence of good-quality city space. Once quality city space is offered, new possibilities for city life open up and people tend to use these possibilities. This relationship between quality, activities, and city life gives an idea on how public spaces should be shaped and how they can be used.

City life on the new frontier

The urban expectations in the twenty-first century include sustainability, health, and safety across the world (Newman and Kenworthy, 1999; Jenks and Dempsey, 2005; Nijkamp and Perrels, 1994; Zetter and Watson, 2006; Kushner, 2007; Pol et al., 2006; Gehl et al., 2006). A lot of research and previous practice recognize the fact that existing urban design policy contributes to obesity, air pollution, traffic congestion, and so on. Many cities are now endeavoring to provide a new vision for transit-oriented urban villages, pedestrian-scale development, traffic calming, and bicycle facilities (Newman and Kenworthy, 1999).With regard to the city life of the twenty-first century and its design implications, Gehl et al. (2006) present ten dimensions:

- *Transport:* walking is an uncomplicated, attractive, and pleasant way to get around the city. It is free, quiet, doesn't take up much room or make heavy demands on infrastructure;
- *Work:* many people still work in city space or have to travel to the city for other compelling reasons. Everyone needs good-quality city space;
- *Sustainability:* good public transport is an important alternative to car traffic. One prerequisite is good public space so that people can walk or cycle safely and comfortably to and from public transport;

- *Health:* getting exercise is easier when walking or cycling can be integrated naturally into a daily routine. A walk in the city is an attractive alternative to the expense of indoor exercise or fitness equipment;
- *Recreation:* other people are the main attraction in urban spaces. Recreation is often more spontaneous and accessible than most other forms. We see an opportunity, respond to it, and stay for a while;
- *Social interaction:* increased privatization of daily life makes the city even more important as a collective meeting place offering all types of contacts between people from quick glimpses to major events;
- *Information and inspiration:* direct contact is an important source of knowledge and insight and a good counterpart to the many indirect digital contacts of modern life. "Seeing things with your own eyes" is still an important dimension;
- *Democracy and diversity:* direct face-to-face meetings with other people of all ages, social statuses, cultures, and ethnic origins are an important element in efforts to strengthen a democratic, diverse, and secure society;
- *Friendliness and a feeling of security:* lively cities are spontaneously sensed as welcoming and safe. Abandoned cities and empty streets put people on their guard. The absence of people and city life is often the cause of real or imagined insecurity;
- *Room for the unexpected:* where there are other people there are always surprises and interesting things to look at. Being near other people gives us a reason to think about life and smile.

Four different scenarios of public space

A look at different cities and cultural patterns in countries where communications, marketplaces, and transportation have undergone radical changes in the last century gives a varied picture of the current uses of public space. The following describes four very different types of cities, using a good measure of simplification, at this time of history.

The traditional city

Considering cities as space in the public realm, the tradition of public space traces back to the Agora of Greece and Forum of Rome, where social solidarity and communal life formed (Kim and Park, 2006). The public space in such ancient cities did not belong to a particular individual, class, or corporation, but was understood to be common. According to Jürgen Habermas, the German philosopher, the public realm indicates that citizens can participate in any political events and thus public space was defined as the spatial reflection of community and became the substance of urban democracy. The marketplace was a representative public space found in traditional cities. It not only has economic functions, such as trade of goods, but also helps communication among citizens. Such commercial activities and political and legal processes occurred in pedestrian-dominated physical settings. Particularly, towns in the Middle Ages emerged on the premise of pedestrian traffic. Streets were adapted to foot traffic and squares tailored to uses that needed space: markets, town meetings, military parades, and religious processions. Venice, Italy is one of the best-known examples of continuing to function as an intact medieval city. Pedestrian-scale development is the most common characteristic in this period in terms of street dimension, distribution of streets and squares, and building details in harmony with human senses and behavior opportunities. In these cities, public spaces have served as meeting place, marketplace, and traffic space simultaneously.

The invaded city

As public spaces have been usurped by cars and subsequent irritants such as dirt, noise, and visual pollution, it didn't take long to impoverish city life. Such auto-dominated cities have continued to grow and sprawl, devouring farm and forest land and creating suburbs that engender considerable ambivalence (Newman and Kenworthy, 1999). More importantly, the reciprocal competition and invasion between the spaces for vehicles and people, transitory or chronic, have accelerated a widespread devastation of urban life. In impoverished public spaces, most of the social and recreational activities disappear completely, leaving only the remnants of the most utilitarian and necessary pedestrian activities. The car invasion of the cities influences many aspects, but particularly environment, public health, and safety, filling the sky with automobile emissions, causing modern disease due to the lack of physical activity, and increasing the number of conflicts between pedestrians or bikes and cars. In addition, there are other forms of invasion which reduce the variety of urban functions, as in an example of large office blocks in Stockholm, Sweden. Although the downtown works well for business, the lack of other vital city functions (e.g., entertainment, residences) causes dead and hollow spots. This fact is also a challenge for many large American cities to overcome. The vacant streets in downtown areas result from the failure to meet the diversity of urban functions offered by public spaces.

The abandoned city

Where urban tradition is weaker and car culture dominates with no constraints in urban planning, a new type of city develops. Where many activities traditionally tied to foot traffic have disappeared completely, public life is ignored. City centers are a sea of asphalt with parking places marking off the space between build-ings. Walking is difficult and would also be unreasonable. Walking distances are too long and walking environments are unsightly, dirty, and possibly dangerous. Sidewalks have disappeared in the city centers as well as residential areas, and all the uses of the city have gradually been adapted to serve the motorist. Transporta-tion and life itself are totally dependent on the car in a drive-in culture. It is difficult to describe the total consequences of this type of urban policy. However, it is important to point out that heavy dependency on the automobile means that children are too young, the elderly too old, and the handicapped find it too difficult to drive, and thus are consigned to a life of being transported by others.

In fact, personal mobility influenced the shift from downtown shopping to suburban shopping. Since their one-story floor plan and onsite parking requires large plots of land that were usually away from the city center, these changing patterns led to a boom of stand-alone shopping centers and, later, shopping malls, many of which were not suited to downtowns (Rybczynski, 1995). Some cities have attempted to bring a new form of shopping environment into the city center, such as shopping arcades or atriums like the Eaton Centre, in Toronto or shops-connected-skywalks in Calgary, Winnipeg, Minneapolis, and Atlanta; and the private setting called "underground city" in Montreal, Toronto, Sapporo, Nagoya, and Osaka. Despite various city-wide endeavors, it is common for most spaces to be private or quasi-public and controlled by unseen surveillance. Unlike traditional marketplaces which can be regarded as sort of open spaces, current shopping centers are by and large closed from outdoor spaces (Kim and Park, 2006). Such changes can be explained as liminality that Zukin (1991) states as extreme phenomena of European cities in the postmodern period. The liminal space where public space is brought into the private marketplaces signifies public spaces are bereft of meaning as spaces for liberal relaxation, mutual understandings, and democratic communication. Even though Victor Gruen, who designed the first shopping center at Northland Center in Detroit, Michigan in 1951, intended to create a community life and outdoor activities within an enclosed space, most of the malls became minimal in space design and not conducive for natural or outdoor experiences (Mitchell, 1995).

On the other hand, public health issues have arisen in these types of cities with more urban inhabitants who are overweight and in poor physical condition. A lot of research reveals that there is a correlation between public spaces and human health, indicating the importance of urban design as a powerful tool for improving human condition (Gehl and Gemzøe, 2000; Jackson, 2003; Moudon et al. 2005; Lee and Moudon, 2004, 2006). An increasing body of evidence suggests that moderate forms of physical activity can have beneficial effects on public health (Frank and Engelke, 2001). Building greenery at the parcel scale (Jackson, 2003), establishing a related policy and intervention program (Moudon et al., 2005), and investigating the determinants that motivate people to walk (Kealey et al., 2005) are all consequences of attempts to enhance civic life. In this sense, abandoned cities may need to rethink public policy approaches to realize health-promoting environments.

The re-conquered city

Over the past 40 years, interest in public spaces and public life have begun to grow again. Paradoxically enough, one source of inspiration came from shopping malls. Back in the 1920s when the first shopping center was built in the USA, customers were lured out of their cars and into car-free shopping streets to concentrate on shopping. It was also true of some of the earliest pedestrian areas in Europe such as Lijnbahn and many German cities in the 1950s. Many other pedestrian areas established in the 1960s and 1970s throughout Europe, including the pedestrian street in mid-Copenhagen from 1962, were also based primarily on the commercial concept. The idea of using public space as social and recreational space grew gradually and was reinforced during the decades that followed. Jane Jacob's seminal book, *The Death and Life of Great American Cities*, was published in 1961 and had tremendous influence. Since the 1970s, an increasing number of pedestrian areas and squares was established in European cities. An important turning point for the traffic situation in cities was the oil crisis starting in 1973. The break in traffic expansion led to planned efforts to limit car encroachment to ensure a better balance between motorists and other forms of transport.

The concept of "re-conquered city" originated in Barcelona, Spain and represents the starting point for a new, intense period for creating or renewing better urban spaces in the last 20 years. During the past few decades many cities, primarily in the Netherlands, Germany, and Scandinavia, have sought experimental types of city space. Urban policy and strategies related to quality of urban life can now be found in cities in North and South America, Asia, and Australia. Nevertheless, the desolate, invaded, or abandoned type of city still coexists with the cities that have fought back by inviting people to return to public spaces. The marked differences from city to city within the same cultural circles underline that successful urban improvements can be made or initiated by visionary individuals or urban programs. In the next section, some exemplary cities with this vision and efforts are described.

Case cities with visionary thinking

European cities where street environments have been thoughtfully and steadily enhanced over the last 30 years provide a sequence of inspirational public spaces. A wide range of efforts have been made to renovate or create public spaces with innovative vision. The following cities demonstrate good examples, treating public spaces and developing associated policy contributing to humanized and dramatized urban landscapes.

Barcelona, Spain

Barcelona is a vibrant city with three million people on the Mediterranean coast. The city center is dense and compact, reflecting centuries of population growth within the confines of city walls and ramparts. The old compact quarters are interlaced with narrow streets lined by tall buildings. Designed as a large grid with wide thoroughfares connecting to the old city, new neighborhoods grew up outside the limits of the old walled city. The new city was built with a radical plan by Idelfonso Cerda, who envisioned a new green and open city with less density, wider streets, and quadratic urban blocks with chamfered corners that create a square at every street intersection.

In Barcelona, public space policy arose from the need for spaces for pedestrians and for gathering people in the democratic tradition. Although the rapid and widespread establishment of public space was initially spurred by political shift from Franco's long dictatorship to new democratic government, the success of public space primarily results from a variety of visionary and imaginative ideas. In the old city center, several new squares were created by tearing down existing buildings to create the space for new meeting places. On the outskirts, new meeting places were centered upon the large sprawling areas that sprung up in the 1960s under the catchphrase "to put a face on the faceless." The new policy contributed to influencing other various private initiatives including urban renewal and renovation of dilapidated buildings. Pasqual Maragall, elected mayor in 1982, expressed the underlying philosophy of the policy: "We want to recreate the lost dignity of the urban landscape and to stimulate and direct the energy of the marketplace." The huge scale of Olympic projects served as an economic locomotive for planning of the entire city. Architecture and sculpture have played a key role in the design of Barcelona's public face. New parks and squares

Figure 10.1 Plaza Real located in the Gothic district of Barcelona. Image courtesy of Jesus J. Lara, 2010.

were created under the motto: "Move museums into the street." The unique characteristics of the squares were emphasized by the design of the space itself as well as the individual art works.

Lyon, France

Greater Lyon is the third largest city in France, with a population of more than 1.3 million, and lies at the confluence of the Rhône and Saône Rivers. The city center was built in the 1600s and 1700s. The comprehensive changes were driven by the poetic, coordinated, and social public policy. As traffic issues and unequal access to the city centre were critical problems, public space policy often worked with traffic policy. It is notable that social efforts were actively engaged in the process of urban public policy. The city council attempted to balance city improvement between the inner city and the suburbs. The policy has been a clear signal to inhabitants that everyone is equal and that no one gives greater priority to the city center than anyone else. The cohesive public space policy was formulated in 1989 by City Councilman Henry Chabert in cooperation with the visionary planner Jean Pierre Charbonneau. One of the remarkable endeavors includes underground multi-story parking lots constructed under the newly renovated squares. The relocated parking spaces not only made the city more pedestrian friendly but also applied quality design standards to the underground space. For instance, Place des Célestins provides a surprising view of a black-and-white striped periscope in the middle of the square. It also features a fascinating swirling ramp reflected by a giant rotating mirror so that people can experience themselves there.

Both green and blue plans are also significant characteristics to improve the city's spatial quality. "Green plans" develop with public spaces and "blue plans" operate with the city's relationship to water. For example, the green space of Place de la Bourse is densely planted with boxwoods in pots, contributing to the overall green structure. On the other hand, Place Antonin Poncet builds a connection all the way to the Rhône River, cutting across varied streams along the riverbank. The springs and fountains of Place des Terreaux produce a unique magical sound and light effect and at the same time give easy access for the people walking between the various bursts of water. Furthermore, a range of soft plans relating to lighting, furnishing, and materials contributed to the functional improvement in public space. The street of Rue de la République represents a successful lighting strategy especially for the course of façades stressing spatial impression by lighting reflection. The lighting plan is being gradually implemented since the relevant building owners need to pay for the initial installment of lighting fixtures, after which they are run and maintained by the municipality. The use of a fixed set of furnishings and materials provides a holistic effect and simplified maintenance. In order for buildings, space types, and landscape features all to be considered together, many different architects, landscape architects, and artists collaborate in the issues of making standard solutions in particular and better outdoor spaces in general.

Figure 10.2 Place des Terreaux is a square located in the center of Lyon. Image
courtesy of Jesus J. Lara, 2010.

Strasbourg, France

As the host city of the European Parliament, the Human Rights Tribunal, and many
other international institutions, Strasbourg has become a European capital. This
new position and obligation have been an important catalyst for extensive urban
renewal. With a regional population of 435,000 including 255,000 city inhabitants,
Strasbourg is not a large city by European standards but has held an important
position in European history and politics for centuries.

A combined strategy for public space and public transport for a new European
capital started in about 1990. The first step was to establish a ring road in 1992
and then the city center was closed to most traffic. Since the introduction of a
brand new collective traffic system, car traffic that took 73 percent of commuting
transportation has been markedly reduced. The goal of new tram lines was combined into one strategy that inspires the rethinking of all the squares, streets, and
roads touched by the tram lines. The first tram line, *Line A* has 22 designated stops
with the speed of 22 km/hour. Only a few years after its introduction in 1994, it
carried 70,000 passengers per day, well beyond the forecasted 50,000. Since 1990,
the use of public transport has increased by 43 percent and the number of trams
has been doubled by adding an extra line. *Line B* was initiated in 2000 with a
12.2 km track and additional lines are being planned for a total track length of
35 km. Adjacent to tram stops there are often important public spaces, including
Place Kléber (main square), Place de l'Homme de Fer (main public transport
interchange area), and Place de la Gare (expansive square junction between the
railway and Line A). The stops underneath the squares are connected to the
stations and underground shopping arcades. A horizontal, transparent glass roof

Figure 10.3 The city of Strasbourg combined strategy for public space and public transport. Image courtesy of Jesus J. Lara, 2010.

allows daylight into the underground area and makes a distinctive presence in the large, simple granite floor of the station square.

Freiburg, Germany

Freiburg is a relatively small city with a population of 200,000 but has many typical European characteristics in respects to design, function, and history. Located in the Rhine Valley in southwestern Germany bordering France and Switzerland, the city has a string of towns built in the 1100s by the Dukes of Zähringer. The towns were particularly based on a set of common planning guidelines characterized by wide main streets and public spaces as a market. In the following centuries, Freiburg also served as a fortification and border town under Austrian, French, and German rules. The city maintained its medieval core, not spilling over into new areas until the nineteenth and twentieth centuries. During World War II, the city was subjected to heavy aerial bombardment, and in November 1944 80 percent of the historic city center was entirely destroyed.

In contrast to many other cities demolished by the war, Freiburg reconstructed the historic network of streets and squares and maintained original building lines. The city policy formulated by Joseph Schlippe rejected the idea of widening streets to meet the demands for growing car traffic. Instead, car traffic was moved to a ring road while trams and bicycles continued to serve the city center. The first car-free streets and squares were established in 1968 around the Town Hall and Cathedral. In 1973 this development evolved into a large interconnected pedestrian area covering almost the entire old city. Freiburg has made extensive efforts to make a green, pedestrian-friendly city, especially during the last quarter century. In 1990, daily bicycle traffic to and from the city center accounted for 43,800 trips and ten years later the number had increased by 63 percent (71,400 trips), with traffic comprising 28 percent for bicycling commuters, 26 percent for public transport, and 46 percent for cars. Special tram lanes ensure faster public transport, a mandated prerequisite for state support. In 1999, a "mobility station" was built in direct connection to the railway and the bridge crossing the railway station. It has bicycle parking space in which train commuters can park their bikes.

A small stream system and pavement decorated with dark stones are the most distinctive visual components connecting streets and squares in the inner city. The small streams, 20–50 cm wide and 5–10 cm deep, diverted from the river Dreisan, run through the city. The stream system was once covered but was re-opened through implementation of a restoration plan. Today's small streams, called "bäckle," make a unique contribution to the street scene, being placed asymmetrically in the streets. The streams function not only as demarcation between pedestrians and tram lines but as urban playgrounds for children. The natural stone in pedestrian areas is another feature employed by city policy. While large surfaces are laid with granite blocks, sidewalk bands of small, primarily dark local stone are used along the facades. These courses of specially selected small stones are an old

Figure 10.4 The small stream system functions not only as demarcation between pedestrians and tram lines but also as an urban playground for children. Image courtesy of Jesus J. Lara, 2010.

German tradition, given a new interpretation and subsequent implementation that are very much characteristic of the Freiburg street scene. The sidewalk bands contain round symbols telling what kind of shops and businesses can be found along the street.

Copenhagen, Denmark

Copenhagen is the capital of Denmark and was founded around 1100. The city grew gradually from a small fishing village to a lively trading port with a population of 1.3 million inhabitants. Large segments of the moats and ramparts of the 1600s and 1700s are still intact and serve as some of the city's parks. Despite the major fires in the eighteenth century, the inner city maintains its medieval streets, dominated by simple neo-classical style from the beginning of the 1800s.

The streets and squares have gradually progressed with many small step-wise decisions in public policy. Although the city center was intensively dominated by car traffic and parking until 1962, many public spaces began to convert to pedestrian areas. Parking was eventually removed from a total of 18 squares, and the car-free streets and squares have increased to almost 100,000 square meters, six times the 15,800 square meters of 38 years ago. While parking has reduced by 2–3 percent annually, bicycle paths have been expanded. One of the new initiatives to promote bicycling is free city bikes financed by sponsors and advertising. Over 125 racks with 2,000 rental bicycles are available with a small deposit throughout the city. From 1970 to 1995, bicycle traffic has increased by 65 percent and car traffic throughout the whole municipality has held constant, despite its extreme increase in many large European cities. Today, Copenhagen is

Figure 10.5 An example of Copenhagen's car-free streets and squares. Image courtesy of Jesus J. Lara, 2010.

a city of biking and foot traffic. About 80 percent of the movements in the city center are by these modes and are the consequence of accumulated efforts in targeted public policy. The many small steps have not only changed people's traffic habits and patterns, but led to an unusually attractive city center, a relatively modest number of cars, and a profusion of public life that is quite extraordinary by Scandinavian standards.

Portland, Oregon, USA

Portland is located in the northwest of the United States. Greater Portland is home to 1.5 million people and has a typical North American grid pattern of streets and squares. However, its urban blocks are smaller and give the city an atypical scale. The city's design guidelines suggest several principles on which public space policy is based. For instance, the "Central City Plan Fundamental Design Guidelines 1990" is a remarkable set of quality criteria for city space design. The guidelines include three categories: city identity, pedestrian priority, and project design. The block structure of 61 by 61 meters is required for new buildings. The sidewalks are divided into several zones to conserve such functions as a street furniture zone

Figure 10.6 Pioneer Courthouse Square, located in the heart of Downtown Portland, is a public space hosting more than 300 programmed events each year. Image courtesy of Jesus J. Lara, 2010.

(sculptures, greenery, and furniture), a central walking zone, and a window-shopping zone along the building facades. The buildings adjacent to parks and squares are required to fit in with outdoor activities and thus create active edge zones.

Portland's Arterial Streets Classification Policy contributed to introducing a diversity of human activities through the transformation of priorities in road capacity. The urban sprawl legislation adopted in 1973 allowed new city functions only within designated areas of the "Urban Growth Boundary." In 1980, such efforts resulted in reinstating trams, discarded over the past three decades. The pedestrian-oriented policy and guidelines were inspired partly by grassroots movements and visionary politicians. Citizen participation and strong involvement of leading politicians have been an impetus for the city's new plans. The Pioneer Courthouse Square is a fine example of such an urban change. Many citizens, activity groups, the Friends of Pioneer Courthouse Square, and private and public agencies contributed to the conversion from car park to a public square. The square serves as a multifunctional space for various users, a central meeting place, a public transport hub, and an expansive living room inviting many different stationary activities.

Curitiba, Brazil

Curitiba is located in southern Brazil and is the administrative center of Parana. The city was founded by Portuguese colonists in 1693. Immigrants from Germany, Italy, Poland, and the Ukraine gradually became an important part of the local population. The population of 120,000 in 1943 tripled in the period from 1965 to 2000 and now it is over 1.5 million. This exponential urban growth necessitated a new city policy and planning ideas to achieve a sustainable living condition. One of the efforts is a five-finger plan for growth control, characterized by tall, dense buildings and diminished height at the edges of the linear growth corridors.

The policy puts a priority on ecological, social, cultural, and economic means for well-designed recreational areas and a pedestrian-friendly city center. The initial city plan developed by Jorge Wilheim in 1965 had objectives to lessen the traffic pressure and preserve the historic core. Those efforts were strengthened by the establishment of an independent planning organization, the Institute for Research and Urban Planning (IPPUC) and a mayor and architect, Jamie Lerner. In his three terms between 1972 and 1992, Jamie Lerner had major influence on the city's extensive and visionary planning.

Due to the flexibility and affordability, buses became more a means of public transport than trams or underground rapid transit. The city developed a bus system called "metro on rubber wheels": The buses have their own lanes separated from the other traffic. Specially designed buses and transparent, pipe-formed bus stops ensure fast, comfortable, and efficient transportation. One special feature is the "gangways" that automatically lower to exactly fit the openings at bus stops.

The bus system is organized around four different types of lines: silver for direct buses, red for express buses, green for cross-town buses, and yellow for the rest. Currently, the buses, with a speed of 30 km/hour, convey 1.7 million passengers daily and 78 percent of commuter traffic.

The city has operated remarkable environmental programs such as green trading: a scheme for the poor, who are given fresh vegetables in exchange for carefully sorted trash. In addition, more attention to good access to parks and public spaces has balanced the high population density. Along with 26 existing woods and parks, newer parks were created and restored from ecologically disturbed areas. Curitiba is distinctive compared to the majority of cities in other parts of the world which are similar in size and economic development because it has managed to control its growth, implemented effective public transport, and improved the urban environment through ecological and sustainable planning measures.

Cordoba, Argentina

Cordoba is the second largest city in Argentina, with a population of 1.5 million. The city is located 650 km northwest of Buenos Aires, on the border between the flat coastal plains and the mountains. Founded by Spanish colonists in 1573, it is laid out as a grid city in 110 by 110 meter blocks, in keeping with colonial tradition. After World War II, the city grew by adding amorphous suburban neighborhoods, while the city center kept its traditional system of urban blocks. The active, versatile, and dense city center still shows a mixture of valuable historical buildings.

The representative characteristics of public space were developed by Miguel Angel Roca with a strategic and unified vision relating to architectural and social policy. The city strategy comprised three cohesive elements with the objectives of encouraging social life and developing the city's identity: (1) strengthening the entire city center as a meeting place; (2) developing linear parks along the Suguia River bank; and (3) bolstering new neighborhoods by building nine suburban centers with decentralized municipal services. The major streets, squares, and parks were unified in a public project in which common design principles, materials, and details reinforced the architectural identity of the city as a whole. Another distinctive feature is revealed in pedestrian streets and squares with a changing variety of characters and treatments at every section. For instance, the reflection of Parliament outlines the chamber and seats on the floor so that people can indicate their political dissatisfaction by stamping on the white marble surfaces, a very direct interpretation of the Parliament of the street. Green roofs are distinct furnishing elements in a more commercial section of pedestrian zones. The plants in green roofs provide shade for pedestrians, reduce the noise from nearby traffic, and form an intimate ground-level space along the shops. The pergola system along the narrow streets is a relatively dominant element but it also hides the obtrusive signs above the shops. Similar treatments were given to the main squares mostly renovated around 1980, such as Plaza San Martin, Plaza Marvinas, and the Plaza Italia.

Melbourne, Australia

Melbourne is Australia's second largest city, with 3.3 million inhabitants. It played a crucial role as the capital until the relocation to Canberra in 1927. The Melbourne metropolitan area has a compact urban core and residential suburban area with single-family homes. The street network was designed in accordance with the traditional block pattern favored by English colonists. The 200 by 200 meter blocks are intersected by a secondary street system running east–west with smaller back lanes. The third network consists of internal arcades cutting through the blocks in a north–south direction. The small back lanes and covered arcades provide rhythm and variation to the otherwise rather rigid street pattern. Another feature is the absence of squares. Instead, the city has a number of large parks and small green areas often found as forecourts to churches and monumental buildings.

Melbourne's public space policy emphasizes street quality and pedestrian friendliness. With political leadership change in 1985, a new Urban Design Branch in charge of the city's public space projects was established and a new active policy was formulated focusing on rivers and parks, older urban quarters, traditional street networks, and the tram system. As a result, Melbourne has become a much greener city despite its already established reputation as a garden city. Along with an underground subway ring, the extensive tram network helps lessen traffic pressure caused by commuters from suburban areas into the concentration of workplaces. More importantly, trams represent Melbourne's particular attempts to preserve and develop the city's traditional values. Started in 1869, trams have continued to operate and old and various newly modeled trams, coupling the history and present of the city, provide colorful, unique street scenes. The city streets have been reinforced as important public spaces. In 1974 the city's first pedestrian mall was built in Bourke Street with a combination walking and tram street. In 1992 the city's main street, Swanston Street, was closed to private car traffic and renamed Swanston Street Walk. Now the street is a pedestrian and tram street with wide refurbished sidewalks. The privately owned squares such as South Bank Centre have occasionally been used for public recreation areas.

Conclusion

It is certainly promising that there are overwhelming interests in, and backing for, new public life in public spaces. In a society where daily life increasingly takes place in the private sphere, the city and public spaces have been given a new and influential role. As seen thus far, the urban shift will continue with changing city life, and undoubtedly it should be a way of promoting more sustainable and livable cities. Streets, parks, meeting areas, public transportation, and all other parts of the city not closed off for private use are vital for urban residents to value. When not valued, they begin to decline as places for social interchange. Advocating pedestrian use, while respecting the historical value of public spaces and improving pedestrian amenities, utilitarian cycling, and green development strategies is becoming more prominent in many neo-traditional cities. The exemplary practices described in this chapter provide many important lessons that other cities can learn from. Fine-grained and human-scaled space design, insightful concerns about social, environmental, and health issues, and quality of life driven by quality of place can be accomplished in other locations that are still experiencing the harmful consequences of urbanization, gigantism, and crudely designed urban landscapes. With an emphasis on "real" streets and squares, integrated functions in cities can bring a rich diversity of city life.

References

Frank, L.D. and Engelke., P.O. (2001). The built environment and human activity patterns: exploring the impacts of urban form on public health. *Journal of Planning Literature*. 16(2), 202–218.

Gehl, J. and Gemzøe, L., (1996). *Public Spaces: Public Life*. The Danish Architectural Press, Copenhagen.

Gehl, J. and Gemzøe, L. (2000). *New City Spaces*. The Danish Architectural Press, Copenhagen.

Gehl J., Gemzøe, L., Kirknæs, S., and Sternhagen, B. (2006). *New City Life*. The Danish Architectural Press, Copenhagen.

Jackson, L.E. (2003). The relationship of urban design to human health and condition. *Landscape and Urban Planning*. 64(4), 191–200.

Jacobs J. (2002). *The Death and Life of Great American Cities*. Reissue ed. Random House, New York.

Jenks, M. and Dempsey, N. (Eds.) (2005). *Future Forms and Design for Sustainable Cities*. Architectural Press, Oxford.

Kealey, M., Kruger, J., Hunter, R., Ivey, S., Satariano, W., Bayles, C., *et al.* (2005). Engaging older adults to be more active where they live: audit tool development. *Preventing Chronic Disease*. 2(2), 1–2.

Kim, I. and Park, S.J. (2006). *Urban Interpretation* (in Korean). GreenWay Press, Seoul.

Kushner, J.A. (2007). *Healthy Cities: The Intersection of Urban Planning, Law, and Health*. Carolina Academic Press, Durham, NC.

Lee, C. and Moudon, A.V. (2004). Physical activity and environment research in the health field: Implications for urban and transportation planning practice and research. *Journal of Planning Literature*. 19(2), 147–181.

Lee, C. and Moudon, A.V. (2006). Environmental correlates of walking for transportation versus recreation purposes. *Journal of Physical Activity and Health*. 3(1), 99–117.

Lekagul, A. (2002). *Toward Preservation of the Traditional Marketplace: A Preference Study of Traditional and Modern Shopping Environments in Bangkok, Thailand*. Doctoral Dissertation of the Virginia Polytechnic Institute and State University.

Mitchell, D. (1995). The end of public space? People's Park, definitions of the public, and democracy. *Annals of the Association of American Geographers*. 85(1), 108–133.

Moudon, A.V., Lee, C., Cheadle, A., Collier, C., Johnson, D., Schmid, T., and Weather, B. (2005). Cycling and the built environment. *Transportation Research D*. 10(3), 245–261.

Newman, P. and Kenworthy, J. (1999). *Sustainability and Cities: Overcoming Automobile Dependence*. Island Press, Washington, DC.

Nijkamp, P. and Perrels, A. (Eds.) (1994). *Sustainable Cities in Europe*. Earthscan, London.

Pol, P.M.J., Mingardo, G., Speller, C.J.M., and and Berg, L.V.D (Eds.) (2006). *The Safe City: Safety and Urban Development in European Cities*. Ashgate Publishing, London.

Rybczynski, W. (1995). *City Life: Urban Expectations in a New World*, Scribner, New York.

Safdie, M. and Kohn, W. (1998). *The City After the Automobile: An Architect's Vision*. Westview Press, Boulder, CO.

Zetter R. and Watson, G.B. (Eds.) (2006). *Designing Sustainable Cities in the Developing World*. Ashgate Publishing, London.

Zukin, S. (1991). *Landscapes of Power: From Detroit to Disney World*. University of California Press, Berkeley.

Chapter 11

Re-urbanization in Thailand

Reconsidering urban development following the tsunami

Khanin Hutanuwatr

Introduction

The 2004 Southeast Asian tsunami has devastated Thailand in various areas. It caused the deaths of 8212 people, leaving 1449 children orphans. Approximately 1000 of 1757 households of indigenous groups and about 400 small-scale fishing communities were damaged. Unfortunately, most are low-income communities where financial power to recover may not be sufficient. The waves destroyed and damaged more than 6800 houses, resulting in over 7000 homeless. Although not the country most devastated by the tsunami, Thailand experienced the second largest economic impact from this extreme event. It was estimated that the impacts cost 2.09 billion USD, resulting in significant long-term livelihood issues. Environmental impacts included coastal ecological systems that suffered from debris of building and infrastructure destruction. The impacts also included damage to the coral reef and sea grass, upon which many marine species rely. In addition, sea water damaged many types of vegetation, changing land conditions and affecting existing agriculture (World Bank, 2006). This caused many agencies to react by providing relief, rehabilitation, recovery, and mitigation. The Thai government and other local and international agencies have responded with emergency assistance and rapid housing projects, redevelopment plans, and the establishment of local and regional early warning systems.

While technical responses (e.g., building techniques, physical modeling, and warning systems) have been heavily discussed, recent literature in hazard and disaster management has expanded to include social, cultural, economic, and political dimensions in the investigation of disasters. This broader approach addresses "vulnerability" (Hewitt, 1983, 1997; Bolin and Stanford, 1998; Wisner et al., 2004) in recent hazard and disaster literature. Since the term vulnerability has been used widely and diversely, it is important to discuss its definition before going into detail.

The following sections provide an overview of this concept along with its relationship with another emerging concept, "resilience." The methodological approach of this study is also described. Later, the chapter discusses the interaction between tourism, land ownership insecurity, and the tsunami in Southeast Asian countries, and provides three specific case studies in Thailand.

Overview of vulnerability and resilience

Although vulnerability and resilience have been used together occasionally, these two concepts are rooted in different disciplines. While vulnerability has been developed mostly through sociology, political ecology, and social geography, resilience is derived mostly from ecology. However, they are strongly related.

In this chapter, vulnerability refers to processes rather than conditions. Here vulnerability is defined as social processes that influence capacity to cope with and recover from extreme events. From this view, causes of disaster are not just about natural events or the lack of structural mitigation systems, but comprise various layers of social processes such as what Wisner et al. (2004) laid out in their Pressure and Release Model demonstrating the progress of vulnerability from root causes to unsafe conditions. Understanding such social processes will then help policy makers to plan ahead of time, to manage resources appropriately, and grab the opportunity to reduce vulnerability (Moser et al., 2008)

On the other hand, resilience has many times been referred to as the opposite of vulnerability. In this study resilience is defined as the ability to "absorb" and at the same time to "adapt" continuously to maintain the survival of the system from disturbance (Resilience Alliance, 2006; Pelling, 2003; Holling, 1973). Originally, this term was used to characterize the behavior of ecological systems. Its key concept is the ability to absorb changes from disturbances. The ecologist Holling (1973, p. 17) said "Resilience . . . is a measure of the ability of the system to absorb changes of state variables, driving variables, and parameters and still persist." In addition to resilience, Holling (1973) defined "stability" as the contrasting behavior of an ecological system. "Stability" means "the ability of the system to return an equilibrium state after temporary disturbance" (Holling, 1973, p. 17). However, it is this author's view that the ability to get back can also mean ability to absorb changes as well. Therefore, the two concepts are not exactly exclusive. As a result, it is not surprising that other ecologists such as Watt and Craig (1986) viewed that in order to protect the stability of the whole system, its components have to be adaptable, or in other words have to be resilient (Wildovsky, 1988).

Adaptability can be viewed as part of the concept of vulnerability or vice versa. Moser et al. (2008) noted that while vulnerability is the function of the ability to cope with external disturbance exposure and sensitivity, the ability to cope with external disturbance depends on "adaptive capacity." In this study, vulnerability is defined as social processes that influence the capacity to cope and recover from extreme events; thus, social processes that influence adaptive capacity can then also influence the capacity to cope with extreme events as well. As the concept of resilience is strongly related to adaptability, the concepts of vulnerability and resilience are related.

Methodological approach

The discussions in the following sections are drawn from preliminary field research in nine sites during June to August 2006 and ongoing research between 2007 and 2010. The study approach is based on Naturalistic Inquiries (Lincoln and Guba, 1985, 2000; Shkedi, 2005; Merriam, 2002; O'Leary, 2004). This means that the study acknowledges (1) multiple realities, (2) the importance of context and time over generalization, (3) the interaction between observers and the observed, (4) complex relationships rather than simple linear relationships, and (5) value-laden inquiries. Consequently, conventional criteria including internal validity, reliability, objectivity, and generalization are not applicable to this study. Instead, it looks for trustworthiness by credibility, dependability, conformability, and transferability. Consequently, data collection methods in this study are based on qualitative approaches, including in-depth interviews and observations in public panel discussions. In order to bring voices of the unheard, most interviewees were community leaders, general community members, and social advocates. Documents (e.g., reports, articles, and books) and field examination were also incorporated into the discussions.

Recovery vulnerability: tourism development, ambiguity in land rights, and recovery challenges in Southeast Asia

After the tsunami, there were significant issues in land rights disputes not only in Thailand but also other Asian countries such as Indonesia, Sri Lanka, and India (Wong, 2009; Brown and Crawford, 2006; Fitzpatrick, 2005; Schulze, 2005). In Thailand alone there were more than 36 communities involved in land disputes during recovery (Rice, 2005). The issue was acknowledged as one of the key obstacles in disaster recovery (Wong, 2009; Brown and Crawford, 2006). The devastation by the tsunami not only made millions of people homeless, but also resulted in displacement and expedited the process of so-called "land grabbing" (Clover and Eriksen, 2009; Brown and Crawford, 2006; Fitzpatrick, 2005).

In many cases, land ownership conflicts involved tourism development. Some serious concern exists that redevelopment plans tried to displace local indigenous communities from coasts in order to promote new tourism development (Rice, 2005; Brown and Crawford, 2006). For example, in Sri Lanka, a new 100-meter setback policy was introduced to coastal communities, which were mostly low-income fishing communities. However, the policy originally gave exceptions for tourism-related construction such as hotels, resorts, and spas (Leckie, n.d.; Rice, 2005; Brown and Crawford, 2006). The plan was later stopped due to local protests (Brown and Crawford, 2006).

Interestingly, even in non-disaster contexts, land grabbing was reported to be related to tourism. In Mozambique, for example, land grabbing was associated with game-based and eco-tourism development (Clover and Eriksen, 2009). Moreover, the practices of land grabbing were also observed to be involved with power and corruption (IIED et al., 2004), in that elite patrons and powerful people managed to take advantage of uncertainty in land rights. Skeptical practices in land administration associated with tourism were found in at least four African countries—Botswana, Zimbabwe, South Africa, and Mozambique (Clover and Eriksen, 2009). This may be the result of the dominating roles of administrative agencies responsible for entitling land rights that make it prone to conspiracy in African countries (IIED et al., 2004).

Although the issue of land grabbing for tourism development has been observed in the previously noted non-disaster context, disasters can provide opportunities to exacerbate this practice (Brown and Crawford, 2006). The author's preliminary fieldwork in Thailand suggests the likelihood of this pattern persisting, as further illustrated in the following section. The background of tourism development and land ownership in Thailand is introduced. Later, the combined pressures between tourism and land right insecurity that consequently influenced tsunami recovery in three Thai case studies are elaborated.

Thai context: tourism and land rights

Development of the southern region of Thailand was heavily influenced by tourism, resulting in the demand for coastal areas. In national, regional, and southern provincial plans, tourism development was among key components (ONESDB,

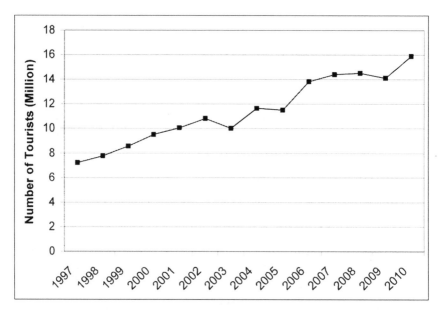

Figure 11.1 The number of tourists. Courtesy of the Department of Tourism, Thailand, 2010.

Figure 11.2 Tourism and related developments at Kaolak, Phang Nga, Thailand. Image courtesy of Khanin Hutanuwatr, 2010.

2006; OSM Andaman, 2010; Krabi City Hall, 2005). The number of international tourists increased almost every year (Figure 11.1). In 2010, there were about 16 million foreign visitors. This growing tourism generated a significant portion of revenues to the state, increasing from approximately $8400 million in 1999 to $17,000 million in 2009 (Kwankong, 2010). Despite threats such as violence, SARS, and other concerns, it was argued that Thai tourism was not seriously impacted in the long run (Rittichainuwat and Chakraborty, 2009; Howard, 2009). Consequently, tourism became a major part of the Thai economy.

This growth in tourism added to the expansion of human activities in the coastal areas of southern Thailand (Green, 2005). It became one of the key drivers in recent coastal urbanization. According to Save Andaman Network's report (SAN, 2005) and the author's field visits, rural areas were increasingly transformed into tourism-related land use such as resorts and hotels and other associated developments (e.g., housing for workers in a hotel, restaurants, tour agent business, photo labs, diving schools, different types of grocery stores, shopping centers, computer stores, etc. (Figure 11.2)). Compared to other regions, southern Thailand was an area where tourist accommodations were mostly concentrated. It is not a surprise then that the nature of this development led to the demand for coastal land for new tourism development.

While there were growing demands for coastal properties, land rights of some communities were insecure. This is similar to the case of Aceh, Indonesia. In Aceh, only 5–10 percent of premises were officially registered (Schulze, 2005). Some communities lived in the areas for a long time and thought that they did not need official land titles (Schulze, 2005). In Thailand, sea gypsy communities settled along coastal areas with little attention to official land titles. Some coastal areas were perceived to be communal space where all community members have access, as exemplified in the Bann Tab Tawan case (see below). Some communities settled on ex-concession zones with unclear official land titles. Other settlements were in conflict with conservation. They claimed that they settled before the declaration of environmental conservation areas (Chalermpak and Sriyai, 2006).

Many of the insecure land ownerships are places on which minorities and low-income fishing communities have settled their communities, and upon which their livelihood depends. Many of these places are located on coasts that are prime areas for tourism development. Pressured by growth in tourism, the ambiguity in rights of these properties created vulnerable conditions for land grabbing during the post-disaster phase. The following discussion of three Thai communities helps to demonstrate how such interactions between tourism development, land right insecurity, the tsunami, and its recovery occurred. These interactions add to the process of the post-disaster vulnerability.

Recovery vulnerability case studies

Bann Tab Tawan

Bann Tab Tawan was a community of "sea gypsies," one of the ethnic minorities in Thailand. The community was located on the coast of Takua Pa District, Phang Nga Province with a population of 314 people. The main livelihood of the community was traditional, small-scale fishing (SAN, 2005, Chalermpak and Khidan, 2006a).

The elderly of Bann Tab Tawan were able to cite the long history of the settlement dating back since their grandparents (Chalermpak and Khidan, 2006a; NTP, 2005). The author's interviews with community members and observation of public panel discussions in which members of Bann Tab Tawan were speakers confirmed those statements from the elderly. Additional evidence includes aerial photographs that show traces of settlements during 1973 (Chalermpak and Khidan, 2006a).

However, the community did not recognize the importance of having official land titles. By the time they started to realize the importance of land titles, in 1955 an individual outside the community had already claimed the official titles and transferred them to many others (Chalermpak and Khidan, 2006a; NTP, 2005). Interestingly, the community members stated that before the tsunami no one showed up to claim the rights of this land plot, according to the interviews, public panel discussion, and related reports (Chalermpak and Khidan, 2006a; NTP, 2005). This statement signals the intensification of land insecurity after disasters.

Not only were their residences insecure, but so also was access to the sea via the old mine pond locally called Kum Kiaw. Interviewed members of Tab Tawan community perceived Kum Kiaw as communal land where most community members parked their fishing boats and gained access to the sea. However, land rights of this pond, like those of their residences, were issued to another individual outside the community around 1975. In 2000, a relative of this individual charged fees for the use of the pond at a rate that most fishermen could not afford. Consequently, they were forced to find other places to leave their boats (Chalermpak and Khidan, 2006a).

Like other coastal communities, Bann Tab Tawan was located in a high potential area for tourism development. During field visits, the author observed that tourism had already come to the areas around the community. Resorts, hotels, bungalows, and other tourism-related businesses were found and a few areas were under new construction for tourist services. The streetscape along the beach was also designed for tourism purposes. With the momentum of tourism increasing, the location of Bann Tab Tawan was clearly one of a few areas of high tourism potential left along the beach (Figure 11.3). As a result this community was under significant pressure from tourism development.

Figure 11.3 An area under pressure for tourism development. Image courtesy of Khanin Hutanuwatr, 2010.

In Bann Tab Tawan, the tsunami completely destroyed over 100 houses out of a total of about 300. Sixty community members died, 12 were lost, and 13 were injured (SAN, 2005). The destruction from the tsunami created conditions for change. One of the key issues was the issue of who would occupy this devastated area. This issue created a challenge to the recovery of the previously existing community.

After the tsunami, conflicts in land rights intensified and consequently influenced the recovery of the existing community. It was reported that representatives of an individual who held "official" land rights made several attempts to claim the ownership by bringing land administration personnel to survey the boundary of the property. Community members perceived these activities as efforts to take away their land and consequently opposed the operations of boundary surveys. In doing so, violence did occur on some occasions. On January 26, 2005 (one month after the tsunami), the provincial office of Social Development and Human Security issued a memo to the community to stop reconstructing houses on these premises because there was an appeal regarding land rights of these plots (NTP, 2005). In addition to residential land, Kum Kiaw, the old mine pond that provides access to livelihoods, was blocked with barbed wire and concrete obstacles (interviews; hearing observation; Chalermpak and Khidan, 2006a; NTP, 2005). This exemplifies the challenge the community encountered which now became more than the destruction from the tsunami alone. When tourism pressure and insecure land rights met with the destruction from the tsunami, the vulnerability of the community's recovery increased.

Bann Nai Rai

Bann Nai Rai is located on the coast of Tai Muang District, Phang Nga Province. It was an ancient Muslim community more than 100 years old, according to the interviews with the local NGOs and the related reports (SAN, 2005; Chalermpak and Khidan, 2006b; NTP, 2005). An old Muslim cemetery is evidence of the age of this settlement (NTP, 2005). It later became a mining site between 1957 and 1974 (Chalermpak and Khidan, 2006b). After the end of the mining period, the community grew gradually. Key livelihoods of the community were aquaculture and fishery in old mines that later filled with water and became ponds and lakes around the area (NTP, 2005; SAN, 2005) (Figure 11.4). Despite the narrative of this historically long settlement, most community members did not acquire official land titles.

With recent growth in tourism industries, in 2002 a tourism developer was able to secure official land titles to this area. Initially land rights were issued to a private sector individual who was a key elite figure. Later land rights were transferred to other private interests and then to a tourism developer. According to related reports and interviews with local NGOs, lawyers, and community actors during July 2006, the developer planned to convert the areas into a large-scale, high-end resort for elderly (Chalermpak and Khidan, 2006b; NTP, 2005). In this plan, the old mine ponds are intended to be a designated area for upscale sail boats, even though

Figure 11.4 Bann Nai Rai community and aquaculture in old mine ponds. Image courtesy of Khanin Hutanuwatr, 2010.

community members' livelihoods have depended on these ponds for years, said local NGOs.

On December 26, 2004 the tsunami devastated most construction in the community. Seventy-two houses were completely destroyed and 38 houses were damaged. Most of the aquaculture equipment was damaged. The tsunami resulted in one death and 11 injuries in this community (NTP, 2005).

Despite the low death toll, their homes and livelihood were not easily recovered. The recovery of the community encountered a significant challenge resulting from the lack of official land rights. After the tsunami, a group of severely impacted community members moved to join the less-impacted members in the same community. However, later a developer claimed the rights of the land and told the community to move out of the area (Chalermpak and Khidan, 2006b). It is interesting that although the official land rights were sold to the developer two years before the tsunami, a community member stated in the public panel discussion that no outsiders claimed the land rights of this area before the tsunami. Similar to Bann Tab Tawan, it is likely that land dispute in this case took place seriously just after the onset of hazards.

Due to such land rights uncertainty, many aid agencies have pulled back their support of the reconstruction of the community (NTP, 2005). Community members, consequently, have suffered in both residential and livelihood dimensions, since areas under dispute include both land and the old mining ponds. Over 100 community members have been sued, being accused of land invasion by the tourism developer (Chalermpak and Khidan, 2006b). This case adds to the pattern of how disaster recovery can be impacted by the interaction between insecure land rights and tourism development.

Pakarang Cape Community

Pakarang Cape Community was a small and dense fishing community located along the beach in Pakarang Cape, Phang Nga Province. The area is not far from Kao Lak, one of the famous tourist destinations in Phang Nga. The environment of Pakarang Cape itself also drew quite a few visitors, which resulted in the establishment of resort hotels just across the street from the community. After growth in tourism around their community, interviewed community members and their leader expressed concerns over attempts to displace the community away from the beach area. These interviews suggest that the community was under pressure of displacement even before the 2004 tsunami.

On December 26, 2004, many community residences were destroyed by the tsunami. With financial support from private and governmental sectors, members

Figure 11.5 Temporary shelters for fishing-related activities at the seaside. Image courtesy of Khanin Hutanuwatr, 2010.

Figure 11.6 Tourist-oriented recreation use in the beach area. Image courtesy of Khanin Hutanuwatr, 2010.

of Pakarang Cape Community finally relocated their settlement inland about seven kilometers from the coast. From field observations and interviews, they commuted daily from the new settlement to the coast to maintain their pre-tsunami livelihood. Although their residences were relocated, the area of old settlement along the beach is needed to recover the community's fishing activities. It was used for temporary shelters, storage of equipment, and fishing-related activities (e.g., producing and repairing fishing gear) (Figure 11.5). These uses of their old settlement became an issue of land disputes between community members and authorities.

Interviews with community members and an advocacy lawyer indicated that fishermen who had temporary shelters on the coast after the tsunami were sued, accused of invading state land. Local activists hypothesized that the temporary shelters of the fishermen block the view from resorts to the sea, and consequently the resorts pressured legal enforcement to remove all shelters along the beach. A fisherman from this community said "perhaps our houses were not beautiful [in the eyes of others], so that they do not want us to be around" (interview 2010).

Another small enterprise owner in the area observed the difference in enforcement between tourism industries and the locals. He pointed out that hotel sectors were able to use the area for recreational facilities of their guests such as a beach volley ball court, massage areas, and sunbathing benches (Figure 11.6) while other locals were prohibited to use the area for their livelihoods.

The interviewed advocacy lawyer, who is experienced in land ownership issues, shared insights by identifying access to information and the minimal community involvement in land entitlement processes as key factors. Years ago, distributions of announcements for land entitlements were geographically limited and the procedure of entitlement at that time mainly involved claimers and officials. Consequently, communities missed opportunities to claim their land rights or appeal other claims during the official entitling period, creating conditions for conspiracy practices. These insights go along with the interview with another fisherman who was also skeptical about the land survey and expressed concerns. This lack of awareness of the process of official land titles was consistent in all three case studies.

Although other sources of information are needed to form concrete conclusions, some common patterns among these three case studies can be seen and provide initial insights for further studies. While communities did not acquire official land titles prior to the tsunami and were under pressure from tourism development, conflicts in land rights were exacerbated after the tsunami. Consequently, support for reconstruction of the communities was held up, except for the case of Pakarang Cape Community since the community was relocated out of coastal areas. Interestingly, holding back reconstruction aid for areas under land rights disputes reflects what occured in the case of Aceh, Indonesia as well (Brown and Crawford, 2006; Schulze, 2005). From recovery difficulties that were associated with a long history of land rights and incoming development, we can see that disasters in these cases were embedded in social, political, and economic contexts rather than just that of a natural disaster.

Conclusion and discussion

This chapter argues that when the unstable condition of land ownership interacts with extreme events such as natural disasters and the pressure of the growth in tourism developments, another threat can surface and make it difficult for marginal communities to recover. Findings from fieldwork support the view that disaster and development are inseparable. While other literature discusses "double exposures" between hazards and globalization (Silva et al., 2010; Schipper and Pelling, 2006), this research demonstrates "triple exposure," between hazards, land rights insecurity, and tourism development, which can be influenced by globalization as well.

Given global trends in transnational trade, pressures for tourism development are not only from internal forces, but also from external drivers that can exacerbate the complexities of the vulnerability process. In international trade policies, such as those seen in the Association of Southeast Asian Nations (ASEAN), the Bay of Bengal Initiative for Multi-Sectoral Technical and Economic Cooperation (BIMSEC) and the World Trade Organization (WTO), tourism is central among international economic collaborative initiatives (ASEAN, 2002, 2004; BIMSEC n.d., 2005; WTO, n.d.). These policies facilitate the opening up of tourism trade to other countries. This growth in international investment in tourism adds to rapid urbanization of coastal areas. Such rapid urbanization consequently increases the demand for coastal land, and more importantly puts marginal coastal communities under greater pressure (Burak et al., 2004; Green, 2005; Freitag, 1994). This growing pressure can play an important role in the process of vulnerability to both disasters and disaster recovery.

Although the fieldwork of this research was in Thailand, the lessons can be transferred to other similar contexts, given global trends in tourism development and coastal urbanization. Thus, in order to reduce vulnerability, greater consideration should be paid to the marginal groups who do not have land right security but may be exposed to hazards and pressures from tourism development. Since issues in land rights and impacts of tourism development existed even prior to the onset of hazards, supporting programs and interventions can be introduced before disasters. Moreover, the ongoing direction of tourism development also should be reconsidered to prevent undesired consequences. This re-emphasizes the pressing need to mainstream disaster-risk/vulnerability reduction into development policies (Mercer, 2010; Parnel et al., 2007; Schipper and Pelling, 2006; Thomalla et al., 2006).

References

ASEAN. (2002) ASEAN tourism agreement 8th summit 2002. Online. Available http://www.aseansec.org/13157.htm (accessed June 25, 2008).

ASEAN. (2004) Appendix I Roadmap for integration of tourism sector. Online. Available http://www.aseansec.org/19432.pdf. (accessed July 15, 2008).

BIMSEC. (n.d.) Proposed plan of action. Online. Available http://www.mfa.go.th/bimstec/bimstecweb/files/plan%20of%20action.pdf (accessed July 11, 2008).

BIMSEC. (2005) Kolkata Declaration on Tourism Cooperation. Online. Available http://www.mfa.go.th/bimstec/bimstecweb/files/Kolkata%20declaration%20on%20tourism%20cooperation.pdf. (accessed July 11, 2008).

Bolin, R. and Stanford, A. (1998) The Northridge earthquake, community-based approaches to unmet recovery needs. *Disasters*, 22: 21–28.

Brown, O. and Crawford, A. (2006) Addressing land ownership after natural disasters, Manitoba Canada: International Institute for Sustainable Development. Online. Available http://www.iisd.org/pdf/2006/es_addressing_land.pdf (accessed February 16, 2010).

Burak, S., Doğan, E., and Gazioğlu, C. (2004) Impact of urbanization and tourism on coastal environment. *Ocean & Coastal Management*, 47: 515–527.

Chalermpak, S. and Khidan, J. (2006a) "Case study: Ban Tab Tawan" in Chalermpak, S. and Sriyai, V. (eds.) *Human Rights Violation Report in Land Ownership Issues: Tsunami Impacted Areas*. Bangkok, Thailand: Office of National Human Rights Commission of Thailand.

Chalermpak, S. and Khidan, J. (2006b) "Case study: Ban Nai Rai" in Chalermpak, S. and Sriyai, V. (eds.) *Human Rights Violation Report in Land Ownership Issues: Tsunami Impacted Areas*. Bangkok, Thailand: Office of National Human Rights Commission of Thailand.

Chalermpak, S. and Sriyai, V. (2006). *Human Rights Violation Report in Land Ownership Issues: Tsunami Impacted Areas*. Bangkok, Thailand: Office of National Human Rights Commission of Thailand.

Clover, J. and Eriksen, S. (2009) The effects of land tenure change on sustainability: human security and environmental change in southern African savannas. *Environmental Science and Policies*, 12: 53–70.

Fitzpatrick, D. (2005). Restoring and confirming rights to land in tsunami-affected Aceh. Online. Available http://know.arsipan.org/dc/articles/20050714_Rights_Land_Tsunami_ Aceh.pdf (accessed January 26, 2011).

Freitag, T. G. (1994) Enclave tourism development for whom the benefits roll? *Annals of Tourism Research*, 21(3): 538–554.

Green, R. (2005) Community perceptions of environmental and social change and tourism development on the island of Koh Samui, Thailand. *Journal of Environmental Psychology*, 25: 37–56.

Hewitt, K. (1983) *Interpretation of Calamity From the View Point of Human Ecology.* Winchester, MA: Allen & Unwin.

Hewitt, K. (1997) *Region of Risk: A Geographical Introduction to Disasters.* London: Addison Wesley Longman.

Holling, C. S. (1973) Resilience and stability of ecological systems. *Annual Review of Ecological and Systematics*, 4: 1–23.

Howard, R. B. (2009) Risky business? Asking tourists what hazards they actually encountered in Thailand. *Tourism Management*, 30: 359–365.

IIED (International Institute for Environmental and Development), NRI (Natural Resources Institute), and RAS (Royal African Society) (2004) Land in Africa: market asset or secure livelihood, summary of conclusions from the Land in Africa Conference, London, November 2004. Online. Available http://pubs.iied.org/pdfs/12516IIED.pdf (accessed February 20, 2010).

Krabi City Hall (2005) Andaman Triangle Provinces Four-year Operational Plan. Online. Available http://app.krabi.go.th/content_images/documents/129/1257358660.pdf (accessed March 23, 2011).

Kwankong, K. (2010) A century of tourism: reflection of Thai economy. Online. Available http://thainews.prd.go.th/view.php?m_newsid=255308020148&tb=N255308&return=ok &news_headline. (accessed March 23, 2011).

Leckie, S. (n.d.) The great land theft. Online. Available http://www.cohre.org/store/ attachments/TheGreatLandTheft-Article.pdf (accessed February 16, 2010).

Lincoln, Y. S., and Guba, E. G. (1985) *Naturalistic Inquiry.* Beverly Hills, CA: Sage.

Lincoln, Y. S., and Guba, E. G. (2000) "Paradigmatic controversies, contradictions, and emerging confluences" in Denzin, N. K. and Lincolnn, S. L. (eds.) *Handbook of Qualitative Research*, 2nd edn, Thousand Oaks, CA: Sage.

Mercer, J. (2010) Disaster risk reduction or climate change adaptation: are we reinventing the wheel? *Journal of International Development*, 22: 247–246.

Merriam, S. B. (2002) "Introduction to Qualitative Research" in S.B. Merriam associates, *Qualitative Research in Practice: Examples for Discussion and Analysis*, San Francisco: Jossey-Bass.

Moser, S. C., Kasperson, R. E., Yohe, G., and Agyeman, J. (2008) Adaptation to climate change in the Northeast United States: opportunities, processes, constraints. *Mitigation and Adaptation Strategies for Global Change*, 13: 643–659.

Mullins, P. (1991) Toursim urbanization. *International Journal of Urban and Regional Research*, 15(3): 326–342.

NTP (The Network of Tsunami-impacted People) (2005) Disaster impacts, experience, and networks, Material in one-year tsunami memorial. Available from Chumchon Thai Foundation, Petch Buri Rd., Bangkok, Thailand.

O'leary, Z. (2004) *The Essential Guide to Doing Research*, Thousand Oaks, CA: Sage.

ONESDB (Office of National Economic and Social Development Board) (2006) The Tenth National Economic and Social Development Plan. Online. Available http://www.nesdb. go.th/Default.aspx?tabid=139 (accessed March 23, 2011).

OSM Andaman (Office of Strategic Management of Andaman Provincial Groups) (2010) Andaman Regional Development Plan 2010–2014. Online. Available http://app.krabi.go. th/content_images/documents/104/1257336929.pdf (accessed March 23, 2011).

Parnell, S., Simon, D., and Vogel, C. (2007) Global environmental change: conceptualizing the growing challenge for cities in poor countries. *Area*, 39: 357–369.

Pelling, M. (2003) *The Vulnerability of Cities: Natural Disaster and Social Resilience*. Sterling, VA: Earthscan.

Resilience Alliance (2006) Assessing resilience in social-ecological systems: a work book for scientists (Draft for testing and evaluation). Online. Available http://www.resalliance. org/1.php. (accessed September 14, 2006).

Rice, A. (2005) Post-tsunami reconstruction and tourism: a second disaster? Online. Available http://www.naomiklein.org/files/resources/pdfs/tourism-concern-tsunami-report.pdf (accessed February 17, 2010).

Rittichainuwat, B. N., and Chakraborty, G. (2009) Perceived travel risks regarding terrorism and disease: The case of Thailand. *Tourism Management*, 30: 410–418.

SAN (Save Andaman Network) (2005) *The People of Andaman, the People of Sea Preservation*. Trung, Thailand: SAN.

Schipper, L., and Pelling, M. (2006) Disaster risk, climate change and international development: scope for, and challenges to, integration. *Disaster*, 30(1): 19–38.

Schulze, K. E. (2005) Between conflicts and peace: tsunami aid and reconstruction in Aceh. Online. Available http://www.lse.ac.uk/Depts/global/Publications/HumanSecurity Report/Tsunami/Aceh%20Tsunami%20Response.pdf (accessed February 20, 2010).

Shkedi, A. (2005) *Multiple Case Narrative: A Qualitative Approach to Studying Multiple Populations*. Philadelphia, PA: John Benjamins.

Silva, J. A., Eriksen, S., and Ombe, Z. A. (2010) Double exposure in Mozambique's Limpopo River Basin. *The Geographical Journal*, 176(1): 6–24.

Thomalla, F., Downing, T., Spanger-Siegfried, E., Han, G., and Rockström, J. (2006) Reducing hazard vulnerability: towards a common approach between disaster risk reduction and climate adaptation. *Disaster*, 30: 39–48.

Watt, K., and Craig, P. (1986) System stability principles. *Systems Research*, 3: 191–201.

Wildavsky, A. (1988) *Searching for Safety*. New Brunswick, NJ: Transaction Books.

Wisner, B., Blaikie, P., Cannon, T., and Davis, I. (2004) *At Risk*. New York: Routledge.

Wong, P. P. (2009) Rethinking post-tsunami integrated coastal management for Asia-Pacific. *Ocean and Coastal Management*, 52: 405–410.

World Bank (2006) Tsunami Thailand: one year later, national response and contribution of international partners. Online. Available http://siteresources.worldbank.org/ INTEASTASIAPACIFIC/Resources/TsunamiTH_One-Year-Later.pdf. (accessed June 3, 2007).

WTO (n.d.) Sector specific commitment. Online. Available http://tsdb.wto.org/simple search.aspx. (accessed March 16, 2009).

Chapter 12

Urban/suburban landscapes

An ecological view

Michael Hough

Introduction

During his lifetime, Ian McHarg frequently described the sprawling American suburbs with a fable. A world cataclysmic event has eliminated every living thing with one exception: groups of amoeba have found refuge in a deep lead-lined crack many hundreds of feet below the surface of the earth. Over time, these creatures begin to discuss the future of life on earth. What, or who, should come next? And what about *Homo sapiens?* The discussion gets hotter and hotter and more and more cantankerous as they struggle with this problem. But at last they reach consensus. Next time, no brains.

Sustainability is a term that has at last begun to have currency for North American cities. It reinforces the notion that an ecological view is an essential component of the economic, political, planning and design processes that shape cities and urbanism in general. The issues facing urban and rural regions, the links between urbanism and nature at both local and regional scales, can only be resolved with such an integrated view. The concerns of this author revolve around three major issues: (1) the impact of urbanization on the various natural systems upon which cities rely, such as energy, water, plant communities and climate; (2) the role of environmental design in creating a rational basis for reshaping city form; and (3) the regional and local urban landscapes that can provide an ecological framework for structuring urban growth.

The forces that have shaped today's urban regions have been governed by unlimited resources of energy and by attitudes that have paid little heed to the necessity for a sustainable future. It is common knowledge that urban growth in North America has been associated with a vision of limitless space – one that we have come to realize is environmentally, economically and socially untenable. Evidence of this myth is clear when we understand the relationships between land areas covered by development, and increases in population. Studies by the Brookings Institute have found that between 1982 and 1997 the amount of land used for development in the United States increased by 45 percent. During that same period, population growth was only 17 percent (Fulsen et al., 2001). Low-density development in New Jersey consumed 130,000 more acres of land than compact urban form, and at an additional cost of $7,400 million for roads and $440 million for sewers and water infrastructure (Houck, 2002). In contrast, between 1990 and 2000 the Portland metropolitan region's population grew by 31 percent, but land consumption increased by only 3 percent (Houck, 2002), which says a great deal for urban growth boundaries.

The destructive consequences for rivers, streams and groundwater, for vegetation and natural processes in general are evident. An unavoidable conclusion about urban natural processes is how intricately they are interwoven with economic and social issues. There are destructive consequences to natural systems from runoff in urbanizing areas and withdrawal of groundwater, on which Tucson, Arizona in the Southwestern United States, was once totally dependent for its water supply. The engineering systems required to control urban stormwater runoff and repair flood damage involve very large financial expenditures. Trees provide an alternative to engineered solutions because of their capacity to store water through their leaves, branches and soil. An ecosystem analysis for the Houston, Texas Gulf Coast region conducted by American Forests assessed the loss of tree canopy over a 27-year period. Tree loss resulted in an estimated increase of 360 million cubic feet of stormwater during a flow peak storm. A 40 percent increase in tree canopy cover would have provided $3.5 billion in one-time stormwater benefits (American Forests, 2000). Studies in Davis California have shown that shaded narrow streets can be as much as 6 degrees Centigrade cooler than unshaded streets and use only half the amount of electricity for air conditioning (Phillco, 1981).

Remaking the urban landscape

These facts and figures illustrate a general point, that thinking ecologically involves the principle of maximum gain for minimum input and effort. There's also a real need to think both locally and regionally in any discussion on remaking the urban landscape because an ecological view is an inherent component of sustainability. Remaking urban landscapes can also be understood as restoring places back to health, or it can mean doing things right in the first place. It's about diversity, connectedness, making the most of opportunities, and making visible the processes that sustain life.

The task of remaking urban landscapes, however, involves a fundamental principle of natural systems – that of evolution and change. This is also an inherent characteristic of cities. Jane Jacobs once observed that cities are laboratories for experimentation and change and are far too complex to be understood by planners and designers (Jacobs, 1961). Robert Fulford (1995), the author of *The Accidental City*, echoes my own conclusions that while those in charge of giving direction to how cities grow may imagine that they're responsible, complex and stable neighborhoods are not the product of grand designs or fast-track developer master plans. They're created by the people who live there, through a multitude of small decisions and choices made by untold numbers of individuals going about their daily business.

The processes of change, whether they are social or natural, seem to respond to similar forces. This line of thought raises several questions. First, if we can only design, or plan, with urban unpredictability in mind, what strategies can we employ for sustainable development in the long term? Second, how can the concept of urban greening be used as a planning and design tool? Maybe one answer to these questions lies in understanding the landscape as infrastructure. The engineering infrastructure of cities – streets, squares, parks, sewers, water and lighting – is the organizing framework that establishes a basic pattern of development and without which urban development in the way that we know it could not exist. Buildings get built and demolished, shops come and go in response to economic imperatives, but the infrastructure in one form or another remains. It is, in fact, a key aspect of site planning. Kevin Lynch (Lynch and Hack, 1984) once said of this, that "its influence outlives that of the individual structure since site organization usually persists for generations." An example of this in operation is the four squares that William Penn laid out when he planned the City of Philadelphia. Much has changed since then but the parks have remained. Thus, in today's terms natural landscapes, parks and squares may be seen as a fundamental structuring element for urban growth.

Green Infrastructure, Greenbelts and Urban Growth Boundaries derive from McHarg's concept of ecological determinism, by which he meant that the biophysical processes that shape the physical landscape should also determine the form and location of towns and cities. In other words, putting nature first, not last, on the design agenda. Green Infrastructure, therefore, is about establishing the landscape on a site in the same way that engineers establish sewers, water, electricity, telephone and other essential services prior to planning development. A key characteristic of Green Infrastructure is the fact that it's relevant at any scale.

Design strategies for a derelict port

The Green Infrastructure concept has been incorporated into many planning projects undertaken by the author because the idea is essentially an ecological approach to urban planning. Several years ago the author collaborated with an organization called the Waterfront Regeneration Trust to provide long-range conceptual planning for Toronto's derelict industrial port. A report was produced called *Greening the Toronto Port Lands* (Hough et al., 1997) whose purpose was to set in place a long-term strategy for future development and economic renewal on the waterfront. The report was later approved in principle by the City Council as official policy for the port's future planning.

The first plan for the port was initiated by the Toronto Harbour Commission in 1912 which involved filling in the existing lakefront marsh. The port was never particularly successful, however, and over the years its economy continued to decline. It has today become a classic case of urban dereliction. In fact, the area has been called "just plain ugly" by the press, and a candidate for waterfront renewal. The location on the city's waterfront was well serviced by roads and

Figure 12.1 Existing condition of the port lands. Image courtesy of Michael Hough.

Figure 12.2a Natural ecological regeneration of the port lands. Image courtesy of Michael Hough.

Figure 12.2b Natural ecological regeneration of the port lands. Image courtesy of Michael Hough.

marine modes of transportation. It was connected to the city's bicycle trail system to the city's residential communities. It was also linked to the Leslie St Spit; a 5 km man-made peninsula of land jutting out into Lake Ontario, made from raw landfill and sand dredged from the lake. The spit was originally built to create a new harbor that never came about and it has evolved on its own over 50 years into one of the most ecologically diverse urban habitats in Canada. By 1992 some 400 species of plants had appeared; 290 species of birds visit and nest here; coyotes have taken up residence; and over 60,000 people migrate to the Spit during the summers.

North of the Port lands is the Don River. A restoration process has been ongoing through a citizen organization called the Task Force to Bring Back the Don, with whom the author worked in the 1990s to create a long-range strategy for future restoration.

The first requirement was to find out what lay beneath the surface aesthetic of physical decay. The area is fascinating for what it reveals of its industrial history and the commercial shipping that had plied the Great Lakes for well over a century. There are industrial artifacts like the bascule bridge, railway spurs, silos and evidence of vernacular humor, all of which represented past and present engineering and architectural technologies associated with the port's activities. The place has a tremendous sense of its waterfront location. And throughout the port area, regenerating vegetation on vacant lands and backfields provides a complex, seasonally changing landscape of remarkable diversity for the thousands of pedestrians and cyclists who travel through it on weekends.

The Green Infrastructure system became the basis for an ecological strategy for revitalizing the Port's economy that will function as an organizing framework for future development of the port. It's conceived as a network of green corridors designed to connect with natural park areas, organized in a hierarchy of wide and narrow corridors, major and minor parks and waterfront promenades. The plan is organized around several key principles that are outlined as follows.

1. Provide a multi-functional framework for development.
   - Improve air quality: Tree canopies greatly improve air quality by absorbing dust and chemicals such as sulfur dioxide and ground ozone by maintaining cool surfaces.
   - Improve microclimate: This includes shelter from lake winds and providing shade from the summer sun.
   - Storm drainage: Using surface, biological treatment at the source, this leads to improved water quality and the creation of aquatic habitats for wildlife.
   - Mitigating soils/groundwater pollution: Soil and groundwater in the port have been polluted from years of industrial activity. Soil and groundwater can be improved by pythoremediation – the use of plants such as poplar.

2. Establishing regional linkages
   - The Green Infrastructure system establishes links between the wildlife sanctuary of the Spit and the Don river valley and reconnects travel ways

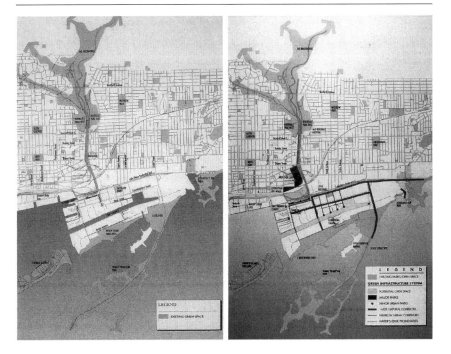

Figure 12.3 Existing green structure. Image courtesy of Michael Hough.

for wildlife and people, reinforcing regional links between regions to the north and to the lake.

3. Plan in the context of the larger river watershed.
   • Recognition of what's happening upstream is essential to planning downstream, from various perspectives, such as dealing with water issues, providing habitats and staging grounds in the port area for birds that migrate in the spring and fall, and reinforcing connections to breeding grounds to the north.

4. Reinforcing the existing sense of place.
   • It is essential, as in any brownfield site, that the underlying industrial character of the port should reflect its unique natural and historic qualities and diversity as a special district in the city.

Conclusion

The concept of Green Infrastructure is where the landscape provides the driving force for the development of the city. It needs to be understood as an organizing framework for city growth and development, rather than the other way around,

Figure 12.4a Green Infrastructure proposals. Image courtesy of Michael Hough.

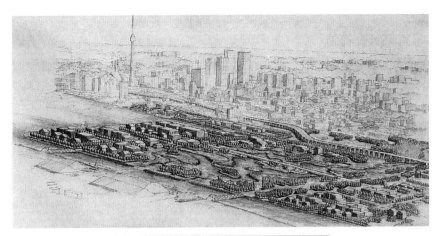

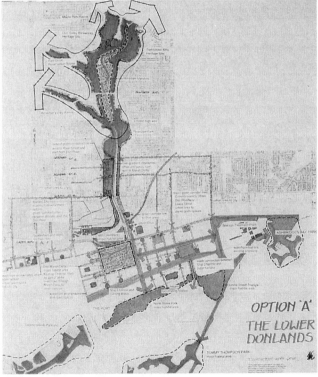

OPTION 'A'
THE LOWER
DONLANDS

Figure 12.4b Green Infrastructure proposals. Image courtesy of Michael Hough.

Figure 12.5 Design details. Image courtesy of Michael Hough.

where the landscape gets fitted into the urban fabric after urban development decisions have been made.

Green Infrastructure provides the appropriate way of dealing with unpredictability, since city development and change requires infrastructure as the organizing framework within which social functions evolve.

It is based on principles of landscape ecology that involve continuity and linkage and has application at both regional and local scales.

It is essentially place related, reinforcing the differences between one district and another and one place and another. It is, therefore, an integrated biological, cultural and economic concept, restoring identity to the regional and local landscape and maintaining ecological and cultural diversity.

There is, therefore, a need to embrace the concept of unpredictability in the art of decision-making and design. There is a need to accept this as a process of design over time, which can be translated to mean adaptive management, a process that sets out long-range goals and agendas, while implementing projects in the context of short-term time frames. It is about learning by doing.

References

American Forests. (2000) *Urban Ecosystems Analysis for the Houston Gulf Coast Region*. Washington, DC: American Forests.

Fulford, R. (1995) *The Accidental City*. Toronto: McFarlane Walter and Ross.

Fulson, W., Pendall, R., Nguyen, M. and Harrison, A. (2001) *Who Sprawls Most? How Growth Patterns Differ Across the U.S.* Washington, DC: The Brookings Institution.

Houck, M. (2002) The Humane Metropolis: People and Nature in the 21st Century. Address to New York University, June 6–7, 2002.

Hough, M., Benson, B. and Evenson, J. (1997) *Greening the Toronto Portlands*. Toronto: Waterfront Regeneration Trust.

Jacobs, J. (1961) *The Death and Life of Great American Cities*. New York: Random House.

Lynch, K. and Hack, G. (1984) *Site Planning*, 3rd Edition. Cambridge, MA: MIT Press.

McHarg, I. (1969) *Design with Nature*. Garden City, NY: Natural History Press.

Phillco, J. (1981) *The Davis Energy Handbook*. Davis, CA: City of Davis, California.

Chapter 13

Tapestries and traditions
Urban ecology and city making

Martin Bryant and Penny Allan

Introduction

It is ironic that urban ecological thinking is an emerging concept and city making is an old tradition. After all, human settlement has nearly always been sited and planned around ecological services such as fresh water, fertile soils or cooling breezes. Yet urban ecology has only been recognised for its importance in the last 30 years (Dramstad et al., 1996; Makhzoumi and Pungetti, 1999). Its theory links cities with the dynamic tapestry of natural elements, the interrelationships between place, vegetation, ground, animals and the order that supports it. But can urban ecology determine urban form? Or should we shape cities based on human settlement functions, and then retrofit ecology? This chapter discusses these ideas at two urban development sites – one greenfield, one brownfield; one unbuilt, the other built. Both address the potential for urban ecology in urban planning, and both use landscape as the design generator.

Urban form making is now under scrutiny as humanity faces environmental issues of potential resource depletion (Mostafavi, 2010) and inexorable population growth (United Nations, 1999). In the absence of certainty, or perhaps because of it, one of the almost-normative theories in urban thinking is the idea that cities operate as open systems: where players, activities and space make up a complex web of interdependencies that are always in a state of flux; where urban land-scapes are 'nodes of interaction rather than bounded places' (Hill, 2005: 141). Sites for urban development sit within this paradigm as places with complex inter-relationships to their past and to their physical and social contexts; places where a multiplicity of forms is possible, where pluralistic social and cultural needs accumulate, and where boundless ecological latency awaits. Urban designers' toolboxes now not only include figure ground representations, but also topologies of space and time integrated at a number of scales. Amongst all this complexity, where are the common threads?

It is remarkable but perhaps unsurprising that the idea of diversity pervades the disciplines of ecology, city making and social justice. Biodiversity is broadly accepted as fundamental to our future, and a cornerstone attribute of the biosphere's resilience. Jane Jacobs' (1961) seminal book attributed good urban life to good urban form, and good urban form to diversity. Richard Weller (2009: 389), in contemplating future plans for Perth, equates diversity with resilience and innovation. Susan Fainstein (2010) considers diversity paramount to social justice in cities, achievable not so much by spreading rich and poor evenly, but by making concentrations with porous boundaries. Lefebvre (1968) called this porosity the 'right to the city', analogising the 'right to nature'. In the course of this chapter we will reflect on the common ground of ecological and urbanism attributes, such as diversity and porosity, and assess two case studies for evidence that these attributes can be woven together spatially.

Strong parallels emerge between the practices of urban design and urban ecology. For urban designers the task of making higher quality, sustainable living environments entails acknowledgement that urban form needs to focus on making diverse, densified, legible, compact, place-oriented cities. Within this vision, urban structure in the public landscape is ordered by streets and parks (Krieger and Lennertz, 1991), which are programmed both from the bottom up and the top down by community and politics. For urban ecologists, publicly owned streets and parks have the potential to be a boundless mosaic of landscape, made up of corridors and patches in a matrix that evolves over time (Dramstad et al., 1996). Corridors grow and shrink connecting to a complex network of patches. Patches provide habitat. Matrices of interconnected patches generate diversity, moving in and out of focus as scales change. To be sustainable, urban ecologies need coarse-grained regions with fine-grained areas within (Forman, 2010: 313). Urban ecologists see streets and parks at various scales as the seed beds for a dynamic order, where landscape integrates programmed activities of the city with the semi-programmed attributes of urban ecology. This is how McHarg would have had it: landscape shapes the city. But in reality, the landscape of cities is often a fragmented complex. Furthermore, territorially fixed governance creates problems for ecology's boundlessness. So how can the requirements of urban ecosystems be achieved spatially? How can we retrofit boundless urban ecology within existing patterns of cities? Or do we need to sprawl differently, as if to start afresh?

The binary debate of brownfield–greenfield, or infill–sprawl, reveals distinct intentions in urbanism and has done so since Howard proposed the Garden City and Haussmann the boulevards of Paris. In the last century positivist planning practices have led capability-based urban development, sited mostly in the outskirts of cities. Many planners now cite the culture-consuming shadow of globalisation and threats to resources of air, water, land and habitat as reason to eschew the car-dependent, land-hungry, anti-cultural and anti-community suburbia in favour of the transit-oriented developments proposed by Peter Calthorpe (1989) or the walkable cities proposed by Jan Gehl (2010). But in a relativist post-modern age of adaptive governance, diverse values drive diverse solutions. For all its apparent shortcomings, suburbia is still probably more, or at least just as safe and healthy as dense urban environments – and cheaper. Suburbia continues to be championed for its market-place neo-liberal politics that contributes to social justice through housing (Kirby, cited in Fainstein, 2010: 31). If we are to integrate urban ecology in city making we need to adapt it to both new and old settings of urban expansion, to multiple political fields, and to diverse economic and multi-cultural societies.

In brownfield infill sites this means ecologies need to be reinterpreted, rebuilt or hybridised as part of development. Paradoxically, Alan Berger (2006) suggests that damaged sites have a latency with potential to allow highly diverse ecologies to flourish. Chris Reed (2010) cites Allen's, Corner's and Lister's Downsview Park Competition entry to show how degraded sites offer the potential to propagate emergent ecologies that could evolve and adapt with increased complexity over time. On the other hand, ecologies in greenfield sites are often more apparent. However, the need to retain the complexities of biodiversity and the interrelational qualities of resilience constrains the potential for cheap, simple and therefore modular suburban development. The problem here is the intensification of ecology: a process requiring both simplification and enrichment. In both cases the challenge for designers is pressing.

The 'design' in urban design behoves us to integrate all factors that influence sustainability. If we take urban ecology as fundamental – as a system that balances and cleans, adapts, diversifies and connects, and match it with the demands for healthy, amenable, connected, sociable environments – then the emergent urban structure will be sustainable and resilient. A more integrated design gives equipoise to both the ecological and the mannerist influences of city making.

Brownfield and greenfield in Sydney

New South Wales (NSW) sits in a temperate zone on the eastern seaboard of Australia. Sydney, its capital, is now home to four million people. The place has witnessed the passing of an ancient culture, the strictures of colonial settlement, industrialisation, the growth of a muscular port within the city, the intensification of working class suburbs, modernism, glass and steel, suburbanism, gentrification, hedonism and the decline of its harbour as a working port. Environmental issues are now prominent on the agenda. Climate change, protection of biodiversity, security of water supply and bushfire threats are entrenched in planning legislation, making the task of development a complicated process. And the demands of an increasing population persist.

This chapter looks at two projects in New South Wales. Victoria Park is 5 km from the centre of Sydney, now mostly built. The unbuilt project at North Hawks Nest sits on the periphery, 200 km north of Sydney. Both are mixed-use developments, intended for housing and commercial uses. Both are on damaged landscapes. Both are driven by traditional urbanist principles but both have been enriched by a design process that sees urban ecology as fundamental to the design of the place. Their layouts may not be much different from traditional parts of the city or the outskirts, but they both have been influenced by ecological planning that weaves its way into urban form.

The two projects adopt differing ecological approaches: Victoria Park, near the centre of Sydney taps into the sometimes hidden biophysical context to create a tapestry of urban ecology within the tight demands of the inner city. The North Hawks Nest project sits beyond the periphery of Sydney and weaves the existing and diverse natural landscapes into low density urban fabric in a way that both protects and enhances biodiversity.

North Hawks Nest

Hawks Nest is a coastal hamlet located 200 km north of Sydney. The Pacific Ocean lies to the east, the Myall River to the west, Port Stephens, a deep water harbour, to the south and Myall Lakes National Park to the north. Hawks Nest is known as the village in a blackbutt forest. The hamlet has about 1000 people living there, plus an itinerant population of holiday makers who activate the place in warm weather. There is even a resident population of koalas, once so prolific they were considered to be pests.

An idyllic spot? Unfortunately, there is a problem: the town is neither economically nor socially sustainable. As the current population ages in place – the average age of the Hawks Nest resident is 55 – there is an increased demand for services that are either unavailable or require long car trips. In winter, the local shop owners and doctors shut early or take holidays. There has been a steady increase in demand for land and housing, mostly from 'sea changers' – baby boomers who want a weekender that will turn into their retirement home as they gradually extricate themselves from work. Sadly, intensification is too slow to attract services, but fast enough to cause the demise of the koala population.

Just north of Hawks Nest, adjacent to Myall Lakes National Park, there is a stretch of bush, of about 1000 hectares, where one could live in either littoral forest or coastal heath and be no more than 15 minutes walk from water. It is a long, thin strip of land with a wealth and abundance of diverse ecologies. The ecologies are ordered by a tapestry of vegetation types. In discernible layers moving east to west from ocean to river, the vegetation succession includes duneland, heathland, eucalypt forests, littoral rainforest and wetland. Within this layering there are Casuarina groves, Tea-tree heath, Banksia heath, Tallowwood forests, Bloodwood forests, Angophora forests, Blackbutt forests and wetlands. All have a rich diversity of faunal populations, including koalas, sugar gliders, wombats, cockatoo, galah and cacophonies of insects. Some have habitats within particular vegetation typologies, some utilise the structural edges of vegetation types for foraging and movement. If there is such a thing as spirit of place it is embodied in North Hawks Nest in the structure of vegetation and the sheer abundance of ecological variety.

Idyllic, maybe even Elysian. With a spike in the permanent population, North Hawks Nest could become a viable community with an economic basis for servicing itself and its delicate, fragile environment. But perhaps the site is too fragile for development? The fragility of the landscape is already past the threshold that will allow it to survive in its current form. For instance, the koala population in North Hawks Nest, studied over a number of years, is in decline (Phillips and Pereglou, 2004). There were 200 twenty years ago but now only 35 remain. In five

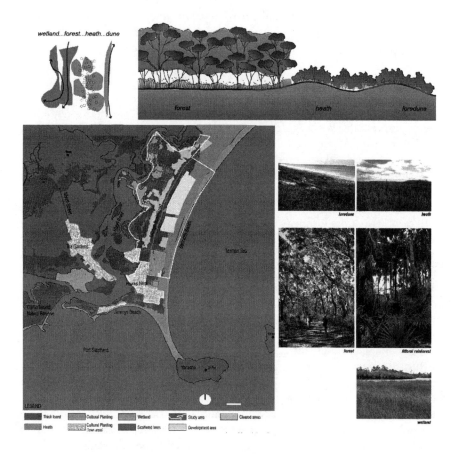

Figure 13.1 North Hawks Nest vegetation complex. Image courtesy of Hassell.

years they will all be gone. Their resilience has no more latitude. One solution is to import koalas to re-establish numbers, but this is not worthwhile without a site-wide management solution. The landscape is also severely susceptible to bushfires. An aeon of ocean deposition processes has left a deep and thirsty sandy soil. Vegetation creates moist microclimates, but the soil dries it out quickly and frequently and the vegetation is often parched. Bushfires occur at alarming frequencies. There has been 265 bushfires recorded in the area in the last ten years. Again, a site-wide management system is needed to keep the biodiversity of the bush.

A management system which considers the whole site is subject, however, to the current multiple ownership constraints. Multiple ownership of land is the bane of ecology, be it urban or rural. In the past this has not always been an issue.

Land entitlement was contrary to the culture of Australia's traditional land owners. Even European cultures once enjoyed the management benefits of large land holdings, albeit at the expense of the people working on them, sometimes at the whim of a totalitarian or oligarchic regime. But the Lockean right of neo-liberal societies to own property commodifies land and constrains holistic management. Can democracy and ecology be reconciled?

At North Hawks Nest there are currently 45 land owners. By amalgamating into one entity, the land holding can be managed as one. At North Hawks Nest that means one system that protects the koala population, manages bushfires, accommodates sugar gliders, wombats, the forests, the heaths and wetlands, and recognises human interaction in the place. It means no more anti-ecological selective slashing of undergrowth, irresponsible removal of koala feed trees, loss of faunal species and numbers, ad hoc building, trampling wetlands beside the river or overuse of the river edges. A single management entity offers a simple and viable way of managing the place's complex interrelated ecologies, protecting and enhancing its biodiversity. But a single entity could only be funded today if it accommodates population growth.

Population growth offers the opportunity to provide the kind of urban services that are dwindling in Hawks Nest. Not a duplication of services that already struggle, but the provision of services, employment and events that foster a permanent population with diverse demands. North Hawks Nest has the potential to be more than a holiday town, because development will spawn urban diversity, and in so doing will protect ecological biodiversity. A vision thus emerges for North Hawks Nest of an ecology that is made up of forests and fauna and employment and residence and environment existing in a symbiotic relationship. New development will create density, but not at the expense of ecology which underpins the site's character and appeal. This vision was established by Andrew Wiesener, a Sydney developer, who bought and amalgamated the land, and has now partnered with the NSW Government in preparing a plan, with Hassell urban designers and landscape architects, that promises to fulfil city-making ideas based on ecological principles.

The footprint of the site's ecological structure was generated by McHargian principles which defined the areas of greatest sensitivity. Wetlands and koala feed forests were excluded from development. Migration corridors were protected. Eighty per cent of forest and of heath were retained as conservation areas in a 900 hectare matrix of undeveloped patches and corridors, which are to be preserved in perpetuity for conservation, removed from private ownership, amalgamated with the National Park and managed holistically. The State Government's Department of Conservation will resume control and implement management of activities that will maximise benefit to the estuarine environment of Myall River and its wetlands, manage bushfires and intervene positively on the wildlife populations to ensure resilience.

The balance of land, which is a 100 hectare footprint, was set aside for residential development. The development footprint is long and thin, bisected by a 100 metre

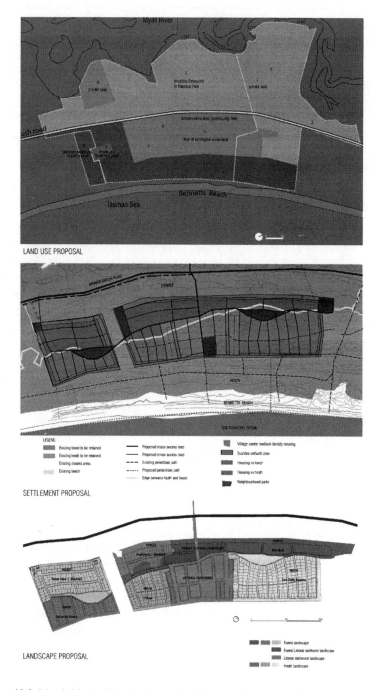

Figure 13.2 North Hawks Nest land use, development footprint, urban structure and landscape. Image courtesy of Hassell.

vegetated corridor, and includes forests and an area that was once used for sand mining but has now recovered a diverse heathland. This long, thin footprint offers ecological and city-making advantages. For the ecology, it provides a long axis running parallel to the structure of the vegetation typologies, thus conserving intact primary corridors for the site's fauna. The short axis provides short distances for wildlife to 'step' over when connecting between the forest and the heath. The footprint also provides an extended edge between development and conservation areas, conserving and enriching biodiversity in both forest and heath conditions. From an urban designer's position the long axis creates a diversity of opportunity for activity along the proposed settlement, and the short axis maximises the opportunity for the proposed village to be close to and in touch with the conservation areas; a concept which, if managed, will generate regard and respect for the context. The configuration of the development footprint has a key role in making both ecology and city making work.

Within the development footprint, the ecologies have been abstracted in the process of designing the landscape of the new village. Once the 900 undeveloped hectares were conserved and managed, the urban settlement could have been shaped like a traditional subdivision. After all, the ecological benefits have been won. The price for this battle would be 1000 houses with a traditional infrastructure of roads, amenity horticulture and services. But this would, of course, reinforce the binary ideas of culture/wilderness, urbanity/ecology, garden/forest. It would reinforce the illusion that amenity horticulture masquerades as ecology, and the delusion that landscaping, as an afterthought, reinstates Eden. Wiesener, however, wanted to infuse the development with an ecology that supported and enhanced the conserved ecologies and, in so doing, reinforce and enrich its reason for being there.

Within the development footprint, diversities in housing density allow conservation of the vegetation's typological transect. The proposed village is designed to achieve an overall yield of ten lots per hectare, similar to that of the extant village of Hawks Nest, to the south. Parts of the site will be denser, where significant ecological reconstruction will occur and town centre activities will take place. Parts will be less dense, where larger patches of remnant habitat are included in the public park system and housing lots can be large enough to retain and supplement forest or heath associations. This approach to diversity of density yields will be organised in a way that ensures that a maximum of habitat is ideally placed in the public domain for community use and ecological benefit. Public open space that follows the perimeter of the development has multiple benefits including the management of bushfire regimes required for settlement and for conservation (two different regimes – one for separation, one for connectivity – together reconciled by the principle of porosity). In addition, a string of fine-grained parks occur along the forest/heath edge within the core of the development footprint. It is a rich interface, where hotspots of ecological biodiversity can be preserved. Each park has a unique floristic nature and a different community purpose. They provide concentrations of ecology within a matrix of diversity.

The designers proposed to arrange the streets in a distorted grid pattern. Normative urban theories champion the grid, especially on relatively flat sites where connectivity and permeability is easily achievable. But the ecological structure of the forest/heath edge that meanders along the long axis of the development footprint deforms the grid. The edge is not only a good site for the fine-grained remnant bushland parks, it is also key ecological connective tissue. It is therefore important that it stays in the public domain where it can be managed, with some additional planting, as an axial street, a wide corridor for movement of fauna from north to south, and the main thoroughfare for movement of people within the town. Elsewhere, in deference to the ecology, the grid is similarly deformed, without losing its porosity. In the forest, long streets will be aligned to conserve existing trees and amplify the labyrinth qualities of the forest. In the heath they are to be short and canted, terminating in the fore dunes, which are unencumbered by built form. The heath vegetation that lines the streets on private lots thus forms a corridor that links the forest to the coast. The streets were designed to be narrow and curb-less, maximising the potential for retention of the integrity of the vegetation, providing at-source infiltration and also retaining the dunal bumps and troughs that slow vehicular movement and provide sharing with pedestrian traffic. The free-draining soils obviated piped solutions, permitting instead natural solutions to stormwater percolation and a series of treatment spots on troughs in roads.

The ecological benefits of the development are imbued in the subdivision pattern and the design of the private lots. Lots were designed, not to maximise efficiency of infrastructure, but to maximise retention of the numerous ecotopes of heath and forest. Housing lots in the forest are to be laid out with narrow frontages and deep yards that allow building setbacks to accommodate existing trees. Prototypes were developed around the idea of a tree house, where elevated living spaces catch the breezes, and the footprint is minimal, permitting access for terrestrial based ground-plane fauna. Discontinuous vegetated fences will become stepping-stones for faunal passage through the landscape. In contrast, the housing lots in the heath are to be short and wide. The wide frontages minimise the number of punctuations for entrance and maximise the continuity of the mosaic of heath that intersperse the lots, providing ecological and amenity benefits. The housing prototype designed for the heath is based on a low-slung courtyard style form, where endemic heath frames the boundaries, and amenity landscape defines the courtyards. Within the forest and heath housing, precincts are to be created based on the prevailing tree or heath association, amplifying the floristic variations that occur across the site (for example, the Angophora precinct, the Tea-tree precinct, the Banksia precinct and so on). The ecotopes generate their own type of light-touch response, and invite limited interventions that permit adaptations that enrich what is already there. While at one level this strategy is a conceit that is intended to amplify character, it also highlights the dominant vegetation species and allows gardens and landscapes to be influenced by their role in the evolving ecology of the broader context.

The success of this place as a community will depend on a thriving centre with higher densities. The plan for the village centre includes intensive accommodation and a variety of services including events, retail, cultural places, restaurants and hotels for businesses that are committed to year round activity, thus guaranteeing year round employment. Three-storey, medium-density buildings were tested and designed to accommodate generous courtyards so that littoral rainforest, an endemic ecology of the area, will be re-introduced where it can be protected from bushfires. Reconstructing this biodiversity is a fundamental part of this project, and doing so in a controlled setting at the village centre will enrich and focus the tapestry of ecologies that are to be adapted and conserved within the development footprint.

The community ownership proposed for the place ensures compliance with community goals that are set out in the agreement for purchase. Community title allows a governing body to maintain the key incentives for conservation and urban ecology. This will ensure that no deleterious influence occurs in private gardens or public spaces. It does not 'set in stone' the development outcomes, but focuses instead on site-wide management of the intent and the dynamic of the ecology, recognising the changing nature of its environmental asset.

Victoria Park

The pressure for housing in New South Wales occurs not only on the periphery, but also in the inner city, where the demand to intensify, gentrify and amplify amenity is urgent. Sydney's infrastructure struggles to meet the demands of its growing population, faltering under the pressure for more housing, more jobs and

Figure 13.3 Victoria Park as it might have been in 1789. Image courtesy of Martin Bryant.

Figure 13.4 Victoria Park 1999. Image courtesy of NSW GAO.

more roads. The argument for urban consolidation and infilling density promises more efficient forms of sustainable development and diverse but compatible land uses. It also intends to maximise existing infrastructure. The trouble with this is that, in Sydney, existing infrastructure is already at capacity, with little room to move in extreme situations. Notwithstanding the sustainability of AAA-rated tapware and energy-efficient glazing, infill necessitates the unsustainable practice of building a whole new infrastructure of roads and pipes.

Green Square is an ambitious post-industrial project initiated in the mid 1990s that intended to establish a dense, mixed-use development that could capitalise on its proximity to the city and existing infrastructures. Sydney may be renowned for its sandstone bluffs that flank its harbour, but Green Square, 10 km south of the city, is largely a low-lying flat area that was once a massive ephemeral wetland, stratified over geological time by layers of alluvial sands and peat. The peat is the remnant of organic material that has been inundated by floods of water and floods of alluvial sand. The sand layers are now conduits and filter fresh water that exfiltrates in the upstream catchment. Soon after European settlement, the fresh water and flat land attracted industry. Industry drained the wetland, mined the water and disposed of excesses methodically in channels and canals, carving a new hydrology for the place. Industry then polluted, disposing of some of the dirtiest contaminants imaginable into the waterways. Industry then left, leaving a landscape of ground-plane concrete slabs and canals. A 1998 master plan proposed to extend the canal network as a way of evoking the authenticity of the place: a romantic validation of industrial processes.

The project at Victoria Park, a 24 hectare slice of Green Square, was intended to provide 1800 dwellings, hundreds of thousands of square feet of commercial space, a hierarchy of parks and a number of community facilities. A 1999 master plan ignored the canal reference, and instead drew reference from the ecological context and history of the site, contemplating a whole new infrastructure of extensive ephemeral wetlands at the surface, indeed almost at the doorstep of

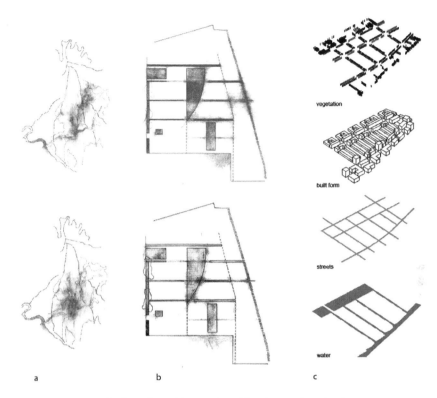

Figure 13.5 Victoria Park ecological integration: (a) ephemeral wetland context; (b) ephemeral wetland intervention on site; (c) infrastructure overlaid on water. Image courtesy of NSW GAO.

apartment buildings. The reconstructed wetlands have integrated functions: they treat stormwater in a way that naturally occurring wetlands do, and they provide amenity and recreation opportunities. Their ephemerality responds to the rhythm of fluctuating ground water levels. Given the premium associated with inner city land, Victoria Park shows that ecological reconstruction can be implemented in conjunction with dense urban living, and in particular, can be integrated with infrastructure and the amenity and recreation needs of incoming populations. The revised master plan set the stage for ecological thinking to be part of every concept plan, every design component detail and every marketing strategy on the site.

The spatial structure at Victoria Park entailed a traditional approach to a tightly squared city grid, with north–south and east–west streets, small block sizes (generally less than 100 m) and four parks/plazas which are addressed by the connecting streets. Accommodation was all built to the street edge. The public domain – the streets and parks – were designed by the NSW Government Architects Office and Hassell and were delivered by the master developer, Landcom, a land agency attached to the State Government. The streets were designed as simple legible connections; the parks were rich and textured with plazas, playgrounds and recreation activity zones. The accommodation blocks were developed by private interests, within a framework set down by the master plan which entailed a perimeter block approach with a courtyard communal space framed by three- to four-storey walk-up apartments and the occasional 12-storey tower.

But before any form was conceived, the site-wide concept for Victoria Park drew inspiration from the biophysical context and, in particular, sought to manage flooding and to clean water by re-establishing the watery ecologies of the area. Integrated in the design were ideas of baffling, infiltration, filtering and polishing water quality. The streets and parks included fine-grained ecological interventions in this site-wide strategy, designed to expose the latent attributes of the site's pre-industrial ecology, its naturally sandy soils and its water table that had been covered up for a century. Some of these fine-grained interventions occurred in the streets which were designed to be wide enough to accommodate 4–6 m wide wetlands and which sponged the water off the streets. Built form was articulated in height so the planting received enough sunlight. The streets are wider than they need to be for efficiency, but the extra width was used to create greater separation between medium-density developments and to provide a rich and complex landscape along the otherwise simply laid out streets. The streets include not only the swales, but also an overlay of shade trees that provide a rich and bio-diverse street. The parks also adopted various roles in the water management regime: they detained water in basins to permit exfiltration and minimise downstream flooding; they also provided a site for community interactive water features and were endowed with wetlands that provide habitat for wildlife, play for children and a sense of 'ecological' identity for all.

One of the key roles of the wetlands is to treat stormwater at source. This is a contrary piece of infrastructure: infrastructures are traditionally built for efficiency, which suggests that it is easier to treat stormwater mechanically, usually at key spots in the catchment or at the end of the catchment, before it enters the sea. The problem is, this process rarely removes all solids and pollutants. It bypasses wetland ecologies, as if there is an excess of process and thereby a lack of efficiency in ecology. The Victoria Park plan sought to introduce the complexities of ecologies at the point of pollution. The plan entailed bio-retention swales with wetlands along the streets, which perform a cleansing function at source.

The wetland swales are ephemeral waterways located as medians and designed to catch road drainage, detain it and allow it to infiltrate and filter, utilising sand (sourced from site) and the ever-regenerating wetland plant root matrices. They operate primarily on first flush stormwater, the water collected by the first rains that carries all the contaminants and sediment that ends up primarily on our road surface and usually, under traditional systems, ends up in the receiving waters of our rivers and harbours. The swales were heavily planted with local wetland species, simulating naturally occurring wetlands, using plants that can sit in water for days, and then survive weeks of drought. An overflow system, coordinated with

Figure 13.6 Ephemeral wetlands in public space and bio-retention swales at Victoria
Park. Image courtesy of Martin Bryant.

bridges that augment pedestrian access, takes the flow from the big storms and
distributes it to traditional stormwater infrastructure. This was a necessary pre-
caution to avoid flooding. The combination of natural systems and traditional city-
making infrastructure provides the basis for the emergence of a system of ecological
planning.

The action of bio-retention swales and basins collecting and filtering stormwater
is regularly tested. Ten years after implementation the swales are working as
intended, successful species are adapting to the system, and avifauna is now

Figure 13.7 'Stormwaters' at Victoria Park. Image courtesy of Patrick Bingham Hall.

abundant on the site. The years of droughts in Sydney over that time have favoured the hardier wetland species. The asset managers appreciate the sieve-like qualities of the wetland in dealing with sediment and leaf litter. The heavy rains in 2009 pushed the system into full operation: recent tests have shown a thin crust of hydrocarbons trapped in the top soil horizons, where it can lay dormant, validating the role of urban ecology in making healthy cities (Tattersall, personal communication, 14 April 2008). The innovation at Victoria Park was about integrating latent ecologies with traditional infrastructure and open space function and character. The demand for accommodation yield was just as important, and led to a machinist approach to urban ecology: one that is now manifest in a tight weave of streets and urban parklands.

To celebrate the reinstated ecologies, the filtered stormwater was collected and reused in a water feature in the main park. Without mains water or chemicals, and with no chance of health risk, the water was designed to flow over shallow ponds and steps, creating an interactive water feature. As the water trickles down the steps in a carefully orchestrated cascade of water play, its history as filtered stormwater gives it an ecological layer that transcends the idea of water as surface.

Early in the development process the marketers and public relations agencies conjured up the notion that this piece of inner-city living had 'added-value' because its ecological qualities suggested healthy living. Before long, the reinterpreted and reconstructed ecologies became not a byword of the development, but a branding tool for the place. Residences sold quickly. The architecture, the character of public space, the quality of public space integrated with the revealed ecologies was an experiment that succeeded. While any one component is difficult to tease out of the marketing mix, it is clear that inner-city 'eco' housing relied on the success of the public space's sustainable systems which heralded integration, resilience, character and public space function.

Conclusion

Urban ecology opens city making to a rich and dynamic tapestry that defines, sustains, invigorates and characterises place. Unlike the prescriptions of human settlement which traditionally err towards a generic code, the demands of ecology are both dynamic and markedly different from place to place. Urban ecology is more than a formula of city-making principles and parameters. It embodies an intertwined complexity that springs from the essence of place. It invites innovation. It champions the particular, the unique, the detailed and the diverse, whereas human settlement planning has traditionally been fed by the legible, the coherent and the simple. As we interrogate urban ecology for its potential influence on the spatial structure of cities, it becomes apparent that landscape is a medium that allows us to understand the systems that will make cities sustainable, because in landscape we easily translate ecological systems while still retaining coherence. Landscape allows a dialectic between the universal and the particular, where one negotiates difference through the other. Landscape can embody diversity of a city by concentrating ecologies and enabling porosity in the connections throughout the city.

Design offers a process for enmeshing urban ecology in city making through an integrated site-wide approach. The case studies described in this chapter show how urban design processes can synthesise the qualities of place with sustainable systems. They show how urban ecology can add options to the machinistic aspects of traditional infrastructure, even in dense environments where land values are at a premium. They show how urban ecology can create urban resilience through community ownership and the inherent adaptability of ecological systems. The diverse landscape and built forms that result demonstrate the potential to integrate a settlement's functions such as amenity and connectivity with ecological principles of diversity and permeability. Above all they show that urban ecology is a design outcome that can shape the spatial structure of the city, and not be an afterthought to the underwhelming process of simplification.

The Victoria Park project demonstrates how a place's natural systems can be reconstructed and can operate in evolving conditions in a dense urban environment. The key findings from this project, which can be applied to other brownfield development sites, are as follows. First, contaminated inner-city sites are full of latent ecologies which emerge, not necessarily according to a prescription, but according to opportunistic design, because the underlying soils and geology and climate can support it. Second, because ecologies have no boundaries, context both spatially and historically is an important factor in their reconstruction, even in heavily transformed sites. Third, fine-grained ecological interventions in dense urban sites are appropriate solutions because they can supplement and possibly replace traditional designs for infrastructure and amenity. Fourth, the case study reveals a solution to the financial issues associated with ecological rehabilitation. The marketing success of Victoria Park suggests that urban ecology can be a community priority rather than an economic burden. The potential for community resilience triggered by ecology is of enormous value. And finally, as a built work it provides a wealth of ongoing ground for testing, an essential tool in understanding the role of active open systems in the city. The project suggests that concepts of site-wide systems of ecology can be applied to brownfield sites to influence the design of settlements.

The North Hawks Nest project gives us a process for retaining delicate and fragile ecologies in greenfield urban settlements, and then enriching them to amplify their main qualities. The factors that show why urban ecology is an important driver of urban settlement design in greenfield sites are as follows. First, the project demonstrates that there is a potential for a mutually supportive relationship between urban ecology and human communities through holistic, adaptive governance. This approach removes one of the main hurdles that has in the past hindered the integration of urban ecology and city making. Second, it suggests that urban ecology does not necessarily entail whole-scale reconstruction, but instead can be a gradual process that intervenes in the existing landscape and adds to and nourishes the qualities of its existing ecologies. Third, it shows the value of diversifying suburban densities so that the processes of conservation and enrichment can be pursued at appropriate places in the city. Finally, the project shows that normative urban theories in street and park design can be adapted in innovative ways to suit ecological systems in greenfield sites.

Both projects recognise the need for a comprehensive understanding of natural systems and a complex process of integrating the detail with sound principles of city making. In both cases this was the subject of a meaningful collaboration between a number of knowledgeable and skilled experts. Both projects show the need for innovation in project procurement and land ownership. Above all these projects rekindle the value of a place-based approach to city making.

References

Berger, A. (2006) 'Drosscape', in C. Wladheim (ed.) *The Landscape Urbanism Reader*, New York: Princeton Architectural Press.

Calthorpe, P. (1989) 'The Pedestrian Pocket', in D. Kelbaugh (ed.) *The Pedestrian Pocket Book*, New York: Princeton Architectural Press.

Dramstad, W.E., Olson, J.D. and Forman R.T.T. (1996) *Landscape Ecology Principles in Landscape Architecture and Land-use Planning*, Washington: Island Press.

Fainstein, S. (2010) *The Just City*, New York: Cornell University.

Forman, R. (2010) 'Urban Ecology and the Arrangement of Nature in Urban Regions', in M. Mostafavi and G. Doherty (eds) *Ecological Urbanism*, Baden, Switzerland: Lars Muller.

Gehl, J. (2010) *Cities for People*, Washington: Island Press.

Hill, K. (2005) 'Shifting Sites', in C. Burns and A. Kahn (eds) *Site Matters*, New York: Routledge.

Jacobs, J. (1961) *The Death and Life of Great American Cities*, New York: Random House.

Krieger, A. and Lennartz, W. (eds) (1991) *Andres Duany and Elizabeth Plater-Zyberk: Towns and Town-Making Principles*, New York: Rizzoli.

Levebvre, H. (1968) 'The Right to the City', in G. Bridge and S. Watson (eds) *The Blackwell City Reader*, Malden, MA: Blackwell.

Makhzoumi, J. and Pungetti, G. (1999) *Ecological Landscape Design and Planning*, London: E&FN Spon.

Mostafavi, M. (2010) 'Why Ecological Urbanism? Why Now?', in M. Mostafavi and G. Doherty (eds) *Ecological Urbanism*, Baden, Switzerland: Lars Muller.

Phillips, S. and Pereglou, F. (2004) 'North Hawkes Nest Koala Plan of Management', unpublished report for Crown Land Developments.

Reed, C. (2010) 'The Agency of Ecology', in M. Mostafavi and G. Doherty (eds) *Ecological Urbanism*, Baden, Switzerland: Lars Muller.

United Nations Population Division Department of Economic and Social Affairs (1999) *The World at Six Billion*. http://www.un.org/esa/population/publications/sixbillion/six billion.htm (accessed February 28, 2011).

Weller, R. (2009) *Boomtown 2050 Scenarios for a Rapidly Growing City*. Western Australia: UWA.

Chapter 14

Urban ecosystems and the sustainable metropolis

Edward A. Cook

Introduction

With the global increase in urbanization, landscape architects, urban planners and ecologists have recently become more interested in the role of urban ecosystems within cities. Historically, cities have existed apart from nature and urban areas have not traditionally been a focus of ecological research. Humans significantly affect ecosystems. This is evident in the development of cities that extract resources from nature and use natural processes to absorb waste. Cities also have a significant impact on ecological function. Urbanization has resulted in landscape fragmentation, deterioration of natural habitat and isolation effect, modification of hydrologic systems, urban heat island effect, poor air quality and many other problems.

The problems associated with maintaining viable ecosystems in urban landscapes are significant. Urban landscapes are a finely structured mosaic of property owners and uses where competing interests for undeveloped land are intense. This chapter examines how embracing nature's deep structure through conservation, restoration and adaptation can provide a foundation for urban sustainability utilizing the planning concept of green networks (Cook, 2002; Jongman and Pungetti, 2004) and articulates typologies for urban ecosystems. Green networks (sometimes referred to as ecological networks, greenways, ecological structure, etc.) can be described as a system of interconnected or related patches and corridors that provide and sustain ecological values within a human-dominated landscape matrix.

Any attempt to restore previously altered ecosystems or protect existing fragments of natural systems must recognize that the most effective way to re-establish or maintain the viability of these systems is to ensure they exist as a part of a larger functioning system. Urban landscapes are generally deficient of areas with significant environmental values, resulting from the anthropocentric orientation of the urban development process. As a consequence, nature (or nature-like) areas are often relegated to remnant patches and corridors, severed from their supporting structure. Normally, constraints to urban development such as extreme slope, flooding and poor soils exclude them from development. Although these remnants may have deteriorated environmental value, it is fortuitous that in many cases the areas with the most significant constraints for urban development are often the richest. Consequently, many urban areas have an existing framework representing nature's deep structure upon which a more comprehensive network can be established (Muerck and Swaffield, 2007; Steiner, 1996).

Urban ecosystems represent an interesting challenge and opportunity for sustainability in cities. We are now just beginning to incorporate the urban landscape into ecological studies, as we are faced with the decline of the benefits they have provided to urban populations throughout history. The challenge is that as a result of fragmentation, invasion of exotic species and general degradation of ecological functions due to human impact, a range of ecosystem services are being lost that urban populations have come to rely upon. Ecologically functional urban ecosystems are critical since society is no longer in a position to move to the next frontier to exploit pristine landscapes, to obtain fresh water, attain cooling air flows, clean and transform our waste and more.

Jordan (1993) notes that we also need ecosystems for a variety of reasons that extend beyond provision of ecosystem services. He emphasizes that our relationship with nature should engage all of our abilities and dimensions, including the physical, mental, emotional and spiritual. A sense of history will increase meaning in our interactions with landscape. Although we differ from other species because of our self-awareness, we too are products of nature and need to be flexible in our relationship with nature, as it is with us. We are dealing with a dynamic system so the nature of the interactions should also be dynamic. Tensions do exist between nature and culture, but for our own benefit it is important to embrace ecological process, especially in urban areas, as a part of our own culture.

One of the greatest challenges we face with urban ecosystems is that we have already caused significant damage in most cases and to restore the systems such that the inherent values that previously existed in these places prior to urbanization is difficult. They have been and are subjected to a variety of increased levels of environmental stresses. They generally exist as highly disturbed systems and may be subject to rapid change in soil and plant cover, temperature and water availability, all essential factors of ecosystem health. Urban ecosystems are also generally characterized by non-native plants and decreased plant density. They are subject to air pollution, road salts and runoff, poor soils, frequent drought, limited sunlight, introduction of toxic substances, loss of habitat and food and frequent disturbance by human activity.

On the other hand, the potential for urban ecosystems is great, but it is important to take a different view of what urban ecosystems are and to consider how we can redefine them, rather than attempting to re-establish a pre-existing condition that will in many cases be unsustainable, expensive and may not provide the range of desired ecosystem services. The metric for urban ecosystems should be more heavily weighted with the values of ecosystems services provided rather than looking for naturalness. There are, of course, situations where naturalness and the presence of native species is viable and desirable in an urban context, but in every circumstance, specific consideration needs to be given to the origin, nature and potential of the system in its current condition and context.

Nature has provided and does provide us with exceptional examples of functional, efficient ecological systems. We can use these to inform the process of design and restoration of urban ecosystems. The more we know about how nature functions, the better we will be at designing systems that will provide the benefits we seek. However, we also have to embrace technology along with natural sciences to develop effective strategies for designing urban ecosystems, resulting in a range of ecosystem types from natural to artificial.

Several authors have discussed the notion of a range of types of urban ecosystems. Turner (1993) suggests four ways of characterizing the differences. Conservation, he describes as something representing a vast resource, both physical and spiritual that must be wisely husbanded to continue to yield rich harvest in the future for humans. Preservation, he sees for the intrinsic value of nature, untouched by humans, inviolate and unpolluted. Restoration embraces the idea of reconstruction of the classical ecosystem. And, the inventionist creates a new ecosystem. While the objective of the preservationist philosophy is often unattainable in an urban context, the intent of these views is to represent practical philosophical viewpoints when considering urban ecosystems. Baldwin et al. (1993) provide a similar perspective utilizing the concepts of preservation, restoration and invention. Preservation, as they describe it, is applicable only in areas where ecosystems are not severely tampered with and are of sufficient size and connected to a larger supporting system. Restoration and invention are consistent with Turner's (1993) view.

Following in this chapter is a framework that embraces the fundamental notions of employing philosophies of preservation, restoration and invention in urban ecosystems, but expands on those concepts to include the concepts of hybrid and regenerated ecosystems and uses examples to demonstrated how these can apply in a practical sense.

Extent, context and content

Regardless of what type of urban ecosystem seems most practical, in every situation several key variables will affect how it evolves and, in turn, the extent of ecosystem services or cultural benefits produced. The key guiding concepts of extent, context and content if properly considered can help to increase the possibility of successful realization of an urban ecosystem in a functional and viable state. Together, they address the potential for successful integration into a transformed urban landscape that may have quite different potential for supporting urban ecosystem functions. Extent relates to the place of an urban ecosystem as a part of a larger interconnected system. Context recognizes the influence that adjacent land uses may have on the function of urban ecosystems. And content is focused on the internal make-up of an urban ecosystem.

Extent is essential to consider for long-term viability of an urban ecosystem. By virtue of being functionally connected as a part of a larger system, an urban ecosystem realizes the possibility for renewal and continuous regeneration. The connective tissue of a larger system facilitates flows within the landscape that bring nutrients, energy and genetic material that are essential to long-term ecological viability. These flows take the form of water, sediment movement and deposit, seed dispersal, animal migration, wind flow and others. The resulting connectivity combats landscape fragmentation and resulting isolation effects and may facilitate exchange with larger source areas. One of the prevailing challenges dealing with urban ecosystems is the lack of recognition that specific ecosystems are part of a larger system connected spatially but also connected between scales with a more extensive hierarchy of systems. Planning and design concepts such a green networks (Cook, 2011), green infrastructure (Benedict and McMahon, 2006), ecological networks (Jongman and Pungetti, 2004), greenways (Hellmund and Smith, 2008) embrace this notion of connectivity of ecosystems in an extended hierarchical system.

Context should be understood in an urban situation as having significant impact on the viability of an urban ecosystem. Urban areas are often sources of toxic material and invasive species. Urban land uses adjacent to urban ecosystems are not just nearby; their influence extends beyond the immediate boundary of the designated land use area. The result can include significant deterioration of urban ecosystems due to edge effects (Esbah et al., 2009). In addition, changes in the context can completely overwhelm an urban ecosystem's normal functions. For example, the hydraulic regime of an urban river or stream may be incapable of accommodating the increased runoff generated by highly urbanized areas with extensive paved surfaces and rooftops resulting in impervious surfaces over an area that may have previously been largely open landscape capable of absorbing or retarding storm flows. The water that does run into the river or stream may also carry contaminants from road surfaces and other areas. Exotic or invasive species of plants and/or animals may also find their way into adjacent ecosystems, perhaps altering the suitability for already established native species to persist. Most ecologists, planners and designers will suggest that consideration of the compatibility of adjacent land uses be taken into account, but also the establishment of buffer zones, preferably external to the urban ecosystem to act as a filter.

Content can best be characterized as the arrangement of physical features of an urban ecosystem. This would include topographic conditions, vegetation, water, soils and geology. The content of an urban ecosystem is dependent on extent and context to a significant degree. Particularly in an urban setting, human needs and expectations become increasingly important as well. The content of ecosystems that are preserved or restored will be reflective of the natural condition and structure. Regardless of the amount of change in original content, extent and context, understanding the origins of the ecosystem will help determine a viable future. Landscapes have memory in the sense that they are often inclined to re-establish some physical characteristics and functions that existed previously. The amount of change to content, extent and context may influence the depth of memory.

The tendency for the physical characteristics to return to some representation of the former ecosystem might also be referred to as the deep structure (Cook, 2011; Steiner, 1996). An ecological design approach to establishing urban ecosystems will embrace this notion of ecological history, recognizing the memory and deep structure of the ecosystem. An urban ecosystem's content will also need to be responsive to human needs and systems that act upon it. The content will provide the possibility of a variety of ecosystem services including water filtration and storage, climate or microclimate amelioration, improved air quality and more.

Green networks, functions and values

The goal of the planning concept of green networks is to preserve or restore the ecological integrity of critical natural systems while allowing for compatible human activities within the network and continued productive (economic) use of adjacent lands. Some of the functions or uses that can be accommodated within these categories are obvious, while others are more obscure. The intent is to accommodate these functions or uses in varied amounts and at varied locations within the ecological carrying capacity.

The most viable way to establish a green network is to ensure the integrity of critical natural systems or the deep structure are retained or re-established while allowing adjacent land uses to continue to function effectively. Clearly, compatibility of adjacent land use is an important issue and where it is possible to modify adjacent lands to make them more ecologically compatible it should be done. Continuous networks can provide greater efficiency for functioning ecosystems, but also preserve the integrity of adjacent uses. The overall goal is to accommodate the greatest level of biodiversity and ecological processes while accommodating compatible uses. A number of potentially compatible functions, benefits or ecosystem services include hydrologic processes, biological diversity, climate amelioration, public recreation, aesthetics, environmental education, human psychology, cultural and historical significance and land use buffers and markers.

The functions of hydrologic processes are among the most critical to preserve and restore. Rivers, streams and drainage corridors are well suited to serve as the foundation of a green network since they are often left as undeveloped because of flood danger. They are also among the most environmentally rich and sensitive. When in a viable state, these areas serve as filters for surface runoff, helping to purify water before it returns to water supply sources. They also serve as sinks for groundwater recharge. Flood containment and protection against soil erosion are also important (Cook, 2007).

Both habitat and conduits for species migration are among the most important ecological functions that can be accommodated. Within an urban context, a green network may not be entirely suitable as primary habitat for all but a few species, but as islands for refuge or places to forage they may be quite suitable if connected to node or primary source areas. Plants and animals both are dispersed through corridors and patches of natural systems. These zones serve as conduits for nutrient, energy and gene flow.

Specifically in urbanized areas, climate modification can be achieved by increasing vegetative cover in appropriate locations. In many metropolitan areas, and particularly in hot arid climates, an "urban heat island effect" has increased average temperatures significantly, reducing human comfort and causing increased energy consumption. Negative effects of wind can also be mitigated through increased plantings (Bowler et al., 2010).

The most commonly recognized human activity that may occur in more natural areas is that of recreation. Suitable activities would likely be passive, such as hiking, cycling, horseback riding, nature observation, picnicking and light camping in specific locations.

Although it is difficult to place specific monetary values on beautiful scenery, it is generally understood that aesthetic qualities are important. Research has shown that properties adjacent to nature areas have increased economic value that may be translated into tax revenues for government. In many cases, the image of an entire district is formed because of the existence, or lack, of natural landscape characteristics. The spiritual or emotional value of beautiful natural areas should also be recognized.

Education and human psychological ties with nature can be reinforced by having nature areas accessible within cities. As society becomes more urbanized, the danger of losing touch with nature becomes real. Functioning nature areas within an urban setting can provide opportunities for city-dwellers to learn more, first-hand, about natural processes and also provide sanctuary from the strains of urban life. In the long term this may promote a stronger environmental ethic in society.

Often, locations of cultural or historical significance are identified and set aside, or should be set aside, to be preserved for use or appreciation by the public and future generations. Trails, monuments, sites of important events and other significant locations are often restored or preserved with the former character of the place as the model. Both ecological and cultural value is often implicit and as a network component its value could be enhanced by its connection to other elements within a system.

Separation of incompatible land uses is a frequent use of open space patches and corridors. They also help delineate property boundaries, changes in use or other cultural phenomena. This is quite common in agricultural areas and is occasionally found in urban areas.

A number of other functions could be identified, but these are some of the most relevant in most urban areas. All of these functions or uses would likely not occur throughout the system. There may be several compatible functions with varying levels of priority in certain segments. However, some places may be critical and single functions may predominate.

Developing green networks

For a green network to be effective it needs to function at several levels or scales. The primary structure occurs at landscape (regional) scale and establishes a network of regionally significant source areas, patches and corridors that have long-term protection and provide the prospect of continued renewal and exchange. At the community level smaller-scale elements are incorporated into the network consistent with the needs of municipal government planning and nature conservation strategies. Specific site-level planning and management is the third level at which ecological networks are relevant. Individual sites are preserved, restored or transformed on an incremental basis to realize the potential of a comprehensive ecological network plan, the overall goal being to achieve some degree of ecological integrity throughout the network.

Landscape-scale planning establishes a broad overview of landscape patterns. Consequently, the grain of the data is somewhat coarse and the extent is broad. The intent is to understand interrelationships of elements within and outside of the study area of "regional" or "landscape-scale" significance. The network formed at this scale becomes the main, and more stable, structure. Other network elements at finer scales may be more transient in nature, varying in ecological value over time.

At the community level (sub-structure) plans are prepared at the municipal level (or portions if too large) to correspond with municipal-level planning and management hierarchy. The grain of data is less coarse. At this scale, planning can be undertaken for interrelated network elements. Scenarios for change of landscape structure of network components can be analyzed to determine how potential network element quality can affect the function of the total system.

Local area planning and management includes specific plans for changes in elements or management plans to preclude deterioration of quality. Individual studies are undertaken that respond to specific site needs and reinforce the objectives of sub-structure (municipal or community-level) plans or landscape-scale plans. The scale at which these plans are undertaken varies with the nature of the network element. They are all subject to management by one entity, however, whether public or private. At this level implementation occurs on an incremental basis, consistent with urban planning development processes. Corresponding management units may be such individuals or groups as park managers, neighborhood associations, utility companies or private development companies.

Landscape morphology, the historical evolution of landscape attributes and dynamics, provides useful information concerning past structure, function and agents of landscape change. Understanding the previous state sometimes provides a baseline from which the current status can be measured. Examination of landscape change and ecological history provides information about previous functioning of ecosystems. Re-establishing previously existing connections or ecosystems (patches and corridors) is a useful way to improve the possible successful rehabilitation of degraded ecosystems. Although it is generally not feasible to attempt to return a degraded ecosystem to some previously existing state at anything other than site scale, understanding the previous landscape structure and its evolution will be useful in making planning and management decisions and adapting to future landscape dynamics.

Historical maps, aerial photographs and other forms of documentation are necessary to understand the earlier ecosystem structure and function. The presence of these reoccurring remnants of natural systems or the deep structure, may mean that forces of nature acting in these elements or systems are stronger or more persistent over time than human intervention. The prospect is that they will likely continue to revert, so human-dominated activity is expensive to maintain and sometimes hazardous. A logical proposition is to recognize the characteristics of these elements and incorporate them as a part of a green network, rather than continuing to battle the forces of nature.

Hough (2004) provides a description of a spectrum of open spaces most often found in cities and illustrates the relative ecological values associated with each. If a worthwhile goal is to establish increased levels of sustainability in our cities, then it follows that, where possible, open spaces should provide an ecological frame or network. This type of system can provide the supporting structure to keep open spaces ecologically viable. Using Hough's framework, it is possible to link different types of open spaces, with existing or potential ecological values, to form an integrated network. Some open spaces, like natural parks, have existing ecological values and need mostly to be managed so that critical resources and functions are preserved and tied in to a larger system to facilitate exchange and regeneration opportunities. Other less natural open spaces, such as cultivated parks, provide greater ecological benefits by pursuing alternative management strategies like organic pest control, less frequent mowing of grassy areas and replacement of some exotic vegetation (in areas not requiring it for critical park functions) with native species.

Urban ecosystem typologies

Urban ecosystems are generally significantly modified from ecosystems that were formerly present and as such should be considered within a modified set of parameters that include significant human intervention due to the urban context. Urban open space systems contribute to the quality of the urban environment in many ways. The range of open space types includes urban plazas and remnant natural open space or natural parks. Each of these plays an important role in the dynamics of an urban landscape. However, urban open spaces which are valued for their natural qualities are in a precarious position. Research has demonstrated that over time the qualities that are so valued in these "natural" places will deteriorate because of fragmentation from the supporting structure resulting in isolation. Thus, it is important to establish methods for preserving and re-establishing natural qualities in functioning, self-sustaining ecosystems. Following are descriptions of typologies for reconsidering urban ecosystems.

Preserved ecosystems

Preserved ecosystems in an urban context are often rare, and when present difficult to maintain at a high level of ecological functioning over time. They would typically be in natural or near-natural condition with intact internal landscape structure or content. Supportive connective systems are also important in order to maintain flows and other functions critical to the process of natural regeneration. This is an important dimension of facilitating dynamic development of the ecosystem. Adjacent land uses or landscape character also have significant influence. Land use compatibility or the existence of buffer zones will be important to filter contaminants, limit the intrusion of invasive species and reduce the potential for other deleterious edge effects. The principle aim is to ensure the ecosystem preserves the ability to function and evolve as if it were still existing and functioning as a natural system in a predominantly natural context. While preservation of natural systems in an urban context with no significant impact is impossible, good planning and effective management can do much to facilitate the preservation of something close to the original.

Fish Creek Provincial Park, located in the southern part of the City of Calgary, Alberta, Canada, is an example of a preserved urban ecosystem. It is one of the largest urban parks in North America, extending 19 kilometers (approximately 11 miles) and occupying about 13.5 square kilometers (5.2 square miles). The park was first proposed in 1966 prior to the expansion of urban development in the southern part of the city around Fish Creek. It is now part of a larger greenway system that ties together corridors along the Bow and Elbow Rivers with plans to extend throughout the entire city to include about 100 kilometers (66 miles) in length (Erickson, 2006). Numerous recreational activities are accommodated within the park. In addition to approximately 80 kilometers (50 miles) of trails, picnic areas with shelters, boat launch ramps, environmental education centers and nature observation points are provided.

An extensive environmental management program started with the initial planning for the park in order to establish land use control (Taylor et al., 1995). Land use control was achieved by acquiring all land within the established park boundaries that extends to the top of the bank or valley landform. Adjacent development, above the upper edge of the valley, is separated by a buffer zone, providing a set back for urbanized areas and the ability to filter and protect. There are other active management programs as well that are intended to control invasive species, preserve and improve habitat, monitor wildlife populations, control erosion, re-establish forest cover, preserve wetlands and manage storm water.

Restored ecosystems

Restored ecosystems are those that are re-established with similar structure and function to the original system. Typically, the original ecosystem has become degraded, modified, replaced or completely destroyed. The original ecosystem may

Figure 14.1 Fish Creek Park with adjacent urban development (top photo) and buffer zone along top of ridge adjacent to housing (bottom photo). Images courtesy of E. Cook.

be used as the model for restoration if there is sufficient knowledge about its former structure and function. If there is insufficient documentation or knowledge about the original system, then another ecosystem with similar conditions as presumed existed in the original can be used as a model. As with a preserved ecosystem, connecting structure that facilitates flows is important to ensure ecological viability. The context should also be evaluated to determine if it is compatible and does not introduce deleterious effects such as increased storm water flow, toxic materials, potential for invasive species and others. In an urban context precise replication of a pre-existing ecosystem is difficult and is uncertain in its infancy. The principle aim should be, to the extent feasible, to allow the restored ecosystem to mimic the original, while accepting that adaptation is required and that over time the ecosystem will naturally evolve and adapt to changing context and functions. Most effective ecosystem restoration projects explore the ecological history to provide sufficient knowledge of the landscape morphology. In this way, it is possible to understand the dynamic nature of the system and appropriately determine what point in the system's evolution should be used as the model for design. The restored ecosystem should be designed so that the structure represents the model, but functions that also previously existed should be restored or preserved so that it acts like the original and is also set in motion so that regenerative capacity is in place.

The Lower Indian Bend Wash Habitat in Tempe, Arizona, USA, located above the confluence with the Salt River, is an example of a restored urban ecosystem. Indian Bend Wash extends for about 20–25 kilometers (30–40 miles) north through Scottsdale and into the foothills at the base of the McDowell Mountains (City of Scottsdale, 1985). The original ecosystem became degraded over time as urbanization encroached and vegetation died or was removed. The original channel structure of this natural drainage corridor or wash was similar to many ephemeral washes with a low flow channel. In areas where water is present, cottonwood trees (*Populus Fremontii*) and willows (*Salix* sp.) are present and associated with higher water tables. On upper terraces but still within the flood plain, vegetation is dominated by mesquite (*Prosopsis* sp.) bosques. The US Army Corps of Engineers and the City of Tempe cooperated in preparation and implementation of the restoration plan (Megdahl, 2005). The model for restoration re-established a channel structure similar to the original condition. The project recreated a riparian forest in low-lying areas where water is more abundant. Understory plants included desert broom, elderberry and other native plants. Understory vegetation in the mesquite bosques outside the low-lying areas includes elderberry, greythorn and wolfberry. While this zone is established primarily to provide wildlife habitat and to restore ecological functions, recreational access is provided through trails and informal viewing stations. The connectivity and flows from the Upper Indian Bend Wash are preserved and connections also exist on the lower end at the confluence with the Salt River. It is intended that these connections will enhance the regenerative capacity of the ecosystem and allow the re-vegetated zone to better sustain itself over time.

Figure 14.2 Lower Indian Bend Wash Habitat restoration, Tempe, Arizona. Mesquite
bosque (top photo) and riparian zone with cottonwoods and willows
(bottom photo). Images courtesy of E. Cook.

Hybrid ecosystems

A hybrid ecosystem exists within a frame or location of a pre-existing ecosystem and restores some of the original ecological functions while accommodating varied landscape context, supporting structure and some functions. In this case, it is recognized that significant changes in context, supporting structure and functions require an alternative approach to preservation or restoration. Because the hybrid ecosystem is within the same frame or location, the inherent characteristics and recurring tendencies of pre-existing natural systems will support the levels of ecological functioning in the ecosystem, working with the deep structure (Cook, 2011; Steiner, 1996) to increase the odds of long-term sustainability. Generally, the use of ecological design principles (observing and documenting patterns and processes of nature to inform design) is helpful. Other ecosystems that have similar structure and functions may be used as models to provide a design framework. Critical design and management concepts might include the predominant use of native vegetation, re-establishment of flows and connectivity, periodic intervention to manage outcomes, and significant initial introduction of some wildlife.

The Rio Salado Project in the Phoenix, Arizona, USA metropolitan area is an example of a project characteristic of a hybrid ecosystem. Several entities are involved in this effort including the US Army Corps of Engineers, the City of Phoenix, the City of Tempe, the City of Mesa and the Salt River Pima Maricopa Indian Community. The US Army Corps of Engineers is partnered with each of the other entities that has geographic jurisdiction over certain segments of the Salt River Corridor as it passes through the Phoenix metropolitan area.

The Salt River originates in the White Mountains of Eastern Arizona and flows westward through the Phoenix area to the confluence with the Gila River west of the metropolitan area. Prior to the 1900s it was a perennially flowing river with abundant riparian vegetation. In the early 1900s flows were diverted through a system of canals to provide irrigation for agriculture. The river was left without perennial flows through the metropolitan area, groundwater levels declined, vegetation disappeared and the river corridor became barren, devoid of water except for occasional years when spring runoff from upstream dams is released.

The Rio Salado plan was initially proposed by students in the Architecture School at Arizona State University in 1966. After years of study, further plan development and funding attempts, this coordinated effort is now being facilitated by the US Army Corps of Engineers and includes numerous segments in various stages of planning and implementation. Some projects are now complete and several key components are in place. The first and most challenging aspect of the project was to secure a water source to re-establish a continuous flow for the low-flow channel that is able to support vegetation. Due to complex water rights issues, all of the water that would naturally flow in the river is allocated for other purposes. Each of the participating entities is engaged in employing creative tactics to re-introduce water to the low-flow channel, including directing nuisance and storm

Figure 14.3 Re-vegetated zones of the Rio Salado Corridor (Salt River) where water has been re-introduced. Images courtesy of E. Cook.

water to the corridor, buying back some water already diverted to canals and introducing reclaimed water. Channel restructuring and re-vegetation strategies are also being employed to simultaneously provide flood protection and create a healthy riparian zone that can support wildlife and ensure higher levels of ecological functioning. While the structure and function of the newly re-established Salt River Corridor is not the same as the original ecosystem, flows and other ecological functions are being returned to the corridor along with numerous culturally oriented functions that bring life and viability back to a largely destroyed ecosystem.

Synthetic ecosystems

Synthetic ecosystems establish critical ecosystem functions through ecological design in locations where similar ecosystems did not previously exist. They may be useful to fill a gap to establish connectivity and flows or to replace a former linkage in a new location and different landscape structure. A synthetic urban ecosystem may also be useful to establish alternative connections within the larger set of urban ecosystems or green network. They exist where there is no opportunity to work with the deep structure in the landscape. They are designed to establish specific ecosystem functions and ecosystem services. They may also provide a variety of other social and cultural benefits embracing the concept of multiple use. Synthetic ecosystems could also comprise technological or invented elements that provide certain ecological or "green" values to society. Buildings and other structures, not normally considered as ecological elements, could also be a part of this type of ecosystem. A synthetic ecosystem also contributes to the overall ecological health of a larger system.

Waitangi Park, situated along the urban waterfront in Wellington, New Zealand occupies approximately three hectares (6.5 acres) and a portion of it includes a synthetic ecosystem. It was established following a design competition held in 2003. It includes a range of park functions typically found in urban parks, but it also includes a wetlands storm water treatment system that cleans water running off from adjacent neighborhoods before it is released back into the harbor. The site where Waitangi Park is now located has gone through many changes. Prior to 1855 it was part of Waitangi Lagoon that was fed by Waitangi Stream. In 1855, an earthquake uplifted the area five feet, altering the water course and wetland. With the site then reclaimed from the sea a variety of functions occupied the site at various times and included a dog pound, city morgue, a works department and a bus park. Storm water runoff from adjacent neighborhoods, encompassing 448 hectares (of which 262 hectares are impervious) was forced underground and piped into the harbor untreated. The buildup of nutrients, heavy metals, sediment and hydrocarbons in the vicinity of the storm water outfall was a concern to local officials for years.

The design of the park included bringing the storm water runoff back to the surface and directing it through a series of treatment wetlands to improve water quality before it was returned to the sea (Cook, 2007). The system includes a variety

Figure 14.4 Waitangi Park, Wellington, New Zealand with overview of water treatment filtration zones along the outer park edge (top photo) and polishing pond (bottom photo). Images courtesy of E. Cook.

of treatment systems since no single treatment technique is able to remove all pollutants. Constructed wetlands like these are intended to mimic the water cleansing capability of natural wetlands. Bio-pits capture the "first-flush" of storm water runoff from roads in adjacent areas at the onset of a storm. The water is then carried through as a series of subsurface and surface wetlands. The subsurface wetlands allow flow of storm water through gravel. Plants on the surface extend roots into the porous material, allowing biofilm to grow which is important to enable pollutant removal through microbial activity. The gravel wetlands also remove grease, solids and sediments and reduce turbidity to levels suitable for ultra violet (UV) disinfection to occur once the water is returned to the surface. The water is again returned to the surface where UV disinfection results in 90–99 percent reduction in bacterial levels. Further filtration, absorption and biological/ chemical transformation occurs in the wetland lagoons. The resulting treated water exceeds fresh water quality guidelines before being discharge into the harbor. The wetlands system also regulates flows so that discharge occurs at more consistent rates rather than with rapid velocity as occurred previously with the underground pipe system. Some of the water is also used to irrigate the landscape of adjacent park grounds. In addition to water treatment, wildlife habitat is provided, public awareness is raised through environmental education and the aesthetic value of the park is enhanced.

Regenerated ecosystems

Regenerated ecosystems allow for nature to take its course and naturally regenerate an ecosystem that has been previously disturbed, modified or compromised. Depending on the nature of the disturbance, the result of natural regeneration may vary substantially. Sometimes the result is unpredictable. Generally, this is the least costly option to re-establish ecological values to a disturbed ecosystem. The trade-off with low cost is accepting the unknown outcome. The time required to re-establish something viable is another variable that can vary with the ecosystem. In some desert landscapes natural regeneration can take generations and then the outcome may be of lesser ecological value. In some cases, where there is potential for undesirable invasive species, natural regeneration may not be a desirable strategy for urban ecosystem renewal. Given the range of possibilities, natural regeneration should, however, be considered as a viable option for re-establishing wild areas in cities (Kowarik, 2005).

Südgelande Naturpark in the Schöneberg district of Berlin, Gemany, now occupies 18 hectares (45 acres) of land that was once a railway switchyard. The switchyard was established in 1889 and for 70 years was one of the busiest in Berlin. It was closed in 1952 and laid fallow. Nature took over and re-established its dominance over the following decades. In 1987, the "Citizens Action Committee Natur-Park Schöneberger Südgelande" was founded. This group began documentation of the regenerated natural qualities of the site and shepherded it through a process that provided recognition of its value and protection for the urban nature

Figure 14.5 Raised permeable walkway introduced after regeneration (top photo) and volunteer vegetation established in and around derelict railway tracks in Südgelande Nature Park in Schöneberg, Berlin, Germany. Images courtesy of E. Cook.

area it had become. In 1995, the land was transferred to Grün Berlin GmbH, a government agency in Berlin. In 1999, it was established as a nature conservation area and opened in 2000 as a nature park.

Now established as an island of wilderness in the heart of the city, Südgelande Nature Park incorporated dry meadows, tall forbs and natural forest communities. Volunteers have documented the presence of 30 species of birds, 57 spider species, 97 wild bee species, 15 grasshopper species, 49 mushroom species and 350 species of plants. The abandoned rail yard is rich in diversity because plants and animals followed green corridors from outlying areas and took up residence in this location. With its establishment as a park, some facilities have been added to ease access but also to encourage visitors to stay on dedicated paths. Raised walkways direct visitors through the diverse plant communities while preventing trampling or other damage. Some other objects, graffiti, activity centers and historical artifacts and derelict railway tracks from the switchyard are also found in the park. Overall, the Südgelande Nature Park provides an unusual opportunity to learn more about the potential of nature for regeneration in an urban context.

Conclusion

The concept of urban green networks addresses the ecological functioning of urban patches and corridors. The best way to ensure the integrity of these systems is to establish the viability of critical ecological systems within the urban landscape context. This requires planning and management at multiple scales. Although the actual scales will vary with the context and the planning problems to be addressed, three levels are generally necessary to properly understand the context (landscape), employ the planning authority (community) and address specific management needs or implementation schemes (local).

To preserve, rehabilitate or restore the various components of a green network, management strategies must be developed for individual sites on the local level. This will include various types of patches and corridors and the landscape matrix. The viability of any green network or system of interconnected patches and corridors is made possible at the local scale. The types of elements that need to be addressed may include pieces of the main ecological structure of an area (i.e., large remnant patches or corridors) or sites of a more ephemeral nature (i.e., vacant lots). The future value or potential may also need to be addressed with sites in need of regeneration or restoration.

The typologies of urban ecosystems provided in this chapter can be useful to help understand the inherent characteristics and qualities of urban ecosystems, but can also be a guide for future transformation. They are important to be used to gauge the level of intervention or investment that may be appropriate and also to be more explicit about expectations or outcomes. Strategies developed for preservation, restoration, regeneration or with the creation of invented ecosystems, such as hybrid and synthetic, will become more realistic with additional base knowledge and well articulated planning and design frameworks.

References

Amici, V. and C. Battisti. (2009). Selecting focal species in ecological network planning following an expert-based approach: a case study and a conceptual framework. *Landscape Research*. 34: 5, 545–561.

Balwin, D., J. De Luce and C. Pletsch. (1993). Introduction: ecological preservation versus restoration and invention. In: D. Balwin, J. De Luce and C. Pletsch (Editors). *Beyond Preservation: Restoring and Inventing Landscapes*. University of Minnesota Press: Minneapolis.

Benedict, M.E. and E.T. MacMahon. (2006). *Green Infrastructure: Linking Landscapes and Communities*. Island Press: Washington, DC.

Bowler, D., L. Buyung-Ali, T.M. Knight and A.S. Pullin. (2010). Urban greening to cool towns and cities: a systematic review of empirical evidence. *Landscape and Urban Planning*. 97, 147–155.

City of Scottsdale. (1985). *Indian Bend Wash*. The City of Scottsdale Communications and Public Affairs: Scottsdale, AZ.

Cook, E.A. (2002). Landscape structure indices for assessing urban ecological networks. *Landscape and Urban Planning*. 58, 269–280.

Cook, E.A. (2007). Green site design: strategies for stormwater management. *Journal of Green Building*. 2: 4, 46–56.

Cook, E.A. (2011). Embracing nature's deep structure in sustainable urbanism. In: A. Dokart, O. Al-Gohari and S. Rab (Editors). *Conservation of Architecture, Urban Areas, Nature & Landscape: Towards Sustainable Survival of Cultural Landscapes*. CSAAR: Amman.

Duerkson, C.J., D.L. Elliot, N.T. Hobbs, E. Johnson and J.R. Miller. (1997). *Habitat Protection Planning where the Wild Things Are*. American Planning Association: Washington, DC.

Erickson, D.E. (2006). *MetroGreen: Connecting Open Space in North American Cities*. Island Press: Washington, DC.

Esbah, H., E. Cook and J. Ewan (2009) Effects of increasing urbanization on the ecological integrity of open space preserves. *Environmental Management* 43: 5, 845–862.

Hellmund, P. and D. Smith (2008) *Designing Greenways: Sustainable Landscapes for Nature and People*. Island Press: Washington, DC.

Hough, M. (2004). *Cities and Natural Process*, Second Edition. Routledge: London.

Jongman, R. and G. Pungetti. (2004). *Ecological Networks and Greenways*. Cambridge University Press: Cambridge.

Jordan, W. (1993) Sunflower Forest: ecological restoration as the basis for a new environmental paradigm. In: D. Balwin, J. De Luce and C. Pletsch (Editors). *Beyond Preservation: Restoring and Inventing Landscapes*. University of Minnesota Press: Minneapolis.

Kerkstra, K. and P. Vrijlandt. (1990). Landscape planning for industrial agriculture: a proposed framework for rural areas. *Landscape and Urban Planning*. 18: 275–287.

Kowarik, I. (2005). Wild urban woodlands: towards a conceptual framework. In: I. Kowarik and S. Korner (Editors). *Wild Urban Woodlands: New Perpectives in Urban Forestry*. Springer: Berlin.

Megdahl, S. (2005) Environmental Restoration Projects in Arizona: The US Army Corps of Engineers' Approach, Final Report – Project Number W912PL04P0045. Water Resources Research Center, University of Arizona, Tucson, AZ.

Muerck, C.D. and S.R. Swaffield. (2007). Cities as complex landscapes: Biodiversity opportunities, landscape configurations and design directions. *New Zealand Garden Journal.* 10: 1, 10–20.

Steiner, F.R. (1996). Connecting infrastructure to deep structure. *Places.* 10: 3, 60–61.

Taylor, J., C. Paine and J. FitsGibbon (1995) From greenbelt to greenways: four Canadian case studies. *Landscape and Urban Planning.* 33, 47–64.

Turner, F. (1993) The invented landscape. In: D. Balwin, J. De Luce and C. Pletsch (Editors). *Beyond Preservation: Restoring and Inventing Landscapes.* University of Minnesota Press: Minneapolis.

Chapter 15

Bringing urban streams back to life!

The use of modern waterway construction technologies in restoring degraded streams

Wolf-Peter Geitz

Introduction

Throughout history humans have been forced by natural powers to limit their existence to areas where they are safe from harm caused by extreme heat, cold, storms or floods. In the course of evolution, humans increasingly moved to more hostile areas and conquered these new habitats. Through intelligence and technical advancement many dangers could be averted, prevented and safeguarded against. Consequently, humans have been convinced of their ability to populate and conquer the entire planet. Unfortunately, or maybe luckily, during recent years humans have been put back in their place more and more frequently by nature. Unusually long periods of extreme heat or cold, severe storms, unpredictable earthquakes, volcano eruptions, and more frequently occurring flood disasters stake the limits that define human existence.

The fact that some of the most threatening environmental dangers today have been caused or at least fueled by human action does not lack a certain irony. These include, for example, climate change, forest dieback, soil erosion, and flood events in urban watersheds where a high degree of impermeable surfaces prohibit natural processes, like the infiltration and retention capacities of the soil. Subsequently, large quantities of water are being flushed into our streams with increasing speed and frequency, whose natural profile is not able to handle the unnatural pressure. The logical and costly results include decreasing groundwater levels, stream erosion, and more frequent flood events which cause huge destruction in the densely developed riparian areas. Many rivers and streams now reflect the changes that the entire environment has undergone mainly in the last two centuries.

Short historic review of waterway construction in Germany

Rhine

Until the beginning of the nineteenth century, even the huge European rivers like the Rhine or the Danube were wild, natural streams. For example, in 1828 the upper reach of the river Rhine near Breisach still had numerous channels, oxbows, gravel banks and islands spread out over the riparian areas in the valley. Starting in 1812, countless "corrections" were implemented following the plans of the famous civil engineer Tulla. The goals of these corrections were to make large parts of the riparian zones useable for development and agriculture, and to eliminate wet areas which were often breeding grounds for epidemic illnesses like malaria. The numerous smaller winding channels of the stream were combined into one wide channel which was able to carry double the amount of water. Levees were built to limit flooding to riparian meadows and forests, preventing developed areas from flooding. There was also a certain political interest in these measures: the new, regulated Rhine finally defined a fixed border to neighboring France. Until 1963, numerous follow-up projects were undertaken, all aimed at improving navigability and power generation. For this purpose, canals were dug and locks and power plants were constructed eliminating migration possibilities for stream organisms.

Today, 87 percent of the flood-water-retaining riparian zones have been lost due to the construction of flood protection dams along the river. The originally 300 km long river reaching from Basel in Switzerland to Karlsruhe in Germany was reduced by 82 km. The velocity was increased by half. As a result, velocities and flood peaks in various connected rivers increased so unfavorably that flooding occurred even more frequently, a result that has to be countered again by more intensive flood protection measures.

Neckar

The Neckar in the southwest of Germany also used to be a wild and roaring river with extreme water level fluctuations and flooding. This is already implicated by the river's name, Neckar, which is derived from the Celtic word "nicra" which means fierce, wicked, quick, raging, wild. Two thousand years ago, in Roman times, first alterations took place to make development and transport of goods easier. These included bank protection treatments, dams, bridges, fords and small weirs. In the middle ages, the importance of the Neckar as a navigable waterway and source of power increased, resulting in the construction of large weirs and rafting channels.

In less than 40 years, between 1925 and 1962, the whole river was engineered to become navigable and to eliminate flooding. The straightened channel was formed into a trapezoidal profile which was lined with concrete. Twenty-seven weirs transformed the river into a chain of artificial lakes and secured a water depth of 3 m, necessary for navigability along the 200 km long stretch.

In the Stuttgart region all oxbows, except for one, were filled in and the fill areas nearly completely developed. Today, nothing even gives a hint to the fact that the Neckar used to be several hundred meters wide and constantly redefined its course by natural dynamics. In 1900, 260 fishermen could still make a living from what they pulled out of the river. Today there is not even one.

This, from the standpoint of aquatic ecology, most disastrous condition was set off in 1950 when the pollution through toxic industrial wastewater and ship traffic on the river began to increase significantly. The quality of aquatic conditions reached its all-time low around 1970. Only 22 fish species of the original 42 could still be found in the river and the current-adapted species were reduced from 18 to four. The anadromous species like Atlantic salmon and sea trout had vanished completely. The oxygen level fell under 2.5 mg/l. In comparison: the oxygen level of a healthy stream would be 8–9 mg/l. Mass fish die-offs were the ultimate consequence.

Only in 1975, with the construction of modern wastewater treatment plants, was action taken to improve the poor water quality conditions. However, due to the artificially constructed, concrete-lined stream channel, the river Neckar has not been able to regain its natural self-purification abilities in its 200 km long navigable section.

Apart from aquatic habitat qualities in the river itself, the economically strong and densely populated Neckar region is also lacking parks and greenways in close proximity to the river. After centuries of focusing solely on economic growth, it has been realized that economically strong regions can only be competitive if they also possess ecological values. Landscapes which are designed taking into consideration natural processes and recreational purposes are therefore mandatory in achieving a satisfying standard of living in densely developed urban areas.

Meanwhile, numerous ideas and programs have been developed and sparked public and political interest. Unfortunately, there are still no constant, long-term-oriented reactions and commitments from political decision makers.

At the moment there are three big initiatives which aim to improve the situation. They are, however, lacking coordination due to abnormal ambitions on administrative and personal levels. They all have two things in common, they claim to have been the first to tackle the topic and, it comes as no surprise, they all do not have a budget for realizing their ideas. First and foremost it is therefore crucial to implement some kind of coordination mechanism to prevent the representatives of the different programs from wasting their energy on competitive battles.

IkoNE Program

Since 1999, the waterways administration has sponsored the Integrierende Konzeption Neckar-Einzugsgebiet – Integrated Conceptual Program for the Neckar Watershed (IkoNE) – an integrated program aimed to improve stream habitats, flood protection, and water quality. As a first step of the program that encompasses 75 projects involving dams and weirs and 79 projects focusing on the river banks and riparian areas, three pilot projects were developed.

Modern natural waterway construction methods

New ideas ask for new tools. In addition to changing the political and social view of the way rivers and streams are treated, it is also important to establish new goals and construction techniques to develop interdisciplinary projects which are described later in this chapter.

Only 20 years ago, modern methods of natural waterway construction that had already been used for a long time, for example in Switzerland, were still widely ignored and absolutely rejected in Germany. The well-known German orderliness led to a very technically and hydraulically oriented view of streams which dominated the aesthetic ideal of the German landscape at the time. Also, civil engineers who often had no or little sense for ecological matters and landscape aesthetics were responsible for rivers and streams. Additionally, rising labor costs and the ever faster accelerating mechanization paved the way for the use of quickly produced, less space-intensive hard structures almost without exception. Hence, numerous rivers and streams were degraded to a concrete "landscape gutter."

Today, landscape architects have infiltrated hard structure engineering and once again made the old, newly discovered bioengineering bank stabilization methods acceptable. In addition to the traditional techniques, there is a variety of new and further developed construction methods. Natural and landscape-adapted construction materials are used for these techniques, leading to nature-like results in stream construction. The goal of using this type of construction is to stabilize stream banks entirely with the help of plants.

Various construction techniques and the combination with other materials help to achieve immediate protection right after construction. After the necessary development period, plants are fully able to stabilize the stream banks. Other materials necessary in the beginning like wood, wire, or geotextiles are left to degrade. The result is a naturally developed plant community with high ecological qualities which is able to fulfill the desired stabilization function.

As well as stabilizing stream banks, bioengineering construction techniques (Schiechtl, 1980; Scheichtl and Stern, 1997) can, by contrast, also be used to trigger or promote dynamic processes in stream development. Stream bank revetments, for example, are specifically used for redirecting currents to initiate desired erosion processes.

Project examples in Germany

Back Water and Fish Passage at the River Neckar in Ludwigsburg "Zugwiesen"

This pilot project is located north of Stuttgart in the area of the lock Poppenweiler. This entire reach of the river Neckar is canalized for large ship traffic and as a result lacks ecological continuity and prohibits stream organisms from migrating up and down the river.

The project aims to restore ecological continuity with the help of a 1700 m long natural fish pass. Approximately 1 m³/s is supposed to flow through the natural-like designed channel which is approximately 5 m wide and 1 m deep. In contrast to technically engineered fish passes, this channel serves as an independent habitat for all stream organisms. The new habitats will feature fast-flowing water and coarse gravel substrate. They are especially designed to attract current-adapted species whose typical habitats have been almost completely lost in the navigable part of the river.

Two large water bodies with a combined water surface of 26,000 m² will be created in the riparian area to serve as habitats and spawning grounds for slack water fish species. Just recently the design was changed to directly connect these water bodies to the Neckar, removing the dam which is currently separating the river from its floodplain. This change was made possible by the involvement of the Federal Waterways Authority. In addition there will be a number of ponds of varying form and size designed to serve as habitat for amphibians.

But not only flora and fauna will benefit from the project. Since the new water bodies will be extremely attractive to recreation-seeking residents, a path system including rest areas, an information point and an observation tower has been sensibly designed to not interfere with the ecological functions. An interregional bike path leading along the project reach will bring visitors from the whole country to the site. It is the hope of the project designers that the experience of traveling

Figure 15.1 View of the southern project area located in May 2012. The newly constructed 1.7 km long fish passage is depicted in the foreground, new amphibian pools and backwater areas can be viewed in the back. The dam separating the Neckar and the new backwater will be removed in the next construction phase. Image courtesy of Peter Geitz.

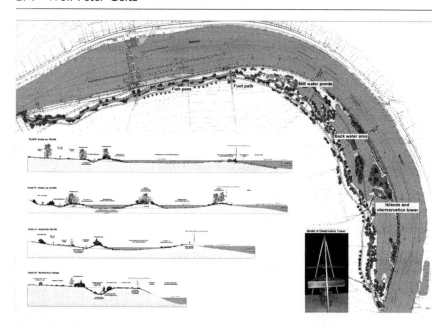

Figure 15.2 Plan view and cross sections of the project; an observation tower will enable visitors to have a wide view from above and observe the fauna which is likely to inhabit the redesigned river floodplain quickly.
Image courtesy of Peter Geitz.

through this area and experiencing it will also help to increase environmental awareness and the acceptance of large-scale environmental projects in urban areas. Construction of the three million euro project started in the summer of 2011.

Restoration of the Neckar in Horkheim

Another project type is planned south of Heilbronn in the city of Horkheim. Ecological migration is disrupted in this case as well, similar to the reach shown before. However, in 1928, a 3 km-long shipping canal was built parallel to the stream channel to serve the lock structure. That way the original natural channel was maintained and still serves as an important refuge with good habitat conditions.

In order to effectively reactivate the original channel by creating the right current structures for the typical species, it is necessary to pipe a sufficient amount of water, approximately 15 m³/s, through this stretch. Because this quantity of water would no longer be available for power generation in the navigable channel, the power company will only agree to the project if a new, small power plant will be built that can use this amount. From the view point of aquatic ecology, this proposal is feasible since ecological continuity will be secured with the help of a new natural-like bypass channel which will only convey 1 m³/s.

In close cooperation with aquatic ecologists, a number of construction techniques were developed to optimize and adapt the design for the reach using the predefined water quantity. The major goal of this work was to provide a maximum of habitat diversity for current-adapted fish species which have become so sparse in the Neckar. The use of a two-dimensional hydraulic program at the University of Karlsruhe was critical for coordinating the needs of hydraulics and aquatic ecology, and to size the structures.

The size of the project is impressive. The same is true for the costs, which were calculated to be 2.5 million euros (approximately US$3.25 million). This is one reason why this project is on hold at the moment, awaiting the necessary political decisions to be made which can carry this endeavor forward.

Restoration of the confluence area of the Elz and the Neckar in Mosbach

Another project type is located approximately 100 km north of Stuttgart in the town of Mosbach. It is important to know for this project reach that the 14 km distance between the locks is far greater than in most cases, and therefore one can find normal flow patterns in this section. Correspondingly, the water level fluctuations between high and low water are very extreme as well.

Originally the banks of the river were armored with concrete paving but maintenance of these structures was neglected over the last few years to save costs. This fact served as an advantage for ecology since bank erosion occurred in some areas, initiating the development of biologically active stream banks. The project area also includes the confluence of the Neckar with the river Elz, an important tributary with very good aquatic habitat qualities. Numerous restoration projects have already been executed along this stream. For the last one, which was undertaken as part of a State Garden Show in 1997, long reaches were completely redesigned using modern waterway construction techniques.

It was the goal of the pilot project to improve aquatic habitat structures in a one km-long reach of the river Elz and to redesign the concrete-lined confluence area creating a nature-like environment with restored migration functions. For this purpose the hard armoring in the confluence area was removed. The confluence section was then structured into three channels of varying width, allowing the Elz to use one or several stream sections depending on the water quantity. Bank stabilizations were not necessary in this case since the intent was to encourage the Elz to create its own course through natural dynamic processes.

A 500 m-long stretch along the right bank of the Neckar was freed of its stone armor. Many bank areas were left unprotected, giving the river room for dynamic development. Other areas prone to erosion had to be protected with bioengineering techniques. A boardwalk with integrated observation platforms was constructed along the river to allow residents to experience the newly created bank habitats. Including recreational elements in environmental restoration areas is the key to

Figure 15.3 Newly created back water habitats right after planting. Image courtesy of Peter Geitz.

acceptance of revitalized water systems in urban areas. Since human beings play an important part in shaping our environment it is of great importance to recognize humans are part of it.

The river Neckar not only lacks typical flow patterns, but also areas that are free of currents which serve as refuge and spawning habitats for special species. That is why a water body measuring 5000 m², with a water depth of up to 2 m was created. It has a connection to the Neckar in the form of a 35 m-wide opening allowing fish and other organisms to migrate freely between the river and newly created habitats.

In order to be able to connect the riparian areas of the Neckar and the Elz, the new water body was extended under a huge highway bridge. To allow for a continuous pedestrian and bike path in these areas, two new bridges had to be built spanning the distance between the highway bridge piers.

The entire cost of the project was 800,000 euros (approximately US$1 million) and was completed in 2002. Seventy percent of that amount was covered by funding from the federal state of Baden-Württemberg. The areas have developed very well. It is impressive to see how quickly the new water body has been populated especially by minnows who find diverse habitat structures, refuge, and food. But not only wildlife enjoys the new habitat. The local residents intensively use the flat banks and boardwalks to safely get close to the water's edge.

Figure 15.4 The redesigned confluence of the Elz with the Neckar during grading work spanning under the highway-bridge. Image courtesy of Peter Geitz.

Figure 15.5 Confluence area after eight years of development (highway-bridge in the background). Image courtesy of Peter Geitz.

Reconstruction of the canalized river Enz in Pforzheim in 1990

The city of Pforzheim is located approximately 60 km northwest of Stuttgart at the northeastern edge of the Black Forest. The State Garden Show in Pforzheim in 1992 provided the background for restoring the Enz in the exhibit area. At the time this project was unique regarding the dimension, the handling as well as the conflicts and problems that had to be solved. Still today this state pilot project is unparalleled.

Until the end of the nineteenth century, the Enz area in the eastern part of Pforzheim was still a natural river landscape. As a result of severe flooding events at the end of the nineteenth century that caused serious damage, the technically oriented canalization of the Enz was undertaken in the downtown area of Pforzheim between 1902 and 1907 with the goal of providing flood safety to the city's inhabitants. Ecological considerations were of no importance. After this construction effort the new, paved, double-trapezoidal profile was able to safely convey the waters of the three rivers Enz, Nagold and Würm which flow through the Black Forest. The watershed of the Enz in Pforzheim is 1500 km^2 in area, the mean discharge equals approximately 17 m^3/s. In comparison, during the 100-year flood event the discharge amounts up to 425 m^3/s. In January of 1990 such an event occurred.

Just five months before construction started, the worst-case scenario was experienced first-hand and demonstrated the nature of river. The roaring masses of water made their way through a nearby wooded area. This event demonstrated that it is important to have respect for the forces this river could unleash.

The approximately 1.8 km-long project reach at the eastern edge of Pforzheim has little attraction for humans and nature alike. The Enz was flowing through the straightened, paved trapezoidal profile between the flood protection dams, lacking any ecological habitat structures or vegetation.

When design ideas for the remodeling of the Enz were submitted as part of a competition in 1987, there was laughter, criticism, and even anger. But, there was also enthusiasm because of the comprehensive approach proposed to restore the entire reach. Admittedly, the designs were rather generous, going beyond the limits of the flood protection dams and as a result offered more space for additional bends and meanders. But the new concept for the Enz did not strike the designers as unrealistic as implied by critical viewers.

The paving in the straight channel was to be removed completely to make way for a new meandering course of the stream initiated by current-deflecting structures and interspersed islands creating a diversity of conditions. The banks were to be redesigned with the help of bioengineering stabilization methods using the entire width of the cross sectional profile between the flood protection dams.

In order to improve the situation for aquatic organisms, the designs included a diversity of flat and deep water zones. To improve the possibility of experiencing the new stream habitats, pedestrian paths and bridges were incorporated.

Figure 15.6 Model of the design conditions. Image courtesy of Peter Geitz.

The planning team and the politicians were euphoric and presented the Enz as the "blue backbone" of the city as part of a marketing campaign. However, the permitting agencies had a hard time warming up to these new ideas. Even on a field trip that we organized to Switzerland with all involved parties to visit very similar, successful projects, the critics could not be convinced. Since the design was so unparalleled in its nature in Germany, it would have been impossible to convince the permitting agencies to give approval using traditional hydraulic calculation patterns. Therefore, it was decided that waterway construction experts at the University of Karlsruhe should conduct a special hydraulic modeling study of the Enz. For this purpose a 30 m-long model at a scale of 1:40 was built and calibrated to match the existing conditions.

In the second modeling phase, the conditions after completion of construction were implemented and tested using different discharge amounts. The different water levels as well as the flow velocities were measured during this process for the entire area.

In the third and last phase, the conditions ten years after construction were simulated to be able to determine how much vegetation could be tolerated to still safely convey the flows. The result of the modeling showed that the existing profile was able to convey approximately 1000 m^3/s but the design event only amounted to a discharge of 540 m^3/s. This great leeway in flood water capacity provided the safety valve and was the basis for the restoration of the Enz.

It took ten months of intensive and controversial discussions between all parties involved to come to an agreement. The playful act of barefooted designers placing more shrubs and trees into the model and the hydraulic engineers taking them out again at a meeting in Karlsruhe reflected the nature and marked the end of a long decision process. In the end, there was a compromise that was able to satisfy all experts involved.

In April of 1990, construction for the 1.8 km-long reach started. In a first step the paved, partially concrete bank treatments were torn up and removed. The organic topsoil was stripped and stored on site for later use. During the construction phase thousands of existing plants were removed in the form of sods and clumps before grading the site.

The whole construction site was located in a drinking water protection zone from which the city of Pforzheim was drawing 40 percent of its drinking water supply. Therefore the extensive grading work, necessary to form the new course of the Enz, had to be conducted using great care and asked for close construction supervision. Other problems and challenges for the construction process were caused by numerous existing infrastructure elements which had to be worked around, such as pipes and bridges.

The newly created stream banks were covered with a mixture of red sandstone gravel. The material was taken from a large gravel bank that had been deposited in the river further downstream during a flood event. Areas which were only exposed to low flow velocities and shear stresses could be left to develop without any bed armoring. Banks exposed to high flow velocities were secured with live stakes and riprap consisting of a specially graded stone mix. Parallel to the stone, layers of live willow stakes were inserted into the gravel to permanently stabilize the bank. Only a few weeks later the stakes had sprouted and secured the banks with their roots.

In the following paragraphs three soil bioengineering treatments using plant material to stabilize stream banks are described in more detail.

Brush fascines

Fascines are constructed using branches which are densely packed together with wire forming approximately 4 m-long bundles. The finished fascines are laid and staked in a trench along the toe of the bank at the mean water elevation. The live fascines are made from freshly cut willow brush material which is able to quickly regenerate and produce roots and shoots securing the banks. In the long term a dense, flexible brush vegetation will establish itself which corresponds to the native plant community.

Another fascine type can be produced from any kind of brush material which is not able to regenerate from woody parts. It is used to prevent scour at the toe of the bank and protect the saplings planted behind the fascines. All types of fascines offer excellent habitat structures for stream organisms which find lots of nooks and crannies in-between the brush material to hide in.

Brush mattress

Brush mattresses are used in combination with fascines. For this treatment, willow branches are closely packed on the bank with their ends tucked under the fascine. Wood poles, stakes, and wire are used to secure the branches and press them close to the soil. The key for successful bioengineering treatments is the professional handling of the construction process. Since a lot of contractors are not familiar with these techniques it is very important to provide close construction supervision. If everything is done right the willow branches sprout and the numerous shoots quickly secure the whole covered bank area.

Reed roll

The reed roll is another bioengineering treatment that works with herbaceous instead of woody plant material. This treatment is used to quickly develop herbaceous plant communities at the water's edge. Strong, up to 4 m-long coconut matting is laid out in a pre-dug trench along the mean water elevation and filled with gravel, soil, and various herbaceous plants which are ideally harvested as sods from nearby sites. The remaining geotextile is laid out on the bank, secured with wooden stakes, and either planted or seeded with appropriate plant species. Protected by the coconut mats the plants can quickly grow and contribute to stabilizing the banks. The coconut matting will biodegrade within approximately five years, leaving only the well-established plant community.

Durable grass-gravel paths were constructed along both banks of the newly restored Enz to allow for maintenance and public access. This type of path is easy and inexpensive to build and does not constitute a barrier for animals. Depending on the conditions and the intensity of use, the grass surface only develops sparsely. The most favorable scenario would be for the grass to cover the whole path surface. In any case, this pathway is suitable for heavy use and is very easy to repair.

The designs also included a very special kind of pathway that could be found in old Roman cities like Pforzheim 2000 years ago. These special stream crossings, called fords, were already established at the Enz to allow for wagons to get to the other side safely. When looking through historic reports, it was determined that such a stream crossing had existed in the project area and a reconstructed ford was thus included in the design.

Due to the high flow velocities reaching 4 m/s or more, most stream banks had to be stabilized using various treatments. In contrast to all the constructed banks, we wanted to create some areas which were completely left to dynamic processes, giving the river space to take its own shape. Several groups of islands were created, only secured at the current exposed end with some large stones. These islands were meant to be left to geomorphic dynamic processes. The construction for the 1.8 km-long and 90 m-wide area only took seven months. Since it was a pilot project the entire cost of approximately two million euros (about US$2.8 million) was covered by funding from the state of Baden-Württemberg.

After three years, the willow growth from the bioengineering treatments was already very dense, securing the banks with their roots. This strong, protecting vegetation was much needed right at that time.

In 1993, not even three years after construction completion, the newly restored reach was put to the test when a flood event with a peak discharge of 550 m³/s hit. This discharge amount was well beyond the design discharge used in the planning process. A site visit after the flood event did not reveal any significant damage. It was proven that the new cross section was able to securely convey even serious floods. Nothing has happened that was not supposed to happen. The majority of the flexible bioengineering treatments were able to withstand the high shear stresses during the flood event. As intended by the designers, the islands completely restructured themselves during flood events. Today, only a couple of very large stones remain of the formerly biggest island.

The Enz has become a highly frequented local recreational area in downtown Pforzheim. Plants, animals, and humans alike enjoy their new habitat. In particular, aquatic organisms have quickly and abundantly inhabited the restored river reach. A scientific study has documented the biological and morphological changes over the course of ten years. However, it is often forgotten or neglected that natural waterway construction does not end when the excavators leave the site. Only adequate and consequent maintenance will lead to the desired development. Although the successful and fast development of the brush vegetation on the banks is pleasing, one also needs to realize that it can constitute a problem when limiting the water carrying capacity of the river.

The river is alive again and its natural dynamics are working. Sandy sediment, for example, can cause problems and limit the water carrying capacity if it is deposited in the wrong spots. Consequently, it is important to achieve the goals laid out in the design process by performing adequate maintenance. It is also important to strive for a permanent balance between flood safety, recreational needs, and environmental protection. A very detailed maintenance and development plan has been worked out for the river Enz. If used by responsible authorities this plan can help to achieve the intended goals and make this project a permanent success story.

After a 14-year development period it is safe to say that the enormous effort and investment has yielded positive results. The river now shows dynamic behavior to a tolerable degree which is required for the development of a healthy stream ecosystem. The redesigned section of the Enz, with special regard to its location in an urban area, shows the extent to which ecological improvements are possible.

Conclusions

The potential of stream and river restoration with the use of natural waterway construction methods in revitalizing urban areas is immense but still has not been fully grasped by all responsible parties. However, a lot of progress has been made in laying the ground for more successful water revitalization projects like the ones described above. It is not only the increased environmental awareness, or the amended state and federal regulations in Germany but also the European Union Water Framework Directive (WFD) which has helped to promote nature-oriented construction techniques. Here it is important to point out an important difference: whereas the state and federal regulations are only applicable for un-navigable streams and rivers, the WFD also demands improvements of the ecological conditions of navigable waterways. In addition, the WFD is the only regulation which gives a time frame in which the ecological improvements have to be implemented. However, the realization process is still in the beginning phase. It will probably take another two decades before enough pilot projects have been built and long-term knowledge about their performance can be gained.

Although the planner still sometimes has to walk a long and winding road to convince the clients and responsible parties of the benefits of nature-oriented techniques, nature-oriented water engineering has gained wide recognition in Europe. A lot has been accomplished already. Thirty years ago conventional hard engineering methods were still used and called for almost without alternative; today they are rarely used anymore in stream and river construction. Alternative methods applying ecologically based treatments are at least considered in the planning process and are often given preference over conventional methods. Over the last 20 years numerous groundbreaking projects have been implemented which demonstrate the enormous spectrum of application and development but also show the limits of capability of nature-oriented techniques. The past has shown clearly that the classic, one-way-oriented examination used for projecting conventional, hard engineered treatment does not lead to success in the design and development process with nature-oriented restoration projects. The factors influencing revitalized streams and rivers are too multifaceted to be defined with simple calculations. Involving an engineer with experience in the understanding of these factors and the application of these techniques is the key to success.

Extensive knowledge of the natural site conditions, the flora and fauna and of the biotechnical performance of the plant material used for the bioengineering techniques is required to guarantee a long-lasting success of a revitalization project. Still, though, the treatments are prone to unpredictable natural forces so that an element of risk always remains. The planning engineer not only has to recognize this risk but also has to implement and respect it in his or her work. However, the most difficult part in the process is to successfully communicate this risk, which takes courage.

References

Schiechtl, H. (1980) *Bioengineering for Land Reclamation and Conservation.* University of Alberta Press: Edmonton.

Schiechtl, H. and R. Stern (1997) *Water Bioengineering Approaches for Watercourse Bank and Shoreline Protection.* Wiley-Blackwell: London.

Chapter 16

Managing the urban/nature border
Sonoran Islands in the urbanized desert

Joseph M. Ewan, John Ball, Michael Underhill, and James P. Burke

Introduction

Rapid global urbanization is resulting in significant expansion of many cities. Phoenix, Arizona, USA is one of the cities coping with this problem. In just 50 years, its population grew from approximately 60,000 to over 1,300,000 (including the surrounding metropolitan area 3.5 million). As the urban area grew, natural open spaces at the historic periphery were enveloped by urban and suburban land uses. The resulting natural islands became increasingly important as open space preserves and recreational areas. Conflicts arose between various competing interests. Many other cities, including fast-growing cities of Asia and Africa, are facing similar situations and may look to recent history for solutions. Described here is a specific example of efforts by city planners and academics to reconcile the challenges faced at the natural and urban edge in metropolitan Phoenix.

Within one of the largest and fastest-growing metropolitan communities in the world lie several islands of preserved mountainous Sonoran Desert. These preserves range in size from just a few acres to over 16,000 acres and one such island preserve is the largest city park in the United States. Managing the interface at the perimeter of the preserves and the surrounding urban built environment has largely been left to the City of Phoenix Parks and Recreation Department. The development and implementation of strategies, master plans, policies, a zoning ordinance, and the means of enforcement have evolved over a period of nearly 20 years, spanning several municipal administrations and a complete economic boom/bust cycle. This chapter reviews that history and attempts to provide lessons learned for contemporary practitioners working at the borders of the urban and the natural.

A short story illustrates the fundamental conflict at the heart of this narrative. One day a City of Phoenix Parks Department landscape architect received two telephone calls within the space of a few minutes from unhappy Phoenix citizens. The first was a call from a hiker's mobile phone in a desert park complaining that a resident in an adjacent single family residence was harassing him from a back yard. The second was from a homeowner adjacent to the same desert park who complained that a hiker was staring into his windows.

Both calls displayed symptoms characteristic of the user conflict at the natural/urban interface. This chapter focuses on that political agenda, as well as the efforts of the City of Phoenix and an Arizona State University joint landscape architecture and architecture studio through design research, master planning, and the modification of zoning ordinances, to mitigate conflicts and maximize the opportunities for a variety of user-communities claiming rights at the urban/natural interface. A journey is recounted that began with recognition by City of Phoenix staff that managing the urban/natural interface was a critical initiative and that the subsequent implementation of master plans and zoning ordinances were required to achieve a goal of balanced use and continued preservation. The process is described, including the reaction by the development community to the new regulatory framework. Arizona State University was engaged to provide a third party assessment of the conflict from a design perspective. Subsequent modification of City policy was undertaken in response to that input.

Ultimately as a result of the recession that began in 2008, the effort and momentum slowed and conflicts were diffused. Once development pressures return, however, it is anticipated that the process will re-engage.

Many urban theorists have challenged designers to look more carefully at suburban sprawl. In *Edge City: Life on the New Frontier*, Joel Garreau (1991) studies American cities seeking to understand new patterns of urban development in areas where there is the most growth—the fringes. In *Beyond the Urban Fringe*, Peirce Lewis (1983) describes contemporary development as a "galactic urban tissue." And in *Making a Middle Landscape*, Peter Rowe (1991) challenges designers to develop a "poetic" for the emerging American suburb that recognizes Arcadian yearnings.

Perhaps the most relevant, Steven Holl (1991), in *Edge of a City*, proposes several interesting theoretical projects that try to make economic, aesthetic, and ecological sense out of the opportunity presented by the border between the city and the landscape. His "Stitch Plan" for Cleveland, "Spatial Retaining Bars" for Phoenix, and "Spiriod Sectors" for Dallas-Fort Worth are suggestions for the use of physical form to adjudicate the border, to formally and programmatically sort out how urbanization meets open space. Holl explains,

> Our exploration . . . attempts a celebration of the landscape of natural occurrences, mystery, and transcendent meanings. The phenomenon of place is an objective that can be given new dimensions in the form and material of architecture.

Holl's efforts mark the boundary and make the juxtaposition of denser development and open space both useful and beautiful. Sculptural shapes contain urban uses but primarily frame or mark the edge, supporting the idea that there should be more, not less, density at the edge. Indeed, the border between urbanization and open space should be a symbolic marking of respect for nature and the place of most public access and activity.

Landscape theorists like Ian McHarg (1969), Phillip Lewis (1983), and Michael Hough (2002) have advocated the awareness of natural processes when designing urban environments. Holl's theoretical proposals are not unlike many realized efforts where natural areas seem more juxtaposed to urban environments rather than integral. The studio embraced Michael Hough's call for integrating the concept of urbanism with nature.

Context

Phoenix has a history of setting aside desert lands. During the city's relatively short history, just over 100 years, more than 25,000 acres of predominantly mountains and hillsides have been set aside as desert parks and preserves. The effort began in the 1920s with the establishment of the 16,500 acre South Mountain Park, the largest municipal park in the country. In 1960 the city was able to secure 350 acres

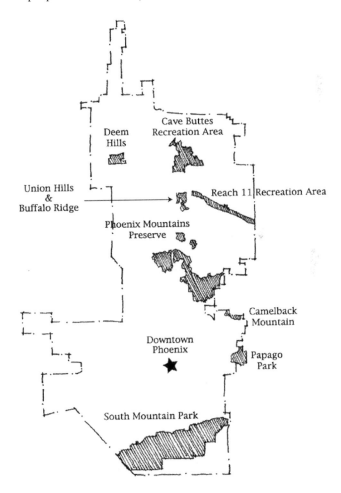

Figure 16.1 Context area. Image courtesy of J. Ewan.

at the top of Camelback Mountain, a landmark that was already encircled by private homes. Then, in 1972, the public voted to expand the Phoenix Mountain Preserves by 10,500 acres with the addition of the North Mountain range. This addition increased opportunities for the city's rapidly growing population to commune with the desert environment.

Some of these areas have sustained extensive damage that has typically been attributed to loving the parks to death. As a result, proper use of the desert preserves is a topic of significant concern and debate. Ironically, linked to the concern about use of the preserves is adequate access to trails within these open spaces. Popular trails are difficult to find because the land is typically surrounded by large-lot residential developments where homeowners seek to protect their privacy. Protection of private property rights and views, and access to public open space are hotly debated topics.

The 2010 U.S. census reports the City of Phoenix currently has a population in excess of 1.4 million spread out over more than 500 square miles, a density of 2,800 people per square mile. Phoenix has historically supported a low density of settlement (Danzig and Saaty, 1973). The pattern for urban development is primarily guided by the Jeffersonian grid, which initially served farming, but is now governing the larger grain of planned community development. An extensive working canal-based irrigation system and remnant citrus orchards, now incorporated into developments, provide hints of the city's agricultural past.

The most prominent interruption in the urban pattern is the desert mountain preserves, which from the air appear to be islands of open space surrounded by urban settlement. Standing at the edge of these preserves provides distant views of open desert, mountains, and skies that are extraordinary. Exemplifying the Arcadian tendencies that Peter Rowe (1991) discusses in *Making a Middle Landscape*, many people move to Phoenix for the climate and enchanting desert. However, the influx of new residents and the low-density sprawling development pattern increasingly threaten air quality and the delicate desert ecology.

Metropolitan Phoenix lies within the Sonoran Desert, where ecosystem processes are closely linked to precipitation patterns. Most vegetation growth occurs in the spring following winter rains; however, some growth occurs during the summer monsoon season. These bimodal rainy seasons enable the land to support diverse and rich plant communities, making the Sonoran Desert the lushest desert in the world.

The Sonoran Desert is classified into six categories defined by natural factors such as temperature, precipitation, geology, and soils (Shreve, 1951; Brown and Lowe, 1982). The majority of metropolitan Phoenix is located within the subdivision referred to as the Lower Colorado River Valley or the microphyllous desert. This area is the largest and most arid subdivision of the Sonoran Desert. Low annual precipitation and high temperatures support relatively sparse vegetation. The average annual precipitation reported for the City of Phoenix is 7.51 inches (Sellers et al., 1985).

Figure 16.2 The existing preserves, North Mountain in the foreground and South in the background, once on the periphery of the metropolitan area, are now surrounded by urban settlement. Image courtesy of the City of Phoenix.

Characteristic species include blue paloverde (*Cercidium floridum*), creosotebush (*Larrea tridentata*), and bursage (*Ambrosia sp.*). South Mountain Park, Camelback Mountain, Squaw Peak, and the vast majority of developed areas within the city are located within this subdivision. In contrast, the northern extent of the city is located in the transition zone between the Lower Colorado River Valley and the Arizona Upland subdivision of the Sonoran Desert.

Despite debates about access and use, there is widespread enthusiasm for preserving open desert. However, there is much less agreement about what to do at the edge in terms of urban development. Because Phoenicians are accustomed to low-density, single family, detached homes, many people assume this should be the development type along the urban side of the preserve boundary. The notion of low-density development adjacent to open space is advocated by many professional and academic groups involved in the process of development and open space preservation locally and nationally as well. A charrette coordinated by the City of Phoenix and Arizona State University proposed a strategy that advocated

Figure 16.3 The existing edge condition in Phoenix primarily consists of single family houses with backyards oriented toward the preserve/public open space, South Mountain Park, Phoenix, Arizona. Image courtesy of J. Ewan.

a spectrum of development intensity in the North Area of the City that had previously been uniformly recommended for the lowest density at the edge of the desert open space (McCarthy et al., 1996). Baschak and Brown (1994) have also proposed an ecological design framework that sets up a similar strategy for minimizing intensity of development at the edge of sensitive habitats or Multiple-Use-Modules (MUMs). Essentially, concentric buffers are intended to protect core areas within open space.

The participants in the struggle over management of the urban/natural interface tend to fall into three groups: (1) recreational users of the desert preserves; (2) existing single family homeowners adjacent to the preserves; and (3) the owners of the developable land at the urban/desert interface. Frequent conflicts arise when land owners feel their privacy is compromised by preserve users while preserve users believe their recreational experience is negatively impacted by behavior on the private side of the edge.

In the existing preserves, providing access is a constant struggle. Many existing access points are constructed well after the need is established. It is unlikely anyone could have envisioned the visitation level in South Mountain Park would soar from 36,000 per year in the 1920s to over 3,000,000 per year currently. Once settled along the edge of the preserve, homeowners, community associations, and developers prefer access to occur anywhere but in their community. As a result, public access points are very far apart, not well defined, and often have inadequate amenities. Further complicating the access issue are the ad hoc access points that have historically appeared along drainage easements and undeveloped properties. While these have provided an important type of neighborhood access in the past, current development tends toward exclusive housing projects, gated communities, and networks of walls that prohibit the greater public from even having a sense of access. In order to mitigate some aspects of the conflict, the Phoenix Parks and Recreation Department developed a plan for a hierarchy of access points for new and existing preserves.

Preserve planning in Phoenix, Arizona

In 1993 the Phoenix City Council approved a new policy establishing a desert preserve for the northern growth areas of the city. This policy recommended that a system of environmentally sound open space lands be preserved that would include all indigenous plant communities and habitat types. This concept was refined and developed with citizen participation through the established boards and commissions, as well as committees established to develop policies on specific issues.

The Desert Preserve Citizen Advisory Committee, appointed by the Parks and Recreation Board, was charged with preparing a report defining which lands were to be included in the desert preserve system. The committee submitted a preliminary plan recommending 11,000 acres of primary and secondary washes, scenic corridors, and utility corridors for the program. The committee did not address mountains and foothills. These areas were considered the charge of the Mountain Preserve Citizens Advisory Committee.

The *Desert Preserve Preliminary Plan* was approved by the Parks and Recreation Board and City Council in 1994. The Parks and Recreation Board designated this new preserve initiative as the Phoenix Sonoran Preserve System. The plan was based on initial environmental inventories and analysis. It used United States Geological Survey (USGS) 7.5 minute maps for a base sheet. Maps were prepared to show slope characteristics at 5 percent slope intervals, proposed streets, the general plan for the area, planned trails and bikeway systems, natural systems and features, and potential archaeological sites. Seven categories of desert lands are identified in the preliminary plan: (1) major washes and floodplains, (2) secondary washes, (3) utility corridors, (4) view corridors, (5) mountains, (6) open space linkages, and (7) scenic corridors.

In 1998 the city committed to forming an even larger preserve at its northern edge. This 21,500 acre network of open space, including saguaro-studded hillsides, creosote flats, and large desert washes, was supported overwhelmingly by Phoenicians despite the estimated 250 million dollars needed for acquisition. The effort received national attention when it was awarded the American Society of Landscape Architects (ASLA) Presidential Award of Excellence for analysis and planning (Engley, 2001). This new preserve also created more than 150 miles of preserve edge condition. While implementation of the Sonoran Preserve progressed, there was also political pressure to assure public access, especially for the vast majority of residents who did not anticipate living at the desert edge.

For the first time in Phoenix's history, the *Sonoran Preserve Master Plan* advocated open space to be configured to preserve natural "systems that function biologically" in an effort to protect the fragile flora and sensitive fauna (Burke and Ewan, 1999). Driving the effort was the fact that Phoenicians live amid some of the most beautiful and biologically rich desert in the world, a valuable resource threatened at an increasing rate. With sensitive planning, a commitment to maintaining quality of life, and quick action, the intent was to accommodate quality growth and preservation of the Sonoran Desert.

The Sonoran Preserve Master Plan was prepared by the PRLD with the Phoenix Sonoran Preserve Committee and was based on the Desert Preserve Preliminary Plan prepared in 1994, additional citizen involvement, and a database and ecological inventory prepared by the Parks, Recreation and Library Department in conjunction with Arizona State University. The plan was presented to the City of Phoenix urban village planning committees and the Environmental Quality Commission and received enthusiastic support. On January 22, 1998, the Parks and Recreation Board and the Phoenix Sonoran Preserve Committee both unanimously approved the plan at a joint meeting. The City Council unanimously approved the plan on February 17, 1998.

The planning process for the Sonoran Preserve incorporated traditional planning techniques (inventory and analysis) with landscape ecological theory. Past open space preservation efforts had been primarily designated by only three criteria: slope, visual prominence, and land ownership. The Sonoran Preserve Master Plan

Figure 16.4 Edge condition. Image courtesy of J. Ewan.

attempted to develop a system that functions biologically—maintaining species diversity and ecological processes—while providing a recreational resource. A significant goal was to avoid the oversights of the past that created "sky islands" with miles of walls separating the mountain preserves from the greater community and the larger natural environment.

Implementation of the plan was partly achieved by the adoption of Design Review Guidelines for the desert edge in the city's zoning ordinance, which occurred in 1999. Political activists had been advocating for more public access to and public use of open space, and convinced the city to adopt an ordinance (known as the 60/40 rule) that required that preserver edges bounded by privately held land be developed so that more than half of the edge remains accessible to the public. The ordinance proposed four options to meet this requirement of 60 percent access: (1) single loaded streets adjacent to the preserve, (2) cul-de-sacs opening to the preserve, (3) private open space adjacent to the preserve, and (4) the final vague catch-all: creative options. In practice the last option was unlikely to be used because the Phoenix development community has been historically reluctant to invest resources in an effort to discover which creative option the city would support.

Design Review Guidelines (DRG) for the desert edge were incorporated into the zoning ordinance, and the city received a modest number of developer applications for site plan review. Anecdotal data from city staff suggested that the public access contemplated and required by the DRG was not well received by the developers intending to create new housing projects along the preserve edge.

Desert edge design studio

In response to developer complaints, the City of Phoenix Planning Department asked Arizona State University's College of Architecture and Environmental Design (now The Design School) to hold a cross-disciplinary studio to consider proposals that could inform new policy guiding urban form at the edge during the summer of 2001. The studio, led by architecture and landscape architecture faculty, and graduate students from environmental planning, architecture, and landscape architecture, was to holistically consider the edge in an effort to inform design that would be sensitive to the fragile Sonoran Desert landscape and simultaneously increase citizen's awareness, understanding, and appropriate use of the desert open space. The charge to the studio was to explore the possibility of accommodating both urban and ecological functions in a coordinated and spatially merged form that treated both sides of the edge as environmentally and culturally significant. The city's challenge presented a unique opportunity to develop design-driven policy that addressed the complex issues affecting development at the desert edge.

The City's *Sonoran Preserve Master Plan* called for "an integration of a preservation ethic into the overall urban form." This statement laid the groundwork for a departure from the common interpretation that nature starts where the city ends. Because the creation of this new preserve was an unusual opportunity, the urban/nature edge could be an example of the private sector and the public sector working together to create valuable places for more people. The open space would create higher land value for adjacent private land, and development could be more sensitive to the needs of the public.

The studio initially focused on natural factors with the intent to identify the relative ecological value of areas within and outside of the preserve. Second, it looked at infrastructure with the ultimate goal to identify areas in proximity to the Preserve that could support a concentration of activities. Subsequently, the analysis was synthesized and indicated where increased intensity of development was appropriate, relative to both ecological concerns for the Preserve and the spatial and economic viability of public facilities and private enterprises. Finally, the studio conducted extensive meetings with homebuilders, developers, open space advocates, and city officials. Four primary issues were identified.

1. *Access.* It was clear issues of access were complex, and there were two opposing arguments beyond the immediate response that there should be access for all. The purpose of creating the desert preserves was to save the delicate natural landscape. However, large numbers of people using the desert can cause irreparable damage. The counter-argument was that access for all enhances efforts to educate the public about the desert, leading to more interest, knowledge, and respect for natural places, and greater concern for preservation.

2. *Security.* The assumption on the part of developers and wealthy homeowners living at the desert edge has been that public access and increased density

increases crime. The counter-argument Jane Jacobs (1961) also made is for more people and eyes on the streets to enhance security. While a large open space might be different than a city street, the analogy was deemed worth testing.

3. *Density.* Historically higher levels of urban density have almost always been considered to be undesirable in Phoenix by many residents and policy-makers. However, it became clear that increasing the density of urban development, especially housing, along the edge of open space could make that space more accessible and perhaps more secure. The studio considered ways to increase density without perpetuating negative impacts on the desert's ecological or aesthetic value.

4. *Environmental impact.* A surprising finding of the study by the studio was that single family home ownership along a nature preserve tends to promote more environmental damage than multi-family ownership. In a study by Koole (2003), it was concluded that some single family residents tend to throw yard clippings and discarded items over their back walls and into the preserves while the residents of multi-family dwellings do not. Koole credits the sense of preserve land "ownership" by the single family dweller as the justification for these actions.

Impact of the DRG

Analysis of then current developer proposals related to public access under the 60/40 rule revealed three common problems: (1) Single loaded roads were infrequently utilized and when used were often characterized by residential facades dominated by garage frontage that contributed little to the quality of the edge, (2) cul-de-sacs were typically located deep inside a network of streets making it virtually impossible for visitors to find access to the preserve; and (3) open spaces were used to accommodate the traditional scheme of backyards facing the edge which ultimately does nothing to improve visual or physical access to the preserve.

Community outreach efforts also revealed that extensive changes in current practice were highly unlikely to be accepted owing to the general entrenchment of all parties in their positions. Therefore, it was determined that incremental changes in zoning and development practices had the greatest promise of realization.

Recommendations

Final recommendations included a proposal with five interrelated components: (1) an overall strategy for coordinated planning for the preserve and future urbanization, (2) strategies for increasing urban density adjacent to the preserve, (3) the need for a specific plan to respond to the edge condition, (4) suggestions for developers to demonstrate how they might build housing near the desert edge to realize the full potential, and (5) a strategy to refine the DRG credit system adopted by the city.

The results of this effort, after extensive meetings with homebuilders, developers, open space advocates, and city officials, were necessarily more modest than initially hoped. The basis was the principle that because the preserve presented a unique opportunity for realizing considerable integration of urban development and nature, it could be an *example* of the private sector and the public sector working together to create valuable places for more people. The open space would create higher land value for adjacent private land, and development could be sensitive to the needs of the public. The most important conclusion was that increasing density in appropriate places at the edge could offer more value for developers *and* make a better edge for the public.

To make the proposal viable, the studio argued that the City should develop a master plan for the edge that identified a tiered system of access points and public facilities for the developers to plan around. Further, it was suggested that in portions of the preserve where natural systems were less sensitive, the City should invite developers to apply for zoning to include higher densities and mixed-use. Finally, the City was urged to consider locating developed parks and schools with outdoor recreational space adjacent to the preserve, combined with higher-density development when feasible.

Improve coordination at the edge

At the edges of the preserve, public sector projects and private sector development should be coordinated. A sense of public access to open space is important since this is public space supported through increased taxes. Access should be of many different types: distant views, scenic corridors through the preserve, and wide views from streets along the edge, various sizes of trailhead facilities and interpretive centers, active pedestrian edges, and neighborhood pedestrian access points.

Strategically increase density

To intensify the public's awareness of the desert and to generate more pedestrians at the edge, more intensive land uses should be strategically introduced. Such intense use could be focused to areas of the preserve that are least sensitive and areas that require partial improvement or restoration. This is where we see the public and private sector really working together. In certain edge situations higher-density housing, commercial uses, public buildings, and retail could be located to activate desert *paseos* along the edge of the preserve.

Develop a desert edge specific plan

The third item is a suggestion that there should be a specific plan. The specific plan would assess Sonoran Preserve land, consider adjacent open space that might be connected, understand the need for different kinds of access to the preserve, and

Figure 16.5 Proposal illustrating a *paseo* along the edge of the preserve where public access could be complemented by commercial or mixed use development. Image courtesy of J. Ewan.

develop a framework or strategy for guiding urbanization at the desert edge. Developers should be able to count on city improvements shown in the plan, and the city should ask developers to respond to opportunities presented by public open space.

While the studio understood the *Phoenix General Plan* has the ability to do much of this, our feeling was a physical plan specifically about the interface between open space and urban development would address the broad range of concerns that were explored in the studio. The current laissez-faire approach toward growth provides little direction for the development community, yielding unchanged forms of development. Unfortunately, this practice has perpetuated the city's reputation as a prime example of inefficient and poor quality urban sprawl. Ultimately, an Edge Coordination Plan could be developed to facilitate an edge that would celebrate the opportunity presented by the Sonoran Preserve.

Without this plan, only voluntary, and therefore unlikely, deviations from traditional development approaches by the private sector would elicit change.

New residential concepts for the desert edge

The studio observed older desert preserves and found the most common condition to be single family detached houses backing up to the open space. This type of urbanization intensified the feel of the sprawling city eating away at the landscape. While the effort to provide affordable housing is laudable, the vision of single family homes on one acre lots has been abstracted to the point that it no longer functions as intended and in reality is affordable now by a limited few. Further, conflicts between public access and community privacy and perceived safety tended to be exacerbated by the development pattern.

While the city's master plan called for developers of new housing communities to hold development away from major portions of the edge, and to provide access points at regular intervals, many in the development community saw those restrictions as a taking; the preserve would increase land value but if the edge cannot be built some of that value is lost. Accordingly, the studio proposed that developers consider single family housing types other than detached houses and proposed that the City allow more density at select points along the desert edge, density that is coordinated with non-residential development to increase the feeling of an active community in harmony with nature.

Revise the DRG weighting system

To legally effectuate the trade-offs the studio suggested amendments to the current Design Review Guideline (DRG) that weight proposed edge treatment by a series of factors. The notion was to allow developers flexibility while creating more variety. The system would give developers incentives to try desirable development patterns by allowing more and better use of the edge of open space, challenging public and private interests to work together to create socially viable development that is sensitive to the ecology and beauty of the desert.

The DRG required that 60 percent of the edge along open space be left un-built, assuring visual and physical access for residents of the sub-divisions near the preserve. This 60/40 ratio was established through a development credit system. The studio proposed a refinement of the guidelines allowing developers more flexibility while asking for more creative visions for living at the edge of the desert. The proposal adjusted the DRG credit system by introducing weighted credits and an expanded number of different open space edge treatments. The weighting system allows inclusion of all viable treatments while encouraging the most desirable.

For example, in the old DRG, spaces left between estate houses did not deserve the same credit as large stretches of private open space, so the treatment got no credit. The studio's proposed weighting system allowed the treatment to be encouraged, but at an appropriate weight. The studio proposed a weighting system that would allow spaces between building envelopes over 50 feet wide to receive 40 percent credit toward the required open edge. If employed on streets that were very accessible to the general public, the spaces could receive 60 percent credit.

Another example is the cul-de-sac. The studio concluded that the DRG gave too much credit for leaving openings at the end of cul-de-sacs. The fear was that the confusion between the private nature of a cul-de-sac and the use of cul-de-sacs to

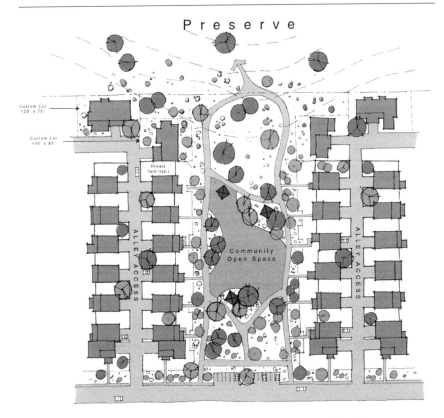

Figure 16.6 Proposal which illustrates how 14 housing units could face the preserve as well as provide neighborhood access in a space where typically four single family homes would back on to the preserve; a modest but significant increase in both density and access given the Phoenix context. Image courtesy of J. Ewan and adapted by Allyce Hargrove.

provide physical access would exacerbate conflicts between visitors and residents. Furthermore, the extended use of this treatment results in a long row of open cul-de-sacs with attendant side walls which is not more aesthetically pleasing than back-up treatment. In the proposed weighting system credit for open cul-de-sacs would be retained, but at a 40 percent rate.

It was the intention of the proposed weighting system to reward developers for careful coordination of the design of housing at the edge. Single loaded roads with houses that face the open space and reduce the negative visual impact of garages would get more credit. Higher-density single family housing would be aggressively encouraged where the preserve can support more access and use.

The proposed weighting system was designed to create incentives for appropriate public visual and physical access to the desert. Careful placement of opportunities for enhanced public access seemed appropriate for such an important public resource, and would actually improve the privacy and safety of housing communities near the preserve.

Furthermore, in an effort to encourage areas of intensity at appropriate points along the edge of open space, the weighting system would give developers an incentive of up to double credit for desert *paseos* with mixed use development. Such places would become examples of coordination between the public and private sectors where the public benefit from appropriate creative development would put them in touch with the desert and publicly owned open space, while private enterprise would fully capitalize on the same asset.

Conclusion

Phoenix, Arizona has recently experienced and managed the type of urban and natural edge conflicts the fast-growing cities of Asia and Africa may only be initially encountering. The development of planning policy based on sound design principles is possible, though challenging to implement owing to the opposing needs of various constituencies. Academia can play an important role by offering a theoretical perspective, independent eyes, and a research orientation. The fundamental lesson Phoenix and other mature cities offer is that the conditions which will arise are fairly predictable. The next generation of planners should proactively design the edge of the urban and natural instead of waiting for conflicts to erupt and attempting to solve them reactively.

References

Baschak, L. and Brown, R. (1994) River Systems and Landscape Networks. In E.A. Cook and H.N. van Lier (eds.) *Landscape Planning and Ecological Networks*, Amsterdam: Elsevier.

Brown, D.E. and Lowe, C.H. (1982) Biotic Communities of the Southwest (map). General Technical Report RM-78. US Forest Service. Fort Collins.

Burke, J. and Ewan, J.M. (1999) Sonoran Preserve Master Plan. City of Phoenix Parks, Recreation and Library Department. City of Phoenix.

Danzig, G.B. and Saaty, T.L. (1973) *Compact City: A Plan for a Liveable Urban Environment.* San Francisco: Freeman and Co. Publishers.

Engley, K. (2001) A Line in the Sand. *Landscape Architecture.* 91:4 pp. 80–85.

Ewan, J. and Underhill, M. (2003) *Exploration of the EDGE.* Horberger Center for Design Excellence, Arizona State University: Tempe.

Garreau, J. (1991) *Edge City: Life on the New Frontier.* New York: Anchor Books.

Holl, S. (1991) *Edge of a City.* Princeton: Princeton Architectural Press.

Hough, M. (2002) *Cities and Natural Form.* London: Taylor & Francis.

Jacobs, J. (1961) *The Death and Life of Great American Cities.* New York: Random House.

Koole, S. (2003) The Edge: Sonoran Preserve, Phoenix, Arizona. Unpublished Master's Thesis. Wageningen University, Netherlands.

Lewis, P. (1983) The Galactic Metropolis. In R.H. Platt and G. Macinko (eds.) *Beyond the Urban Fringe*, Minneapolis: University of Minnesota Press.

McCarthy, J., Shetter, K. and Steiner, F. (1996) *Findings of the North Sonoran Preserve Land Use Character Charrette*. Herberger Center for Design Excellence, Arizona State University: Tempe.

McHarg, I. (1969) *Design with Nature*. Garden City, NY: Natural History Press.

Rowe, P. (1991) *Making a Middle Landscape*. Cambridge, MA: Massachusetts Institute of Technology.

Sellers, W.D., Hill, R.Hh. and Rae, M.S. (1985) *Arizona Climate: The First Hundred Years*. Tucson: University of Arizona Press.

Shreve, F. (1951) *Vegetation of the Sonoran Desert*. Washington, DC: Carnegie Institute of Washington.

Part

F

Conclusions

Chapter 17: Edward A. Cook and Jesus J. Lara
Global prospects for the metropolis

Chapter 17

Global prospects for the metropolis

Edward A. Cook and Jesus J. Lara

Remaking Metropolis is about how cities can move forward to reinvent, rehabilitate, retrofit and reconceive in ways that are sustainable and reflective of the global forces that influence how they have evolved and will transform in the future. Many of the most pressing global environmental problems, such as population growth, pollution, waste generation and resource consumption have coalesced in and around cities (Grimm et al., 2008). Cities are a microcosm of the changes that are occurring globally. Cities also hold the most promise for working through social, economic and environmental issues and achieving a sustainable future. This book has provided a discussion of the current state of cities, external influences, over-arching concepts for achieving sustainable futures, specific techniques or strategies for improving quality of life of urban residents and ensuring long-term viability. The range of geographic, political and environmental conditions presented makes it clear that there are many challenges facing cities in a dynamic global context. Contributors provided examples of specific responses to local conditions, but in each case there are global drivers at work and opportunities for lessons to be learned for others in more distant locales (Germundsson et al., 2011). The authors describe innovative strategies that are employed to help cities move toward a more sustainable future. There are some important lessons to be learned from contributors in this volume that help to highlight future possible solutions in the quest to attain sustainability in cities in a global context. The aim has been to demonstrate that while each challenge requires a nuanced and tailored response to local conditions, global connections are important and should be understood and embraced in the urban landscape.

Global sustainability as a goal is widely agreed to be critical to increase the possibility of a satisfactory quality of life for future generations. The term sustainability is used by many different disciplines and has different implications in varied contexts. What is clear and consistent, however, is that to achieve sustainability, social, economic and environmental perspectives must all be addressed and today's needs must be met without compromising the needs of future generations (WCED, 1987). Context will dictate that the actions taken to achieve this goal must respond explicitly to the local conditions, resources and needs. Therefore, it is important to recognize that ties to the place should drive solutions while contributing to a larger view of a connected system at multiple temporal and spatial scales. If global systems are failing, interrelationships at the local scale become unpredictable and unstable. A collection of local actions that do not take into consideration a larger global impact ultimately lead to unpredictable and unstable global systems. While these relationships all exist in their particular contexts, a common set of principles can guide actions undertaken by policy makers, planners, designers and others to help achieve the goal. Brown et al. (1987) articulate some classic common themes that emerge that include the possibility of (1) continued support of human life on earth, (2) long-term maintenance of biological resources, (3) stable human populations, (4) limited growth economies, (5) an emphasis on small-scale self-reliance and (6) continued quality in the environment and ecosystems. These themes are all addressed in varying degrees in the contributions here and while not comprehensive in nature, provide some points of dialogue to further the movement toward more sustainable futures for cities.

Any prospect at arriving at the goal of global sustainability needs to recognize the role of cities both as a fundamental part of the problem and as the avenue toward solutions. Transformation is needed in the way cities are conceived, not just in the administrative and economic structure, but also in the design of urban systems and structures. As Berg (1991) and Thayer (1997) have both argued, we need city metamorphosis that takes cities from gray to green, both physically and in spirit. Cities need to become places where regeneration occurs for both people and natural ecosystems and where the intrinsic value of all life is integral to the daily activities of the urban population and reflected in planning for the future evolution of the city, region and planet. The traditional view that nature and urbanism are separate and somehow incompatible is no longer valid and a new direction is emerging where a symbiotic relationship between humans and nature exists and is essential to attaining a high quality of life in cities.

What is a sustainable future for cities and the ever-increasing global population? There is no single perspective that is widely accepted about what a sustainable city looks like, how it is governed or how its residents inhabit the place. Every city will likely be different because of its regional context, history, political and economic system. A sustainable city probably needs to be different from most of the cities of the world that currently exist. Existing urban centers will need to be retrofitted to become more sustainable and new urban developments will need to follow a different development process that leads to new types of urban form. Some currently less-used types of transport may gain favor, those powered by dwindling and polluting fuels may decline and some entirely new transport systems will emerge. The position of the pedestrian will likely take greater prominence in the adaptation and creation of future urban development. A fundamental characteristic of sustainability must be to ensure that the city is a healthy urban environment that sustains or improves people's physical health and emotional well-being. Many of the characteristics of life that have formerly been taken for granted have been lost in many cities. Both social and environmental change will be necessary to reduce negative aspects of urban life such as disease, pollution, stress and vulnerability to climate change and natural disaster. Access to green spaces, healthy food, good sanitation, clean air for exercise, access to transportation, educational and economic opportunities, social acceptance and equity, shared burdens in society and access to resources are not always certain and in many cities, and for much of the population are becoming rare.

The role of nature in cities will increase as it is embraced as a central organizing force in the future urban landscape. The human–nature relationship will become more intimate. It will be critical that we learn to sustain urban life and co-exist with natural systems through adaptation of human activity that ensures the integrity of the systems for the future. Nature can also provide inspiration and models for design and implementation of urban systems. Hough (Chapter 12) makes a case for using an ecological framework for structuring cities, both existing urban areas and areas of new growth. One of the key concepts that operationalizes the idea is the planning strategy of green infrastructure or green networks. Martinez Uriarte (Chapter 7) incorporates this as a central organizing element to be retrofitted to the vast urban fabric of Mexico City in the proposal for a sustainable future for that city. As we continue to learn more about how nature functions and how we impact natural systems, we can do more to preserve it in a form that provides the numerous benefits cities rely upon without depleting future resources. With greater understanding of natural systems, we can help nature sustain the city and the planet.

Thayer (Chapter 3) explains that if cities embrace their bioregion, as defined by land not political boundaries, they will be able to establish a new direction. Bioregionalism recognizes that unique watersheds, soils, flora, fauna, climate, seasonal dynamics and enduring processes are particular to each geographic region. Cities should develop strategies that consume regionally available resources in accordance with the needs and population. The approach should be a reciprocal process with nature in which the city gives back as it takes. Within that context cities can become more self-reliant and sustainable, managing problems locally and using resources drawn from the region. There is no one-size-fits-all approach. Local initiatives are central to building toward sustainability. A key component of urban sustainability is keeping problems contained without passing along deleterious effects to other communities or spreading them beyond the region. One example provided by Geitz (Chapter 15) deals with urban river restoration. He demonstrates clearly how decisions to channelize river and stream corridors simply pass problems like flooding downstream and actually create additional problems like increasing sedimentation and reduced water quality. The remedies of re-naturalization of rivers and streams accept the river or stream as a system within the region that has inherent value and by embracing the resource for what it is. Ecosystem services that benefit society are provided while sustaining it in a viable state for the future. The bioregion as the basic context for food security, energy and other resources encourages wise local knowledge and management of resources and reduces potential vulnerabilities to interruptions in support systems. Collaboration between cities and regions is also important to build a knowledge and skill base and to infuse new ideas and resources where appropriate. Particularly in developing world cities where resilience of support systems is less sure, embracing bioregionalism can go some distance to ensure more consistent and equitable access to resources and improve overall quality of life.

Great strides have been made in industrial and technological development since the industrial revolution. Cities, industry and technology are linked together in a mutually beneficial and destructive relationship that provides jobs for urban residents and markets for industry. At the same time, this relationship causes decline in public health due to pollution and sometimes hazardous work environments. Early reactions to this phenomenon led to new city planning concepts like the Garden City Movement (Howard, 1902) championed by such visionaries as Ebenezer Howard and others. These planning strategies were a reaction to poor living and working conditions in cities. Many of the same challenges persist today with the added layer of complexity resulting from global economic systems, global-scale environmental problems and a dynamic and unpredictable geo-political environment. In many ways, the call for bioregionalism reaches back and draws on some of Howard's Garden City principles originally intended to improve the health and overall quality of life, but at the same time contributed to some important concepts that are now considered essential to achieve urban sustainability. Howard's "town-country" principle linked the town and the surrounding countryside in a mutually beneficial relationship. The surrounding agricultural landscape provided fresh, locally grown food to the town residents, while the town provided a ready market for the farmers from the countryside. A corollary principle of "limited size" reinforces this relationship and establishes a kind of regional basis for population and land area limits. Each garden city would accommodate 32,000 people, 30,000 in the town and 2,000 in the surrounding agricultural zone. The land area was also fixed at about 6,000 acres, 1,000 for the town and 5,000 for agriculture. While this principle is somewhat arbitrary about size and in that sense is not entirely consistent with bioregionalism which suggests community size is based on capability of a region to support a certain population level, it does suggest that there should clearly be local ties between the landscape's ability to support a population and its ultimate size. Other principles such as "spaciousness," that suggest provision of green space in the town, are also consistent with recommendations by many that sustainable cities should incorporate a network of green spaces within the urban fabric.

Two key differences exist for most cities now in the early stages of the twenty-first century: more advanced technology and global influences. Contemporary cities are working hard to incorporate new technology, but it will be important to incorporate it wisely. Technological advancement has generally been viewed positively since it often reduces tedious work and magnifies the potential to acquire and manipulate information. It is also recognized that with some of the benefits come challenges and changes that society has not fully recognized or addressed. One of the most recent trends influencing approaches to sustainable city development is making cities smart. Steinert et al. (2009) outline a framework for "Making Cities Smart and Sustainable." They start with the overarching concept of innovation, defined as a new or significantly improved product, service or process. Recognizing and utilizing the growing availability of information can improve efficiency of systems, drive economic opportunities and effectively manage resources contributing to environmental sustainability. There are six areas in which Steinert et al. (2009) note that the European Union is now engaged in the development of smarter cities that also contribute to the aim of urban sustainability. First, "smart governance" envisions interconnectivity of governmental organizations, increasing opportunities for communication and collaboration while improving community access to services and information about government activity. Second, "smart people" increases inclusion in public processes and opportunities by extending e-learning educational experiences to a broader spectrum of the population, increasing capabilities so that urban residents can become empowered and provide more informed insight and contributions. Third, "smart environment" reduces energy consumptions through technological innovations while promoting conservation and reuse of materials. Fourth, "smart mobility" promotes use of more efficient and intelligent transportation systems and new types of public perceptions about car sharing, car pooling, bicycle use and car–bike combinations. Fifth, "smart economy" creates business opportunities by leveraging information networks to improve business processes through e-banking, e-shopping, e-auction and others. Sixth, "smart living" provides access to improved health care, home automation and better access to business and social services. The result of these smart city initiatives will lead to reduced carbon emissions and more durable economic growth. Of course, the potential application of these new technologies will have unanticipated deleterious effects that will be discovered in time and should be evaluated for the impact on people, cities and the global context.

The use of technology in contemporary cities also applies to the way we develop, manage and co-exist with ecological systems. As noted by Hough (Chapter 12), Bryant and Allen (Chapter 13), Cook (Chapter 14) and Geitz (Chapter 15), we are learning more about urban ecological systems and are developing technological approaches to intervene following patterns and processes of nature. Ecological systems provide what is needed to support human life as well as that of the many other organisms on the planet. The planet's biodiversity is important to sustain all life, but urban biodiversity is also critical. Rachel Carson (1962) pointed out in her classic book *Silent Spring* that plants and animals are warning systems or indicators of the relative health of the environment. Maintaining the heath of these systems is essentially maintaining the health of our support systems. We live in the same environment and are part of the urban ecology. In some cases, it is possible to create alternative systems that perform similar functions to natural systems. The emerging concept of biomimicry is gaining acceptance, yielding new approaches to design. Many landscape architects have for some time been using lessons from nature to inform design and other design disciplines are now studying organisms and natural processes to provide models and inspiration for creating products, buildings and systems for human use. In urban situations, the human–nature relationship needs to be balanced and the human place in nature recognized as integral but not dominant. Place-based knowledge and science will allow humans to intervene to adapt existing natural systems without compromising their inherent capability to provide ecosystem services upon which society is dependent. Ecological restoration also requires place-based knowledge and science to be effective. While it is sometimes possible to re-establish ecological systems in compromised urban landscapes that reflect the original, often it is more practical to employ scientific knowledge to introduce some technological solutions using nature as a model and ecological design process.

People, public life and public engagement are central to achieving sustainability in any context. People are the life of the city and facilitating their participation in the process of moving toward sustainability and overall quality of life will encourage ownership and citizenship. Ensuring that local actions lead to positive global transformations starts with the participation and engagement of individuals. Flows of ideas and resources need to go in both directions, but implementation is undertaken at a local level, even if influenced by national policy or global initiative. Urban populations can and should be a force in any process of global change and the ultimate success of any movement for change will require engagement of local populations. Change that affects individuals is already occurring at the local level in cities everywhere. Some of it is positive, but there are also many negative transformations occurring as a result of forces acting at a global level. Pijawka et al. (Chapter 6), Gemzoe and Park (Chapter 10) and Hutanuwatr (Chapter 11) all address the critical role and specific challenges people face in changing urban and urbanizing environments. Central to the discussion is how people can be more engaged to help their own urban futures to move toward a better quality of urban life. Urban life in future cities will be both recognizable and different from what current urban residents are now accustomed to. Quality of life is achieved in many different ways and perceived differently in varied locales and with different populations. It is becoming clear, however, that while it is important to provide this for people living in cities for their own well-being, it is also becoming important to help establish identity for cities and to draw sustainable economic enterprises that help reinforce positive trajectory that cities establish.

The future is urban. It is not the urban that exists today. It will need to become more flexible to adapt to rapidly changing global, regional and local conditions. The urban of the future will also need to be integral with nature. It will not be possible to continue on the path where in the city traditional human systems dominate natural systems. Future urban systems will need to allow natural systems to continue to function or become more like hybrid or synthetic systems that function in the same ways. The urban of the future will need to be embedded in the region, drawing on local resources and managing waste internally. Knowledge and science will need to be integral to encourage more informed decision-making. The economy of the future city will also need to be based on a less consumptive, more sustainable, foundation that encourages smart investment in people and systems. In the final analysis, the quality of life of the people of the city will be the ultimate measure of success of remaking the metropolis in the global landscape.

References

Berg, P. (1991) A Metamorphosis for Cities: From Gray to Green. *Trumpeter*, 8:1, pp. 9–12.

Brown, B., M. Hanson, D. Liverman and R. Meredith (1987) Global Sustainability: Toward Definition. *Environmental Management*, 11:6, pp. 713–719.

Carson, R. (1962) *Silent Spring*. Boston: Houghton Mifflin.

Germundsson, T., P. Howard and K. Olwig (2011) Introduction: Reassessing Landscape Drivers and the Globalist Environmental Agenda. *Landscape Research*, 36:4, pp. 395–399.

Grimm, N. S. Faeth, N. Golubiewski, C. Redman, J. Wu, X. Bai and J. Briggs (2008) Global Change and the Ecology of Cities. *Science*, 319: 756–760.

Howard, E. (1902) *Garden Cities of To-Morrow*. London: Faber and Faber.

Steinert, K., R. Marom, P. Richard, G. Viega and L. Witters (2009) Making Cities Smart and Sustainable. In: S. Dutta (Editor). *The Global Innovation Index 2011*. Fountainebleu: Insead.

Thayer, R. (1997) *Gray World, Green Heart: Technology, Nature and the Sustainable Landscape*. New York: John Wiley and Sons.

WCED (1987) *Our Common Future*. Oxford: Oxford University Press.

Index

References in **bold** indicate tables, in *italics* indicate figures and followed by a letter n indicate end of chapter notes.